Fodor's 1st Edition

W9-BLO-832

Puerto Rico

The complete guide, thoroughly up-to-date

Packed with details that will make your trip

The must-see sights, off and on the beaten path

What to see, what to skip

Mix-and-match vacation itineraries

City strolls, countryside adventures

Smart lodging and dining options

Essential local do's and taboos

Transportation tips, distances, and directions

Key contacts, savvy travel tips

When to go, what to pack

Clear, accurate, easy-to-use maps

Background essays

Fodor's Travel Publications • New York, Toronto, London, Sydney, Auckland
www.fodors.com

Fodor's Puerto Rico

EDITOR: Matt Lombardi

Editorial Contributors: Mary Dempsey, Karen English, Stephen Fowler, Delinda Karle, Karl Luntta, John Marino

Editorial Production: Linda K. Schmidt

Maps: David Lindroth, *cartographer*; Robert Blake and Rebecca Baer, *map editors*

Design: Fabrizio La Rocca, *creative director*; Guido Caroti, *art director*; Jolie Novak, *photo editor*

Cover Design: Pentagram

Production/Manufacturing: Angela McLean

Cover Photograph: Dave G. Houser

Copyright

Copyright © 2001 by Fodor's Travel Publications

Fodor's is a registered trademark of Random House, Inc. All rights reserved under International and Pan-American Copyright Conventions. Published in the United States by Fodor's Travel Publications, a division of Random House, Inc., New York, and simultaneously in Canada by Random House of Canada Limited, Toronto. Distributed by Random House, Inc., New York.

No maps, illustrations, or other portions of this book may be reproduced in any form without written permission from the publisher.

"When I Was Puerto Rican" reprinted from *When I Was Puerto Rican* by Esmeralda Santiago, copyright © 1993 by Esmeralda Santiago. Reprinted by permission of Perseus Books Publishers, a member of Perseus Books L.L.C.

First Edition

ISBN 0–679–00720–2

ISSN 1531–0396

Special Sales

Fodor's Travel Publications are available at special discounts for bulk purchases for sales promotions or premiums. Special editions, including personalized covers, excerpts of existing guides, and corporate imprints, can be created in large quantities for special needs. For more information, contact your local bookseller or write to Special Markets, Fodor's Travel Publications, 280 Park Avenue, New York, NY 10017. Inquiries from Canada should be directed to your local Canadian bookseller or sent to Random House of Canada, Ltd., Marketing Department, 2775 Matheson Boulevard East, Mississauga, Ontario L4W 4P7. Inquiries from the United Kingdom should be sent to Fodor's Travel Publications, 20 Vauxhall Bridge Road, London SW1V 2SA, England.

PRINTED IN THE UNITED STATES OF AMERICA

10 9 8 7 6 5 4 3 2 1

Important Tip

Although all prices, opening times, and other details in this book are based on information supplied to us at press time, changes occur all the time in the travel world, and Fodor's cannot accept responsibility for facts that become outdated or for inadvertent errors or omissions. So **always confirm information when it matters,** especially if you're making a detour to visit a specific place.

CONTENTS

Maps

ON THE ROAD WITH FODOR'S

Every trip is a significant trip. Acutely aware of that fact, we've pulled out all stops in preparing *Fodor's Puerto Rico*. To guide you in putting together your Puerto Rican experience, we've created multiday itineraries and neighborhood walks. And to direct you to the places that are truly worth your time and money, we've rallied the team of endearingly picky know-it-alls we're pleased to call our writers. Having seen all corners of the regions they cover for us, they're real experts. If you knew them, you'd poll them for tips yourself.

An itch to travel has carried journalist **Mary Dempsey,** the writer of the Eastern Puerto Rico chapter, throughout Latin America and the Caribbean. Her writings from those journeys have appeared in numerous publications, including the *Los Angeles Times, Travel and Leisure, Americas,* and *Conde Nast Traveler.* She tackled her Fodor's assignment after spending two years in Puerto Rico, where she wrote for the island's English-language daily, the *San Juan Star.* She's currently an editor at *Latin Trade* magazine, a Miami-based monthly covering business and investment in the Caribbean and Central and South America.

A native of Michigan, **Delinda Karle** discovered the tropics on her first job in journalism, with a Puerto Rican weekly business newspaper. She returned to the cold latitudes to pursue a career as a business reporter, but found herself traveling to the Caribbean every chance she could get. She left the *Cleveland Plain Dealer* in 1991 to return to Puerto Rico, and she's been there ever since, writing for the *San Juan Star,* the Associated Press, and Reuters. She wrote the Southern and Northwestern Puerto Rico chapters here.

For the past 10 years, **Karl Luntta** has traveled to Puerto Rico to hit the beaches and savor the sounds of salsa—and to cover the island for Fodor's. On a favorites scale, he ranks San Juan (which he covers here, as well as working on the Destination chapter and Gold Guide), as "so hip it hurts." In addition to his published travel guides to Jamaica, St. Lucia, the Virgin Islands, and the Caribbean region, he writes a newspaper column and has frequently written about his home, Cape Cod and the islands of Martha's Vineyard and Nantucket, for Fodor's and other travel publications.

John Marino, who reviewed San Juan restaurants and wrote the Destination introduction for this book, is city editor at the *San Juan Star.* He has written extensively about Puerto Rico and the Caribbean for several publications, including the *Washington Post,* the *New York Times, Gourmet, New York Newsday,* and Reuters. He lives with his wife and son in San Juan.

Don't Forget to Write

Keeping a travel guide fresh and up-to-date is a big job. So we love your feedback—positive and negative—and follow up on all suggestions. Contact the Puerto Rico editor at editors@fodors.com or c/o Fodor's, 280 Park Avenue, New York, NY 10017. And have a wonderful trip!

Karen Cure
Editorial Director

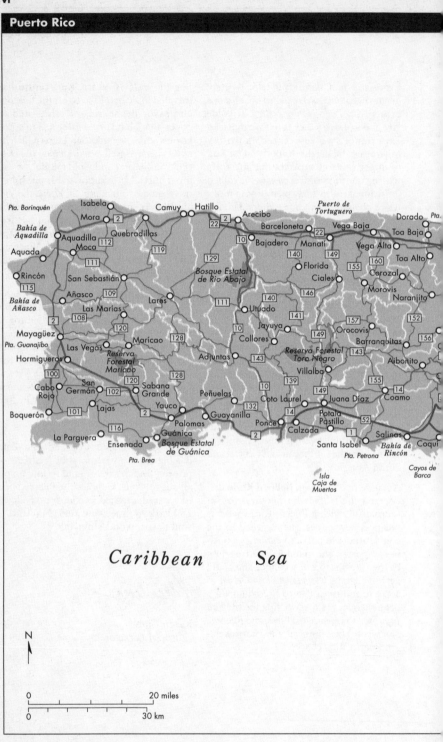

Pta. Borinquén

Isabela
Mora
Camuy
Hatillo
Arecibo
Puerto de Tortuguero
Dorado
Pta.
Toa Baja

Bahía de Aquadilla
Aquadilla
Quebradillas
22
2
Barceloneta
Vega Baja
22
Vega Alta
Toa Alto

Aquada
112
Moca
10
Bajadero
Manatí
140
149
155
160
Corozal

Rincón
111
119
129
Florida
Ciales
146
Morovis
Naranjito

115
San Sebastián
Bosque Estatal de Río Abajo
140
141
157
152

Bahía de Añasco
Añasco
109
Lares
111
Utuado
Jayuya
149
Orocovis
Barranquitas
156

Mayagüez
108
Las Marías
120
10
Collores
143
Reserva Forestal Toro Negro
143
Aibonito

Pta. Guanajibo
Las Vegas
Maricao
128
Adjuntas
143
Villalba
155
14
Coamo

Hormigueros
Reserva Forestal Maricao
120
128
139
10
149
Juana Díaz

Cabo Rojo
San Germán
102
Sabana Grande
Peñuelas
Coto Laurel
Potala Pastillo
52
14

Boquerón
101
Lajas
Yauco
132
14
1
Salinas

La Parguera
116
Palomas
Guánica
Guayanilla
Ponce
2
Calzada
Santa Isabel
Bahía de Rincón
Coquí

Ensenada
Bosque Estatal de Guánica
Pta. Petrona
Cayos de Barca

Pta. Brea

Isla Caja de Muertos

Caribbean   Sea

N

0   20 miles
0   30 km

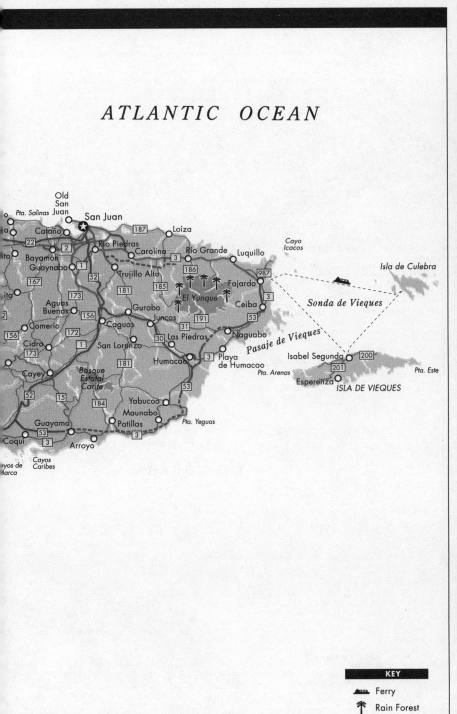

ATLANTIC OCEAN

KEY

🚤 Ferry

🌴 Rain Forest

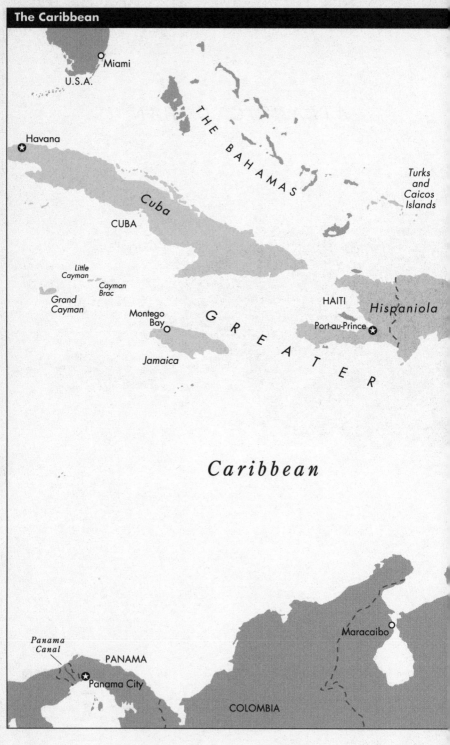

The Caribbean

Miami

U.S.A.

THE BAHAMAS

Turks
and
Caicos
Islands

Havana

Cuba

CUBA

Little
Cayman

Cayman
Brac

Grand
Cayman

Montego
Bay

HAITI

Hispaniola

Port-au-Prince

G R E A T E R

Jamaica

Caribbean

Panama
Canal

PANAMA

Maracaibo

Panama City

COLOMBIA

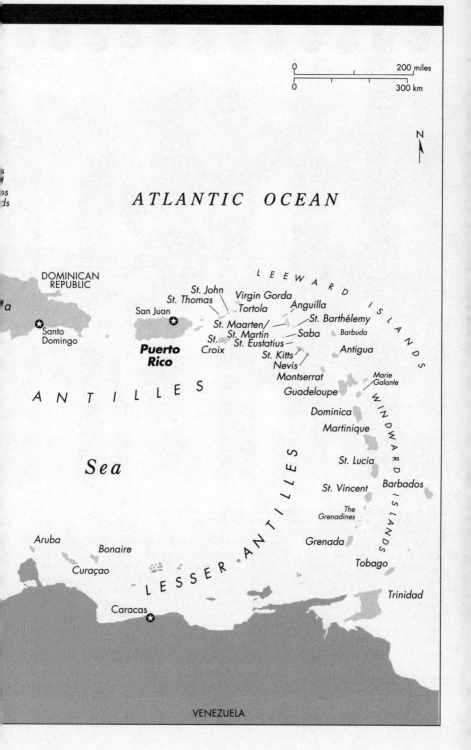

ATLANTIC OCEAN

DOMINICAN
REPUBLIC

Santo
Domingo

San Juan

**Puerto
Rico**

St. John
St. Thomas
Virgin Gorda
Tortola
Anguilla
St. Maarten/
St. Martin
St. Barthélemy
Saba
St. Eustatius
St.
Croix
St. Kitts
Nevis
Montserrat
Guadeloupe
Barbuda
Antigua
Marie
Galante

A N T I L L E S

LEEWARD ISLANDS

WINDWARD ISLANDS

Sea

Dominica
Martinique
St. Lucia
Barbados
St. Vincent
The
Grenadines
Grenada
Tobago
Trinidad

Aruba
Bonaire
Curaçao

LESSER ANTILLES

Caracas

VENEZUELA

0   200 miles
0   300 km

N

World Time Zones

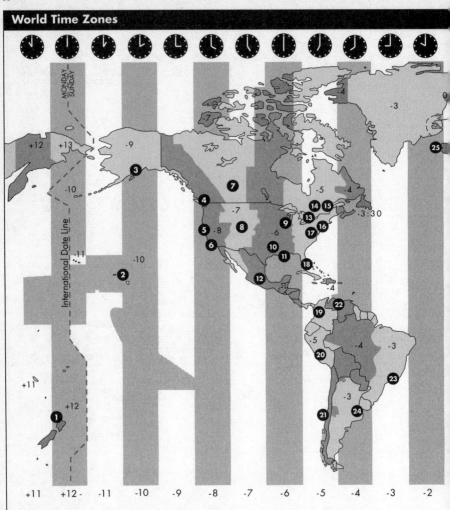

Numbers below vertical bands relate each zone to Greenwich Mean Time (0 hrs.).
Local times frequently differ from these general indications,
as indicated by light-face numbers on map.

Algiers **29**	Caracas **22**	Jakarta **53**	Mexico City **12**
Anchorage **3**	Chicago **9**	Jerusalem **42**	Miami **18**
Athens **41**	Copenhagen **33**	Johannesburg **44**	Montréal **15**
Auckland **1**	Dallas **10**	Lima **20**	Moscow **45**
Baghdad **46**	Delhi **48**	Lisbon **28**	Nairobi **43**
Bangkok **50**	Denver **8**	London	New Orleans **11**
Beijing **54**	Dublin **26**	(Greenwich) **27**	New York City **16**
Berlin **34**	Edmonton **7**	Los Angeles **6**	Ottawa **14**
Bogotá **19**	Hong Kong **56**	Madrid **38**	Paris **30**
Budapest **37**	Honolulu **2**	Manila **57**	Perth **58**
Buenos Aires **24**	Istanbul **40**	Mecca **47**	Reykjavík **25**

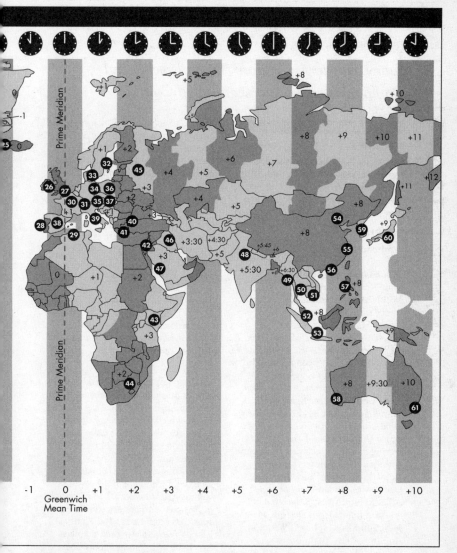

SMART TRAVEL TIPS A TO Z

*Basic Information on Traveling in Puerto Rico,
Savvy Tips to Make Your Trip a Breeze, and
Companies and Organizations to Contact*

AIR TRAVEL

BOOKING

When you book **look for nonstop flights** and **remember that "direct" flights stop at least once.** Try to avoid connecting flights, which require a change of plane.

CARRIERS

San Juan's Luis Muñoz Marín International Airport is large and busy, with **multiple daily flights** arriving from North America and around the world. Most air traffic to Puerto Rico comes from the east coast of the United States, and a majority of people fly in on American Airlines, the busiest carrier to the island and to the rest of the Caribbean. Luis Muñoz Marín is American's regional hub. The airline flies nonstop from New York, Boston, Newark, and Miami, as well as connecting through many other North American cities. Other major United States–based carriers serving San Juan include Continental, with daily nonstop service from Newark, Houston, and Cleveland; Delta, with nonstop service from Atlanta; Northwest, offering daily nonstop flights from Detroit, Memphis, and Minneapolis; TWA, nonstop from New York, Boston, Orlando, Fort Lauderdale, Los Angeles, and St. Louis; United, daily nonstop from Chicago and weekends from New York and Washington, DC; and US Airways, flying nonstop daily from Pittsburgh, Philadelphia, and Charlotte.

Canada's Montréal and Toronto are connected to San Juan by Air Canada Vacations, and Canadian Airlines also flies to San Juan, with a stop in Miami, from Toronto, Vancouver, and Calgary. **Europe and the U.K.** are connected to San Juan by British Air out of London, and Lufthansa's partner Condor out of Germany. LACSA, the airline of Costa Rica,

connects San Juan to San José, as well as to Miami (with a stop in San José), Cancún, and Panama. Your best bet for flying to San Juan from **Australia and New Zealand** is with Qantas Airways. Qantas flies out of Sydney, Brisbane, Perth, Melbourne, and several other Australian cities, with direct connections to Honolulu and Los Angeles. From there you can connect on an associated airline (booking all through Qantas) to Boston, Chicago, Miami, New York, Toronto, Vancouver, and Washington, DC, with further connections to Puerto Rico. Qantas also flies from Auckland, New Zealand, to Los Angeles, with associated airline connections on to Puerto Rico.

Puerto Rico is also a good spot from which to hop to other Caribbean islands on **small interisland connectors** such as American Airline's American Eagle, which flies to many of the Lesser Antilles islands; Cape Air, which connects San Juan to St. Thomas and St. Croix; ALM, traveling to Jamaica, Aruba, Bonaire, and its base in Curaçao; and Leeward Islands Air Transport (LIAT), based in Antigua with connections to San Juan and nearly all Lesser Antilles islands. Vieques Air-Link connects San Juan with Puerto Rico's eastern islands of Vieques and Culebra. For local phone numbers of airlines serving Puerto Rico, *see* San Juan A to Z *in* Chapter 2.

➤ Major U.S. Airlines: **American Airlines** (☎ 800/433–7300), **American Trans Air (ATA)** (☎ 800/883–5228), **Continental** (☎ 800/231–0856), **Delta** (☎ 800/241–4141), **Northwest** (☎ 800/447–4747), **TWA** (☎ 800/892–4141), **United** (☎ 800/538–2929), **US Airways** (☎ 800/428–4322)

➤ Smaller Airlines: **ALM** (☎ 800/327–7230), **American Eagle** (☎ 800/433–7300), **Cape Air** (☎ 800/352–

0714), **LIAT** (☎ 800/468–0842), **Martin Air** (☎ 787/723–7474), **Vieques Air-Link** (☎ 787/723–9882 or 787/863–3020).

➤ FROM ELSEWHERE IN THE WORLD: **Air Canada Vacations** (☎ 800/774–8993 in North America), **British Airways** (☎ 800/247–9297 in the U.S.; 0845/7222–111 in the U.K.), **Canadian Airlines** (☎ 800/426–7000 in North America), **Condor** (☎ 800/645–3880 or 800/524–6975 in the U.S.; 06107/939–229 in Germany), **LACSA** (☎ 800/225–2272; 506/231–0033 in Costa Rica), **Qantas** (☎ 800/227–4500 in the U.S.; 800/062–241 in Australia; 09/357–8700 in Auckland, 0800/808–767 elsewhere in New Zealand).

CHECK-IN & BOARDING

For Americans, Puerto Rico is, in essence, a domestic destination, but it's best to show up at least an hour and a half before flight time to check in. Assuming that not everyone with a ticket will show up, airlines routinely overbook planes. When everyone does, airlines ask for volunteers to give up their seats. In return, these volunteers usually get a certificate for a free flight and are rebooked on the next flight out. If there are not enough volunteers, the airline must choose who will be denied boarding. The first to get bumped are passengers who checked in late and those flying on discounted tickets, so **get to the gate and check in as early as possible,** especially during peak periods.

Always **bring a government-issued photo I.D. to the airport.** You may be asked to show it before you are allowed to check in.

CUTTING COSTS

The least expensive airfares to Puerto Rico must usually be purchased in advance and are non-refundable. It's smart to **call a number of airlines, and when you are quoted a good price, book it on the spot**—the same fare may not be available the next day. Always **check different routings** and look into using different airports. Travel agents, especially low-fare specialists (☞ Discounts & Deals, *below*), are helpful.

Consolidators are another good source. They buy tickets for scheduled international flights at reduced rates from the airlines, then sell them at prices that beat the best fare available directly from the airlines, usually without restrictions. Sometimes you can even get your money back if you need to return the ticket. Carefully read the fine print detailing penalties for changes and cancellations, and **confirm your consolidator reservation with the airline.**

When you **fly as a courier,** you trade your checked-luggage space for a ticket deeply subsidized by a courier service. There are restrictions on when you can book and how long you can stay.

Airline charter companies operate flights to Puerto Rico, and their fares can offer savings over regularly scheduled airlines. The disadvantage is that charter-flight packages are often coupled with hotel or resort stays limited to those chosen by the airline, though you can in many instances opt to buy the flight and not the entire package. A further disadvantage is that many charter companies operate on a once-per-week basis, departing for the island on, for example, Saturday only. This means you must return the following Saturday. There are penalties to pay for an added week's stay, and more penalties for cancellation. In some cases, flights can be cancelled 10 days in advance if the company doesn't fill the seats, and can be delayed by as long as 48 hours while the charter company fills up its plane.

If you plan to use Puerto Rico as a base for **exploring other Caribbean islands,** look for island-hopping special fares from LIAT; their Caribbean Super Explorer program discounts flights on unlimited travel for 30 days to any LIAT destination. ALM also has, in the past, offered discounts on multiple Caribbean destinations within one trip.

➤ CONSOLIDATORS: **Cheap Tickets** (☎ 800/377–1000). **Discount Airline Ticket Service** (☎ 800/576–1600). **Unitravel** (☎ 800/325–2222). **Up & Away Travel** (☎ 212/889–2345). **World Travel Network** (☎ 800/409–6753).

➤ COURIERS: **International Association of Air Travel Couriers** (✉ 220 S. Dixie Hwy. #3, Box 1349, Lake Worth, FL 33460, ☎ 561/582–8320).

➤ DISCOUNT PASSES: **ALM** (☎ 800/327–7230), **LIAT,** (☎ 800/468–0842).

ENJOYING THE FLIGHT

For more legroom, **request an emergency-aisle seat.** Don't sit in the row in front of the emergency aisle or in front of a bulkhead, where seats may not recline. If you have dietary concerns, **ask for special meals when booking.** These can be vegetarian, low-cholesterol, or kosher, for example. On long flights, try to maintain a normal routine, to help fight jet lag. At night, **get some sleep.** By day, **eat light meals, drink water** (not alcohol), and **move around the cabin.**

FLYING TIMES

Nonstop flights to San Juan from New York are 3¾ hours; from Miami, 1½ hours; from Atlanta, 3¾ hours; from Boston, 4 hours; from Chicago, 4¾ hours; from Los Angeles, 8 hours; from the United Kingdom, 5 hours. There are no nonstop flights from Australia or New Zealand.

HOW TO COMPLAIN

If your baggage goes astray or your flight goes awry, complain right away. Most carriers require that you **file a claim immediately.**

➤ AIRLINE COMPLAINTS: U.S. Department of Transportation **Aviation Consumer Protection Division** (✉ C-75, Room 4107, Washington, DC 20590, ☎ 202/366–2220, airconsumer@ost.dot.gov, www.dot.gov/airconsumer). **Federal Aviation Administration Consumer Hotline** (☎ 800/322–7873).

RECONFIRMING

Airlines flying in and out of Puerto Rico are reliable, but it's always best to reconfirm flights. Several San Juan and island hotels offer flight reconfirmation as a service of the concierge.

AIRPORTS

Luis Muñoz Marín International Airport (airline code SJU), minutes east of downtown San Juan in the coastal section of Isla Verde, is one of the **easiest and cheapest destinations in the Caribbean.** It's a bustling airport, with a new terminal for American Airlines, which uses San Juan as its Caribbean hub. San Juan's other airport is the small **Fernando L. Rivas Dominici Airport** in Isla Grande, near the Miramar section of the city, where you can catch Vieques Air-Link to Culebra and Vieques, as well as small charter flights to spots in Puerto Rico and the Caribbean. Several smaller airlines fly to other airports around the island, including **Mercedita** in the south coast town of Ponce, **Eugenio María de Hostos** in the west coast's Mayagüez, and **Rafael Hernández** in Aguadilla in the northwest corner of the island.

➤ AIRPORT INFORMATION: **Luis Muñoz Marín International Airport** (☎ 787/791–4670), **Aeropuerto Fernando L. Rivas Dominici** (☎ 787/729–8711), **Aeropuerto Mercedita** (☎ 787/842–6292), **Aeropuerto Eugenio María de Hostos** (☎ 787/833–0148), **Aeropuerto Rafael Hernández** (☎ 787/891–2286).

TAXIS & SHUTTLES

From the Airport: into San Juan, **Taxi Turísticos** charges set rates based on zones, so the fare depends on the destination. Uniformed and badged officials help you find a cab at the airport (look for the Tourism Company booth) and hand you a slip with your fare, which you can present to your driver. To other points in Isla Verde, the fare is $8; to Condado, $12; to Old San Juan, $16. If you don't hail one of these cabs, you're at the mercy of the meter and the driver.

Other options are the **Airport Limousine Service** (☎ 787/791–4745), which provides minibus service to hotels in the Isla Verde, Condado, and Old San Juan areas at basic fares of $2.50, $3, and $3.50, respectively; the fares do vary, depending on the time of day and number of passengers, and you may have to wait until the van fills before leaving the airport. Limousines of **Dorado Transport Co-op** (☎ 787/796–1214) serve hotels and villas in the Dorado area for $20 per person.

Many hotels provide transfers for their guests (either free or at a cost), and will meet you at the airport to zip you away to the hotel; when booking your room, get the low-down.

If you're heading directly out onto the island, consult with your hotel about transportation. The large resorts run regular shuttles; other than that, your best bet may be to rent a car (☞ Car Rental, *below*).

DUTY-FREE SHOPPING

Puerto Rico is not a duty-free island, but duty-free shops are found at Luis Muñoz Marín International in San Juan. The duty-free shops are in the terminal boarding areas, where you'll have to show your boarding pass before loading up on watches, liquor, and perfume.

BIKE TRAVEL

Selected areas of Puerto Rico lend themselves to bike travel (the central mountains, small towns), but, in general, the roads are congested, distances are vast, and you will find travel by other means more efficient and safer. This is particularly true of the San Juan metro area.

BIKES IN FLIGHT

Most airlines accommodate bikes as luggage, provided they are dismantled and boxed. For bike boxes, often free at bike shops, you'll pay about $5 from airlines (at least $100 for bike bags). International travelers can sometimes substitute a bike for a piece of checked luggage at no charge; otherwise, the cost is about $100. Domestic and Canadian airlines charge $25–$50.

BOAT & FERRY TRAVEL

The ferry **between Old San Juan (Pier 2) and Cataño** costs a mere 50¢ one-way. It runs every half hour from 6 AM to 10 PM. The 400-passenger ferries of the Fajardo Port Authority run between that east coast town and the islands of **Vieques and Culebra.** They carry cargo as well as passengers, and make the 90-minute trip between Fajardo and Vieques three times daily ($2 one-way). They make

the 90-minute run from Fajardo to Culebra twice daily with three runs from Culebra to Fajardo on weekends ($2.25 one-way).

FARES & SCHEDULES

Get schedules for the Culebra and Vieques ferries by calling the Port Authority in Fajardo, Vieques, or Culebra. Tickets are bought at the ferry dock before entering; you'll find weekend and holiday traffic heavier than on weekdays, but getting space on the boats is generally not a problem. You can make reservations by calling the Port Authority.

➤ BOAT & FERRY INFORMATION: **Cataño Ferry** (☎ 787/788–1155), **Fajardo Port Authority** (☎ 787/863–4560 in Fajardo; 787/742–3161 in Culebra; 787/741–4761 in Vieques).

BUS TRAVEL

The **Autoridad Metropolitana de Autobuses** (AMA, or Metropolitan Bus Authority) operates *guaguas* (buses) that thread through San Juan. Buses run in exclusive lanes on major thoroughfares, stopping at signs marked PARADA or PARADA DE GUAGUAS. The main terminals are the Covadonga parking lot and Plaza de Colón, in Old San Juan, and Capetillo Terminal in Río Piedras, next to the central business district. Destinations are indicated above the windshield; those marked A5 and B21 cover the popular San Juan beach and hotel areas of Isla Verde, Condado, and Old San Juan. A-3 covers Río Piedras and Hato Rey. Most buses are air-conditioned and have wheelchair lifts and lock-downs.

Bus travel to outlying areas in Puerto Rico is generally unavailable. Your best bet for travel to other parts of the island is by rental car, which affords you the most flexibility, or by *publicos* (public cars), which are sort of a cross between a private taxi and a bus. In other words, they operate regularly, but not on schedules, and carry more than one passenger. Call the following San Juan *publicos* for schedule and fare information: **Blue Line** (☎ 787/765–7733) for trips to Aguadilla and the northwest coast, **Choferes Unidos de Ponce** (☎ 787/

764–0540) for Ponce transport, **Linea Caborrojeña** (☎ 787/723–9155) for trips to Cabo Rojo and the southwest coast.

FARES & SCHEDULES

In San Juan, bus fares are 25¢ or 50¢, depending on the route, and are paid in exact change upon entering the bus. (Try to have a few quarters on hand. Credit cards are not accepted.) Buses adhere to their routes, but schedules are fluid, to say the least. Count on a bus passing your stop every 15–30 minutes, less frequently on Sunday and holidays. Buses start their morning runs between 5 AM and 6 AM, and the last run for most city buses is between 9 PM and 10 PM. For more information on specific schedules, call the AMA or pick up a schedule at the nearest bus station.

➤ BUS INFORMATION: **Autoridad Metropolitana de Autobuses** (Metropolitan Bus Authority; ☎ 787/729–1512 or 787/767–7979).

BUSINESS HOURS

For the wide range of shops, stores, and businesses on the island, hours will vary. But count on convenience stores staying open late into the night, seven days a week. Supermarkets are often closed on Sunday, although some remain open 24-hours, seven days a week. Souvenir shops, boutiques, and many other nonessential businesses are closed on Sunday.

BANKS & OFFICES

Banks are open weekdays 8:30–2:30 and Saturday 9:45–noon. **Post offices** are open weekdays 7:30–4:30 and Saturday 8–noon. **Government offices** are open weekdays 9–5.

GAS STATIONS

Gas is readily available all over the island, from stations with internationally known names such as Mobil, Texaco, and others. Station hours vary, but most are open daily from early in the morning until 10 PM or 11 PM, and numerous stations in the metro areas of San Juan, Ponce, and other cities are open 24 hours. In cities, payment may be made in cash or by credit card. In rural areas, expect to use cash.

MUSEUMS & SIGHTS

Museum and attraction hours vary considerably around the island, but as a general rule you can expect many San Juan area museums to be **closed on Monday,** and, in some cases, Sunday. Hours otherwise are 9 or 10 to 5, often with an hour off for lunch, sometime between noon and 2. Other sights, such as Fuerte San Felipe del Morro (El Morro) and San Cristóbal, which are managed by the National Park Service, are open daily 9–5.

PHARMACIES

Pharmacies are located in urban areas throughout the island and generally keep the same hours as shops—open until 6 or 7 in the evening weekdays and Saturday. **Walgreens** operates numerous pharmacies around the island, some of which remain open 24 hours. Among them are the Walgreens at 1130 Avenida Ashford (☎ 787/725–1510) in Condado; Plaza Carolina (☎ 787/769–4122) in Carolina; Mayagüez Mall (☎ 787/832–2072) in Mayagüez; and Av. Fagot (☎ 787/841–2135) in Ponce.

SHOPS

Street **shops** are open Monday–Saturday 9–6 (9–9 during Christmas holidays); mall stores tend to stay open later, until 8 or 9 in most cases.

CAMERAS & PHOTOGRAPHY

Puerto Rico was made for the camera. With its turquoise sea, lush rain forests, and expansive mountain views, you can't help but take home a few good shots. The **sun is not your friend,** however, so consult your camera's guide to help prevent overexposure and glare—early in the morning or just before dusk are good times to let nature help out with a softer light and intriguing shadows. Your subjects will be wide and varied, from mountain views to street festivals, and when they involve individuals not known to you, be prepared to **ask permission** before taking the photo.

➤ PHOTO HELP: **Kodak Information Center** (☎ 800/242–2424). *Kodak Guide to Shooting Great Travel Pictures,* available in bookstores or from Fodor's Travel Publications (☎

800/533–6478; $16.50 plus $5.50 shipping).

EQUIPMENT PRECAUTIONS

Always **keep your film and tape out of the sun.** Carry an extra supply of batteries, and **be prepared to turn on your camera or camcorder** to prove to security personnel that the device is real. Always **ask for hand inspection of film,** which becomes clouded after repeated exposure to airport X-ray machines, and **keep videotapes away from metal detectors.**

When taking your camera to the **beach,** be wary of sand and salt spray—keep the camera and film in a sealed container or bag when not in use. As well, when not using you camera, **do not leave it locked it your rental car** all day—heat can reduce the quality of the film. Never leave your camera gear unattended on the beach, and lock it in your hotel room safe when out of the room.

FILM & DEVELOPING

Film of all types is widely available in supermarkets, drugstores, souvenir shops, and photo shops. Count on paying about $8 for a 24-exposure roll of color-print film. In San Juan and other urban areas, numerous one-hour film developing shops and drugstores will get your prints made promptly.

VIDEOS

The local standard for video players is the same as on the U.S. mainland—NTSC. Travelers from Australia, Britain, and New Zealand, where PAL is the standard, will have to wait until returning home to view their vacation.

CAR RENTAL

A **valid driver's license** from your native country can be used in Puerto Rico for three months. In some cases the driver must be at least 25 years old. Rental rates can start as low as $35 a day (plus insurance), with unlimited mileage. Discounts are offered for long-term rentals, and insurance can be waived for those who rent with American Express or certain gold credit cards (be sure to check with your credit-card company before renting). Some discounts are offered for AAA membership or for booking more than 72 hours in advance. Dozens of agencies are represented at San Juan's airport, and most car rentals have shuttle service to or from the airport and the pickup point. **Speed limits are posted in miles, distances in kilometers; gas prices are per liter.** Note that many service stations in the central mountains don't take credit cards.

You can rent just about any sort of car you'd like, from a four-wheel-drive off-road vehicle to a compact car. Most are available with either automatic or standard transmission. Four-wheel drive will not be necessary unless you plan to go way off the beaten path; in most cases **a standard car will do the trick,** but opt for air-conditioning—you'll be glad you did when it's high noon and you're in a San Juan traffic jam.

All major U.S. car-rental agencies are represented on the island, but **don't forget local companies**—most are perfectly reliable and less expensive than international companies.

➤ MAJOR AGENCIES: **Alamo** (☎ 800/522–9696; 0181/759–6200 in the U.K.). **Avis** (☎ 800/331–1084; 800/879–2847 in Canada; 02/9353–9000 in Australia; 09/525–1982 in New Zealand). **Budget** (☎ 800/527–0700; 0870/607–5000 in the U.K., through affiliate Europcar). **Dollar** (☎ 800/800–6000; 0124/622–0111 in the U.K., through affiliate Sixt Kenning; 02/9223–1444 in Australia). **Hertz** (☎ 800/654–3001; 800/263–0600 in Canada; 020/8897–2072 in the U.K.; 02/9669–2444 in Australia; 09/256–8690 in New Zealand). **National Car Rental** (☎ 800/227–7368; 020/8680–4800 in the U.K., where it is known as National Europe).

➤ LOCAL AGENCIES: **Charlie Car Rental** (☎ 787/791–1101 or 800/289–1227). **L & M Car Rental** (☎ 787/791–1160 or 800/666–0807). **Target** (☎ 787/728–1447 or 800/934–6457).

CUTTING COSTS

To get the best deal, **book through a travel agent who will shop around.** Do **look into wholesalers,** companies that do not own fleets but rent in bulk from those that do and often offer better rates than traditional car-rental operations. Payment must be made before you leave home.

➤ WHOLESALERS: **Auto Europe** (☎ 207/842–2000 or 800/223–5555, FAX 800–235–6321, www.autoeurope. com).

INSURANCE

When driving a rented car you are generally responsible for any damage to or loss of the vehicle as well as for any property damage or personal injury that you may cause. Before you rent see what coverage your personal auto-insurance policy and credit cards already provide.

REQUIREMENTS & RESTRICTIONS

Several rental agencies require the driver to be at least 25 years of age, so call ahead to check if you're in Puerto Rico on spring break.

SURCHARGES

Before you pick up a car in one city and leave it in another, **ask about drop-off charges or one-way service fees,** which can be substantial. Note, too, that some rental agencies charge extra if you return the car before the time specified in your contract. To avoid a hefty refueling fee, **fill the tank just before you turn in the car,** but be aware that gas stations near the rental outlet may overcharge.

CAR TRAVEL

Using a car is the easiest, most efficient way to get to get around Puerto Rico. At about $35 per day, you'll be spending less than you would on taxi travel, and you'll have the ease of coming and going at will. Roads are well marked by name or route number, and cover all points on the island, north to south and east to west, through the central mountains with panoramic vistas or along the coast. Road signs are most often in Spanish.

Several multilane **highways link populations centers:** Route 26 is the main artery through San Juan, linking Condado and Old San Juan to Isla Verde and the airport in the east. Route 22 moves traffic east–west between San Juan and Aguadilla, and Route 52 runs north–south between

San Juan and Ponce. These two are toll roads, with tolls averaging 35¢– 50¢ per booth. Route 2, a smaller highway but still a main road, covers the west coast, and Routes 3 and 53 traverse the east coast. The island's tourism authorities have designated five routes and highways as particularly appealing to tourists, and have given them names: La Ruta Panorámica (Panoramic Route) east–west through the central mountains; Ruta Cotorra (Puerto Rican Parrot Route) along the north coast; Ruta Paso Fino (Paso Fino Horse Route, after a horse breed) north–south and west along the south coast; Ruta Coquí (Coquí Route, after the famous Puerto Rican tree frog) along the east coast; and Ruta Flamboyán (Flamboyant Route), from San Juan to the east coast through the mountains. These are public, otherwise standard highways, but afford wonderful views and panoramic overlooks.

Traffic around cities, particularly around the San Juan, Ponce, and Mayagüez metro areas, is **heavy at rush hours** (weekdays 7–10 and 4–6)—an unavoidable problem if you need to get around at these times.

U.S. and international laws rule the roads. Driving is on the right.

AUTO CLUBS

➤ IN AUSTRALIA: **Australian Automobile Association** (☎ 02/6247–7311).

➤ IN CANADA: **Canadian Automobile Association** (CAA, ☎ 613/247–0117).

➤ IN NEW ZEALAND: **New Zealand Automobile Association** (☎ 09/377–4660).

➤ IN THE U.K.: **Automobile Association** (AA, ☎ 0990/500–600). **Royal Automobile Club** (RAC, ☎ 0990/722–722 for membership; 0345/121–345 for insurance).

➤ IN THE U.S.: **American Automobile Association** (☎ 800/564–6222).

EMERGENCY SERVICES

For extreme emergencies, call 911. If your car breaks down, call the rental company for a replacement. Before renting, make sure you investigate the company's policy regarding replacement vehicles and repairs out on the island, and ask about surcharges that might be incurred if you break down in a rural area and need a new car.

GASOLINE

Puerto Rico's gas stations are much the same as those in the continental United States. Gas, however, is **sold by the liter** (currently an average 35¢, working out to about $1.33 per gallon), and is readily available in stations all over the island, from familiar brand-name suppliers such as Mobil and Texaco.

All types of fuel are available, from unleaded regular to unleaded super-premium to diesel. Most stations have both full- and self-service. Station hours vary, but **most are open daily** from early in the morning until 10 PM or 11 PM, and numerous stations in the metro areas of San Juan, Ponce, and other cities are open 24 hours. Gas stations are fewer and farther between in the central mountains and other rural areas, but you'll never be too far from a station. Payment can be made in cash or, in the cities, by credit card.

ROAD CONDITIONS

Roads in Puerto Rico are some of the best-maintained in the Caribbean—they will seldom be the source of problems. After heavy rains or hurricane activity, **roads might be washed out or damaged,** but repairs are generally made quickly—the island has a great deal of experience overcoming bad weather.

ROAD MAPS

Most car-rental agencies give you an adequate **free map** with your car, but more detailed maps are available in bookstores and in many souvenir shops. One of the better maps is the **Puerto Rico Mapa de Carreteras** (about $7), by Metro Data Maps, which features an island map, a large metro map of San Juan, and inset maps of Aguadilla, Mayagüez, Arecibo, Ponce, and other large towns. You can find free **Puerto Rico Travel Maps,** better than the map issued by rental agencies, at Tourism Company offices and information booths around the island.

RULES OF THE ROAD

U.S. driving laws apply in Puerto Rico, and you'll find no problems with signage or directionals. Street and highway signs are most often in Spanish but use international symbols; brushing up on a few key Spanish terms before your trip will help. The following words and phrases are useful when driving in Puerto Rico: *calle* (street), *calle sin salida* (dead end, no exit), *cruce de peatones* (pedestrian crossing), *cuidado* (caution), *desivío* (detour), *estació de peaje* (toll booth), *no entre* (do not enter), *prohibido adelantar* (no passing), *salida* (exit), *trásito* (one way), *zona escolar* (school zone).

Speed limits, **posted in miles per hour,** reach 55 mph on major highways and less in the cities, but city traffic is often determined by congestion rather than posted speed limits. Remember, distances are posted in kilometers (1.6 km to 1 mi). Speeding penalties are much the same as in North America, and speed limits, as well as drunk driving laws, are enforced. Remember, driving is on the right side of the road.

CHILDREN IN PUERTO RICO

Puerto Ricans are very family oriented, and island hotels and resorts are increasingly sensitive to visitors traveling with children. With miles of beach and plenty of outdoor activities, the island is a paradise for the entire family. These days, many of the larger resorts and hotels offer **children's activity centers, kids' programs, and baby-sitting services** (at extra cost). When planning, be sure to talk extensively with your hotel representative to establish what on-site activities are available for the children. Baby food, diapers, and other infant necessities are easy to find. If you are renting a car, don't forget to **arrange for a car seat** when you reserve.

➤ LOCAL INFORMATION: The Puerto Rico Tourism Company's free publication *Qué Pasa* regularly lists special activities and events for children. The magazine is available at all Tourism Company offices.

THE GOLD GUIDE / SMART TRAVEL TIPS

FLYING

If your children are two or older, **ask about children's airfares.** As a general rule, infants under two not occupying a seat fly at greatly reduced fares or even for free. When booking, **confirm carry-on allowances** if you're traveling with infants. In general, for babies charged 10% of the adult fare you are allowed one carry-on bag and a collapsible stroller; if the flight is full, the stroller may have to be checked or you may be limited to less.

Experts agree that it's a good idea to use safety seats aloft for children weighing less than 40 pounds. Airlines set their own policies: U.S. carriers usually require that the child be ticketed, even if he or she is young enough to ride free, since the seats must be strapped into regular seats. Do **check your airline's policy about using safety seats during takeoff and landing.** And since safety seats are not allowed everywhere in the plane, get your seat assignments early.

When reserving, **request children's meals or a freestanding bassinet** if you need them. But note that bulkhead seats, where you must sit to use the bassinet, may lack an overhead bin or storage space on the floor.

FOOD

Puerto Rican cuisine includes many dishes that children tend to enjoy. However, children who shy away from spicy, exotic foods can find their respite in the Burger Kings, Pizza Huts, and any number of U.S.-based **chain restaurants** found all over the country. **Fresh fruit** is available for pennies in markets and supermarkets, and the island's modern supermarkets stock all the cereals, snacks, and other foods that many children crave. Most restaurants, including those in hotels, offer **children's menus.**

Note that the legal drinking age in Puerto Rico is 18.

LODGING

Children are, in general, welcome in island resorts and hotels—many offer children's programs, activity centers, and wading pools for the toddlers. Ask specific questions about children's programs. Many hotels offer activity centers that are much like pre-school rooms, with games, craft stations, and big pillows for naps. Others offer **innovative exploring programs** such as walks on the beach to identify and collect shells, or excursions to locals sights. Many resorts have in-room "movies on demand" systems (for about $9), with a wide range of movies for children, as well as systems to block adult titles. Ask about video games for children as well. Children's menus in resort restaurants are the rule, not the exception.

Most hotels allow children under a certain age to stay in their parents' room at no extra charge, but some charge for them as extra adults; be sure to **find out the cutoff age for children's discounts.** The cutoff age generally lies between 12 and 16. Also ask about cribs, extra beds, and cots to accommodate the family.

Many of the island's resorts have special children's programs. In San Juan these include the Condado Plaza, Marriott, Wyndham El San Juan, and San Juan Grand resorts. Others out on the island include the Westin Río Mar, Wyndham El Conquistador, Palmas del Mar, and Ponce Hilton.

➤ BEST CHOICES: **Condado Plaza Hotel and Casino** (✉ 999 Av. Ashford, Condado 00902, ☎ 787/721–1000; 800/468–8588; or 800/624–0420 direct to hotel), **Palmas del Mar Resort & Villas** (✉ Rte. 906, Box 2020, 00792, ☎ 787/852–6000), **Ponce Hilton** (✉ Rte. 14, 1150 Av. Caribe, Box 7419, 00732, ☎ 787/259–7676 or 800/445–8667), **San Juan Grand Beach Resort and Casino** (✉ 187 Av. Isla Verde, Box 6676, Isla Verde 00914, ☎ 787/791–6100, 800/544–3008, or 800/443–2009), **San Juan Marriott Resort and Stellaris Casino** (✉ 1309 Av. Ashford, Condado 00907, ☎ 787/722–7000 or 800/228–9290), **Westin Río Mar Beach Resort** (✉ 6000 Río Mar Blvd., Box 2006, Barrio Palmer, 00721, ☎ 787/888–6000), **Wyndham El Conquistador Resort and Country Club** (✉ 1000 Av. El Conquistador, Box 70001, 00738, ☎ 787/863–1000, 800/996–3426, or 800/468–5228), **Wyndham El San Juan Hotel and Casino** (✉ Av. Isla Verde, Box 2872,

Isla Verde 00902, ☎ 787/791–1000, 800/468–2818, or 800/996–3426).

SIGHTS & ATTRACTIONS

Places that are especially appealing to children are indicated by a rubber duckie icon in the margin.

COMPUTERS ON THE ROAD

Puerto Rico's electric system is, like the mainland's, 110-volt 60 cycles, and many hotels these days are equipped with completely safe **dedicated fax/modem lines** and plenty of outlets for plugging in. Still, it's a good idea to carry an extra battery, as well as a small extension cord for those cases when the only outlet is behind the headboard of the bed.

CONSUMER PROTECTION

Whenever shopping or buying travel services in Puerto Rico, **pay with a major credit card** so you can cancel payment or get reimbursed if there's a problem. If you're doing business with a particular company for the first time, **contact your local Better Business Bureau and the attorney general's offices** in your own state and the company's home state as well. Have any complaints been filed? Finally, if you're buying a package or tour, always **consider travel insurance** that includes default coverage (☞ Insurance, *below*).

➤ BBBs: **Council of Better Business Bureaus** (✉ 4200 Wilson Blvd., Suite 800, Arlington, VA 22203, ☎ 703/276–0100, ℻ 703/525–8277, www.bbb.org).

CRUISE TRAVEL

Puerto Rico is a major cruise destination, and an embarkation point for several cruise lines that ply the Caribbean. Cruising is certainly a relaxing way to visit a destination, though it's not a way to get to know a place. The reason is time—most cruise ships call at several ports per trip, spending a day or part of a day in port. Your experience on shore is limited to a few hours of sightseeing and, generally, shopping.

However, millions of people embark on cruises each year; cruises offer open air, sunshine, entertainment, and plenty of good food and drink, all at one price—all the elements of total relaxation. For details, see Fodor's *Best Cruises 2001*; the Cruise Primer chapter is helpful for first-time cruise passengers.

For the best deals in cruise travel, consult a travel agent who deals exclusively with cruise lines.

➤ CRUISE LINES: **American Canadian Caribbean Line** (✉ Box 368, Warren, RI 02885, ☎ 401/247–0955 or 800/556–7450); **Carnival Cruise Lines** (✉ 3655 N.W. 87th Ave., Miami, FL 33178, ☎ 305/599–2600 or 800/327–9501); **Celebrity Cruises** (✉ 5200 Blue Lagoon Dr., Miami, FL 33126, ☎ 305/262–8322 or 800/437–3111); **Clipper Cruise Line** (✉ 7711 Bonhomme Ave., St. Louis, MO 63105, ☎ 800/325–0010); **Club Med Cruises** (✉ 40 W. 57th St., New York, NY 10019, ☎ 212/750–1687 or 800/258–2633); **Commodore Cruise Lines** (✉ 800 Douglas Rd., Suite 700, Coral Gables, FL 33134, ☎ 305/529–3000 or 800/832–1122); **Costa Cruise Lines** (✉ World Trade Center 80 S.W. 8th St., Miami, FL 33130, ☎ 305/358–7352 or 800/462–6782); **Cunard Line** (✉ 555 5th Ave., New York, NY 10017, ☎ 800/728–6273 or 800/221–4770); **Dolphin/Majesty Cruise Line** (✉ 901 South America Way, Miami, FL 33132, ☎ 305/358–2111); **Holland America Line** (✉ 3000 Elliot Ave. W, Seattle, WA 98119, ☎ 800/426–0327); **Norwegian Cruise Line** (✉ 95 Merrick Way, Coral Gables, FL 33134, ☎ 305/445–0866 or 800/327–7030); **Premier Cruise Line** (✉ Box 517, Cape Canaveral, FL 33134, ☎ 800/222–1003 or 800/258–8006); **Princess Cruises** (✉ 10100 Santa Monica Blvd., Suite 1800, Los Angeles, CA 90067, ☎ 310/553–1770 or 800/421–0522); **Radisson Seven Seas Cruises** (✉ 600 Corporate Dr., Suite 410, Fort Lauderdale, FL 33334, ☎ 800/333–3333); **Royal Caribbean Cruise Line** (✉ 1050 Caribbean Way, Miami, FL 33132, ☎ 305/539–6000 or 800/327–6700); **Seabourn Cruise Line** (✉ 55 Francisco St., Suite 710, San Francisco, CA 94133, ☎ 415/391–7444 or 800/929–9595); **Windstar Cruises** (✉ 300 Elliott Ave., Seattle, WA 98119, ☎ 800/258–7245).

THE GOLD GUIDE / SMART TRAVEL TIPS

➤ ORGANIZATIONS: **Cruise Lines International Association** (✉ 500 5th Ave., Suite 1407, New York, NY 10010, ☎ 212/921–0066).

CUSTOMS & DUTIES

If you're coming from outside the United States, **keep receipts** for all purchases. Upon reentering the country, **be ready to show customs officials what you've bought.** If you feel a duty is incorrect or object to the way your clearance was handled, note the inspector's badge number and ask to see a supervisor. If the problem isn't resolved, write to the appropriate authorities, beginning with the port director at your point of entry.

IN AUSTRALIA

Australian residents who are 18 or older may bring home $A400 worth of souvenirs and gifts (including jewelry), 250 cigarettes or 250 grams of tobacco, and 1,125 ml of alcohol (including wine, beer, and spirits). Residents under 18 may bring back $A200 worth of goods. Prohibited items include meat products. Seeds, plants, and fruits need to be declared upon arrival.

➤ INFORMATION: **Australian Customs Service** (Regional Director, ✉ Box 8, Sydney, NSW 2001, ☎ 02/9213–2000, FAX 02/9213–4000).

IN CANADA

Canadian residents who have been out of Canada for at least seven days may bring home C$500 worth of goods duty-free. If you've been away less than seven days but more than 48 hours, the duty-free allowance drops to C$200; if your trip lasts 24–48 hours, the allowance is C$50. You may not pool allowances with family members. Goods claimed under the C$500 exemption may follow you by mail; those claimed under the lesser exemptions must accompany you. Alcohol and tobacco products may be included in the seven-day and 48-hour exemptions but not in the 24-hour exemption. If you meet the age requirements of the province or territory through which you reenter Canada, you may bring in, duty-free, 1.14 liters (40 imperial ounces) of wine or liquor *or* 24 12-ounce cans or bottles of beer or ale. If you are 16 or older you may bring in, duty-free, 200 cigarettes and 50 cigars. Check ahead of time with Revenue Canada or the Department of Agriculture for policies regarding meat products, seeds, plants, and fruits.

You may send an unlimited number of gifts worth up to C$60 each duty-free to Canada. Label the package UNSOLICITED GIFT—VALUE UNDER $60. Alcohol and tobacco are excluded.

➤ INFORMATION: **Revenue Canada** (✉ 2265 St. Laurent Blvd. S, Ottawa, Ontario K1G 4K3, ☎ 613/993–0534, 800/461–9999 in Canada, FAX 613/957–8911, www.ccra-adrc.gc.ca).

IN NEW ZEALAND

Homeward-bound residents 17 or older may bring back $700 worth of souvenirs and gifts. Your duty-free allowance also includes 4.5 liters of wine or beer; one 1,125-ml bottle of spirits; and either 200 cigarettes, 250 grams of tobacco, 50 cigars, or a combination of the three up to 250 grams. Prohibited items include meat products, seeds, plants, and fruits.

➤ INFORMATION: **New Zealand Customs** (Custom House, ✉ 50 Anzac Ave., Box 29, Auckland, New Zealand, ☎ 09/359–6655, FAX 09/359–6732).

IN PUERTO RICO

Clearing U.S. Customs in Puerto Rico is fast and efficient, provided you've filled out all customs forms and declared all items, including fruits and vegetables, plants and plant products, meat and meat products, and live animals, birds, and wildlife products. The United States enforces certain restrictions on bringing pets into its territories.

U.S. citizens and legal residents need not clear customs in Puerto Rico when arriving from the mainland.

When leaving Puerto Rico for the mainland, you must pass your bag through a checkpoint of the USDA's Animal and Plant Health Inspection Service (APHIS). The list of organic products that can be transported from Puerto Rico to the States includes avocados, bananas, breadfruits, citrus fruits, ginger, papayas, and plantains.

Pets and other live animals and birds can enter Puerto Rico subject to certification, permits, inspection, and quarantine rules that vary with the animal and its origin.

➤ INFORMATION: **U.S. Customs Service** (✉ 1300 Pennsylvania Ave. NW, Washington, DC 20229, www.customs.gov; inquiries ☎ 202/354–1000; complaints c/o ✉ Office of Regulations and Rulings; registration of equipment c/o ✉ Resource Management, ☎ 202/927–0540).

IN THE U.K.

From areas outside the EU, including Puerto Rico, you may bring home, duty-free, 200 cigarettes or 50 cigars; 1 liter of spirits or 2 liters of fortified or sparkling wine or liqueurs; 2 liters of still table wine; 60 ml of perfume; 250 ml of toilet water; plus £136 worth of other goods, including gifts and souvenirs. If returning from outside the EU, prohibited items include meat products, seeds, plants, and fruits.

➤ INFORMATION: **HM Customs and Excise** (✉ Dorset House, Stamford St., Bromley, Kent BR1 1XX, ☎ 0171/202–4227).

DINING

In San Juan and other cities and at the large resorts you'll find restaurants serving a wide range of international cuisines. Elsewhere on the island, the emphasis is on traditional food of the region, including simple, well-prepared meat and seafood, plantains and other fresh produce, and rice and beans.

The restaurants we list are the cream of the crop in each price category. Properties indicated by an ✕🏠 are lodging establishments whose restaurant warrants a special trip.

MEAL TIMES

Unless otherwise noted, the restaurants listed in this guide are open daily for lunch and dinner.

RESERVATIONS & DRESS

Reservations are always a good idea: we mention them only when they're essential or not accepted. Book as far ahead as you can, and reconfirm as soon as you arrive. We mention dress

only when men are required to wear a jacket or a jacket and tie.

WINE, BEER, & SPIRITS

Puerto Rico is not a notable producer of wine, but there are several well-crafted local beers to choose from, and the rum produced here is known worldwide. The drinking age in Puerto Rico is 18.

DISABILITIES & ACCESSIBILITY

As a commonwealth of the United States, **Puerto Rico complies with regulations** of the Americans with Disabilities Act (ADA).

Parking for travelers with disabilities is readily available in most places, and in many towns curbs have been cut to accommodate wheelchairs. A notable exception is Old San Juan, where the cobblestone streets, narrow alleys, and steep hills are problematic for travelers in wheelchairs.

➤ LOCAL RESOURCES: For ADA and accessible information in Puerto Rico, contact the **Northeast Disability and Business Technical Assistance Center** of the United Cerebral Palsy Associations of New Jersey (✉ 354 S. Broad St., Trenton, NJ 08608, ☎ 800/949–4232).

LODGING

Many of the newer accommodations in Puerto Rico offer rooms that comply with ADA rules. However, as is the case in all hotel bookings, don't simply ask whether the room in question is accessible, but ask specific questions. Many hotels are genuinely accessible in the ADA sense, while others are not.

RESERVATIONS

When discussing accessibility with an operator or reservations agent, **ask hard questions.** Are there any stairs, inside *or* out? Are there grab bars next to the toilet *and* in the shower/tub? How wide is the doorway to the room? To the bathroom? For the most extensive facilities meeting the latest legal specifications, **opt for newer accommodations.**

SIGHTS & ATTRACTIONS

Public attractions and sites such as museums, beaches, and galleries are subject to ADA regulations, and in

SMART TRAVEL TIPS / THE GOLD GUIDE

many cases the attractions, as well as rest rooms and public phones, are able to be used by travelers in wheelchairs. However, not all attractions are up to code, and **not all are truly accessible.** In a quick survey of top attractions in the country—Hacienda Buena Vista in Ponce, Las Cabezas de San Juan in Las Croabas, El Morro in Old San Juan, San Juan Cathedral in Old San Juan, and El Yunque at the eastern end of the island—it appears that the phrase "limited accessibility" applies to all. While some portions of the sites are accessible, notably rest rooms, many of their walking areas, trails, and displays are not fully accessible by travelers with mobility, vision, or hearing issues. A notable exception is famous Luquillo Beach, east of San Juan, which operates a program called Sea Without Barriers, with special equipment and entry systems designed to get those with mobility issues onto the beach and into the water.

TRANSPORTATION

San Juan's Luis Muñoz Marín International Airport is well equipped for travelers with disabilities. Visitors disembark on flyways straight into the airport, thus avoiding the steep steps of airplane stairways and the long walk across the Tarmac to the terminal. The public rest rooms and phones are accessible. Airport personnel help travelers in wheelchairs through the long walkways, through baggage claim, and through customs and immigration (if necessary). **Make sure you request wheelchairs and escorts when booking your flights.**

Most public buses are equipped with wheelchair lifts and lockdowns. The few that are not are older buses bought more than 10 years ago. Taxis and publicos can fit chairs in the trunk. Public parking lots have designated spots for travelers with disabilities. Car-rental agencies do not issue tags or placards, but you can use yours from home. Reputable car-rental agencies such as Avis (☞ Major Agencies, *above*) can equip cars with hand controls and other devices for travelers with mobility problems. Give advance notice of at

least a week. Avis and other airport agencies will deliver the car to you at the arrivals area.

Wheelchair Getaway (☎ 787/883–0131) in San Juan offers wheelchair transport from airports and cruise-ship docks to San Juan hotels, as well as city sightseeing tours.

➤ COMPLAINTS: **Disability Rights Section** (✉ U.S. Department of Justice, Civil Rights Division, Box 66738, Washington, DC 20035-6738, ☎ 202/514–0301 or 800/514–0301; TTY 202/514–0301 or 800/514–0301, FAX 202/307–1198) for general complaints. **Aviation Consumer Protection Division** (☞ Air Travel, *above*) for airline-related problems. **Civil Rights Office** (✉ U.S. Department of Transportation, Departmental Office of Civil Rights, S-30, 400 7th St. SW, Room 10215, Washington, DC 20590, ☎ 202/366–4648, FAX 202/366–9371) for problems with surface transportation.

TRAVEL AGENCIES

In the United States, the Americans with Disabilities Act requires that travel firms serve the needs of all travelers. Some agencies specialize in working with people with disabilities.

➤ TRAVELERS WITH MOBILITY PROBLEMS: **Access Adventures** (✉ 206 Chestnut Ridge Rd., Rochester, NY 14624, ☎ 716/889–9096, dltravel@prodigy.net), run by a former physical-rehabilitation counselor. **CareVacations** (✉ 5-5110 50th Ave., Leduc, Alberta T9E 6V4, ☎ 780/986–6404 or 877/478–7827, FAX 780/986–8332, www.carevacations.com), for group tours and cruise vacations. **Flying Wheels Travel** (✉ 143 W. Bridge St., Box 382, Owatonna, MN 55060, ☎ 507/451–5005 or 800/535–6790, FAX 507/451–1685, thq@ll.net, www.flyingwheels.com). **Tomorrow's Level of Care** (✉ Box 470299, Brooklyn, NY 11247, ☎ 718/756–0794 or 800/932–2012), for nursing services and medical equipment.

➤ TRAVELERS WITH DEVELOPMENTAL DISABILITIES: **New Directions** (✉ 5276 Hollister Ave., Suite 207, Santa Barbara, CA 93111, ☎ 805/967–2841 or 888/967–2841, ℻ 805/964–7344, newdirec@silcom.com, www.silcom.com/ânewdirec/). **Sprout** (✉ 893 Amsterdam Ave., New York, NY 10025, ☎ 212/222–9575 or 888/222–9575, ℻ 212/222–9768, sprout@interport.net, www.gosprout.org).

DISCOUNTS & DEALS

Be a smart shopper and **compare all your options** before making decisions. A plane ticket bought with a promotional coupon from travel clubs, coupon books, and direct-mail offers may not be cheaper than the least expensive fare from a discount ticket agency. And always keep in mind that what you get is just as important as what you save.

DISCOUNT RESERVATIONS

To save money, **look into discount reservations services** with toll-free numbers, which use their buying power to get a better price on hotels, airline tickets, even car rentals. When booking a room, always **call the hotel's local toll-free number** (if one is available) rather than the central reservations number—you'll often get a better price. Always ask about special packages or corporate rates.

➤ AIRLINE TICKETS: ☎ **800/FLY–4–LESS.** ☎ **800/FLY–ASAP.**

➤ HOTEL ROOMS: **Hotel Reservations Network** (☎ 800/964–6835, www.hoteldiscounts.com). **Players Express Vacations** (☎ 800/458–6161, www.playersexpress.com). **RMC Travel** (☎ 800/245–5738, www.rmcwebtravel.com). **Steigenberger Reservation Service** (☎ 800/223–5652, www.srs-worldhotels.com).

PACKAGE DEALS

Don't confuse packages and guided tours. When you buy a package, you travel on your own, just as though you had planned the trip yourself. Fly/drive packages, which combine airfare and car rental, are often a good deal.

ECOTOURISM

The Puerto Rico government and numerous private organizations are concerned about and actively combatting the degradation of the island's natural resources. The Conservation Trust of Puerto Rico has accumulated, for the purposes of preservation and education, properties around the island that have unique ecological and historic qualities. Among them are Las Cabezas de San Juan in Las Croabas, which contains marshes, forest, and several different ecological environments common to Puerto Rico, and sections of the Bahía Fosforescente (Phosphorescent Bay) in La Parguera. The 28,000-acre Caribbean National Forest, commonly know as El Yunque, is managed by the U.S. Forest Service, and is lush with tropical trees and plants, waterfalls, and miles of hikes through the hills.

ELECTRICITY

Puerto Rico uses the same 110-volt AC (60-cycle), two-prong-outlet electrical system as in North America. European guests who have traveling appliances that use other systems should bring adapters and converters, or call ahead to confirm that their hotel has them on hand.

EMERGENCIES

Emergencies are handled by dialing 911. You can expect a quick response by police, fire, and medical personnel.

➤ CONTACTS: **Ambulance, police, and fire:** ☎ 911.

Hospitals and clinics: Ashford Memorial Community Hospital (✉ 1451 Av. Ashford, Condado, San Juan, ☎ 787/721–2160), **Bella Vista Hospital** (✉ Cerro las Mesas, Mayagüez, ☎ 787/834–6000), **Eastern Medical Associates** (✉ 267 Av. Valero, Fajardo, ☎ 787/863–0669), and **San Juan Health Centre** (✉ 200 Av. de Diego, San Juan, ☎ 787/725–0202).

Pharmacies: Puerto Rico Drug Company (✉ 157 Calle San Francisco, Old San Juan, ☎ 787/725–2202). **Walgreens** (✉ 1330 Av. Ashford, Condado, San Juan, ☎ 787/725–1510). This Walgreens is open 24 hours; the chain also has more than 30 other locations on the island.

ENGLISH-LANGUAGE MEDIA

If you don't read Spanish, you won't be lost in Puerto Rico. While there are a number of good Spanish newspapers, the island also offers numerous English

THE GOLD GUIDE / SMART TRAVEL TIPS

dailies, including its own *San Juan Star* as well as U.S. newspapers either imported from the States or printed in Puerto Rico under agreements.

Television programming is in Spanish and English. Some local shows broadcast in English, but the majority of English programming comes from cable-transmitted HBO, CNN, and others.

BOOKS

Most bookstores carry books in both English and Spanish, and you'll find the standard English paperbacks at supermarkets and drugstores, with prices comparable to those in the United States.

➤ BOOKSTORES: **Borders** (⊠ Plaza Las Américas, 525 Av. Franklin Delano Roosevelt, Hato Rey, ☎ 787/777–0916), **Cronopios** (⊠ 255 Calle San José, Old San Juan, ☎ 787/724–1815), **Thekes** (⊠ Plaza Las Américas, 525 Av. Franklin Delano Roosevelt, Hato Rey, ☎ 787/765–1539).

NEWSPAPERS & MAGAZINES

Puerto Rico's Pulitzer prize–winning *San Juan Star* is printed daily (35¢) in Spanish and English, and is one of the **most informative** newspapers in the Caribbean. It carries local and syndicated columnists, and a good mix of local and international news. Its weekend edition is a font of information on goings on around San Juan and the island. In addition, you can get copies of the *Wall Street Journal, New York Times, USA Today, Miami Herald,* and other dailies, most often at hotels and drugstores.

RADIO & TELEVISION

Most local television programs are in Spanish, and consist of a mix of news, game shows, movies, soaps, and music video programs. In addition, cable has brought CBS, NBC, ABC, HBO, CNN, and a wealth of U.S. programming to the island.

Radio programs run the gamut of Spanish talk shows, Miami-based English news broadcasts, evangelical religious broadcasts, reggae stations in English and Spanish, and Spanish pop music.

ETIQUETTE & BEHAVIOR

Puerto Ricans have, in general, a **strong sense of religion**—as evidenced by the numerous Catholic patron-saint festivals held throughout the year. Puerto Rican family ties are also strong, and it's not unusual to see families piling onto the beaches on weekends for a day of fun and barbecue. Puerto Ricans tend to proffer a great deal of respect to elders, in formal greetings and language and in general attitude.

Many **islanders are somewhat conservative** in dress and manners, despite a penchant for frenetic music and dance. Typical greetings between female friends and male and female friends and relatives is a **handshake or kiss on the cheek,** and the greeting "Buenos días" (Good day) or "Buenos tardes" (Good afternoon), among a host of formal and less formal colloquial greetings. The phrases are also said in departing.

Islanders' knowledge of U.S. culture is thorough. Many Puerto Ricans have spent a great deal of time Stateside, and those who haven't inevitably have relatives or friends living on the mainland. U.S. music, dress, and attitudes have infiltrated the island in many ways, especially among the young, but the overriding cultural cues are Spanish-Caribbean. Indeed, Puerto Ricans have a strong sense of island identity, marked by often-ferocious debates over Puerto Rico's political destiny.

FESTIVALS & SEASONAL EVENTS

Puerto Rico's festivals are colorful and inclined toward lots of music and feasting. The towns and villages are particularly loyal to their patron saints, and every year each of the island's 78 municipalities celebrates a **fiesta patronale** (patron saint festival). Though religious in origin, these festivities feature processions, sports events, folklore shows, feasting, music, and dance. They last about 10 days, with more activities on weekends than on weekdays. San Juan's fiesta patronale honors San Juan Bautista in late June; Ponce honors Nostra Señora de la Guadalupe in mid-December. Several towns and regions also have pre-Lenten **Carnivals,** complete with parades, folk music, local dishes, a Carnival Queen pageant, and music competitions. All are in early-to-late February, sometimes into March. Ponce's Carnival is widely considered to be the most vivid and energetic. Contact the tourist office (☞ Visitor Information, *below*) for a complete list of fiestas patronales and other events.

In addition to the patron saint festivals, Old San Juan holds an annual **San Sebastián Street Festival** in January, several nights of live music in the plazas, food festivals, and *cabezudos* parades recalling folk legends with performers wearing oversize masks. **Emancipation Day** on March 22 honors the abolition of slavery. The **Casals Festival,** held at the Luis A. Ferré Performing Arts Center in San Juan in early June, honors the late, great cellist with 10 days of classical music. In mid-November you can find the annual **Festival of Puerto Rican Music** in San Juan and other venues, celebrating the vibrancy of Puerto Rico's *plena y bomba* folk music and dance, highlighted by a contest featuring the *cuatro,* a traditional guitar. Sport anglers will want to keep the annual **International Billfishing Tournament** in mind; held in August and September, this gamefishing tournament attracts anglers from the world over competing for prizes for the biggest marlin and other billfish.

GAY & LESBIAN TRAVEL

San Juan is a cosmopolitan and sophisticated city, and gays and lesbians will find it an **easy city in which to mingle.** There are gay-friendly hotels and gay clubs throughout downtown and the suburbs, and the beach at Ocean Park tends to attract a gay crowd. You can even find scuba diving outfits for gays and lesbians. However, normal precautions regarding overt behavior stand; Puerto Ricans are often conservative about matters of sexuality and dress.

➤ GAY- & LESBIAN-FRIENDLY TRAVEL AGENCIES: **Different Roads Travel** (✉ 8383 Wilshire Blvd., Suite 902, Beverly Hills, CA 90211, ☎ 323/651–5557 or 800/429–8747, ⅁X 323/651–3678, leigh@west.tzell.com). **Kennedy** Travel (✉ 314 Jericho Tpke., Floral Park, NY 11001, ☎ 516/352–4888 or 800/237–7433, ⅁X 516/354–8849, main@kennedytravel.com, www.kennedytravel.com). **Now Voyager** (✉ 4406 18th St., San Francisco, CA 94114, ☎ 415/626–1169 or 800/255–6951, ⅁X 415/626–8626, www.nowvoyager.com). **Skylink Travel and Tour** (✉ 1006 Mendocino Ave., Santa Rosa, CA 95401, ☎ 707/546–9888 or 800/225–5759, ⅁X 707/546–9891, skylinktvl@aol.com, www.skylinktravel.com), serving lesbian travelers.

HEALTH

Although both Spanish and English are Puerto Rico's official languages, Spanish prevails. English is widely spoken, especially among professionals such as doctors and nurses. At all hospitals and medical centers you'll find English-speaking medical staff, as well as in emergency services. In addition, most large hotels have an English-speaking doctor on call to take care of guests' medical problems.

Health care in Puerto Rico is among the best in the Caribbean.

DIVERS' ALERT

Do not fly within 24 hours of scuba diving.

FOOD & DRINK

Tap water is generally fine on the island; just avoid drinking it after storms (when the drinking-water supply might become mixed with sewage). Thoroughly wash or peel produce you buy in markets before eating it.

OVER-THE-COUNTER REMEDIES

All the **familiar brand names** of over-the-counter medicines (Tylenol, Motrin, Nyquil, etc.) are available in pharmacies (many of which are open 24 hours), supermarkets, and convenience stores, exactly as in mainland North America. Popular brands of sunscreen are also available at all of the above, as well as at souvenir shops in tourist centers.

PESTS & OTHER HAZARDS

Most health problems encountered by visitors to Puerto Rico involve the trio

rum, sun, and blisters. Overindulgence has probably sidelined more travelers than any other health hazard—use common sense. The sun is hot and you should take precautions while outdoors, whether on the beach or hiking through the rain forest. Limit your tanning to 20 minutes at a time, and wear a T-shirt on the beach when the going gets rough. Use a strong sunscreen and carry extra, wear a lightweight hat, and carry plenty of drinking water to guard against dehydration. Wear comfortable walking shoes when hiking.

The **ocean presents its own types of hazards.** Some beaches along the north and west coasts are rough, with strong waves more suitable for surfing, and undertows not suitable for small children. Signs are posted where and when areas are too dangerous for swimming.

Avoid the black, long-spined sea urchin, often found in shallow water near shore, hidden among coral and rocks. The strong barbs will pierce the skin and break off, resulting in painful swelling. Remove the fragments immediately and soak the affected area, and treat with antiseptic as soon as possible. Then see a doctor. Also, **stay clear of all forms of jellyfish,** which often wash up on shore. They're nice to look at but not to touch. Their tentacles are equipped with stinging organisms that detach when brushed. Splash the affected area with drying agents such as alcohol, talcum powder, even sand, but avoid rubbing your skin or you may activate detached stingers. Then see a doctor.

When snorkeling or diving, **avoid touching live coral,** for the organism's safety as well as your own. All corals can be harmful, either causing a slow-healing gash or releasing toxins on contact. Avoid even the smooth-looking coral. Fire corals and stinging corals do what their names suggest and should be avoided. If you accidentally touch them, seek treatment. Likewise, breaking coral, kicking it with your fins, or brushing it with your underwater camera can traumatize the delicate ecological balance of the reef.

Bugs are, primarily, annoying— mosquitoes and sand gnats (no-see-ums) are the biggest problems, and they can be warded off with a good repellent, available in all drugstores and pharmacies. Mosquito coils are also sold throughout the island.

HOLIDAYS

Puerto Rico observes **all U.S. federal holidays, as well as local religious and other holidays.** Most government offices and businesses shut down on holidays, with the exception of convenience stores, some supermarkets, pharmacies, and restaurants. Public transportation runs on abbreviated schedules, just as on Sunday. Public holidays in Puerto Rico include: New Year's Day, Three Kings Day (Jan. 6), Eugenio María de Hostos Day (Jan. 8), Dr. Martin Luther King Jr. Day (3rd Mon. in Jan.), Presidents' Day (3rd Mon. in Feb.), Palm Sunday, Good Friday, Easter Sunday, Memorial Day (last Mon. in June), Independence Day (July 4), Luis Muñoz Rivera Day (July 16), Constitution Day (July 25), José Celso Barbosa Day (July 27), Labor Day (1st Mon. in Sept.), Columbus Day (2nd Mon. in Oct.), Veteran's Day (Nov. 11), Puerto Rico Discovery Day (Nov. 19), Thanksgiving Day, and Christmas.

INSURANCE

The most useful travel insurance plan is a comprehensive policy that includes coverage for trip cancellation and interruption, default, trip delay, and medical expenses (with a waiver for preexisting conditions).

Without insurance you will lose all or most of your money if you cancel your trip, regardless of the reason. Default insurance covers you if your tour operator, airline, or cruise line goes out of business. Trip-delay covers expenses that arise because of bad weather or mechanical delays. Study the fine print when comparing policies.

If you're traveling internationally, a key component of travel insurance is coverage for medical bills incurred if you get sick on the road. U.K. residents can buy a travel insurance policy valid for most vacations taken during the year in which it's purchased (but check pre-existing-condition coverage). British and Australian citizens need extra medical coverage when traveling overseas. Always **buy travel policies directly from the insurance company**; if you buy them from a cruise line, airline, or tour operator that goes out of business you probably will not be covered for the agency or operator's default, a major risk. Before making any purchase, **review your existing health and homeowner's policies** to find what they cover away from home.

➤ TRAVEL INSURERS: In the U.S.: **Access America** (✉ 6600 W. Broad St., Richmond, VA 23230, ☎ 804/285–3300 or 800/284–8300, FAX 804/673–1583, www.previewtravel.com), **Travel Guard International** (✉ 1145 Clark St., Stevens Point, WI 54481, ☎ 715/345–0505 or 800/826–1300, FAX 800/955–8785, www.noelgroup.com). In Canada: **Voyager Insurance** (✉ 44 Peel Center Dr., Brampton, Ontario L6T 4M8, ☎ 905/791–8700; 800/668–4342 in Canada).

➤ INSURANCE INFORMATION: In the U.K.: **Association of British Insurers** (✉ 51–55 Gresham St., London EC2V 7HQ, ☎ 0171/600–3333, FAX 0171/696–8999, info@abi.org.uk, www.abi.org.uk). In Australia: **Insurance Council of Australia** (☎ 03/9614–1077, FAX 03/9614–7924).

INTERNATIONAL TRAVELERS

CONSULATES & EMBASSIES

➤ AUSTRALIA: Australia has no embassy in Puerto Rico.

➤ CANADA: ✉ 107 Ceriepo St., Alturas de Santa Maria, Guaynabo, 00969, ☎ 787/790–2210.

➤ NEW ZEALAND: New Zealand has no embassy in Puerto Rico.

➤ UNITED KINGDOM: ✉ Bank Trust Plaza, Suite 807, 265 Av. Ponce de León, Hato Rey, 00917, ☎ 787/721–5193).

CURRENCY

The dollar is the basic unit of U.S. currency. It has 100 cents. Coins include the copper penny (1¢); the silvery nickel (5¢), dime (10¢), quarter (25¢), and half-dollar (50¢); and the golden $1 coin, replacing a now-rare silver dollar. Bills are denominated $1, $5, $10, $20, $50, and $100, all green and identical in size; designs vary. The exchange rate at press time was $1.52 per British pound, 68¢ per Canadian dollar, 59¢ per Australian dollar, and 47¢ per New Zealand dollar.

ELECTRICITY

The U.S. standard is AC, 110 volts/60 cycles. Plugs have two flat pins set parallel to each another.

EMERGENCIES

For police, fire, or ambulance, **dial 911.**

INSURANCE

☞ Insurance, *above.*

MAIL & SHIPPING

You can buy stamps and aerograms and send letters and parcels in post offices. Stamp-dispensing machines can occasionally be found in airports, bus and train stations, office buildings, drugstores, and the like. You can also deposit mail in the stout, dark blue, steel bins at strategic locations everywhere and in the mail chutes of large buildings; pickup schedules are posted.

For mail sent within the United States, you need a 33¢ stamp for first-class letters weighing up to 1 ounce (22¢ for each additional ounce) and 20¢ for domestic postcards. For overseas mail, you pay 60¢ for ½-ounce airmail letters, 50¢ for airmail postcards, and 35¢ for surface-rate postcards. For Canada you need a 52¢ stamp for a 1-ounce letter and 40¢ for a postcard. For 50¢ you can buy an aerogram—a single sheet of lightweight blue paper that folds into its own envelope, stamped for overseas airmail.

To receive mail on the road, have it sent c/o General Delivery at your destination's main post office (use the correct five-digit zip code). You must pick up mail in person within 30 days and show a driver's license or passport.

PASSPORTS & VISAS

Visitor visas are not necessary for Canadian citizens or for citizens of Australia, New Zealand, and the United Kingdom staying fewer than 90 days. For complete passport information, *see* Passports & Visas *below*.

TELEPHONES

All U.S. telephone numbers consist of a three-digit area code and a seven-digit local number. For complete information about local and long-distance calling procedures, *see* Telephones, *below*.

LANGUAGE

Puerto Rico is caught betwixt and between languages—the official languages are Spanish and English, in that order. Spanish prevails in everyday conversation, in commerce, and in the media. And although English is widely spoken, you'll probably want to take a Spanish phrase book along on your travels to the rural areas of the island. Hotel front desk staff and restaurant staff in large facilities speak English. Most business and government telephones are manned by people who speak English (or will find someone who does), and telephone answering systems are bilingual.

If you're stumped, call the **Tourist Information Line** (☎ 787/766–7777) or **Traveler's Aid** line (☎ 787/791–1054), both in English, where someone can help.

LANGUAGES FOR TRAVELERS

A phrase book and language-tape set can help get you started.

➤ PHRASE BOOKS & LANGUAGE-TAPE SETS: *Fodor's Spanish for Travelers* (☎ 800/733–3000 in the U.S.; 800/668–4247 in Canada; $7 for phrasebook, $16.95 for audio set).

LODGING

In Puerto Rico you have your choice between large, full-service resorts on the coast, medium-size resorts and inns on the coast or in the central rural areas and mountains, and a wide range of hotels and resorts in the cities.

San Juan's high-rise hotels on the Condado and Isla Verde beach strips cater primarily to the cruise-ship and casino crowd, though several target business travelers. Outside San Juan, particularly on the east coast, you'll find self-contained luxury resorts that cover hundreds of acres. In the west,

southwest, and south—as well as on the islands of Vieques and Culebra—smaller inns, villas, and condominiums for short-term rentals and government-sponsored **paradores** are the norm.

Some paradores are rural inns offering no-frills apartments, and some are large hotels, but all must meet certain standards, such as proximity to an attraction or beach. Most have a small restaurant that serves local cuisine. They're great bargains (prices range from $60 to $125 for a double room). You can make reservations for all paradores by contacting the tourist board's **Paradores of Puerto Rico** (✉ Box 4435, Old San Juan 00902, ☎ 800/443–0266 in North America; 787/721–2884 in San Juan; 800/981–7575 elsewhere in Puerto Rico, www.prtourism.com). When booking a room, note that beachfront rooms or rooms overlooking the pool will be more expensive than so-called "garden" or "mountain-view" rooms, which are essentially rooms without ocean views. As well, consider your needs: are you concerned about a children's program or a wading pool for the toddlers? Do you want a hotel with a vigorous nightlife, casino, or floor shows? Must the hotel be on the beach, or do you want to save money by being only within driving distance? Do the room windows open, and can you shut off the air-conditioning without having to call the front desk? Do you want cable TV to keep up with CNN's financial news? A refrigerator in the room? Make a list of your desires, and call the hotel directly, or direct your travel agent to do the same.

The lodgings we list are the cream of the crop in each price category. We always list the facilities that are available—but we don't specify whether they cost extra: When pricing accommodations, always ask what's included and what costs extra.

Assume that hotels operate on the **European Plan** (EP, with no meals) unless we specify that they use the **Continental Plan** (CP, with a Continental breakfast), **Modified American Plan** (MAP, with breakfast and dinner), or the **Full American Plan** (FAP, with all meals).

APARTMENT & VILLA RENTALS

If you want a home base that's roomy enough for a family and comes with cooking facilities, **consider a furnished rental.** These can save you money, especially if you're traveling with a group. Home-exchange directories sometimes list rentals as well as exchanges.

➤ INTERNATIONAL AGENTS: **At Home Abroad** (✉ 405 E. 56th St., Suite 6H, New York, NY 10022, ☎ 212/421–9165, FAX 212/752–1591, athomabrod@aol.com, http://member.aol.com/athomabrod/index.html). **Europa-Let/Tropical Inn-Let** (✉ 92 N. Main St., Ashland, OR 97520, ☎ 541/482–5806 or 800/462–4486, FAX 541/482–0660). **Hideaways International** (✉ 767 Islington St., Portsmouth, NH 03801, ☎ 603/430–4433 or 800/843–4433, FAX 603/430–4444, info@hideaways.com www.hideaways.com; membership $99). **Hometours International** (✉ Box 11503, Knoxville, TN 37939, ☎ 865/690–8484 or 800/367–4668, hometours@aol.com, http://thor.he.net/áhometour/). **Vacation Home Rentals Worldwide** (✉ 235 Kensington Ave., Norwood, NJ 07648, ☎ 201/767–9393 or 800/633–3284, FAX 201/767–5510, vhrww@juno.com, www.vhrww.com). **Villas and Apartments Abroad** (✉ 1270 Avenue of the Americas, 15th floor, New York, NY 10020, ☎ 212/897–5045 or 800/433–3020, FAX 212/897–5039, vaa@altour.com, www.vaanyc.com). **Villas International** (✉ 950 Northgate Dr., Suite 206, San Rafael, CA 94903, ☎ 415/499–9490 or 800/221–2260, FAX 415/499–9491, villas@best.com, www.villasintl.com).

➤ LOCAL AGENTS: **Puerto Rico Vacation Apartments** (✉ Marabella del Caribe Oeste S-5, Isla Verde 00979, ☎ 787/727–1591 or 800/266–3639, FAX 787/268–3604). **Island West Properties** (✉ Rte. 413, Km 1.3, Box 700, Rincón 00677, ☎ 787/823–2323, FAX 787/823–3254). **Connections** (✉ Box 358, Esperanza, Vieques 00765, ☎ 787/741–0023).

CAMPING

It is not legal, and not safe, simply to pitch a tent in the woods or on a seemingly deserted beach. The island's designated camping sites are most often found at the various *balnearios* (public beaches). Campsites typically have bare grounds where you can pitch your own tent, or sites designated for RVs. Some spots rent tents as well. Most have cooking grills and public bath houses for campers. Weekend camping at balnearios is popular among Puerto Ricans, and you'll find that the crowds are usually in a party mood, with lots of music and general merriment—it's not a setting for peaceful communion with nature. Other camping areas include nature reserves, such as Refugio de Vida Silvestre de Humacao or Bosque Estatal Carite in the interior, and a limited number of private camps located along the north and northeast coast. No overnight camping is allowed at El Yunque.

HOME EXCHANGES

If you would like to exchange your home for someone else's, **join a home-exchange organization,** which will send you its updated listings of available exchanges for a year and will include your own listing in at least one of them. It's up to you to make specific arrangements.

➤ EXCHANGE CLUBS: **HomeLink International** (✉ Box 650, Key West, FL 33041, ☎ 305/294–7766 or 800/638–3841, FAX 305/294–1448, usa@homelink.org, www.homelink.org; $98 per year). **Intervac U.S.** (✉ Box 590504, San Francisco, CA 94159, ☎ 800/756–4663, FAX 415/435–7440, www.intervac.com; $89 per year includes two catalogues).

HOSTELS

Currently, no hostels in Puerto Rico, youth or otherwise, are sanctioned by local or international organizations.

HOTELS

In the most expensive room categories we've listed, your room will be large enough for two to move around comfortably, with a king or queen bed (*cama matrimonial*) (possibly two doubles), air-conditioning (*aire acondicionado*), phones (*teléfono*), a private bath (*baño particular*), an in-room safe, cable TV, a hair dryer, iron and ironing board, room service (*servicio de habitación*), shampoo and toiletries, and possibly a view of the water (*vista al mar*). There will be a concierge and at least one hotel restaurant and lounge, a pool, shops, and an exercise room or spa facility. In Puerto Rico's smaller inns, rooms will have private baths with hot water (*agua caliente*), air-conditioning or fans, double to king beds, possibly room service, and Continental breakfast included in the rates. You might encounter cases where the hotel has several rooms sharing baths—it's a good idea to ask before booking the room.

All hotels listed have private baths unless otherwise noted.

RESERVING A ROOM

➤ TOLL-FREE NUMBERS: **Best Western** (☎ 800/528–1234, www.bestwestern.com). **Choice** (☎ 800/221–2222, www.hotelchoice.com). **Doubletree and Red Lion Hotels** (☎ 800/222–8733, www.doubletreehotels.com). **Embassy Suites** (☎ 800/362–2779, www.embassysuites.com). **Hilton** (☎ 800/445–8667, www.hiltons.com). **Holiday Inn** (☎ 800/465–4329, www.holiday-inn.com). **Hyatt Hotels & Resorts** (☎ 800/233–1234, www.hyatt.com). **Marriott** (☎ 800/228–9290, www.marriott.com). **Le Meridien** (☎ 800/543–4300, www.forte-hotels.com). **Quality Inn** (☎ 800/228–5151, www.qualityinn.com). **Ramada** (☎ 800/228–2828, www.ramada.com). **Renaissance Hotels & Resorts** (☎ 800/468–3571, www.hotels.com). **Ritz-Carlton** (☎ 800/241–3333, www.ritzcarlton.com). **Sheraton** (☎ 800/325–3535, www.sheraton.com). **Sleep Inn** (☎ 800/753–3746, www.sleepinn.com). **Wyndham Hotels & Resorts** (☎ 800/822–4200, www.wyndham.com).

MAIL & SHIPPING

Puerto Rico uses the **U.S. postal system,** and all addresses on the island carry Zip codes. Major post office branches are at 153 Calle Fortaleza in Old San Juan, 163 Avenida Fernandez Juncos in San Juan, 60 Calle McKinley in Mayagüez, and 102 Calle Garrido Morales in Fajardo. The **general information number** for postal services is 787/793–0444.

OVERNIGHT SERVICES

Post offices in major Puerto Rican cities offer Express Mail next-day service to the U.S. mainland and to Puerto Rican destinations, and most often they can be counted on to deliver. In addition, you can send letters and packages via Federal Express or UPS, as well as through private mail companies such as Mail Boxes, Etc. Find courier services in major towns, or call for pick-up.

The quickest way to ship via courier services is to inquire with the concierge or front desk of your hotel. They can call for pickup. Hotels that offer business services will take care of the entire ordeal for you.

➤ MAJOR SERVICES: For pickup in San Juan, call **Federal Express** (☎ 787/793–9300) or **UPS** (☎ 787/253–2877). Find FedEx offices at the Condado Plaza Hotel on Avenida Ashford and the El Caribe building, Calles Palmera and San Gerónimo in San Juan. UPS offices are at the Royal Bank building on Avenida Ponce de León in Hato Rey.

POSTAL RATES

The island uses U.S. postage stamps and has the same mail rates as the mainland: 20¢ for a postcard, 33¢ for a first-class letter to the U.S.; 40¢ for a postcard and 46¢ for a letter to Canada; 35¢ and 40¢, respectively, to Mexico; and 50¢ for a postcard and 60¢ for a letter to the United Kingdom, Australia, New Zealand, and other international destinations.

SHIPPING PARCELS

You can easily ship your packages and purchases home from the island. Many shops will ship for you, particularly those doing business in San Juan, Old San Juan, and other major cities. Shipping services are especially common at art galleries. There might be an extra cost (as much as $50, depending on weight), but judge its worth against hunting down packaging, a post office or a courier service, and paying for it yourself anyway. Pay by credit card and save your receipts. Make sure the proprietor insures the package against loss or damage, and ships it first class or by courier. Grab a business card with the proprietor's name and phone number.

MONEY MATTERS

Puerto Rico is a good bargain for Americans. The U.S. dollar is used on the island. Prices of most items are stable and comparable to those in the States, and that includes restaurants and hotel rates. The practice of giving discounts at attractions to seniors, children, and those with disabilities is prevalent on the island.

As in many places, city prices might be higher than those in rural areas, but you're not going to go broke staying in the city. Sample items: soft drink $1, cup of coffee $1, glass of beer in a bar $2, museum admission $2, local newspaper 35¢.

Prices throughout this guide are given for adults. Substantially reduced fees are almost always available for children, students, and senior citizens. For information on taxes, *see* Taxes, *below.*

ATMS

ATMs are readily available in the cities, and reliable; many are attached to banks, but you can also find them on the streets and in supermarkets and other stores. Just about every casino on the island has one—the better to keep people in the game—and several of the larger hotels have them as well.

ATMs are found less frequently in rural areas. Look to local banks such as Banco Popular.

CREDIT CARDS

Throughout this guide, the following abbreviations are used: **AE**, American Express; **D**, Discover; **DC**, Diner's Club; **MC**, Master Card; and **V**, Visa.

➤ REPORTING LOST CARDS: **American Express** (☎ 800/327–1267), **Discover** (☎ 800/347–2683), **Diner's Club** (☎ 800/234–6377), **Master Card** (☎ 800/307–7309), **Visa** (☎ 800/847–2911).

CURRENCY

Puerto Rico, as a commonwealth of the United States, uses the U.S. dollar as its official currency.

OUTDOORS & SPORTS

BICYCLING

In general, you'll want to stay away from the main highways and streets of San Juan and Old San Juan for biking—the traffic is too heavy and the automobile fumes too thick. However, in the countryside, particularly along the southern coast, biking is a great way to get around. The broad beach at Boquerón makes for easy wheeling, and the entire southwestern coast, in the area of Cabo Rojo, makes for good biking, although you should keep your eye out for traffic.

➤ INFORMATION: Bike rentals: **Boquerón Balnearios** (✉ Dept. of Recreation and Sports, Rte. 101, Boquerón, ☎ 787/722–1551 or 787/722–1771). **Ponce Hilton** (✉ Rte. 14, 1150 Av. Caribe, Ponce, ☎ 787/259–7676).

HIKING

El Yunque's 13 hiking trails loop past giant ferns, exotic orchids, sibilant streams and waterfalls, and broad trees reaching for the sun. You can even hike to the top of El Toro, the highest peak in the forest at 3,532 ft. Other trails include the Bosque de Toro Negro (Toro Negro Forest) in Jayuya.

➤ INFORMATION: **El Portal visitors center, El Yunque** (✉ Rte. 191, Palmer, ☎ 787/888–1810 or 787/888–1880); **Bosque de Toro Negro** (✉ Rte. 143, Jayuya, ☎ 787/867–3040).

GOLF

For aficionados worldwide, Puerto Rico is known as the birthplace of golf legend Chi Chi Rodriguez. Currently you'll find nearly 20 courses on the island, including several championship links at island resorts. There are no public courses in San Juan. Be sure to call ahead for details on reserving tee times; hours vary and several hotel courses only allow guests to play or give preference to guests.

➤ INFORMATION: **Wyndham Palmas del Mar** (✉ Rte. 906, Humacao, ☎ 787/852–6000). There are four attractive Robert Trent Jones–designed 18-hole courses shared by the **Hyatt Dorado Beach and the Hyatt Regency**

Cerromar Beach hotels (⊠ Rte. 693, Km 10.8 and Km 11.8, Dorado, ☎ 787/796–1234, ext. 3238, or 3016). **Bahia Beach Plantation** (⊠ Rte. 187, Km 4.2, Río Grande, ☎ 787/256–5600). **Berwind Country Club** (⊠ Rte. 187, Km 4.7, Río Grande, ☎ 787/876–3056). **Westin Río Mar Beach Resort and Country Club** (⊠ 6000 Río Mar Blvd., Río Grande, ☎ 787/888–6000).

SCUBA DIVING AND SNORKELING

The diving is excellent off Puerto Rico's south, east, and west coasts as well as off its offshore islands. Popular among divers is tiny **Desecheo Island,** about 24 km (15 mi) off the coast of Rincón in the west. At depths of 20 ft–120 ft, the rocky ocean floor around the base of the islet is full of coral and tropical fish, as well as several rock terraces and caverns. **The Cracks,** just off the coast from Humacao in the east, are indeed large cracks in the reef that create massive channels in which fish and other marine life feed.

➤ INFORMATION: **Boquerón Dive Shop** (⊠ Main St., Boquerón, ☎ 787/851–2155). **Caribe Aquatic Adventures** (⊠ Radisson Normandie Hotel, corner of Av. Rosales and Av. Muñoz Rivera, Puerta de Tierra, ☎ 787/724–1882 or 787/281–8858). **Dive Copamarina** (⊠ Copamarina Beach Resort, Rte. 333, Km 6.5, Guánica, ☎ 787/821–6009), where hotel-dive packages are available. **Mundo Submarino** (⊠ Laguna Garden Shopping Center, Av. Baldorioty de Castro, Carolina, ☎ 787/791–5764).

PACKING

Casual is the operative word for vacation clothes in Puerto Rico, but you'll soon note that local men rarely wear shorts on weekdays, even if they're hanging out, and local women tend to be conservative in dress. Puerto Ricans, particularly in the cities, dress up for going out to restaurants; shows; casinos; and, for that matter, to church. Wearing resort clothing outside the hotel or at the casino will peg you as a tourist. Bring some dressy casual slacks and shirts, summer skirts for women, casual clothes for the resort, at least two bathing suits (to avoid having to wear that wet one from yesterday), and sturdy shoes for walking. Consider a light sweater or jacket if you're staying in the mountainous areas, where the nights can get cool.

In your carry-on luggage, **pack an extra pair of eyeglasses or contact lenses** and **enough of any medication you take** to last the entire trip. You may also ask your doctor to write a spare prescription using the drug's generic name, since brand names may vary from country to country. In luggage to be checked, **never pack prescription drugs or valuables.** To avoid customs delays, carry medications in their original packaging. And don't forget to carry with you the addresses of offices that handle refunds of lost traveler's checks.

CHECKING LUGGAGE

How many carry-on bags you can bring with you is up to the airline. Most allow two, but not always, so make sure that everything you carry aboard will fit under your seat or in the overhead bin, and get to the gate early. Note that if you have a seat at the back of the plane, you'll probably board first, while the overhead bins are still empty.

If you are flying internationally, note that baggage allowances may be determined not by piece but by weight—generally 88 pounds (40 kilograms) in first class, 66 pounds (30 kilograms) in business class, and 44 pounds (20 kilograms) in economy.

Airline liability for baggage is limited to $1,250 per person on flights within the United States. On international flights it amounts to $9.07 per pound or $20 per kilogram for checked baggage (roughly $640 per 70-pound bag) and $400 per passenger for unchecked baggage. You can buy additional coverage at check-in for about $10 per $1,000 of coverage, but it excludes a rather extensive list of items, shown on your airline ticket.

Before departure, **itemize your bags' contents** and their worth, and label the bags with your name, address, and phone number. (If you use your home address, cover it so potential thieves can't see it readily.) Inside each bag, **pack a copy of your itinerary.** At check-in, **make sure that each bag is correctly tagged** with the destination airport's three-letter code. If your bags arrive damaged or fail to arrive at all, file a written report with the airline before leaving the airport.

PASSPORTS & VISAS

When traveling internationally, **carry your passport even if you don't need one** (it's always the best form of I.D.) and **make two photocopies of the data page** (one for someone at home and another for you, carried separately from your passport). If you lose your passport, promptly call the nearest embassy or consulate and the local police.

ENTERING PUERTO RICO

Puerto Rico is a commonwealth of the United States; **U.S. citizens do not require passports** to visit the island—however, it is always a good idea to carry a valid passport when traveling. Canadians need proof of citizenship (preferably a valid passport; otherwise bring a birth certificate with a raised seal along with a government-issued photo ID). Citizens of Australia, New Zealand, and the United Kingdom must have passports.

PASSPORT OFFICES

The best time to apply for a passport or to renew is in fall and winter. Before any trip, check your passport's expiration date, and, if necessary, renew it as soon as possible.

➤ AUSTRALIAN CITIZENS: **Australian Passport Office** (☎ 131–232, www.dfat.gov.au/passports).

➤ CANADIAN CITIZENS: **Passport Office** (☎ 819/994–3500 or 800/567–6868, www.dfait-maeci.gc.ca/passport).

➤ NEW ZEALAND CITIZENS: **New Zealand Passport Office** (☎ 04/494–0700, www.passports.govt.nz).

➤ U.K. CITIZENS: **London Passport Office** (☎ 0990/210–410) for fees and documentation requirements and to request an emergency passport.

REST ROOMS

Rest rooms you encounter in Puerto Rico will be not unlike those at home—some clean, some not so clean. Most public rest rooms at government facilities will be accessible for travelers with disabilities. Spanish for toilet is *baño*; men's room doors are labeled *caballeros*, ladies' room doors *damas*.

SAFETY

San Juan and Ponce, like any other big cities, have their share of crime, so guard your wallet or purse on the city streets. Puerto Rico's beaches are open to the public, and muggings can occur at night even on the beaches of the posh Condado and Isla Verde tourist hotels. Although you certainly can, and should, explore the cities and beaches, use common sense. Don't leave anything unattended on the beach. Leave your valuables in the hotel safe, and stick to the fenced-in beach areas of your hotel. Always lock your car and stash valuables and luggage out of sight. Avoid deserted beaches at night.

WOMEN IN PUERTO RICO

Women traveling alone in Puerto Rico are likely to encounter some interest in their solo status. This might take the form of simple interest, or, in some cases, might turn to annoyance and harrassment. It is not always dangerous, but it's certainly unsettling. In the cities, such as San Juan or Ponce, women traveling solo are less likely to attract a great deal of attention, yet men might still, in places such as bars and nightclubs, approach and attempt to make conversation. Women can avoid trouble, and danger, by avoiding places where there's the greatest likelihood for trouble to exist: Walking deserted beaches at night, or dark streets in unknown areas, or drinking alone in a bar, are as risky in Puerto Rico as they are anywhere else. Getting into an unmarked car identified by the driver as a taxi is a bad idea. Wearing swimming suits away from the water, or other revealing attire in public, is commonly a magnet for attention.

Unwanted attention can be discouraged in many of the same ways women discourage it at home—a simple "No, thanks," or variations on that theme (in English or in Spanish) usually will be enough to achieve the desired result. Be polite but firm.

SENIOR-CITIZEN TRAVEL

To qualify for age-related discounts, **mention your senior-citizen status up front** when booking hotel reservations (not when checking out) and before you're seated in restaurants (not when paying the bill). When renting a car, ask about promotional car-rental discounts, which can be cheaper than senior-citizen rates.

➤ EDUCATIONAL PROGRAMS: **Elderhostel** (✉ 75 Federal St., 3rd floor, Boston, MA 02110, ☎ 877/426–8056, 𝖥𝖠𝖷 877/426–2166, www.elderhostel.org). **Interhostel** (✉ University of New Hampshire, 6 Garrison Ave., Durham, NH 03824, ☎ 603/862–1147 or 800/733–9753, 𝖥𝖠𝖷 603/862–1113, www.learn.unh.edu).

SHOPPING

Puerto Rico isn't a duty-free island, so you won't find bargains on electronics and perfumes. You can, however, find excellent prices in San Juan on china, crystal, fashions, designer items, and jewelry. Look to the streets of Old San Juan for the city's largest collection of shops. In Condado, Avenida Ashford is a good bet for artisans' shops, designer clothing boutiques, and art galleries, as well as T-shirt and curio stores.

Shopping in Puerto Rico differs little from shopping in North America—cash of course is always accepted, and in most cases traveler's checks and major credit cards are fine. Vendors who sell crafts and other items on the streets, primarily in Old San Juan, are likely to accept cash only, and are likely to bargain. Bargaining for items in shops and boutiques is not as common—while you are always welcome to suggest a reasonable price, don't be surprised if the store owner's marked price is the final one.

KEY DESTINATIONS

You'll find the island's best shopping in **San Juan**; the city's old section, **Old San Juan,** is full of shops, especially on Calles Cristo, Fortaleza, and San

Francisco. The Old City is perhaps the best single destination for the serious shopper in San Juan—the stores are all within walking distance of each other, and trolleys are at your beck and call. On Old San Juan's streets you'll find everything from T-shirt emporiums to selective crafts stores, bookshops to art galleries, jewelry boutiques to shops specializing in Panama hats made to order. Since Old San Juan is also one of the premier cruise-ship stops in the Caribbean, you'll often find yourself among groups of shoppers, which of course makes bargains harder to find.

In the township of Carolina, a few minutes east of San Juan, you'll find a **Mercado Artesanal** (Artisans' Market) and cultural fair every Sunday 1–5 at the Julia de Burgos Memorial Park on Avenida Roberto Clemente (corner of Paseo de los Gigantes). In addition to craft and food booths, live bands perform and there's often entertainment for the children.

For a more mundane but certainly complete shopping experience, head to San Juan's **Plaza Las Américas,** which has 200 shops including the largest JC Penney store in the chain, The Gap, Sears, Banana Republic, Macy's, Border's Books and Music, Godiva, and Old Navy, as well as restaurants and movie theaters.

SMART SOUVENIRS

Shopping for local crafts can be gratifying: you'll run across a lot of tacky items, but you can also find some treasures, and in many cases you can watch the artisans at work. For guidance, contact the **Puerto Rico Tourism Company's Asuntos Culturales** (Cultural Affairs Office, ☎ 787/723–0692). Popular items include *santos* (small hand-carved figures of saints or religious scenes), hand-rolled cigars, Panama hats, handmade *mundillo* lace from Aguadilla, *veijigantes* (colorful masks made of papier-mâché and coconut husks and used during Carnival and local festivals) from Loíza, east of San Juan, and fancy men's shirts called *guayaberas*. Also, some folks swear that Puerto Rican rum is the best in the world, and locally grown and processed coffee is of a very high quality.

WATCH OUT

Remember, Puerto Rico is not duty-free, and shopkeepers who tell you otherwise are trying to scam you.

STUDENTS IN PUERTO RICO

Puerto Rico is well within the budget of students and is tailor-made for the adventurous. To beat the costs of traveling alone, hook up with educational institutions that use the island for research. Educational trips where you help out in projects are often inexpensive but might require a time commitment of several weeks.

➤ I.D.s & Services: **Council Travel** (CIEE; ✉ 205 E. 42nd St., 14th floor, New York, NY 10017, ☎ 212/822–2700 or 888/268–6245, FAX 212/822–2699, info@councilexchanges.org, www.councilexchanges.org) for mail orders only, in the United States. **Travel Cuts** (✉ 187 College St., Toronto, Ontario M5T 1P7, ☎ 416/979–2406 or 800/667–2887, www.travelcuts.com) in Canada.

TAXES

Accommodations incur a tax: for hotels with casinos it's 11%, for other hotels it's 9%, and for government-approved paradores it's 7%. Ask your hotel before booking. The tax, in addition to the standard 10%–18% service charge applied by most hotels, can add a hefty 20% or more to your bill.

There is no sales tax in Puerto Rico.

Airport departure taxes are not collected at the airport but should be tagged on to the cost of your airline ticket.

TELEPHONES

Puerto Rico's area code is 787—for **North Americans, dialing the island is the same as dialing another state or Canadian province:** simply dial 1, then the area code, and the number. When calling the U.S. and Canada from Puerto Rico, dial 1, plus the area code and number. Calling many other Caribbean islands will be the same routine. For calling other international destinations such as the United Kingdom, Australia, and New Zealand, dial 011, the country code, city code, and the number.

In August 2001, Puerto Rico will put into effect a **second area code, 939.** This code will be used for new numbers; existing numbers will be unchanged. From that time forward you will have to include the area code for all calls on the island.

Toll-free numbers (prefix 800, 888, or 877) are widely used in Puerto Rico, and many can be accessed from North America; the reverse is also true. Many North American toll-free numbers can be called from Puerto Rico.

DIRECTORY & OPERATOR ASSISTANCE

Dial 411 for directory assistance, and dial 0 for operator-assisted calls. Operators speak English.

INTERNATIONAL CALLS

To dial international calls, you can either dial direct (011 + country code + city code + number or 1 + area code + number), or dial 00 for the international long-distance operator.

LOCAL CALLS

Use your hotel phone or pay phones to make local calls. (Note that many hotels charge exorbitant rates for calls.)

LONG-DISTANCE CALLS

All numbers in Puerto Rico are seven digits. Long-distance charges will be calculated as you talk. Note that, these days, everyone on the island seems to have an ear buried in a cellular telephone. Cell phones are a viable alternative to using local service if you need to keep records of your bills. Call your cell phone company before departing to get information about activation and roaming charges. Some cell phone companies such as Cellular One, Sprint, and others have service on the island.

LONG-DISTANCE SERVICES

AT&T, MCI, and Sprint access codes make calling long-distance relatively convenient, but you may find the local access number blocked in many hotel rooms. First ask the hotel operator to connect you. If the hotel operator balks, ask for a local operator, or dial the local operator yourself. One way to improve your odds of getting connected to your long-distance carrier is to travel with more than one company's calling card (a hotel may block

Sprint, for example, but not MCI). If all else fails, call from a pay phone.

➤ ACCESS CODES: **AT&T Direct** (☎ 787/725–0300). **Cellular One** (☎ 787/505–2273 or 787/505–4636) **MCI WorldPhone** (☎ 787/782–6244 or 800/939–7624). **Sprint International Access** (☎ 800/473–3037 or 800/298–3266).

PHONE CARDS

Phone cards are useful and widely available. In Puerto Rico, the Puerto Rico Telephone Company sells **Ring Cards** (☎ 800/981–9105), available in various denominations, that can be used for both local and international calls. Cards are available in shops, supermarkets, and drugstores, as well as from the phone company.

PUBLIC PHONES

Pay phones use coins or operate with prepaid telephone cards called Ring Cards, available at many souvenir shops, drugstores, and other stores. You can also use Ring Cards for international calls.

TIME

Puerto Rico operates on Atlantic standard time, which is one hour later than the U.S. Eastern standard time during the winter months. The island does not adjust for the U.S.'s Daylight Savings time. This means that when it is noon on a winter day in New York, it is 1 PM in Puerto Rico. In summer, when the United States is on Daylight Savings, Puerto Rico and the east coast of the United States, are on the same time, and three hours ahead of the west coast. Sydney is 14 hours ahead of Puerto Rico, Auckland is 16 hours ahead, and London is 4 hours ahead.

Call **787/728–9595** in Puerto Rico for the exact time.

TIPPING

Some hotels automatically add a 10%–15% service charge to your bill. Check ahead to confirm whether this charge is built into the room rate or will be tacked on at check out. Some smaller hotels might charge extra (as much as $5 per day) for use of air-conditioning, called an "energy tax." Tips are expected, and appreciated, by restaurant waitstaff (15%–20% if a service charge isn't included), hotel porters ($1 per bag), maids ($1–$2 a day), and taxi drivers (10%–15%).

TOURS & PACKAGES

Because everything is prearranged on a prepackaged tour or independent vacation, you'll spend less time planning—and often get it all at a good price.

BOOKING WITH AN AGENT

Travel agents are excellent resources. But it's a good idea to collect brochures from several agencies as some agents' suggestions may be influenced by relationships with tour and package firms that reward them for volume sales. If you have a special interest, **find an agent with expertise in that area**; ASTA (☞ Travel Agencies, *below*) has a database of specialists worldwide.

Make sure your travel agent knows the accommodations and other services of the place they're recommending. Ask about the hotel's location, room size, beds, and whether it has a pool, room service, or programs for children, if you care about these. Has your agent been there in person or sent others whom you can contact?

Do some homework on your own, too: local tourism boards can provide information about lesser-known and small-niche operators, some of which may sell only direct.

BUYER BEWARE

Each year consumers are stranded or lose their money when tour operators—even large ones with excellent reputations—go out of business. So **check out the operator**. Ask several travel agents about its reputation, and try to **book with a company that has a consumer-protection program**. (Look for information in the company's brochure.) In the United States, members of the National Tour Association and the United States Tour Operators Association are required to set aside funds to cover your payments and travel arrangements in the event that the company defaults. It's also a good idea to choose a company that participates in the American Society of Travel Agents' Tour Operator Program (TOP); ASTA will act as mediator in any disputes between you and your tour operator.

Remember that the more your package or tour includes the better you can predict the ultimate cost of your vacation. Make sure you know exactly what is covered, and **beware of hidden costs**. Are taxes, tips, and transfers included? Entertainment and excursions? These can add up.

➤ TOUR-OPERATOR RECOMMENDATIONS: **American Society of Travel Agents** (☞ Travel Agencies, *below*). **National Tour Association** (NTA; ✉ 546 E. Main St., Lexington, KY 40508, ☎ 606/226–4444 or 800/682–8886, www.ntaonline.com). **United States Tour Operators Association** (USTOA; ✉ 342 Madison Ave., Suite 1522, New York, NY 10173, ☎ 212/599–6599 or 800/468–7862, ᴬˣ 212/599–6744, ustoa@aol.com, www.ustoa.com).

GUIDED TOURS

You can see Old San Juan from the free trolley or on a self-guided walking tour (look for tours in a copy of *Qué Pasa*, available at all tourist offices and hotels). You can also board the **Caribbean Carriage Company** (☎ 787/797–8063), an operation that gives tours of the old city in open horse-drawn carriages. It's a bit hokey, but offers a chance to get off your feet. Call them or find them at Plaza Dársenas near Pier 1 in Old San Juan. They give three tours of differing lengths; cost is $30–$60 per couple.

To explore the rest of the city and the island, rent a car and head out on your own. (You should, however, consider taking a guided tour of the vast El Yunque rain forest.) If you'd rather not do your own driving, there are several tour companies you can call. Most San Juan hotels have a tour desk that can make arrangements for you. The three standard half-day tours ($20–$30) are of Old and "new" San Juan; Old San Juan and the Bacardi Rum Plant; and Playa Luquillo and El Yunque rain forest. All-day tours ($25–$45) can include a trip to Ponce, a day at El Comandante Racetrack, or a combined tour of the city and El Yunque rain forest.

Leading tour operators include **Normandie Tours, Inc.** (☎ 787/722–6308), **Rico Suntours** (☎ 787/722–2080 or 787/722–6090), **Tropix Wellness Outings** (☎ 787/268–2173), and **United Tour Guides** (☎ 787/725–7605 or 787/723–5578). **Cordero Caribbean Tours** (☎ 787/786–9114; 787/780–2442 evenings) runs tours in air-conditioned limousines for an hourly rate. **Wheelchair Getaway** (☎ 787/883–0131) offers wheelchair transport from airports and cruise-ship docks to San Juan hotels, as well as city sightseeing trips.

TRAIN TRAVEL

As of this writing, the only operating trains on the island are small-gauge sugarcane trains used for hauling crops from the fields. San Juan, however, has embarked on construction of a $1.6-billion urban train system that will connect major suburbs of the city. The first phase of the elevated train system, due for completion in 2002, will connect Bayamón, Guaynabo, and Santurce. The second phase, due to be completed in 2004, will connect Río Piedras to the municipality of Carolina, and later to Luis Muñoz Marín International Airport. The system will eventually comprise an estimated 16 city stops.

TRANSPORTATION AROUND PUERTO RICO

If you're staying in **San Juan, you can get around on foot or by bus, taxi, and hotel shuttle. If you venture out on the island, a rental car is your best option.** Roads in Puerto Rico are generally well marked (just keep in mind that distances are posted in kilometers, while road speed signs are in miles per hour). A good road map, however, will be helpful in more remote areas. Some car-rental agencies give you a free island map when you pick up your car, but these maps lack detail and are often out-of-date. Head to the nearest gas station or book store to buy a better one. **Buses** are fine for travel around the cities, but for island travel buses prove to be inefficient and time-consuming, with hard-to-fathom or non-existent schedules. **Públicos** (public cars), with yellow license plates ending in "P" or "PD," scoot to towns throughout the island, stopping in each town's main plaza. These 17-passenger vans operate primarily during the day, with routes and fares fixed by the Public Service Commission. In San Juan, the main terminals are at the airport and at Plaza Colón on the waterfront in Old San Juan.

The Puerto Rico Tourism Company's authorized taxis, painted white and displaying the *garita* (sentry box) logo and **Taxi Turistico** label, charge set rates depending on the destination; they run from the airport and the cruise-ship piers to Isla Verde, Condado/Ocean Park, and Old San Juan, with rates ranging from $6 to $16. City tours start at $30 per hour. Metered cabs authorized by the Public Service Commission start at $1 and charge 10¢ for every additional ⅓ mi, 50¢ for every suitcase. Waiting time is 10¢ for each 45 seconds. The minimum charge is $3.

If your feet fail you in Old San Juan, climb aboard the free open-air trolleys that rumble through the narrow streets. Departures are from La Puntilla and from the marina, but you can board anywhere along the route.

TRAVEL AGENCIES

A good travel agent puts your needs first. Look for an agency that has been in business at least five years, emphasizes customer service, and has someone on staff who specializes in your destination. In addition, **make sure the agency belongs to a professional trade organization.** The American Society of Travel Agents (ASTA), with 27,000 agents in some 170 countries, is the largest and most influential in the field. Operating under the motto "Integrity in Travel," it maintains and enforces a strict code of ethics and will step in to help mediate any agent-client disputes if necessary. ASTA also maintains a Web site that includes a directory of agents. (If a travel agency is also acting as your tour operator, *see* Buyer Beware *in* Tours & Packages, *above*.)

➤ LOCAL AGENT REFERRALS: American Society of Travel Agents (ASTA; ☎ 800/965–2782 24-hr hot line, FAX 703/684–8319, www.astanet.com). Association of British Travel Agents

(✉ 68–71 Newman St., London W1P 4AH, ☎ 0171/637–2444, FAX 0171/637–0713, information@abta.co.uk, www.abtanet.com). **Association of Canadian Travel Agents** (✉ 1729 Bank St., Suite 201, Ottawa, Ontario K1V 7Z5, ☎ 613/521–0474, FAX 613/521–0805, acta.ntl@sympatico.ca). **Australian Federation of Travel Agents** (✉ Level 3, 309 Pitt St., Sydney 2000, ☎ 02/9264–3299, FAX 02/9264–1085, www.afta.com.au). **Travel Agents' Association of New Zealand** (✉ Box 1888, Wellington 10033, ☎ 04/499–0104, FAX 04/499–0827, taanz@tiasnet.co.nz).

VISITOR INFORMATION

In addition to the Puerto Rico Tourism Company's *Qué Pasa*, pick up the Puerto Rico Hotel and Tourism Association's *Bienvenidos* and *Places to Go*, as well as the magazine *Where*. Among them you'll find a wealth of information about the island and activities. All are free and available at tourist information offices and often as not at your hotel's front desk.

➤ TOURIST INFORMATION: **Puerto Rico Tourism Company** (✉ Box 902-3960, Old San Juan Station, San Juan, PR 00902-3960, ☎ 787/721–2400; www.prtourism.com). From the States, you can call the New York office toll-free at ☎ 800/223–6530. Other branches: ✉ 3575 W. Cahuenga Blvd., Suite 560, Los Angeles, CA 90068, ☎ 213/874–5991; ✉ 901 Ponce de León Blvd., Suite 601, Coral Gables, FL 33134, ☎ 305/445–9112.

WEB SITES

Do check out the World Wide Web when you're planning. You'll find everything from current weather forecasts to virtual tours of famous cities. Fodor's Web site, www.fodors.com, is a great place to start your on-line travels. When you see a 🕸 in this book, go to www.fodors.com/urls for an up-to-date link to that destination's site.

WHEN TO GO

The busy tourism, or high, season in Puerto Rico is roughly the winter season, defined as mid-December through mid-April. Winter hotel rates are 25%–40% more than off-season rates, and hotels tend to be packed. As well, San Juan is a commercial town, and hotels, save for the short season around Christmas and New Year's, are busy year-round with international business travelers. Which is not to say the island will not have rooms in winter—rarely is space completely unavailable, but if you plan to beat that winter sleet in Duluth, make arrangements for flights and hotel space at least a couple of months ahead of time.

A fun and often less expensive time to visit the island is during the "shoulder" seasons of fall and spring, when the weather is—still—perfect and the tourist crush is less intense.

CLIMATE

Puerto Rico's weather is moderate and tropical year-round, with an average temperature of about 82°F (26°C). Essentially, there are no seasonal changes on the island, although winter sees cooling (not cold) breezes from the north, and higher elevations cooled by as much as 20 degrees. Hurricane season in the Caribbean runs July through November.

The following are average daily maximum and minimum temperatures.

SAN JUAN

Jan.	70F	21C	May	74F	23C	Sept.	75F	24C
	80	27		84	29		86	30
Feb.	70F	21C	June	75F	24C	Oct.	75F	24C
	80	27		85	29		85	29
Mar.	70F	21C	July	75F	24C	Nov.	73F	23C
	81	27		85	29		84	29
Apr.	72F	22C	Aug.	76F	24C	Dec.	72F	22C
	82	28		85	29		81	27

➤ FORECASTS: **Weather Channel Connection** (☎ 900/932–8437), 95¢ per minute from a Touch-Tone phone.

1 DESTINATION: PUERTO RICO

MORE THAN JUST A DAY AT THE BEACH

WHAT MAKES Puerto Rico distinctive among Caribbean destinations is the shear breadth of experiences available to you. If you crave a luxury resort, you'll find several world-class options to choose from. If you're a nature lover, you'll find an abundance of wonders to explore. If you're a surfer or an art aficionado, a golfer or a history buff, a deep-sea diver or a gourmet, you'll find satisfaction here. And perhaps foremost, lending a distinctive flavor to any Puerto Rico experience, you'll find a sophisticated, centuries-old culture—a mix of Native American, Spanish, African, and contemporary U.S. influences that's unique to the island.

Puerto Rico's role as part of the New World began early. Somewhere along the western coast (the spot is disputed), Christopher Columbus landed on his second voyage, claiming the island for Spain on November 19, 1493. Another famous explorer, Ponce de León, had a more lasting impact, helping to establish Spanish rule when not searching for the elusive Fountain of Youth. But for many generations before the arrival of European settlers, there was a thriving indigenous culture here. The Taínos, believed to have numbered 30,000 at the time of Columbus's landing, called the island Boriquén, and to this day Puerto Ricans refer to themselves as Boricuas. Most historical accounts have the Taínos quickly dying out after Spanish settlement, but current University of Puerto Rico studies suggest that Taíno DNA is still evident in the genetic makeup of present-day Puerto Ricans. Researchers say this may indicate that the Taínos were far more numerous than was previously thought, and that they did not disappear so soon after the arrival of Europeans.

Spain would ward off Dutch and English aggression to rule the island until 1898, when the United States took it over as part of the spoils from the Spanish-American war. Since 1952 Puerto Rico has had U.S. commonwealth status, calling itself an *estado libre asociado* (free associated state)—a term that conveys some of the complexities and contradictions of the relationship. Puerto Ricans are U.S. citizens, but their single representative in Congress has only a symbolic vote. The island receives government funds for social, health, education, and infrastructure programs, and Puerto Ricans are found in the U.S. military in numbers proportionately greater than those of many full-fledged states. But Puerto Rico residents don't pay federal taxes, and they aren't allowed to vote in presidential elections.

In day-to-day life, the contrast between U.S. influences and the more long-standing Spanish, African, and Native American cultural mix is in ample evidence: American-style malls and fast-food restaurants compete with small, family-run places that have a distinctly traditional feel. Spanish is the mother tongue, but English is also an "official language" and is widely spoken, particularly in and around San Juan. For tourists from the mainland United States, the relationship provides undeniable advantages—you don't need to clear customs or exchange currency, and when you touch down in San Juan's Luis Muñoz Marín International Airport you'll be in an easily negotiated bilingual environment.

If you're like most visitors, your discovery of Puerto Rico will begin in Old San Juan, a largely restored historic city dating from the 16th century that's a magical place for tourists and Puerto Ricans alike. Perched on a mile-square peninsula to the northwest of the greater metropolitan area, it has open plazas and parks, a sweeping bayside promenade, and some of the best examples of Spanish architecture in the New World.

The Old City's bluestone streets climb from San Juan Bay to a long headland overlooking the Atlantic. The oceanside bluff, which runs along Avenida Norzagaray, is bound at either end by two great fortresses, San Cristóbal to the east and El Morro to the west, testifying to the city's past as a military stronghold. El Morro in particular is a dominating presence, its massive walls melding with the promontory on which it sits, rising to split San Juan Bay from the Atlantic.

As you explore the city, at every turn you're likely to encounter a new pleasure, from the central Plaza de Armas, where you can linger over a *café con leche* and watch schoolchildren chase the pigeons, to the lush, serene gardens of La Casa Blanca, built originally as a home for Puerto Rico's first governor, Ponce de León, in 1521, to the extraordinary folk-art collection of the Museo de las Américas. Along with the fortresses, you'll find an array of other impressive structures, including 19th-century Spanish colonial mansions, Art Deco masterpieces from the 1930s, and the Iglesia de San José, erected in 1532. Yet most buildings are only one or two stories tall, painted in bright pastels that radiate under the Caribbean sun. These structures of a more modest scale are part of the reason why visitors tend to remember the Old City as an intimate place.

Old San Juan is filled with historical treasures, but it doesn't live in the past; it's a thriving cultural center, with the greatest concentration of top-flight restaurants, galleries, shops, and nightspots on the island, attracting artists, intellectuals, and all manner of other *sanjuaneros*. On weekends, particularly, the city can feel like one big party after dark, with salsa and jazz pulsing from doorways and revelers spilling onto the streets. Young gallants strut side by side with San Juan's professional set and distinguished elders who have seen it all a thousand times before. The people you encounter on these streets are even more fascinating and varied than the beautiful buildings that surround them.

Venturing beyond the Old City, you'll find greater San Juan to be a thriving modern metropolis—an urban anomaly in the Caribbean. There are, of course, the trademark beaches, from the Miami-style Condado and Isla Verde areas—rightfully magnets for tourists—to low-key Ocean Park and undeveloped Piñones. But in and around San Juan you can also watch major-league baseball stars in action during Puerto Rico's Winter League, take in a world-class ballet or theatrical production, go to the horse races, or visit one of several fine museums. And everywhere

from makeshift clubs to concert halls, there's music in the air.

The Santurce area, San Juan's urban center, is in the throes of a revival, with old theaters and grand, pre-war apartment buildings undergoing renovation. The summer of 2000 saw the opening of the Puerto Rico Museum of Art; the largest art museum on the island (bigger than the renowned museum in Ponce), it's dedicated exclusively to the works of Puerto Ricans, from the 17th century to the present. It joins Puerto Rico's premier music and theater venue, the Luis A. Ferré Center for the Performing Arts, to make Santurce perhaps the preeminent spot for high culture in the Caribbean.

Hato Rey, home of Puerto Rico's financial district, a single row of office towers known as the Golden Mile, has some of San Juan's finest restaurants, which cater primarily to the district's businesspeople. The range of dining choices reflects the city's cosmopolitan character: there's everything from Chinese to Italian to Mexican to Middle Eastern to Spanish.

In Río Piedras you'll find the main campus of the University of Puerto Rico, built in the fashion of traditional British and U.S. schools, but with beautiful tropical landscaping. There are music, theater, and other performances given at university facilities, which also include museums and libraries.

Overall, San Juan's rapid, urban pulse is what distinguishes life there from life *en la isla* (out on the island)—the term Puerto Ricans use for everything that's not part of the city. The distinction is as much psychological as geographical; it implies a freedom from stress, an embrace of tradition, and a respect for the power and beauty of nature.

WHETHER YOU'RE driving up the northern face of the Cordillera mountain range for a lunch of roast pork, fried rice, and chickpeas on the back porch of a mountain inn, or rumbling down the range's southern side toward the Caribbean coastline, where the water is gentler, calmer, and bluer than in the north, you'll know *en la isla* when you find it. It's a place that includes virgin rain forests, bioluminescent bays, labyrinthine limestone caves, and mile after mile of white sand beaches. You can also find it on the tip of your tongue—just try a fried-fish *empanadilla* washed back by a cold beer at one of the wonderful open-air food stalls scattered along the coasts from Boquerón in the west to Luquillo Beach in the east.

Among the natural attractions, star treatment goes to the Caribbean National Forest, popularly known as El Yunque. This rain forest encompasses a huge, anvil-shape mountaintop that dominates the skyline on the roadway east from San Juan to Fajardo. The Taínos considered the area sacred ground, and as you hike the numerous trails you understand why. Cascading waterfalls slice through the lush forest; mammoth bamboo and ferns, pines and Sierra palms refract the sunlight through a lime-green canopy; more than 200 species of birds make the forest home, including the rare Puerto Rican green parrot. El Yunque is less than an hour's drive from downtown San Juan, but it feels like the other side the world.

On the eastern coast, the Fajardo region is a hot spot for boating and diving, and nearby Playa Luquillo is one of the prettiest and most popular beaches in Puerto Rico. Fajardo also serves as the departure point for trips to the offshore islands of Vieques and Culebra. Both are known as places to get away from it all, considered by some to be the last pieces of unspoiled paradise in the Caribbean—a status that's ironically due in part to the presence of the U.S. Navy, which has kept much of the land undeveloped in order to use it for bombing exercises. (The navy discontinued exercises on Culebra some years ago; its activities on Vieques are currently a subject of heated controversy.) At night, thousands of tiny bioluminescent dinoflagellates light up Vieques's Mosquito Bay, creating one of Puerto Rico's most novel and spectacular natural phenomena.

F YOU TRAVEL SOUTH of the central mountains, you enter a part of the island that is noticeably removed from the influences of San Juan. The urban center here is Ponce, which has a long history as an important port and a center of commerce. The overland trip from the north was until recently an arduous jour-

ney, which in large part explains the distinctive identity of Ponce and the south. The climate here is also different, both drier and warmer. Where the north has El Yunque, the south has the Guánica Dry Forest, a United Nations Biosphere Reserve that's a strangely beautiful collection of twisted, bonsailike trees and towering cacti, and is also a haven for rare birds.

Ponce itself has a well-preserved historic downtown, with a large main square, Plaza las Delicias, that's filled with broad tile walkways, shade trees, and flower gardens. Its centerpiece is an opulent fountain with water-spewing lions built for the 1939 World's Fair, but its most photographed landmark is undoubtedly the Parque de los Bomberos, a red-and-black Victorian-style firehouse that dates from 1883.

In its heyday, from the 1850s through the 1930s, Ponce was a center of politics and culture as well as commerce, spawning some of Puerto Rico's most revered artists and civic leaders. The period also marked an architectural flowering that is still abundantly evident in the neighborhoods surrounding the main plaza, where you'll see an often whimsical mix of Caribbean, European, and North American influences in the carefully maintained houses. To the north of the city you'll find two historical treasures: Hacienda Buena Vista, a restored 19th-century coffee plantation, and Tibes Indian Ceremonial Center, a pre-Taíno burial ground dating from AD 700 that's the most important archaeological site in the Caribbean.

To the west of Ponce, in the island's southwest corner, are some of Puerto Rico's finest beaches, stretching from Guánica to Cabo Rojo. The Caribbean coast is calmer than the north, and its shallow waters are filled with reefs that teem with sea life. A vast underwater shelf extending from Ponce to the Mona Channel west of the island provides wonderful opportunities for snorkeling and scuba diving.

The western coast has Mayagüez, Puerto Rico's third-largest city, and, farther north, the hip, charming town of Rincón, epicenter of the island's surfing scene. Karst country, extending along the northwest corridor, is marked by haystack-shape hills and an extended network of caves that were formed many millennia ago as the island rose out of the sea; you can explore them at the Camuy Cave Park. Also in the region is a man-made wonder, Arecibo Observatory, home to one of the world's largest satellite dishes, spanning more than 20 acres.

If you're looking for cool breezes and majestic views, spend some time in the central mountains, which undulate between 1,000 ft and 3,000 ft above sea level as they span the island east to west. There are many inns throughout the area, some of them renovated plantation homes, as well as a number of restaurants and outdoor barbecues of high repute that can be reached on a day trip from San Juan. You'll also be rewarded by the vistas; at some points you can see both the Caribbean Sea and the Atlantic from the same location.

F YOU SPEND THE TIME to enjoy even a few of Puerto Rico's treasures, you'll inevitably get a feel for the Puerto Rican people as well. It's immediately clear that the island has its own vibrant, self-sustaining culture; no one could mistake it for a developer's attempt to create a tourist fantasy. The hotels, restaurants, and nightclubs have been designed with an eye toward the tastes of the locals—a strong market on an island where tourism accounts for less than 10% of the economy. On a personal level, this means you're as likely to meet a Puerto Rican staying at your hotel as one working there. The same goes for restaurants and bars—which makes it all the easier to get to know Puerto Ricans, who rank among the best hosts in the world. They are genuinely friendly and proud of their island, and they can impress you on many levels, from their delicious local *criollo* (creole) cuisine, to their achievements in the fine and performing arts, to the rich variety of wonderful island music, whether salsa, *bomba,* jazz, or pop.

Puerto Ricans are masters at having a good time; you can feel the whole island coming alive on typical weekend nights. If you have the opportunity, attend one of the *fiestas patronales* (patron saint festivals) that towns large and small hold throughout the year. They're a mix of good food, good drink, and great music, often provided by the island's top performers and usually free of charge.

Puerto Rico will wow you with its gorgeous beaches and deep blue waters. If all you want is to sit on the sand and enjoy a piña colada, there's no better place to do it. But if you want something more, Puerto Rico is rich with possibilities.

–John Marino

NEW AND NOTEWORTHY

San Juan

The opening of the **Puerto Rico Museum of Art** in Santurce in the summer of 2000 marked a significant change in the cultural landscape. The museum should develop into San Juan's premier center for the visual arts.

The initial phase of San Juan's **urban train system** is nearing completion, much to the relief of city commuters. The first phase of the $1.6 billion elevated train network, due to open in 2002, will connect Bayamón, Guaynabo, and Santurce. The second phase, due to be completed in 2004, will connect Río Piedras to the municipality of Carolina, and a third phase will link the city's 16 stops to Luis Muñoz Marín International Airport. A stop will be located near, but not in, Old San Juan.

The newest accommodation in Old San Juan, the **Hotel Milano,** opened in 1999. The 30-room, European-style hotel is located on Calle Fortaleza in the thick of the Old City, and features a rooftop bar and restaurant, the Panorama.

In other hotel news, the **Caribe Hilton** reopened in late 1999 after being closed eight months for a $50 million renovation. It now features an expanded beachfront; a widened open-air lobby; a tri-level swimming pool; and, in the rooms, new paint, carpets, and decor. The Hilton did not reopen a casino.

Old hands to San Juan will remember La Concha Hotel and Convention Center as landmarks of the Condado area. The structures have been closed and deteriorating for years. Recent petitions to demolish them to make way for a $225 million **Condado Beach resort** have been held up due to infighting between San

Juan City Hall and the central government's tourism company. The issue resides in court as of this writing.

Eastern Puerto Rico

Vieques is seeing a burst of **hotel development.** The extent of the new construction hinges on whether the U.S. Navy will withdraw from the island, where it has been conducting military exercises for more than half a century.

At the beginning of 2000 the largest guest house in Vieques had only 35 rooms. New hotel proposals include two or three boutique properties to be developed by the owner of the Inn on the Blue Horizon; a $49-million resort called Martineau Bay, which will add 156 rooms to the hotel roster; and a hotel project that has been discussed for years without moving past the drawing board is now being redesigned as an eco-lodge.

Culebra, too, is being eyed by hotel investors. The 164-room Costa Bonita Hotel and Villas is slated to open in 2001.

Officials at the Vieques tourism office acknowledge that the navy's departure—and the end to live bombing and other military exercises—would make Vieques an attractive investment for international hotel chains. But leaders hasten to add that they won't let the island's charm be jeopardized by mega-resorts.

Southern Puerto Rico

The new 18-hole **Coamo Springs Golf Course** near the town of Coamo has lots of sanjuaneros running to the south coast to test it out, especially when it is raining on the north coast. Located on the drier part of the island and designed by Ferdinand Garbin, the course is gaining a reputation for its rugged beauty and challenging holes.

Northwest Puerto Rico

The Río Camuy Cave Park has opened another cave in its vast network, the **Cueva Catedral.** It's geared for more adventurous visitors—you rappel into it and then explore the intricate galleries and passageways. Cathedral Cave has paintings made by indigenous Indians thousands of years ago.

WHAT'S WHERE

San Juan

San Juan, buffed by Atlantic Ocean currents and gentle trade winds, sits on the northeast coast of the island, a bit more than a two-hour drive from the west coast, about an hour's drive from the east coast, and about an hour from the town of Ponce, on the south coast. It is, generally, a flat town, with mountain ranges to the east and to the south, near the center of the island.

Eastern Puerto Rico

In rectangular Puerto Rico, the east coast begins east of San Juan along the northern coast and follows the Atlantic Ocean down to where it meets the Caribbean. Outer island Vieques sits squarely off the central coast, while smaller sister island Culebra floats east of the northeasternmost corner of the "main island." The coastline is placid at points, banked by the remains of coconut plantations, and rugged in other spots, especially north of Fajardo, where bluffs overlook the ocean. Much of the coast lies in the foothills of mountains, including El Yunque rain forest.

Although the east coast encompasses several thriving communities, all have a slower pace and more provincial outlook on life. They also tend to hang on to older traditions harder, something that is reflected in the music, food, and art of the region.

Southern Puerto Rico

Stretching from Puerto Rico's central mountains to the Caribbean Sea and some 90 mi along the southern coast, southern Puerto Rico encompasses lush forests, such as in the Bosque Estatal Carite in the southeastern part of the island, as well as tropical dry forests such as the Bosque Estatal de Guánica on the southwestern coast. In general, this area is drier than other parts of the island, and numerous forms of cacti are abundant. You'll find homes scattered through the area, picturesque mountain towns, seaside fishing villages, and Puerto Rico's second-largest urban area, Ponce.

Heading west of San Juan on Highway 22, northern coastal Puerto Rico skirts the Atlantic Ocean. The area was formerly the home of many coconut and fruit plantations, and trees are still abundant in the area, shading many of the beaches. Some of the island's oldest resorts are located along this coast, and, not coincidentally, some of its best golf courses have been built here. Inland from the coast, north central Puerto Rico is dominated by limestone karst terrain. Huge cliffs and sinkholes in the porous ground create a surreal feeling; the Río Camuy Cave Park found here is one of the island's natural wonders. Farther inland, lush tropical vegetation and striking mountains make up the area near the Cordillera Central, the central mountain range, where the island's tallest peak, Cerro de Punta, looms 4,390 ft above sea level. Western Puerto Rico's jagged coastline holds world-class surfing beaches. A casual, laid-back atmosphere has developed in this vacation center, which is dotted with small hotels and restaurants.

PLEASURES AND PASTIMES

Beaches

A Puerto Rico visit isn't complete without some time in the sand and sun. By law, all Puerto Rican *playas* (beaches) are open to the public. The government maintains more than a dozen *balnearios* (public beaches) around the island, with dressing rooms; lifeguards; parking; and in some cases picnic tables, playgrounds, and camping facilities. Admission is free, parking is $2. Hours vary, but most balnearios are open 9–5 daily in summer and Tuesday–Sunday the rest of the year.

Beaches rim the island; the west coast near the town of Rincón is noted for its big waves and is popular with surfers. To the south, the beaches of Cabo Rojo are wide and inviting, with plenty of beachside bars and restaurants where you can while away the hours. Boquerón Beach, on the southwest coast, is a popular stretch with hard-packed sand fringed with coconut palms. In the northeast, crescentshape Luquillo Beach is one of the island's

most popular and bound to be crowded with Puerto Ricans on weekends out for a day in the sun. With coconut-palm shade, picnic tables, and a nearby string of small kiosks selling tasty local fast food, it's an ideal spot for families. Nearby is Seven Seas Beach, an elongated beach with picnic tables and area water-sports outfits.

Sanjuaneros have attractive beach options as well—the city's beaches are among the best on the island, popular with city folk on weekends and often abuzz with jet skiing, waterskiing, and other activities. The beaches line the north coast of the city from Carolina in the east through the neighborhoods of Isla Verde, Ocean Park, Condado, and Puerta de Tierra. Those seeking beach solitude will find it on the outer islands of Vieques and Culebra, where the beaches are wide, spectacular, and often uncrowded.

Dining

Many Puerto Rican chefs have taken cues from the international set, and "world cuisine" is the buzzword at trend-conscious restaurants. Throughout the island you'll find everything from French haute cuisine to sushi bars, as well as superb local eateries serving *comidas criollas,* traditional Caribbean-creole meals.

If you're looking for authentic Puerto Rican cuisine, one indication is the *mesón gastronómico* label used by the government to recognize restaurants that preserve culinary traditions. There are more than 40 such establishments island-wide, and while not every one is of the highest quality, there are fine restaurants in the system.

Puerto Rican cooking uses lots of local vegetables: plantains are cooked a hundred different ways—as *tostones* (fried green), *amarillos* (baked ripe), and as chips. Rice and beans with tostones or amarillos are basic accompaniments to every dish. Locals cook white rice with *habichuelas* (red beans), *achiote* (annatto seeds), or saffron; brown rice with *gandules* (pigeon peas); and *morro* (black rice) with frijoles *negros* (black beans). Garbanzos and white beans are served in many daily specials. Assorted yams and other root vegetables such as yucca and yautía are served baked, fried, stuffed, boiled, mashed, and whole. *Sofrito*—a garlic, onion, sweet pepper, coriander, oregano, and tomato puree—is used as a base for practically everything.

Beef, chicken, pork, and seafood are rubbed with *adobo,* a garlic-oregano marinade, before cooking; the practice is said to date back to the Taínos. *Arroz con pollo, sancocho* (beef or chicken and tuber soup), *asopao* (a soupy rice gumbo with chicken or seafood), and *encebollado* (steak smothered in onions) are all typical plates. Other traditional favorites, found in abundance during the Christmas holidays, are *lechón* (roast pork) and *pastelles,* a kind of Puerto Rican tamale made of meat and condiment stuffed inside plantain paste, which is then wrapped in a plantain leaf and tied off for boiling. The Cayey barrio of Guavaté, a pleasant 45-minute drive from San Juan, is known for its roast pork, and another favorite, *morcilla,* a black spicy sausage.

Fritters are a Puerto Rican specialty served in snack bars along the highways and beaches as well as at cocktail parties. You may find *empanadillas* (stuffed fried turnovers), *surrullitos* (cheese-stuffed corn sticks), *alcapurias* (stuffed green banana croquettes), and *bacalaitos* (codfish fritters).

Puerto Rican cuisine, as might be expected, also relies on local catches. Caribbean lobster (not as sweet as the Maine variety) is available mainly at small coastal restaurants, and there is always plentiful fresh dolphinfish and red snapper. Conch is prepared in a chilled ceviche salad or stuffed inside fritters with tomato sauce. Local *pan de agua* is an excellent French-style bread, best hot out of the oven. It's also good toasted and should be tried as part of a *cubano* sandwich (roast pork, ham, Swiss cheese, pickles, and mustard). Local desserts include flans, puddings, and fruit pastes served with native white cheese.

Puerto Rico is also known for a number of trademark drinks. The renowned locally grown coffee is excellent served espresso-black or generously cut *con leche* (with hot milk). Legends trace the birthplace of the piña colada to any number of San Juan establishments, from the Caribe Hilton to Gran Hotel El Convento to a Calle La Fortaleza bar. Puerto Rican rum is popular mixed with cola (known as a *cuba libre*), soda, tonic, juices, or water, or served on the rocks or even straight up.

Rums range from light mixers to dark, aged sipping liqueurs. Look for Bacardi, Don Q, Ron Rico, Palo Viejo, and Barrilito.

Gambling

The time when one of the main tourism activities in Puerto Rico was gambling has passed, but casinos still draw crowds. Today, rather than high rollers out for a week of intense dice and card games, the casinos tend to be filled with couples looking for fun and a chance to hit the jackpot.

By law, all island casinos are in hotels, and the majority of the island's gaming halls are in San Juan or the larger hotels of the east and west coasts. In addition to slot machines, typical games include blackjack, roulette, craps, Caribbean stud poker (a five-card stud game), and *pai gow* poker (a combination of American poker and the ancient Chinese game of pai gow, which employs cards and dice). Hotels that house casinos have live entertainment most weekends, restaurants, and bars; drinks are usually served in the casino to players.

Dress for the larger casinos tends to be on the more formal side, and the atmosphere is refined. The law permits casinos to operate noon–4 AM, but individual casinos set their own hours. The minimum age is 18.

Music

Music is the heart and soul of Puerto Rico. One of the island's first musical forms was *bomba y plena,* folk music that originated with slave groups on the island and utilizes drums, scratch gourds, and the *cuatro,* a five-double-string Spanish guitar. The form is still heard at island music and cultural festivals and in the countryside.

The brash Latin sound today is best exemplified by salsa, as interpreted by a flock of internationally known Latin entertainers. Puerto Rico's contributions include pop sensation Ricky Martin and the late, great Tito Puente. Salsa, Spanish for "sauce," meaning the sauce that energizes the party, is a fusion of West African percussion and jazz with a swing beat and is eminently danceable. Other Latin beats heard on the island, with origins in the Caribbean, Latin America, and Spain, are mambo, merengue, flamenco, cha-cha, and rumba. Bands both small in the country tradition and large in the Big Band tradition play at local hotels, casinos, and concert halls throughout the island.

Shopping

What would a vacation be without a few souvenirs to carry home? You will find unique buys in Puerto Rico. Popular local items include *santos,* which are small, hand-carved figures of saints or religious scenes used in religious festivals. Hand-rolled cigars are always a good bet, and the craftsmen that create them can be seen at work in several spots. *Veijigantes* (colorful masks made of papier-mâché and coconut husks and used during Carnival and local festivals) are one-of-a-kind buys, and exquisitely crafted Panama hats are sure to set the tropical mood. Local fine art follows the Puerto Rican tradition of passion and dignity—and the island has plenty of art galleries.

San Juan is the island's shopping center, with numerous designer boutiques, art galleries, souvenir shops, and specialty stores, and Old San Juan, with its cobblestone streets lined with galleries, boutiques, and cafés, is the island's premier shopping spot. It's not a duty-free port, and you won't find bargains on electronics and perfumes. You can, however, find excellent prices on china, crystal, fashions, and jewelry.

FODOR'S CHOICE

No two people will agree on what makes a perfect vacation, but it's fun and helpful to know what others think. We hope you'll have a chance to experience some of Fodor's Choices yourself in Puerto Rico. For detailed information about each entry, refer to the appropriate chapter.

Dining

★ **Café Blu, Vieques.** Take scrumptious food, add an elegant setting, and you've got this posh restaurant. From the sea bass to the tuna to the trout, every dish is exquisite. *$$$$*

★ **Horned Dorset Primavera, Rincón.** The five-course prix-fixe dinner here is known throughout the island. French cuisine is laced with tropical touches to create subtle, sophisticated meals. *$$$$*

★ **El Picoteo, Old San Juan.** El Convento Hotel's stylish tapas bar is one of the most pleasant places in Old San Juan, and it's nothing if not flexible—stop in for an early cocktail and an appetizer, have a full meal, or end the evening with dessert and a nightcap. *$$–$$$$*

★ **Ajili Mojili, San Juan.** Here you'll find classic Puerto Rican dishes given an upscale twist and served with a mix of efficiency and island charm. *$$$*

★ **La Fontanella, Fajardo.** This Sicilian eatery takes garden ingredients and turns them into garlic- and spice-laden masterpieces. If you can't find a dish that overwhelms you, then you just aren't trying. *$$$*

★ **Mark's at the Meliá, Ponce.** This restaurant gets points for being right in the center of town in the Meliá Hotel on Ponce's Plaza las Delicias. Award-winning chef Mark French serves up consistently outstanding food—an eclectic mix of Caribbean and international cuisine. *$$$*

★ **The Parrot Club, Old San Juan.** The relaxed yet stylish environment here seems to have struck a chord with sanjuaneros, who are quickly turning this Nuevo Latino restaurant into an institution. *$$$*

★ **Café Media Luna, Vieques.** For lovers of exotic spices, this local favorite is heaven. Everything from Asian to Middle Eastern fare joins tropical cuisine for a meld that is incomparable. *$$*

★ **The Sand and the Sea, Cayey.** The open balcony at this mountaintop restaurant may have the best view on the island—it's especially breathtaking at sunset. Piano music, a fireplace, and good food make for a memorable experience. *$$*

★ **La Fonda del Jibarito, Old San Juan.** There are excellent family-run restaurants serving traditional Puerto Rican fare all over the island—this happens to be one of the best. *$*

Lodging

★ **Copamarina Beach Resort, Guánica.** The setting is lovely, the service is friendly, and everything is at your fingertips here, from an on-site dive shop to a gorgeous public beach, Caña Gorda, right next door. *$$$$*

★ **El Convento Hotel, Old San Juan.** You wouldn't recognize the El Convento as the Carmelite convent it was 350 years ago; today it's luxurious and hip, a fine example of what sensitive planning and a good decorator can achieve. *$$$$*

★ **Horned Dorset Primavera, Rincón.** The only Relais & Chateaux property on the island, this west-coast inn is the place to go to get away from it all in luxury. There are no phones, TVs, or radios in the antique-trimmed rooms, a secluded beach is steps away, and plunge pools dot the beautifully manicured grounds. *$$$$*

★ **Inn on the Blue Horizon, Vieques.** No phones, no televisions, no noise—just privacy and pampering at this hotel made up of four villas. *$$$$*

★ **Wyndham El Conquistador Resort and Country Club, Fajardo.** Many visitors contend that this resort boasts the most stunning location on the island, hanging off a bluff just above the Atlantic Ocean. With nearly a thousand rooms, it's a giant, largely self-contained complex that aims to meet all of your needs—and succeeds. *$$$$*

★ **Wyndham El San Juan Hotel and Casino, San Juan.** Put on your dancing gear and salsa the night away in the immense, paneled lobby of the landmark El San Juan, where on Saturday night it's the place to see and be seen. It's also one of San Juan's finest hotels. *$$$$*

★ **Gallery Inn, Old San Juan.** This converted 300-year-old Spanish town house is funky, quirky, and welcoming. Without a doubt, it's unlike any other hotel you've stayed in, thanks to the wonderful art of owner Jan D'Esopo that adorns the walls, and to the lush interior courtyards and hidden rooms. *$$–$$$$*

★ **Hacienda Tamarindo, Vieques.** A tamarind tree rises up through three stories in the hotel lobby and the outdoor pool is touted as one of the most beautiful in Puerto Rico, sitting on a hilltop overlooking Vieques. It's a formula for whimsical bliss. *$$$*

★ **Mary Lee's by the Sea, Guánica.** Tranquillity reigns at this colorful complex of apartments and suites with fully equipped kitchenettes. A wonderful place to escape after a day of sun and sea. *$$$*

★ **Bahía Salinas Beach Resort, Cabo Rojo.** You're closest neighbor at this hotel on the southwestern tip of Puerto Rico is the Cabo Rojo Lighthouse. The dry landscape of natural salt flats is amazing, and there's often a lovely pink tinge to the sand on the beach. The resort itself is a fanciful mix of buildings, pools, and walkways. *$$–$$$*

★ **Villas del Mar Hau, Isabela.** The Caribbean doesn't get much better than at this secluded spot. A row of brightly colored cottages lines the Montones Beach, and the whole area is dotted with palm and pine trees. There are outdoor sports facilities where active children and adults can work up a sweat, and horseback riding is available. *$$*

Museums and Cultural Attractions

★ **Fuerte San Felipe del Morro, Old San Juan.** The old fort is solid as a rock and even today seems impenetrable. Take a guided tour and see why San Juan was able to fend off invaders for 400 years.

★ **Hacienda Buena Vista, Ponce.** The grounds of this former corn and coffee plantation are meticulously maintained, and the guided tours, offered in English and Spanish, are as informative as they come. You'll know how it felt to be a settler taming the wilderness.

★ **Museo de Arte Contemporáneo de Puerto Rico, San Juan.** The range of good contemporary art in Puerto Rico is profound, and nowhere is it showcased better than at this art museum on the grounds of the Universidad del Sagrado Corazón (Sacred Heart University) in Santurce.

★ **Museo de Arte de Ponce.** The breadth and quality of both European and Puerto Rican art found here is unequalled anywhere else in the Caribbean. The collection of Pre-Raphaelite paintings is truly world class.

★ **Museo de las Américas, Old San Juan.** The Museum of the Americas, housed in the impressive 1864 Cuartel de Ballajá military barracks in Old San Juan, has on display extraordinary folk art collected from throughout North and South America.

Beaches

★ **Balneario de Luquillo.** This beautiful beach has all the trimmings—including lifeguards, change houses, and nearby kiosks where you can find tasty local cuisine and piña coladas. It also has something extra: ocean access for wheelchair users.

★ **Cabo Rojo Beaches.** The strips of sand stretching along such beaches as Balneario Boquerón, El Combate, Buyé, and the more secluded La Playuela are some of the most gorgeous on the island.

★ **Crashboat Beach, Aguadilla.** The picturesque boats lining the shores here are just part of the appeal. The water has a shimmering, glasslike look and is great for swimming and snorkeling. The shoreline has picnic tables and playground areas.

★ **Isla Verde Beach, San Juan.** There's a reason this spot is the site for some of the toniest resorts in San Juan—the beach, wide and warm and kissed by the surf, seems to go on forever.

★ **Playa Flamenco, Culebra.** Imagine a long curve of white sand and clear, azuretinted water. Palm trees wave in the wind. No one is there to claim the spot as theirs. That's what you'll find at this Culebra beach.

Natural Wonders

★ **Bosque Estatal de Guánica.** While not filled with the lush greenery you might expect in the tropics, this dry forest is an amazing site with its various forms of cacti and abundant bird life. Hiking here may not be for everyone—it's hot and arid—but you'll love it if you're interested in exotic flora and birds.

★ **Centro de Información El Portal, El Yunque.** This exhibit pavilion at the entrance to El Yunque rain forest offers a stupendous multi-media presentation. Even if you're not a nature nut, you're bound to find something that fascinates you here. It's a great way to begin your visit to El Yunque, one of Puerto Rico's treasures.

★ **Mosquito Bay, Vieques.** The magnificence of gliding through the sparkling sea creatures at this bioluminescent bay is almost beyond description. Forget special effects and high-tech trickery; here Mother Nature beats them all hands down.

★ **Parque de las Cavernas de Río Camuy, Arecibo.** The caves are nestled in the island's limestone karst country just south of Arecibo. The tram ride down to them—through wild bamboo and banana plants—is worth the price of admission alone. The large Clara Cave de Empalme is a natural wonder of stalactites, stalagmites, and unique cave life.

FESTIVALS AND SEASONAL EVENTS

Six times per year, the Puerto Rico Tourism Company publishes *Qué Pasa!*, a guide to events, activities, accommodations, and restaurants. Copies are free at any tourism company office, and in many hotels around the island. Also see the Weekend Portfolio section in the Thursday edition of the *San Juan Star*, the island's award-winning daily newspaper.

Local festivals in honor of patron saints are held year-round in the island's 78 towns and municipalities. These 10-day **Fiestas Patronales** feature costume processions, sports events, folklore shows, feasts, music, and dance, and often highlight local crafts, such as the delicate mundillo lace of Aguadilla. One of the island's biggest patron saint festivals is late June's **San Juan Bautista Day,** honoring San Juan's patron John the Baptist with a week of parades; music; dance; and, ultimately, a traditional backward walk into the ocean to bring good luck in the ensuing year. Loíza's **St. James Festival,** held in July, honors Puerto Rico's African traditions and the apostle St. James with a carnival of street parades, music, and dancing. The Puerto Rico Tourism Comany can provide a complete list of Fiestas Patronales as well as specific dates for all of the annual events listed here.

WINTER

➤ DEC.: The Puerto Rico National Folkloric Ballet performs its highly anticipated **Annual Criollísimo Show** regularly during the month. The dance blends modern ballet with Puerto Rican and Caribbean music and themes. Look to the Tapia Theater in Old San Juan or the Luis A. Ferré Performing Arts Center in Santurce for schedules.

➤ MID-DEC.: Cataño's Bacardi Rum company hosts the **Bacardi Artisan's Fair.** The fair, with local crafts, children's activities, folk bands, and food and drink kiosks, is arguably the Caribbean's largest craft fair.

➤ MID-DEC.: If you've got a hankering for loud engines and sea spray, visit the exciting **Puerto Rico International Offshore Cup** speed-boat races held every year in Fajardo, where local and international teams compete for prize money and prestige.

➤ LATE DEC.: **Navidades,** or Christmas, features costumed nativity processions, music concerts, and other festivities island-wide during the week leading to one of the busiest holidays of the year.

➤ LATE DEC.: The annual **Hatillo Festival** honors the mask-making tradition of the northwestern town of Hatillo, where colorful masks used in religious processions have been crafted for centuries.

➤ JAN. 6: The traditional **Three Kings Day** is a time of gift-giving and celebration. Sculptures of the gift-bearing three wise men, in wood or wire decorated with Christmas lights, appear in towns around the island, accompanied by music, puppet shows for children, and feasts. In San Juan, children gather at La Fortaleza, the governor's mansion, for activities and the dispensing of gifts.

➤ JAN.: The annual season of the **Puerto Rico Symphony Orchestra** begins, with classical and pop performances by the island's finest orchestra. Concerts are held in San Juan.

➤ LATE JAN.: The annual **San Sebastián Street Festival,** named after the street in Old San Juan where the festival originated, features several nights of live music in the plazas, food festivals, and *cabezudos* parades, where folk legends are caricatured in oversize masks.

➤ LATE JAN.–EARLY FEB.: Each year the Puerto Rico film industry picks talent to honor in the **Puerto Rico International Film Festival.** International stars such as Chita Rivera and the late Raoul Julia attest to the power of Puerto Rican influence in the arts, and the San Juan film festival showcases island-made films and works from around the world.

➤ EARLY FEB.: Coamo's **San Blas de Illescas Half Marathon** has been running, literally, since 1957. The race, in honor of the town's patron saint and part of its fiesta patronale, covers 13 mi in the hills of the central town; it's so popular that runners from the world over come to compete, and the streets are lined with some 200,000 spectators.

➤ MID-FEB.: Ponce's **Danza Week** of cultural activities celebrates the danza, a colonial-era dance similar to the waltz.

➤ LATE FEB.: The mountain towns of Maricao and Yauco, centers of the island's coffee-growing region, host the annual **Coffee Harvest Festival**, honoring the crop and the farmers who labor in the industry. Coffee, a major cash crop on the island, is important to the culture and the local cuisine. The festival takes place at the towns' plazas, with exhibits of coffee, harvesting equipment, local bands, folk crafts, and food and drink kiosks.

➤ FEB.–EARLY MAR.: The weeks preceding Lent have special significance for Catholicism and other religions, and Puerto Rico celebrates its **Carnivals** with vigor. The flamboyant celebrations, held island-wide but with particular energy in Ponce, are complete with float parades, folk music, local foods, Carnival Queen pageants, and music competitions.

SPRING

➤ MAR.: The two-day **Dulce Sueño Paso Fino Fair**, showcasing the island's famous Paso Fino horses, is held in the town of Guayama. Paso Finos are bred and trained to walk with a distinctive, smooth gait, and the horses and their trainers are held in high regard.

➤ MID-MAR.: The Puerto Rico Tourism Company sponsors the annual **International Artisans' Festival**, with folk art, carvings, leather work, and other crafts and exhibits from islanders and international artists. The festival, held at the tourism company's offices at La Princesa in Old San Juan, was initiated in 2000. Festivities include music and dance demonstrations and locally made refreshments.

➤ APR.: Fajardo's **Kite Festival** features demonstrations and flying competitions, as well as food and drink booths.

➤ LATE APR.: Not only for professionals in the tourism industry, the annual **Tourism Fair** highlights island attractions and activities, as well as local crafts and artisans' creations. The fair is held on the grounds of the Puerto Rico Tourism Company's headquarters at Paseo de la Princesa in Old San Juan.

➤ LATE APR.–MAY: Isabela's **Bobbin Lace Festival** showcases delicate, woven lace (called mundillo) with weaving demonstrations and exhibits.

➤ LATE MAY–EARLY JUNE: The annual **Heineken JazzFest** attracts some 15,000 aficionados of the cool to San Juan each year for four days of outdoor concerts. The JazzFest features workshops conducted by leading musicians and teachers, as well as a wide variety of performances by the likes of David Sánchez, George Benson, and Spyro Gyra.

SUMMER

➤ EARLY JUNE: The annual **Casals Festival,** held at the Luis A. Ferré Performing Arts Center in San Juan, honors the late, great cellist Pablo Casals, who lived in Old San Juan. The 10 days of classical music performances feature the Puerto Rico Symphony Orchestra as well as soloists from the island and around the world.

➤ LATE JUNE–JULY: Gardenias, lilies, begonias, and thousands of tropical plants are showcased at Aibonito's annual **Flower Festival.** Live music, crafts, and refreshment kiosks accompany the flower fest.

➤ EARLY JULY: Río Grande celebrates a **Carnival,** *Carnivale* in Spanish, between the first and second week of July with music competitions, parades, and feasts.

➤ MID-JULY: The annual **Barranquitas Artisans' Fair** offers spots to more than 200 local artisans to display their pottery, wood carvings, leather bags and belts, basketry, and other handiwork. Also on hand to liven up the festival are bands and refreshment booths.

➤ LATE AUG.–EARLY SEPT.: Anglers of all stripes try their hand at snagging blue marlin and other game fish in the largest fishing competition in Puerto Rico, the **International Billfish Tournament.** The strongest tackle might prevail—marlins can weigh as much as 900 pounds. The contest sponsor is Club Náutico in San Juan.

AUTUMN

➤ LATE OCT.: The **National Plantain Festival** highlights this versatile staple of Puerto Rican cuisine. The festival, held during the plantain season, also features folk music and dance, local crafts, and exhibits of dishes made with green and ripe plantains, which are relatives to the banana. Corozal, in the north, hosts the festival.

➤ OCT.: The north coast town of Arecibo holds the **Ceti Festival,** named after a tiny, sardinelike fish found along the north coast, considered a culinary delicacy.

➤ LATE OCT.–JAN.: The boys of summer are actually the boys of winter in Puerto Rico: in October the **baseball season** commences. Fans follow the games, played at various island stadiums, with the fervor of sports enthusiasts anywhere. Major-league players often travel to Puerto Rico to play with the island's six pro teams.

➤ MID-NOV.: The **Festival of Puerto Rican Music,** held in San Juan and other locations, celebrates the vibrancy of Puerto Rico's folk music, highlighted by a contest featuring the cuatro, a traditional guitar with five double strings.

➤ MID-NOV.: The **National Bomba y Plena Festival** turns the spotlight on Puerto Rico's lively African-influenced music and dance. The Ponce festival also features a parade, crafts exhibits, and food and drink booths.

➤ LATE NOV.: Luquillo hosts the three-day **Festival of Typical Dishes,** highlighting food and drink prepared with coconut. Music, dance, and revelry accompany the festival.

➤ LATE NOV.: The central mountain areas hold an annual **Joyuya Indian Festival,** honoring the island's indigenous Taíno culture with crafts demonstrations, ceremonies, and guided visits to Taíno sites in the area.

2 SAN JUAN

Beneath the surface, beneath the highways and malls, beneath the Pizza Huts and K-Marts and Texaco gas stations, it's there. It's in the beat-heavy salsa thumping from your taxi driver's radio, in the insouciant swagger of a young *sanjuanero* walking down the boulevard, in the limpid waters of San Juan Bay and the swaying palm trees beachside at the El San Juan Hotel. This is the Caribbean, the Latin Caribbean, home of mambo and merengue, hot coffee, and a sugared mallorca. It's paradise's baby in an urban comforter, with a U.S. uncle and a Spanish mother.

by Karl Luntta

S AN JUAN IS THE CAPITAL AND LARGEST CITY in Puerto Rico, home to more than a third of the island's 3.9 million people. The sprawling urban area lies on the north coast of the oblong island, just east of center, bordered to the north by the Atlantic Ocean, and to the east and west by ocean bays and lagoons. The city is both modern and antique, a busy commercial and residential center characterized by highways, gleaming office complexes, and blocky housing tenements, and, in the Old San Juan sector, by 350-year-old colonial buildings steeped in history.

By 1508 the explorer Juan Ponce de León had established a colony in the area now known as Caparra, southeast of present-day San Juan, but he soon moved the settlement north to a more hospitable location on the Old San Juan peninsula. The Spaniards originally called the island San Juan Bautista, in honor of St. John the Baptist, and the area now known as San Juan was named Puerto Rico, or "rich port." Ponce de León, who became the first governor in 1521, switched the names to those we know today.

Through the early history of the New World, European powers vied for domination in the Caribbean. Yet with San Juan as its administrative and population center and the imposing Fuerte San Felipe del Morro, commonly known as El Morro, as its primary bastion of defense, the island remained a Spanish possession until 1898, when it came under U.S. control as a spoil of the Spanish-American War.

Centuries of Spanish rule left an indelible imprint on Old San Juan, as will be readily apparent when you set foot on its blue cobblestone streets. Countless examples of Spanish colonial architecture evoke the grandeur of bygone days—but they are also a testament to the intensive preservation and restoration efforts of the last 50 years. Thanks to these efforts, it's no exaggeration to say that Old San Juan is as beautiful today as at any other time in its history.

Although the Old City exists in large part as a monument to the past, the metropolitan area that has grown around it stands firmly in the here and now. The years since the establishment of U.S.-commonwealth status have seen economic growth everywhere on the island but foremost in San Juan, where an influx of business and industry has triggered a significant migration of Puerto Ricans from elsewhere on the island. Today the city is vibrant and growing—not without growing pains, traffic being the most evident. But on the whole, both Old San Juan and the greater metropolis are the happy result of successful urban planning and the civic pride of *sanjuaneros*.

Pleasures and Pastimes

Architecture

San Juan has been under construction for nearly 500 years. From early settlements established by the Spanish explorer Juan Ponce de León in 1508 to the founding of Old San Juan in 1521 and the subsequent half-millennium of growth under Spanish and U.S. colonialism, the city has become a combination of the ancient and the ultra-modern. Old San Juan's 300-year-old Spanish row houses, brick with plaster fronts painted in pastel blues, oranges, and yellows, stand tall over narrow streets and alleys paved with *adoquines* (blue-gray stones originally used as ballast in Spanish ships). Several of the city's churches, including the 1540 Catedral de San Juan, were built in the ornate Spanish Gothic style of the era. The walled city has been a U.S. National Historic Zone since 1950, and ongoing efforts to renovate its buildings have made it one of the best-preserved collections of Spanish colonial architecture in the New World. Newer buildings include the massive, white-marble El Capitolio, the home of Puerto Rico's legislature, completed in 1929. Newer still are the gleaming high-rise resorts and condo complexes of Condado and Isla Verde, and the glistening steel-and-glass banking and financial centers of downtown's Hato Rey. Interspersed among this marriage of antiquity and modernity are cinder-block tenements and the residential neighborhoods of tin-roof houses found in central downtown and along Route 26, the main east–west artery through northern San Juan.

Beaches

Just because you're staying in the city doesn't mean you'll have to forgo your tanning time—San Juan's beaches are among the best on the island, popular with city folk on weekends and abuzz with Jet Skis, waterskiing, and other activities. The beaches line the north coast of the city from Carolina in the east to, heading west, the neighborhoods of Isla Verde, Ocean Park, Condado, and Puerta de Tierra.

Note that, by law, all Puerto Rican beaches, *playas* in Spanish, are open to the public. The government maintains 13 *balnearios* (public beaches)—two in the San Juan metro area—which are gated and have dressing rooms, lifeguards, parking, and in some cases picnic tables, playgrounds, and camping facilities. Admission is free, parking is $2. Hours vary, but most balnearios are open 9–5 daily in summer and Tuesday–Sunday the rest of the year. For more information you can contact the **Department of Recreation and Sports** (☎ 787/722–1551 or 787/721–2800).

Balneario de Carolina, a government-run beach east of San Juan, sits near the airport and features miles of sand, picnic gazebos, lifeguards, and daily parking fees, and is easily accessed by car or bus. The vast Isla Verde and Condado beaches sit in front of strings of high-rise resorts and hotels, as well as smaller beach inns and bars, and are wide open, with beach-chair rentals, water-sports outfits, and vendors selling cold drinks. Ocean Park, wedged between Isla Verde and Condado, has a small and quiet public beach adjacent to a park. Near Old San Juan, the new Parque de Tercer Milenio (Third Millennium Park), on the Puerta de Tierra section, hosts Balneario Escambrón, where you'll find restaurants, bathhouses, lifeguards, and parking.

Dining

In San Juan you'll find everything from Italian to Thai to Middle Eastern, as well as superb local eateries serving comida criolla. Although each of San Juan's large hotels has two or more fine restaurants, some of the city's best dining is found at stand-alone establishments, and smaller, lesser known hotels often present good options. Family restaurants, largely specializing in local food, compete against a mind-boggling array of U.S. chains, from Chile's to McDonald's to Pizzeria Uno. No matter what your price range or taste, San Juan is a great place to eat.

WHAT TO WEAR

Dress codes vary greatly, though a restaurant's price category is a good indicator of its formality. For less expensive places, anything but beachwear is fine. You can always head straight from the beach to the drive-through or counter of a Pollo Tropical (a local fast-food chain) for a satisfying pollo sandwich with a side of succulent amarillos. There are many casual family-owned restaurants, specializing usually in seafood or *comida criolla* (creole cooking), where dress is unimportant. Ritzier eateries will expect collared shirts for men (jacket and tie requirements are rare) and chic attire for women. However, Puerto Ri-

cans enjoy dressing up for dinner, so chances are you'll never feel over-
dressed. This is the tropics, however.

CATEGORY	COST*
$$$$	over $45
$$$	$30–$45
$$	$15–$30
$	under $15

per person for a three-course meal, excluding drinks and service

✎ *following the text of a review is your signal that the property has
a Web site, where you will find details and, usually, images; for a link,
visit www.fodors.com/urls.*

Lodging

San Juan is a busy town, with plenty of visitor traffic from tourists,
cruise-ship passengers, and business travelers. Just about every type of
accommodation is available, from high-rise, high-end, beachside resorts
to nondescript business hotels on busy side streets. The city prides itself on its clean, comfortable, and plentiful accommodations, and city
hoteliers, by and large, aim to please. San Juan, however, is not inexpensive. For a high-end beach-resort room, expect to pay at least $200
for a double in high season (roughly mid-December through mid-
April). For smaller inns and hotels, expect to start at $100 for a dou-
ble. As a general rule, if your room is less than $50 in high season, then
the quality and security of the hotel might be questionable. In the most
expensive categories below, rooms will be adequately large, with king-
or queen-size beds (possibly two doubles), air-conditioning, phones,
private baths, in-room safes, cable TV, hair dryers, irons and ironing
boards, room service, shampoo and toiletries, and possibly even a
view of the water. There will be a concierge and at least one hotel restaurant and lounge, a pool, shops, and an exercise room or spa facility.
In the less expensive categories, rooms will have private baths, air-conditioning or fans, double to king beds, possibly room service, and
Continental breakfast included in the rates.

CATEGORY	COST*
$$$$	over $225
$$$	$150–$225
$$	$75–$150
$	under $75

*All prices are for a double room in high season, excluding 9% tax (11% for
hotels with casinos, 7% for paradores) and 10%–15% service charge.*

Music

Music is a source of Puerto Rican pride, and it seems that, increasingly,
everyone wants to live that *vida loca* espoused by Puerto Rico's own
Ricky Martin. The brash Latin sound is best characterized by the
music/dance form salsa, which shares not only its name with the word
"sauce," but is also a zesty, hot flavor. This fusion of West African percussion, jazz (especially swing and Big Band), and other Latin beats
(mambo, merengue, flamenco, cha-cha, rumba) is sexy and primal. Dancing to it is a chance to let go of inhibitions.

Live music can be heard virtually any night of the week in San Juan.
Look to the major hotels in Condado and Isla Verde for salsa bands
turning the night into a white-hot party of dance. The El San Juan Hotel
in Isla Verde is, in particular, an institution—Saturday night is the night
for *sanjuaneros* to dress up, step out, and salsa the night away in the
vast and ornate lobby. Other hotels feature salsa and other Latin
sounds in their nightclubs and casinos. Jazz is popular, too, in small

bars and clubs such as Carli Café Concierto and Café Tabac in Old San Juan, and Café Matisse on Avenida Ashford in Condado.

EXPLORING SAN JUAN

San Juan, home to 1.5 million people, lies on Puerto Rico's northeastern coast. The city is busy and congested, laced with highways and wide avenues. It is graced by centuries-old neighborhoods and blighted by the modern urban sprawl common to cities of its size everywhere. San Juan's metro area stretches for a dozen miles along the north coast, and defining the city is rather like assembling a puzzle—its neighborhoods are irregular and sometimes overlapping, not easily pieced together.

If you are like most visitors, you will spend the majority of your time in the northernmost coastal neighborhoods stretching from Isla Verde in the east to Old San Juan in the west—the popular beach and shopping areas. West from Luis Muñoz Marín Airport along Route 37, north of the large Laguna San José, is the main Isla Verde area, a stretch of high-rise apartment complexes and hotels, many of which sit directly on a superb, sandy beach. West of Isla Verde you will find the more sedate Ocean Park, a residential neighborhood of low-lying buildings on another fine patch of beach, with several outstanding small hotels and restaurants and a few shops. South of Ocean Park lies the suburb of Santurce, a combined residential and business district with wide roads and plenty of commercial activity. The urban core of San Juan is several miles to the south of Santurce, in a collection of neighborhoods including Hato Rey, a busy financial district where you'll find the large Plaza las Americas Mall, and the mostly residential Río Piedras, home of the University of Puerto Rico and its museum and botanical garden.

West of Ocean Park, back on the north coast, is Condado, on a thin strip of land between the ocean and the Condado Lagoon. Here the buzz is all about tourism: hotels crowd the beach, and tony shops and restaurants line the main drag, Avenida Ashford. Heading west from Condado will bring you to the Puerta de Tierra Peninsula, between the ocean to the north and San Juan Bay to the south, where there are several resort hotels and two noteworthy parks, the Parque de Tercer Milenio (Third Millennium Park) and the Parque Muñoz Rivera, a long stretch with a promenade and several monuments and bandstands. Finally, west of Puerta de Tierra is famous Old San Juan, the focal point and showplace of the island's rich history, where you will find in one concentrated area the city's finest museums and shops, as well as excellent dining and lodging.

Great Itineraries

IF YOU HAVE 3 DAYS

If you're coming to the Caribbean, you will likely want to spend some time on a beach—choose from the city's finest at Condado, Ocean Park, or Isla Verde, and park yourself in a rented beach chair with a good book, a cold drink, plenty of sunscreen, and a day to do nothing but. On your second day, head to Old San Juan for sightseeing and shopping, making sure not to miss El Morro, officially Fuerte San Felipe del Morro, the original fortress on a rocky promontory on the northwestern tip of the old city. Built by the Spaniards between 1540 and 1783, the fort's labyrinth of dungeons, ramps, turrets, towers, and tunnels can take the better part of the day to explore. Take your camera for expansive views of the harbor from the fort. Spend the rest of the day ambling through Old San Juan's cobblestone streets and its many shops—Calle Fortaleza (*calle* is Spanish for street) and Calle Cristo are stacked with jewelry stores, designer clothing outlets, and art galleries.

For your third day, take a day trip to El Yunque (☞ *see* Chapter 3), the 28,000-acre Caribbean National Forest about an hour east of San Juan. You'll find a rain forest of 100-ft-high trees, dramatic mountain ranges, and walking trails leading to waterfalls. (Bring a bathing suit; you can change at the park's visitors centers.)

IF YOU HAVE 5 DAYS

Follow the three-day itinerary, but give yourself another two days in and around Old San Juan. The city's myriad museums and galleries are enough to fill several days of sightseeing at a leisurely pace. Make sure to walk down the Paseo de la Princesa at the south side of the Old City. This promenade passes by La Princesa, once the city's main jail and now home to the Puerto Rico Tourism Company, as well as a gallery with rotating exhibits by prominent Puerto Rican artists. On its west end a picturesque fountain depicts the ethnic groups of Puerto Rico, and just past the fountain the *paseo* connects to a shoreline walk that hugs the city's southwestern *la muralla* (wall) and passes through the massive antique gates that once protected it from attack. Then head to the north end of the city and the Plaza de San José. Here you'll find the 1532 Gothic-style Iglésia de San José, which once held the remains of the explorer Juan Ponce de León, and you can visit several museums, including the Museo Pablo Casals, dedicated to the famous cellist who lived in Puerto Rico for the last 16 years of his life, and the Museo de Nuestra Raíz Africana, which explores Puerto Rico's African heritage. Next door is the massive Cuartel de Ballajá, a vast former military barracks completed in 1864, now the home of the Museo de las Américas, an extraordinary collection of folk art and historical displays from Latin America. If the steep streets begin to wear you down, remember you can always board the free trolleys that wend their way through Old San Juan. Give yourself half a day to visit the Bacardi Rum Plant in Cataño, a short ferry ride from Old San Juan across the bay (it's 50¢ one way). The plant offers tours of its operations and small museum, and of course you can sample the wares.

IF YOU HAVE 7 DAYS

With the luxury of a week in San Juan, consider day trips to outlying areas, with perhaps the option of spending a night on the coast or in the central mountains. If, however, you're committed to your hotel in San Juan, follow the five-day itinerary, leaving plenty of time to enjoy all the sights of Old San Juan. Then head to the southern suburb of Río Piedras, where the University of Puerto Rico maintains its 75-acre Jardín Botánico (Botanical Garden). Gravel paths loop through the extensive gardens, connecting 200 species of tropical and subtropical vegetation in a lotus lagoon, a bamboo promenade, an orchid garden with some 30,000 plants, and a palm garden. Signs are in Spanish and English. Take another day to head off to Luquillo Beach (☞ *see* Chapter 3), about a 45-minute drive east from San Juan and a popular weekend spot for *sanjuaneros* decompressing from city life. The beach is thick with coconut palms, and there are changing rooms, lockers, showers, picnic tables, and tent sites. Perhaps the biggest attractions at Luquillo are the small *quioscos* (kiosks) that sell such savory Puerto Rican delicacies as *bacalaítos* (fried cod fritters) and empanadillas. You can wash them down with fresh coconut milk or a cold beer.

When to Tour San Juan

The high season in San Juan is roughly the winter season, defined as mid-December through mid-April. Winter hotel rates are 25%–40% higher than in the off season, and hotels tend to be packed. San Juan is a commercial center, and save for the short season around Christmas and New Year's, hotels are busy year-round with business travelers. Which is not to say that San Juan will not have rooms in winter—rarely is there no space available—but if you plan to beat that winter sleet in Duluth, you should play it save and arrange your flight and hotel at least a couple of months ahead of time. Visiting in winter will allow your participation in several colorful annual events that loom large on the San Juan social calendar. The January **San Sebastián Street Festival,** held in Old San Juan, features several nights of live music in the plazas, food festivals, and *cabezudos* (parades), in which folk legends are caricatured using oversize masks. A near-winter festival, the mid-November **Festival of Puerto Rican Music,** is held both in San Juan venues and out on the island. The festival celebrates Puerto Rico's traditional *plena* and *bomba* folk music with competitions and concerts.

A fun and often less expensive time to visit San Juan is during the "shoulder" seasons of fall and spring, when the weather is—still—perfect and the tourist crush is less intense. Weather is San Juan is moderate and tropical year-round, with an average temperature of about 82°F (26°C). And while it's true that much of the summer encompasses the hurricane season, San Juan is still an attractive destination during those months—many accommodations charge the lowest rates of the year, restaurant reservations are less hard to come by, and the streets are free of tourists.

Old San Juan

It's almost inevitable that if you're visiting San Juan you will eventually be drawn to Old San Juan's 16th-century cobblestone streets, its ornate Spanish town houses with wrought iron balconies, its busy plazas, and it museums, the repositories of the island's history. Founded in 1521 by the Spanish explorer Juan Ponce de León, Old San Juan (Viejo San Juan in Spanish) sits on a high, rocky promontory at the northwestern end of the city, separated from "new" San Juan by a couple of miles and a couple of centuries. While technically part of the greater metropolitan area, it has a culture unto itself, reflecting the sensibilities of the stylish professionals, the bohemian art crowd, and the skateboarding teenagers who populate its streets. Ironically, Old San Juan feels youthful and vibrant. You'll find more streetside cafés and restaurants, more contemporary art galleries, more musicians playing in plazas, than anywhere else in San Juan.

At the northwest end of city, Calle Norzagaray leads to El Morro, the old city's defense bastion. On the north side of Calle Norzagaray, you'll note a small neighborhood at the foot of an embankment, bordering the ocean—this is La Perla, a rough neighborhood that you would do best to avoid. The west end of the Old City faces San Juan Bay, and it's here where the stone walls of the original city are most in evidence. On Old San Juan's south side, you'll find the commercial and cruise-ship piers that jut into San Juan Harbor.

Numbers in the text correspond to numbers in the margin and on the Old San Juan map.

A Good Walk

The best place to start any Old San Juan walking tour is the central **Plaza de Armas** ①, bordered by Calles San Francisco, San José, and Cruz. From here you can branch out, much like following the spokes of a wheel, to various parts of the Old City. On the north side of the plaza is the **Alcaldía** ②, the former city hall built between 1604 and 1789. On the west side of the plaza, the regal **La Intendencia** ③, once the Spanish Treasury building, now houses Puerto Rico's State Department.

Old San Juan

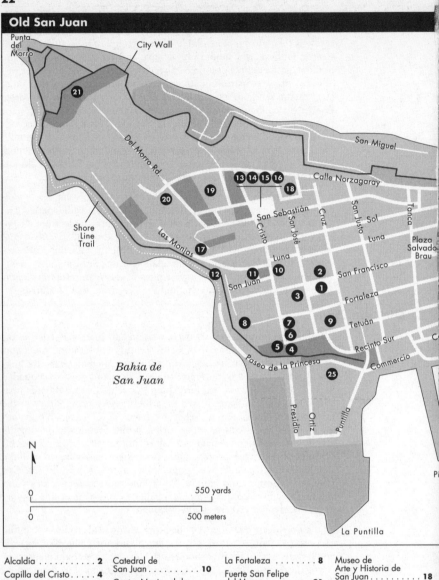

Punta del Morro

City Wall

Del Morro Rd

San Miguel

Calle Norzagaray

Shore Line Trail

Las Monjas

San Sebastián

Cristo

San José

Cruz

San Justo

Sol

Tanca

Luna

Plaza Salvado Brau

San Juan

Luna

San Francisco

Fortaleza

Tetuán

Recinto Sur

Commercio

Bahia de San Juan

Paseo de la Princesa

Presidio

Ortiz

Puntilla

N

La Puntilla

| 0 | 550 yards |
| 0 | 500 meters |

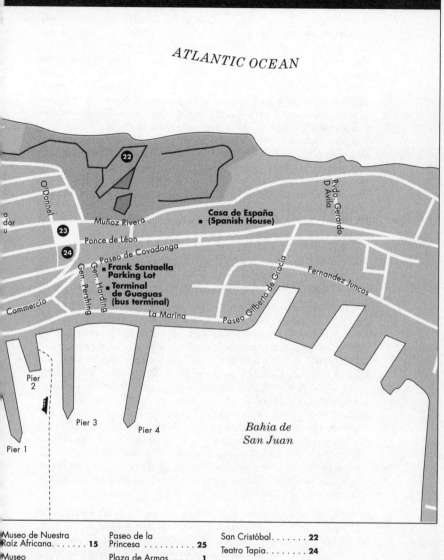

ATLANTIC OCEAN

O'Donnel

a dor u

22

Muñoz Rivera

23

Ponce de Léon

24

Paseo de Covadonga

Gen. Harding
Gen. Pershing

**Frank Santaella
Parking Lot**

**Terminal
de Guaguas
(bus terminal)**

Commercio

La Marina

Pier 2

Pier 1

Pier 3

Pier 4

**Casa de España
(Spanish House)**

Rvdo. Gerardo
D'Avila

Paseo Gilberto de Gracia

Fernandez Juncos

*Bahia de
San Juan*

A block to the west is Calle Cristo, where many of the city's galleries and designer-clothes outlets are found. Heading south on Cristo to the end of the street brings you to **Capilla del Cristo** ④, an ornate 18th-century chapel and monument to the Christ of Miracles. You can gaze through the chapel gates at the ornate altar, but note that the gates are open only on Tuesday. To the right of the chapel is the **Parque de las Palomas** ⑤, roost for many of the city's pigeons. A few steps north of the Capilla and Parque de las Palomas, also on Calle Cristo, is the sedate **Casa del Libro** ⑥, home to rare books and exhibits on 18th-century bookbinding. Next door, the **Centro Nacional de Artes Populares y Artesanías** ⑦ displays island crafts, many of which are for sale. Walk a block north from the Casa del Libro and go left on Calle Fortaleza and right on Calle Recinto Oeste for **La Fortaleza** ⑧, the imposing former bastion now used as the governor's residence. (If you're in a hurry, you might bypass Fortaleza—many of the rooms are closed to the public, and the entire house is, on occasion, taken over for state functions.) Head east on Calle Fortaleza and south on Calle Cristo back to the Parque de las Palomas. A block and a half east of the parque on Calle Tetuán is the **Casa de Ramón Power y Giralt** ⑨, the restored home of an 18th-century naval hero and politician. The home is now the headquarters of the Conservation Trust of Puerto Rico, where you can find interactive displays highlighting the natural wonders of Conservation Trust properties around the island.

From Casa de Ramón Power y Giralt, head back west to Calle Cristo and walk north for two blocks to find the looming **Catedral de San Juan** ⑩. A church has stood on this spot since the 1520s, and the structure today holds the remains of Ponce de León. Across the street from the church is the El Convento Hotel, once a Carmelite convent and now one of the Old City's premier hotels. The plaza adjacent to the hotel, Plaza de Catedral, is the site of the small but absolutely child-friendly **Museo del Niño** ⑪, which features natural-history exhibits and interactive displays on such popular topics as the food groups and building techniques. Heading west from the Museo del Niño on Caleta de las Monjas you'll find a small plaza, the **Plazuela de la Rogativa** ⑫. The statue here of a priest and three women commemorates the historic moment when British attackers were frightened off by torches of a religious procession, or *rogativa*, which they mistook for Spanish reinforcements.

Head north on Calle Cristo (which runs in front of the Museo del Niño) until you reach the white stucco **Iglesia de San José** ⑬ on the Plaza San José. The church, built in 1532, is one of the oldest in the Western Hemisphere. On the east end of the plaza are two museums worth noting: the two-story **Museo Pablo Casals** ⑭ celebrates the life and art of the famous cellist, who lived the last years of his life in Puerto Rico; and the **Museo de Nuestra Raíz Africana** ⑮ investigates African influences on Puerto Rico's culture. Also on the plaza, to the west of the church, is the 1532 **Convento de los Dominicos** ⑯ building, now home to the bookshop of the Instituto de Cultura Puertorriqueña (Institute of Puerto Rican Culture), where you can also buy religious *santos* and other Puerto Rican folk crafts. From here, a short walk west on Calle San Sebastián will bring you to the famous **Casa Blanca** ⑰, originally built in 1521 as a home for Ponce de León, who died before he had a chance to live in it. The present structure was built soon after a hurricane destroyed much of the original in 1523.

Traveling north on Calle Cristo from Plaza San José will bring you to Calle Norzagaray; to the east is the **Museo de Arte y Historia de San Juan** ⑱, once a bustling marketplace and now an art and history museum where music concerts are occasionally held. West on Calle Norza-garay, you'll pass the large Plaza de Quinto Centenario, a tribute to the quincentennial of Columbus's voyages. On the west side of the plaza is the Cuartel de Ballajá, an imposing three-story structure that once served as a military barracks, with a massive interior courtyard. Today the second floor is home to the **Museo de las Américas** ⑲, which features rotating exhibits of Latin American art. The next building west of the Cuartel is the old Asilo de Beneficencia, once a hospital for indigents and now the headquarters of the Instituto de Cultura Puertorriqueña. Inside, on the first floor to the right, is the tiny **Museo del Indio** ⑳, a museum that traces the indigenous Taíno culture of Puerto Rico through artifacts and a short video presentation. (Those trying to complete the tour in a day might skip this small museum.) Finally, look to the west across a wide field. The massive stone structure on the hill is **Fuerte San Felipe del Morro** ㉑, also known as El Morro, the city's premier defense bastion, built between 1540 and 1783. The fort is the highlight of any visit to Old San Juan; tours are given in Spanish and English.

Head east from El Morro along Calle Norzagaray to the eastern side of the Old City, where you'll find Old San Juan's second fort. **Fuerte San Cristóbal** ㉒, built in the 18th century, guarded the north end of the city. At the base of the fort, bordered by Calle San Francisco and Calle O'Donell, is the **Plaza de Colón** ㉓, with a large statue of Christopher Columbus. At the south end of the plaza, across Calle Fortaleza on Calle Recinto Sur, stands the **Teatro Tapia** ㉔, which was built in 1832 and has been presenting live performances ever since. Head south and east on Calle Recinto Sur to **Paseo de la Princesa** ㉕, a long and wide promenade that stretches to San Juan Bay, and passes La Princesa, once the Old City's jail and now home to the Puerto Rican Tourism Company's offices.

TIMING AND PRECAUTIONS

Old San Juan is, in effect, a small neighborhood, approximately seven city blocks square with numerous side streets, alleys, and hidden plazas. In strictly geographical terms, it's easily traversed in a day, but lingering is what Old San Juan is all about. To truly appreciate the numerous museums, galleries, and cafés requires two or three days—and the walk described above is designed with that kind of time commitment in mind. If you're limited to a day, you'll need to pick and choose sights according to your interests. It can be done—it's just not quite so rewarding.

Don't consider driving in Old San Juan unless you have a penchant for sitting in traffic jams for much of the waking day. Old San Juan is a walking city, with narrow one-way streets, narrower alleys, sparse parking, and sights and shops all packed together in an area hardly larger than half a square mile. Some of the streets are steep, and the cobblestones will wreak havoc on high heels, so you'll want to take your time and dress comfortably for this tour. Wear walking shoes and carry a hat or sunscreen, as well as drinking water—the afternoon sun can be hot any time of year. Old San Juan is generally a safe area, but keep in mind that pickpockets visit the same places as tourists, with a different goal in mind—keep money and credit cards in money belts and avoid carrying open handbags. Street hustlers are few and far between, but you will find the occasional, mostly harmless, indigent asking for money.

If you get tired, remember the free trolleys that swing through Old San Juan all day, every day—they depart from the Covadonga parking lot at the main bus terminal area across from Pier 4 and take two routes through the Old City. One route heads north to Calle Norzagaray then west to El Morro (the trolley does not go into El Morro, but drops you off at the long footpath leading to the fort), then south along Calle Cristo to Fortaleza, San Justo, and back along Calle Gilberto Concepción de Gracia (also called Calle la Marina) to the piers. Another takes riders to central Old San Juan to the Plaza de Armas, south on Calle San José, then back to the piers. Both make regular stops (at signs marked *parada*) on their routes. When you're finished touring, taxis can be found in several spots: in front of Pier 2, on the Plaza de Armas, or on Calle O'Donell near the Plaza de Colón.

Sights to See

❷ Alcaldía. This city hall was built between 1604 and 1789. In 1841, extensive renovations were done to make it resemble Madrid's city hall, with arcades, towers, balconies, and a lovely inner courtyard. Recent renovations were completed in 1999 to refresh the facade of the building and some interior rooms, but the architecture remains true to its colonial style. A municipal tourist information center and an art gallery with rotating exhibits are on the first floor. ⊠ *Calle San Francisco, north side of Plaza de Armas,* ☎ *787/724–7171, ext. 2391.* ☒ *Free.* ⊙ *Weekdays 8–4.*

❹ Capilla del Cristo. According to legend, in 1753 a young horseman named Baltazar Montañez, carried away during festivities in honor of San Juan Bautista (St. John the Baptist), raced down Calle Cristo and plunged over its steep precipice. A witness to the tragedy promised to build a chapel if the young man's life could be saved. Historical records maintain the man died, but legend contends that he lived. (Another version of the story has it that the horse miraculously stopped before plunging over the cliff.) Regardless, this chapel was built, and inside it is a small silver altar dedicated to the Christ of Miracles. ⊠ *South end of Calle Cristo,* ☎ *no phone.* ☒ *Free.* ⊙ *Tues. 10–3:30.*

⓱ Casa Blanca. The original structure on this site, not far from the ramparts of El Morro, was a frame house built in 1521 as a home for Ponce de León. But he died in Cuba never having lived in it, and it was virtually destroyed by a hurricane in 1523, after which his son-in-law had the present masonry home built. His descendants occupied the house for 250 years. From the end of the Spanish-American War in 1898 to 1966, it was the home of the U.S. Army commander in Puerto Rico. A museum devoted to archaeology is on the second floor. Select rooms, with period furniture, are open for viewing as well. The lush surrounding garden, cooled by spraying fountains, is a tranquil spot for a restorative pause. ⊠ *1 Calle San Sebastián,* ☎ *787/724–4102.* ☒ *$2.* ⊙ *Tues.–Sat. 9–noon and 1–4:30.*

❻ Casa del Libro. This 18th-century building, the House of Books, contains exhibits of books and bookbinding techniques—it's dedicated to the artistry of the printed word. The museum's 6,000 books, sketches, and illustrations include some 200 rare volumes produced before 1501, as well as what appears to be legal writing on a fragment of clay, thought to date from the time of Christ. Also on hand are several antique printing presses, one constructed in 1812 in France and brought to Puerto Rico in the mid-19th century. ⊠ *255 Calle Cristo,* ☎ *787/723–0354.* ☒ *$2 donation suggested.* ⊙ *Tues.–Sat. 11–4:30.*

🤚 ❾ Casa de Ramón Power y Giralt. The restored home of 18th-century naval hero Don Ramón Power y Giralt is now the headquarters of the Conservation Trust of Puerto Rico. On site are several displays highlighting the physical, cultural, and historical importance of land and properties on the island under the trust's aegis. You'll find a display of musical instruments that you can play, a bird diorama with recorded bird songs, an active beehive, and a seven-minute movie discussing the trust's efforts on the island. Displays are in Spanish; the movie is in English or Spanish. A gift shop sells toys and Puerto Rican candies. ⊠ *155 Calle Tetuán,* ☎ *787/722–5834.* ⊡ *Free.* ☉ *Tues.–Sat. 10–4.*

⑩ **Catedral de San Juan.** The Catholic shrine of Puerto Rico had humble beginnings in the early 1520s as a thatch-top, wooden structure. Hurricane winds tore off the thatch and destroyed the church. It was reconstructed in 1540, when the graceful circular staircase and vaulted Gothic ceilings were added, but most of the work on the present cathedral was done in the 19th century. The remains of Ponce de León are in a marble tomb near the transept. ⊠ *153 Calle Cristo,* ☎ *787/722–0861.* ⊡ *$1 donation suggested.* ☉ *Weekdays 8:30–4; masses Sat. at 7 PM, Sun. at 9 AM and 11 AM, weekdays at 12:15 PM.*

❼ **Centro Nacional de Artes Populares y Artesanías.** Run by the Institute of Puerto Rican Culture, the Popular Arts and Crafts Center is in a colonial building next to the ☞ **Casa del Libro,** and is a superb repository of island crafts, some of which are for sale. ⊠ *253 Calle Cristo,* ☎ *787/722–0621.* ⊡ *Free.* ☉ *Mon.–Sat. 9–5.*

⑯ **Convento de los Dominicos.** Built by Dominican friars in 1523, this convent often served as a shelter during Carib Indian attacks and, more recently, as headquarters for the Antilles command of the U.S. Army. Now home to some offices of the Institute of Puerto Rican Culture, the beautifully restored building contains religious manuscripts, artifacts, and art. The institute also maintains a book and music shop on the premises, and occasionally classical concerts are held here. ⊠ *98 Calle Norzagaray,* ☎ *787/721–6866.* ⊡ *Free.* ☉ *Mon.–Sat. 9–5.*

❽ **La Fortaleza.** Sitting on a hill overlooking the harbor, La Fortaleza, the western hemisphere's oldest executive mansion in continuous use, was built as a fortress. It was attacked numerous times and taken twice, by the British in 1598 and by Dutch invaders in 1625. The original primitive structure, constructed in 1540, has seen numerous changes over the past four centuries, resulting in the present collection of marble and mahogany, medieval towers, and stained-glass galleries. The building is still the official residence of the island's governor, and much of its interior is closed to visitors—guided tours will take you through the extensive gardens and selected rooms not in use. The tours are conducted every hour on the hour in English, on the half hour in Spanish; both include a short video presentation. ⊠ *Calle Recinto Oeste,* ☎ *787/721–7000, ext. 2211 or 2358.* ⊡ *Free.* ☉ *Weekdays 9–4.*

★ ☜ **㉑** **Fuerte San Felipe del Morro.** On a rocky promontory at the northwestern tip of the old city is El Morro (which translates as "promontory"), a fortress built by the Spaniards between 1540 and 1783. Rising 140 ft above the sea, the massive six-level fortress covers enough territory to accommodate a nine-hole golf course. It is a labyrinth of dungeons, ramps, barracks, turrets, towers, and tunnels. Built to protect the port, El Morro has a commanding view of the harbor. You're free to wander throughout. The cannon emplacement walls are thick as a child's arm is long, and the dank secret passageways are a wonder of engineering. The fort's small but enlightening museum offers displays of ancient Spanish guns and other armaments, military uniforms, and blueprints for Spanish forts in the Americas. There's also a gift shop. The fort is a national historic site administered by the U.S. Park Service. Tours and a video are available in English. ⊠ *Calle Norzagaray,* ☎ *787/729–6960.* ⊡ *$2.* ☉ *Daily 9–5.* ☙

⑬ **Iglesia de San José.** With its vaulted ceilings, this church is a splendid example of 16th-century Spanish Gothic architecture. It was built under the supervision of Dominican friars in 1532, making it one of the oldest churches in the Western Hemisphere. The body of Ponce de León, the Spanish explorer who came to the New World seeking the Fountain of Youth, was buried here for almost three centuries before being removed in 1913 and placed in the ☞ **Catedral de San Juan.** ⊠ *Calle San Sebastián, Plaza de San José,* ☎ *787/725–7501.* 🎫 *$1 donation suggested.* ☉ *Mon.–Sat. 8:30–4; mass Sun. at 12:15 PM.*

❸ **La Intendencia.** From 1851 to 1898, this three-story neoclassical building was home to the Spanish Treasury; now it's the headquarters of Puerto Rico's State Department. You can go inside, where the wide interior courtyard, typical of the colonial architectural style, is framed by the high arcades of the perimeter walkways. ⊠ *Calle San José at Calle San Francisco,* ☎ *787/722–2121, ext. 230.* 🎫 *Free.* ☉ *Weekdays 8–noon and 1–4:30. Tours in Spanish at 2 and 3, in English at 4.*

⓲ **Museo de Arte y Historia de San Juan.** A bustling marketplace in 1855, this handsome building is now the modern San Juan Museum of Art and History. You'll find exhibits of Puerto Rican art and audiovisual shows that present the island's history. Concerts and other cultural events take place in the huge interior courtyard. ⊠ *Calle Norzagaray at Calle MacArthur,* ☎ *787/724–1875.* 🎫 *Free.* ☉ *Tues.–Sun. 10–4.*

★ ⓳ **Museo de las Américas.** One of the finest collections of its type in Puerto Rico, the Museum of the Americas is housed on the second floor of the imposing former military barracks, **Cuartel de Ballajá,** at the west end of Old San Juan near El Morro. Most exhibits rotate, but the focus is on the popular and folk art of Latin America. The permanent exhibit, Las Artes Populares en las Américas, features religious figures, musical instruments, basketwork, costumes, and farming and other labor implements of the Americas. The old military barracks, big and boxy in a neoclassical style and painted green and peach, was built between 1854 and 1864, and its immense inner courtyard is used for concerts and private events such as weddings. ⊠ *Calle Norzagaray and Calle del Morro,* ☎ *787/724–5052.* 🎫 *Free.* ☉ *Tues.–Fri. 10–4, weekends 11–5.*

⓴ **Museo del Indio.** The Instituto de Cultura Puertorriqueña (Institute of Puerto Rican Culture) maintains this small Museum of the Indian as a repository of ancient Taíno artifacts and information regarding Taíno life some 500 years ago. The short tour starts with a five-minute video describing the geophysical origins of the island, and displays include Taíno religious figures carved from rock, digging and fishing implements, and a replica of a Taíno home. The museum is in the institute's headquarters in the **Asilo de Beneficencia building,** once a hospital for the poor. ⊠ *Calle Beneficencia at Calle del Morro,* ☎ *787/724–0700.* 🎫 *$1.* ☉ *Tues.–Sat. 10–4.*

👋 ⓫ **Museo del Niño.** This three-floor, hands-on "museum" is pure fun for kids. There are games to play, clothes for dress-up, a mock plaza with market, even a barber shop where children can play (no real scissors here). One of the newer exhibits is an immense food-groups pyramid, where children can climb to place magnets representing different foods. Older children will appreciate the top-floor garden where bugs and plants are on display, and the little ones can pretend to go shopping or to work at a construction site. For infants, there's a playground. Note that the museum's ticket window closes an hour before the close of the museum. ⊠ *150 Calle Cristo,* ☎ *787/722–3791.* 🎫 *$2.50.* ☉ *Tues.–Thurs. 9–3:30, Fri. 9–5, weekends 12:30–5.*

⓯ **Museo de Nuestra Raíz Africana.** The Institute of Puerto Rican Culture created this Museum of Our African Roots to help Puerto Ricans understand African influences in island culture. On display over two floors are African musical instruments, documents relating to the slave trade, and a list of African words that have made it into popular Puerto Rican culture *(mofongo, calalu).* The building stands next to the ☞ **Museo Pablo Casals.** ✉ *Calle San Sebastián, Plaza de San José,* ☎ *787/ 724–0700, ext. 4239.* 🎫 *Free.* ☉ *Tues.–Sat. 9:30–5, Sun. 11–5.*

⑭ Museo Pablo Casals. The small, two-story Pablo Casals Museum contains memorabilia of the famed cellist, who made his home in Puerto Rico from 1956 until his death in 1973. Manuscripts, photographs, and his favorite cellos are on display, in addition to recordings and videotapes (shown on request) of Casals Festival concerts, which he instituted in 1957. The festival is held annually in June. ✉ *101 Calle San Sebastián, Plaza de San José,* ☎ *787/723–9185.* 🎫 *$1.* ☉ *Tues.–Sat. 9:30–5:30.*

⑤ Parque de las Palomas. Never have pigeons had it so good. The small, shaded park bordering Capilla del Cristo features a large stone city wall with pigeonholes cut into it. Hundreds of pigeons roost here, and the park is full of cooing local children chasing the well-fed birds. There's a small kiosk where you can buy refreshments and bags of seed to feed the *palomas.* Stop to enjoy the wide views over the bay. ✉ *Calle Cristo.*

㉕ Paseo de la Princesa. This street down at the port is spruced up with flowers, trees, benches, street lamps, and a striking fountain depicting the various ethnic groups of Puerto Rico. Take a seat and watch the boats zip across the water. At the west end of the paseo, beyond the fountain, is the beginning of a shoreline path that hugs the Old City's walls and leads to the city gate at Calle San Juan.

❶ Plaza de Armas. This is the original main square of Old San Juan, once used as military drilling grounds. The plaza, bordered by Calles San Francisco, Rafael Codero, San José, and Cruz, has a lovely fountain with 19th-century statues representing the four seasons, as well as a bandstand and a small outdoor café. This is a central meeting place in Old San Juan, and you're likely to encounter everything from local bands to artists sketching caricatures to street preachers imploring the wicked to repent.

NEED A BREAK?   Stop in at the open-air **Café 4 Estaciones,** on the Plaza de Armas in Old San Juan. Tables and chairs sit under a canvas canopy, and the café is surrounded by potted plants, a perfect spot to put down your shopping bags and rest your tired feet. Grab a *café con leche* (coffee with hot milk), an espresso, or cold drink, and watch the children chase the pigeons.

㉓ Plaza de Colón. A statue of Christopher Columbus stands atop a high pedestal in this bustling square. Originally called St. James Square, it was renamed in honor of Columbus on the 400th anniversary of his arrival in Puerto Rico. Bronze plaques on the base of the statue relate various episodes in the life of the great explorer. On the north side of the plaza is a terminal for buses to and from San Juan. ✉ *On pedestrian mall of Calle Fortaleza.*

⑫ Plazuela de la Rogativa. According to legend, the British, while laying siege to the city in 1797, mistook the flaming torches of a rogativa for Spanish reinforcements, and beat a hasty retreat. In this little plaza, statues of a bishop and three women commemorate the legend. The monument was created in 1971 by the artist Lindsay Daen to mark the Old City's 450th anniversary. ✉ *Caleta de las Monjas.*

㉒ San Cristóbal. This stone fortress, built between 1634 and 1785, guarded the city from land attacks. Even larger in structure (but not in area covered) than El Morro, San Cristóbal was known in the 17th and 18th centuries as the Gibraltar of the West Indies. Five free-standing structures are connected by a labyrinth of tunnels, and restored units include an 18th-century barracks. You're free to explore the gun turrets, officers' quarters, and passageways. Along with El Morro, Old San Juan's other major fortification, San Cristóbal is a national historic site administered by the U.S. Park Service. Guides conduct tours in Spanish and English. ⊠ *Calle Norzagaray,* ☎ *787/729–6960.* ▣ *$2.* ⊙ *Daily 9–5.* ⊛

㉔ **Teatro Tapia.** This municipal theater was named after the Puerto Rican playwright Alejandro Tapia y Rivera. Built in 1832 and remodeled in 1949 and again in 1987, it showcases ballets, plays, and operettas. Stop by the box office to find out what's showing. ⊠ *Calle Fortaleza at Plaza de Colón,* ☎ *787/722–0407.*

Greater San Juan

Modern San Juan is a study in congested highways and cement-block housing complexes, mingled with the ritzy resorts of the Condado and Isla Verde shoreline. Sightseeing in the modern city requires more effort than it does in Old San Juan—the sights are scattered in the suburbs, accessible by taxi, bus, or a rental car, but not by foot. Avenida Muñoz Rivera, Avenida Ponce de León, and Avenida Fernández Juncos are the main thoroughfares that cross Puerta de Tierra, just east of Old San Juan, to the business and tourist districts of Condado and Isla Verde. Dos Hermanos Bridge connects Puerta de Tierra with Condado's Avenida Ashford and Route 37 (Avenida Isla Verde), which goes through Ocean Park and on to Isla Verde. The G. Esteves and San Antonio bridges also connect Puerta de Tierra to "new" San Juan. Isla Grande Airport, from which you can take short hops to Culebra, Vieques, and other islands, is on the bay side of the bridges. Due south of the Condado Lagoon is Miramar, a residential area with fashionable turn-of-the-20th-century homes and a few hotels and restaurants. East of Miramar and south of Ocean Park is Santurce, another business and residential area characterized by high-rise office and apartment complexes. South of that is the Golden Mile—Hato Rey, the city's financial and banking hub. Isla Verde, with its glittering beachfront hotels, casinos, discos, and public beach, is to the east, near the airport.

Numbers in the text correspond to numbers in the margin and on the Greater San Juan map.

A Good Tour

Heading east from Old San Juan on Avenida Ponce de León brings you to **El Capitolio** ㉖, Puerto Rico's magnificent capitol building of white marble with Corinthian columns. Look for a display of Puerto Rico's constitution. At the east end of Puerta de Tierra is the Caribe Hilton hotel, where you'll find the small bastion **Fuerte San Gerónimo** ㉗, which once guarded an entrance to San Juan Bay. Avenida Baldorioty de Castro (Rte. 26) leads into Miramar, then Santurce, where the Route 37 exit (Avenida José de Diego) brings you to the **Museo de Arte de Puerto Rico** ㉘, a former hospital that has been transformed into the most ambitious art museum on the island. Farther south on de Diego at Avenida Ponce de León is the **Centro de Bellas Artes Luis A. Ferré** ㉙; the modern performing-arts center, big and boxy and white, is the largest of its kind in the Caribbean—stop by the ticket office for a list of current shows. Just minutes from the arts center, west on Avenida Fernández Juncos, then left on Calle Sagrado Corazón, is the Universidad del Sagrado Corazón (Sacred Heart University) and its **Museo de Arte Contemporáneo de Puerto Rico** ㉚. One of the finest collections of contemporary Puerto Rican art on the island, the museum showcases paintings, sculpture, photography, and "new media" art. From the university, it's a straight ride south on Avenida Ponce de León (Rte. 25) to the suburb of Río Piedras, where you'll find the **Universidad de Puerto Rico** and its **Museo de Historia, Antropología y Arte** ㉛. Less than a mile to the west, at the junction of Routes 1 and 847, is the university's **Jardín Botánico** ㉜, a 75-acre garden with foot trails and more than 30,000 plants, many of them labeled. If you're looking for a place to jog or play tennis, visit the **Parque Central Municipo de San Juan** ㉝ in Miramar, at the Calle Cerra exit off Avenida John F. Kennedy (Rte. 2), northwest of the university. With several miles of trails and inexpensive courts, as well as a refreshments shop, it's a good place to work off some of San Juan's wonderful, rich desserts.

TIMING

Depending on what mode of transportation you choose, you can see these sights in a day, two if you linger. Buses are the least expensive way to travel, but the most inconvenient and time-consuming. Taxis are more convenient and you won't get lost—consider hiring a taxi by the hour and covering your selected sights in a couple of hours. Taxis charge $30 per hour for city tours, but the rate can be negotiable for long stretches of time. If you choose to rent a car, get a good map, available at most rental agencies for free, or at bookstores. San Juan's roads are well marked, but one-way streets pop up out of nowhere and traffic jams at rush hour are frequent.

Sights to See

㉖ **El Capitolio.** In Puerta de Tierra, Puerto Rico's capitol is a white marble building that dates from the 1920s. The grand rotunda, with mosaics and friezes, was completed in the late 1990s. The seat of the island's bicameral legislature, the capitol contains Puerto Rico's constitution and is flanked by the modern buildings of the Senate and the House of Representatives. There are spectacular views from the observation plaza on the sea side of the capitol. Pick up a booklet about the building from the House Secretariat on the second floor. Guided tours are by appointment only. You can also watch the legislature in action—note that the action is in Spanish—on select session days, most often Monday and Tuesday. ⊠ *Av. Ponce de León, Puerta de Tierra,* ☎ 787/724–8979. ☎ *Free.* ☉ *Daily 8:30–5.*

㉙ **Centro de Bellas Artes Luis A. Ferré.** This completely modern facility, the largest of its kind in the Caribbean, has a full schedule of concerts, plays, and operas, including performances by many internationally acclaimed artists (☞ Nightlife and the Arts *below*). ⊠ *Corner of Av. José De Diego and Av. Ponce de León, Box 41287, Minillas Station, Santurce 00940,* ☎ 787/725–7334.

㉗ **Fuerte San Gerónimo.** At the eastern tip of Puerta de Tierra, behind the splashy Caribe Hilton, this tiny fort is perched over the Atlantic like an afterthought. Added to San Juan's fortifications in the late 18th century, the structure barely survived the British attack of 1797. Restored in 1983 by the Institute of Puerto Rican Culture, it's now leased by the Caribe Hilton for private functions. The buildings are empty and the structure itself is the attraction, but it's free and open to the public (accessed from the Caribe Hilton entrance). ⊠ *Calle Rosales, Puerta de Tierra,* ☎ 787/724–5477.

★ ㉚ **Museo de Arte Contemporáneo de Puerto Rico.** Santurce, the area that lies between Miramar on the west and the Laguna San José on the east, is a busy mixture of shops, markets, and offices. The Universidad del Sagrado Corazón (Sacred Heart University) is the home of the Museum

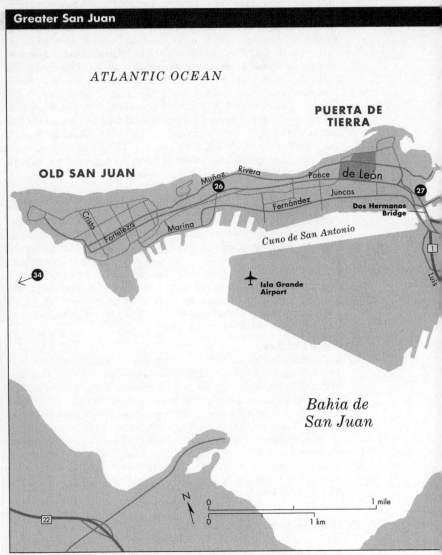

ATLANTIC OCEAN

PUERTA DE TIERRA

OLD SAN JUAN

Muñoz   Rivera   Ponce   de León
26
Fernández   Juncos
27
Crista
Forteleza
Marina
Cuno de San Antonio
Dos Hermanos Bridge
1
Luis
34
Isla Grande Airport

Bahia de San Juan

N

22

| 0 | | 1 mile |
| 0 | | 1 km |

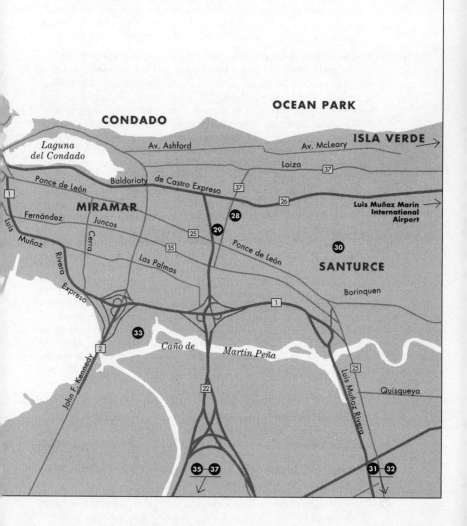

OCEAN PARK

CONDADO

ISLA VERDE

Laguna del Condado

Av. Ashford

Av. McLeary

Loiza

37

Ponce de León

Baldorioty de Castro Expreso

37

1

26

Luis Muñoz Marín International Airport

MIRAMAR

Fernández

Juncos

28

Luis Muñoz

Cerra

25

29

30

Rivera Expreso

35

Las Palmas

Ponce de León

SANTURCE

Borinquen

1

33

2

Caño de Martin Peña

John F. Kennedy

25

Quisqueya

22

Luis Muñoz Rivera

35 37

31 32

of Contemporary Puerto Rican Art, an exceptional opportunity to see a wide range of painting, sculpture, photography, and new media art produced by established and up-and-coming Puerto Rican artists, including Francisco Rodón, Rafael Ferrer, and Pablo Rubio. Exhibits, in several rooms on the large second floor of the university's Barat Building, change once or twice per year. ⊠ *Calle Sagrado Corazón, Barat Bldg., Santurce,* ☎ 787/268–0049. ☞ *Free.* ⊙ *Mon.–Sat. 9–5.* ⊛

★ ㉘ **Museo de Arte de Puerto Rico.** After four years and $55.2 million of construction, this ambitious 130,000-square-ft art museum opened its doors in summer 2000. The west wing is the former San Juan Municipal Hospital, a 1920s neoclassical building that, following top-to-bottom renovation, now houses the museum's permanent collection of Puerto Rican art dating from the 17th century to the present. The newly constructed east wing is dominated by a five-story-tall stained glass window, the work of local artist Eric Tabales, that towers over the museum's Grand Hall and faces a 5-acre garden. In the east wing there are galleries for traveling exhibits, an interactive Family Gallery, and a 400-seat theater that's worth seeing for the stage's remarkable lace curtain alone. The garden has a sculpture trail, a pond, and a variety of native flora. Overall the museum gives Puerto Rican art a showplace unlike anything the island has seen before. Although there are bound to be kinks to work out in its first few years of existence, the Museo de Arte de Puerto Rico is a must-see if you plan to spend time in San Juan. ⊠ *300 Av. José De Diego, Santurce,* ☎ 787/977–6277. ☞ *$5.* ⊙ *Tues., Thurs.–Sun. 10–5, Wed. 10–8.*

㉝ **Parque Central Municipo de San Juan.** Southeast of Miramar, Avenida Muñoz Rivera skirts along the northern side of the mangrove-bordered San Juan Central Municipal Park, dry and dusty but a convenient place for jogging, biking, and tennis. The park was built for the 1979 Pan-American Games. Inside you'll find a sports shop and a cafeteria. ⊠ *Calle Cerra (exit on Rte. 2), Santurce,* ☎ 787/722–1646. ☞ *75¢ per vehicle.* ⊙ *Mon. 2–10, Tues.–Thurs. 6:30 AM–10 PM, Fri. 6:30 AM–9 PM, weekends 6:30 AM–6 PM.*

Universidad de Puerto Rico. Río Piedras, a southern suburb, is home to the University of Puerto Rico, between Avenida Ponce de León and Avenida Barbosa. The campus is one of the two performance venues for the Puerto Rico Symphony Orchestra. (The other is the ☞ **Centro de Bellas Artes Luis A. Ferré** in Santurce.) Theatrical productions and other concerts are also scheduled here.

㉛ The University of Puerto Rico's **Museo de Historia, Antropología y Arte** (Museum of History, Anthropology, and Art) has archaeological and historical exhibits that deal with the Native American influence on the island and the Caribbean, the colonial era, and the history of slavery. Art displays are occasionally mounted; the museum's prize exhibit is the painting *El Velorio* (The Wake), by the 19th-century artist Francisco Oller. ⊠ *Next to main university entrance on Av. Ponce de León, Río Piedras,* ☎ 787/764–0000, ext. 2452. ☞ *Free.* ⊙ *Mon.–Wed. and Fri. 9–4:30, Thurs. 9–9, weekends 9–3.*

㉜ The university's main attraction is the **Jardín Botánico** (Botanical Garden), a lush 75-acre forest of more than 200 species of tropical and subtropical vegetation. Gravel footpaths lead to a graceful lotus lagoon, a bamboo promenade, an orchid garden with some 30,000 plants, and a palm garden. Signs are in Spanish and English. Trail maps are available at the entrance gate, and groups of 10 or more can arrange guided tours ($25). ⊠ *Intersection of Rtes. 1 and 847 at entrance to Barrio Venezuela, Río Piedras,* ☎ 787/767–1710. ☞ *Free.* ⊙ *Daily 9–4:30.*

Western San Juan Environs

The metro suburbs of Cataño, Bayamón, and Guaynabo, west and south of San Juan, are separate municipalities but in many ways are indistinguishable from the city itself. Cataño, bordered by San Juan Bay in the north, is an industrial suburb, most noted these days for its massive Bacardi Rum plant. Bayamón, 15–30 minutes from central San Juan depending on traffic, has an attractive central park bordered by historic buildings. Guaynabo is a mix of residential and industrial areas, and is worth visiting for its historical importance—Juan Ponce de León established the island's first settlement here, and you can visit the ruins of the original fortification.

A Good Tour

Make your way to Old San Juan and Pier 2 at the south end of the old city for the ferry to Cataño. Once on the Cataño side of San Juan Bay, take a quick taxi or bus ride to the **Bacardi Rum plant** ㉞. The plant tour will lead you through the process of distilling the spirits, and its small museum displays the history of the Bacardi family.

To reach the 42-acre **Parque de las Ciencias Luis A. Ferré** ㉟ (Luis A. Ferré Science Park), take Route 22 (Expreso de Diego) south from San Juan's Avenida Ponce de León to Bayamón and go south on Route 167. A great stop for children, the science park features a planetarium and a science and physics museum examining the wonders of space. Also in Bayamón, the city's central park on Calle Santiago Veve features several historic buildings and a church, as well as, in the old city hall, the **Museo de Arte y Historia de Francisco Oller** ㊱ (Francisco Oller Art and History Museum), dedicated to the life and work of the famous Puerto Rican artist. From the Science Park, head south again on Route 167, then left, or east, on Route 2 into Guaynabo. You'll come to the **Caparra Ruins** ㊲, the site of one of San Juan's first settlements, with its small **Museo de la Conquista y Colonización de Puerto Rico** (Museum of the Conquest and Colonization of Puerto Rico).

TIMING

Cantaño's Bacardi Rum plant is best seen by taking the ferry from Pier 2 in Old San Juan across San Juan Bay to the city. The ferry is a mere 50¢ each way, and runs every 30 minutes from 6 AM until 10 PM. Plan half a day for traveling and the plant tour, especially if you sample the product. Once on the Cataño side, look for buses or taxis for the five-minute ride to the plant. You'll need a rental car or taxi to see sights in Bayamón and Guaynabo, about 30 minutes from central San Juan.

Sights to See

㉞ **Bacardi Rum plant.** The fist Bacardi rum distillery was built in 1862 in Cuba by the Bacardi family. The original plant was confiscated by the Castro regime in 1960 and the Bacardi family was exiled, but over the years the rum brand has continued to grow, with distilleries in Spain, Mexico, Panama, and Brazil. The Puerto Rico plant was built in the 1950s and is one of the largest in the world, with the capacity to produce 100,000 gallons of spirits a day and 221 million cases each year. You can take a 45-minute tour of the bottling plant, museum (called the Cathedral of Rum), and distillery, and there is a gift shop. (Yes, you'll be offered a sample.) ⊠ *Bay View Industrial Park, Rte. 888, Km 2.6, Cataño,* ☎ *787/788–1500 or 787/788–8400.* ⊡ *Free.* ☉ *Tours every 30 mins Mon.–Sat. 9–10:30 and noon–4.*

㊲ **Caparra Ruins.** In 1508 Ponce de León established the island's first settlement here. The ruins—a few crumbling walls—are what remains of an ancient fort, and the small **Museo de la Conquista y Colonización** de Puerto Rico (Museum of the Conquest and Colonization of Puerto Rico) contains historical documents, exhibits, and excavated artifacts. (You can see the museum's contents in less time than it takes to say the name.) Both the ruins and the museum are maintained by the Puerto Rican government's museums and parks division. ⊠ *Rte. 2, Km 6.6, Guaynabo,* ☎ *787/781–4795.* ☎ *Free.* ☉ *Tues.–Sat. 8:30–4:30.*

㊱ **Museo de Arte y Historia de Francisco Oller.** In Bayamón's central park you'll find the 18th-century Catholic church of Santa Cruz and the neo-classical former city hall, which now houses the Francisco Oller Art and History Museum. Oller (1833–1917) was one of the most accomplished artists of his time, and in Puerto Rico is best known for his painting *El Velorio* (*The Wake,* on display at the Museo de Historia, Antropolgía y Arte at the University of Puerto Rico), which depicts the futility of a wake for a peasant child. ⊠ *Calle Santiago Veve, Bayamón,* ☎ *787/787–8620.* ☎ *Free.* ☉ *Tues.–Sat. 9–4.*

㊳ ㉟ **Parque de las Ciencias Luis A. Ferré.** The 42-acre Luis A. Ferré Science Park contains a collection of intriguing activities and displays such as the **Transportation Museum,** featuring antique cars and the oldest bicycle on the island; the **Rocket Plaza,** where children can experience a flight simulator; and the **planetarium,** where the solar system is projected on the hemispheric ceiling. On site as well are a small zoo and a natural science exhibit. The park is popular with Puerto Rican schoolchildren, and, although it's a bit of a drive from central San Juan, it's a good activity for the family. ⊠ *Rte. 167, Bayamón,* ☎ *787/740–6878.* ☎ *$5.* ☉ *Wed.–Fri. 9–4, weekends and holidays 10–6.*

DINING

By John Marino San Juan has the variety of dining options that you would expect from a cosmopolitan city—there are restaurants featuring cuisines from around the world and representing all levels of both sophistication and price. Wherever you go, it's *always* good to make reservations in the busy season, mid-November–April, in restaurants where they are accepted.

Old San Juan

Asian

$$–$$$ ✕ **Royal Thai Restaurant.** This long, narrow restaurant, decorated with mirrors and murals of aquarium scenes, sits on Old San Juan's restaurant row. In most dishes on the menu the fire has been turned down to suit the local palate, but if you're a fan of spicy Thai cuisine you can ask to have it turned back up. The coconut shrimp and the *kari gang ped* chicken, served in a pungent curry sauce, are two specialties, and the *tom kha gai,* a coconut herb soup with sliced chicken breast, chili, and *galangar,* is excellent. The service is superb. ⊠ *415 Recinto Sur,* ☎ *787/725–8401. AE, D, MC, V.*

$$–$$$ ✕ **Yukiyú.** The only Japanese restaurant in Old San Juan manages to maintain high standards despite the lack of competition. If you're craving sushi, you should make a beeline for this establishment; if you prefer your meals cooked, you'll also find satisfaction in the selection of beef, chicken, and seafood dishes, all prepared under the watchful eye of chef Igarashi. There's a bit of a Zenlike austerity to the surroundings, but service is friendly, and overall the ambience is relaxed and unpretentious. ⊠ *311 Recinto Sur,* ☎ *787/721–0653. AE, D, MC, V.*

Cafés

$–$$ ✕ **Café Berlin.** This casual café, bakery, and delicatessen overlooks the Plaza Colón. Tasty vegetarian fare prevails—try one of the creative salads—but a wide assortment of nonvegetarian dishes is also available.

The café's pastries, desserts, fresh juices, and Puerto Rican coffees are the perfect treats after a day of touring Old San Juan. ✉ *407 Calle San Francisco,* ☎ *787/722–5205. AE, MC, V.*

$ ✕ **La Bombonera.** This landmark restaurant with an ornate facade was established in 1903 and is known for its strong Puerto Rican coffee and excellent pastries. It's open every day from 7:30 AM until early evening, and full breakfasts are served until 11. It's a favorite Sunday-morning gathering place. The grumpy uniformed waiters give the appearance of having worked here since day one. ✉ *259 Calle San Francisco,* ☎ *787/722–0658. AE, MC, V.*

★ $ ✕ **Cafeteria Mallorca.** This small neighborhood cafeteria features an attentive staff in crisp green uniforms and caps. The specialty here is in its name—the *mallorca,* a sweet pastry that's buttered and grilled, then sprinkled with powdered sugar. Try the breakfast mallorca, with ham and cheese, washed down with one of the city's best cups of café con leche. ✉ *300 Calle San Francisco,* ☎ *787/724–4607. MC, V. Closed Sun.*

Contemporary

$$$ ✕ **La Ostra Cosa.** The menu here ranges from oysters to burgers, but the large, succulent prawns, grilled and served with garlic butter, are the specialty—they take a bit of work to eat, but they're well worth the effort. The restaurant is housed in the rear of a mini-mall in a historic building, and it spills out onto a back courtyard. With the bougainvillea and moonlight, it's one of the prettiest spots to dine outside in the Old City. The owner, Alberto Nazario, brother of pop star Ednita Nazario, is a gregarious host who truly enjoys seeing his guests satisfied. ✉ *154 Calle Cristo,* ☎ *787/722–2672. AE, MC, V.*

$$–$$$ ✕ **Amadeus.** A trendy, fashionable crowd enjoys the nouvelle Caribbean menu here. The front dining room is attractive—whitewashed walls, dark wood, white tablecloths, ceiling fan—but you'll do even better if you go through the outside passage to the romantic back dining room with printed tablecloths, candles, and exposed brick. The roster of appetizers includes buffalo wings and plantain mousse with shrimp. Escargots, cheese ravioli with a goat cheese–and–walnut sauce, and Cajun-grilled mahimahi are a few of the delectable entrées. ✉ *106 Calle San Sebastián,* ☎ *787/722–8635. AE, MC, V. No lunch Mon.*

★ $$–$$$ ✕ **Carli Café Concierto.** One of a set of new, hip joints in the Old City, this intimate bistro, with rust-hue walls and black-marble tables, sits under the Banco Popular building, which dominates the Old San Juan skyline. You can dine—indoors or on the streetside patio—on international savories such as juicy seared loin of lamb or a light spinach and ricotta ravioli in pesto sauce. The genial owner and host, Carli Muñoz, is a pianist (he's toured with the Beach Boys—note the gold album on the wall) who plays his Steinway grand most evenings. Visiting singers and musicians often join in the fun. ✉ *Plazoleta Rafael Carrión, Calle Recinto Sur (corner of Calle San Justo),* ☎ *787/725–4927. AE, MC, V.*

Continental

$$$–$$$$ ✕ **Chef Marisoll.** Set on two sides of a Venetianesque courtyard surrounded by ornate balconies (you can dine inside or out), this restaurant with dark-wood decor and high ceilings serves gourmet international cuisine. You might start with a duck Caesar salad or a cream of exotic mushroom soup, followed by beef tenderloin or salmon fillet. For dessert, try chef Marisoll's specialty: crème caramel. ✉ *202 Calle Cristo,* ☎ *787/725–7454. AE, MC, V. Closed Mon. No lunch Sun.*

Old San Juan Dining & Lodging

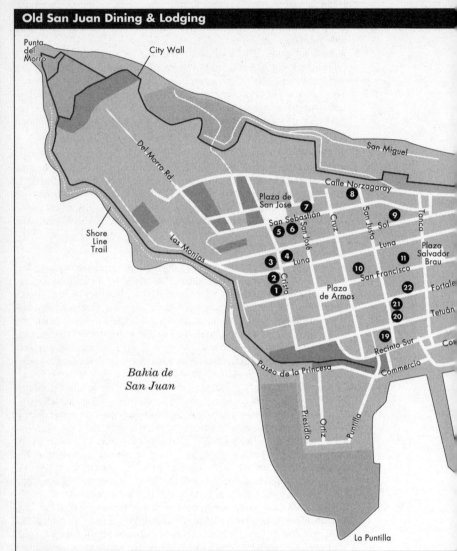

Punta del Morro

City Wall

Del Morro Rd.

San Miguel

Shore Line Trail

Calle Norzagaray

Las Monjas

Plaza de San Jose

San Sebastián

San Justo

Cruz

Sol

Tanca

Luna

Plaza Salvador Brau

San José

Luna

San Francisco

Fortale

Crista

Plaza de Armas

Tetuán

Recinto Sur

Bahia de San Juan

Paseo de la Princesa

Commercio

Co

Presidio

Ortiz

Puntilla

La Puntilla

Dining

Amadeus **6**
La Bella Piazza **12**
The Blue **7**
La Bombonera **10**
Café Berlin **13**
Cafeteria Mallorca **11**
Carli Café
Concierto **19**
La Chaumiêre **15**
Chef Marisol **1**
La Fonda del Jibarito . . . **9**

La Mallorquina **20**
La Ostra Cosa **2**
The Parrot Club **14**
El Patio de Sam **5**
Il Perugino **4**
El Picoteo **3**
Restaurant Galería **21**
Royal Thai
Restaurant **16**
Yukiyú **17**

Lodging

El Convento Hotel **3**
Gallery Inn **8**
Hotel Milano **22**
Wyndham Old
San Juan
Hotel & Casino **18**

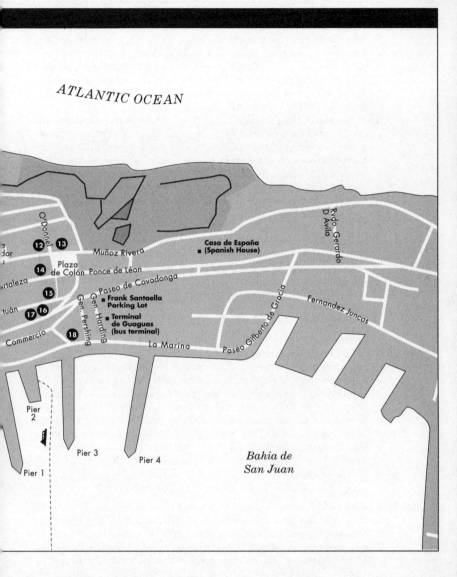

ATLANTIC OCEAN

O'Donnel

12 13

Muñoz Rivera

Casa de España
■ (Spanish House)

Rvdo. Gerardo
D'Avila

Plaza
14   de Colón   Ponce de Léon

rtaleza

15

Paseo de Covadonga

tuán   ■ Frank Santaella
17 16   Parking Lot

■ Terminal
de Guaguas
(bus terminal)

Fernandez Juncos

Commercio   18

La Marina

Paseo Gilberto de Gracia

Pier
2

Pier 3

Pier 4

Bahia de
San Juan

Pier 1

Eclectic

$$–$$$ ✕ **Restaurant Galería.** This stylish, airy restaurant, with marble floors, white walls, and dark-wood accents, is lit by a central atrium. Chef Jesus prepares Italian and other Continental cuisines, including fresh pastas (try the signature pasta *galería*, with alfredo sauce and calamari), risottos, and seafood dishes. Finish with a delicious local dessert such as flan, *arroz con dulce* (rice pudding), or a fruit tart. ✉ *205 Calle San Justo,* ☎ *787/725–0478. AE, MC, V. Closed Mon.*

$$$ ✕ **The Blue.** Classic jazz flows through this attractive place, and artwork on the walls features some of jazz's great figures. The pleasant atmosphere, well-stocked bar, and delicious food will reward you amply for hanging around. A changing menu commonly features such appetizers as escargots burgundy and mussels in white wine with chorizo and cilantro. Entrées include filet mignon in a green peppercorn sauce and individual paellas with red snapper and lobster tail. ✉ *9 Plaza de Mercado,* ☎ *787/723–9962. AE, MC, V. Closed Sun., Mon.*

$–$$ ✕ **El Patio de Sam.** A warm dark-wood and faux-brick interior and a wide selection of beers make Sam's a popular late-night spot. The menu is mostly steaks and seafood, with a few native dishes mixed in. Try the Samuel's Special pizza—mozzarella, tomato sauce, beef, pepperoni, and black olives (it feeds two or three). The flan melts in your mouth. There's live entertainment (usually a guitarist singing old Spanish standards) every evening but Sunday. ✉ *102 Calle San Sebastián,* ☎ *787/723–1149. AE, D, DC, MC, V.*

French

$$$–$$$$ ✕ **La Chaumière.** Reminiscent of a provincial French inn, this intimate two-story restaurant with black-and-white tile floors, heavy wood ceiling beams, and floral curtains serves some of the best French food to be found on the island. The menu features such classic dishes as onion soup, oysters Rockefeller, rack of lamb, scallops Provençale, and poached salmon in vermouth, in addition to daily specials. La Chaumière is located behind the Teatro Tapia and has been under the same management since 1969. All that experience makes the service quite smooth. ✉ *367 Calle Tetuan,* ☎ *787/722–3330. AE, DC, MC, V. Closed Sun. No lunch.*

Italian

$$$–$$$$ ✕ **La Bella Piazza.** This friendly restaurant is a slice of Italy in the middle of Old San Juan. The narrow, beautifully restored dining room has Roman columns, gold-leaf flourishes, and arched doorways leading to an interior terrace, all of which contribute to the Old World atmosphere. The highlight among the appetizers is the outstanding *calamari in padella,* lightly breaded squid sautéed in olive oil, parsley, and garlic. Fresh pastas include *fusilli amatriciana,* with a crushed bacon, tomato, and red-pepper sauce, and *linguine al profumo,* with mixed seafood in either a red- or white-wine sauce. Couples often share an appetizer and a pasta before moving on to main courses such as *saltinbocca alla romana* (veal and prosciutto in a sage, white-wine, and butter sauce) and *medaglioni al Chianti* (beef medallions in a spicy Chianti sauce). ✉ *355 Calle San Francisco,* ☎ *787/728–8203. AE, MC, V.*

★ **$$$–$$$$** ✕ **Il Perugino.** A small, intimate eatery set in a 200-year-old building, Il Perugino is among the finest Italian restaurants in all of the Caribbean. Classic carpaccios, homemade pastas (try the black fettuccine with crayfish and baby eels), hearty main courses (such as rack of lamb in a red-wine sauce with aromatic herbs), and exquisite desserts (particularly the tiramisu) all combine to make this a must for serious gourmets. The extensive wine cellar, housed in the former cistern, is sure to contain the perfect complement to your meal. ✉ *105 Calle Cristo,* ☎ *787/722–5481. MC, V.*

Latin

★ $$$ ✕ **The Parrot Club.** This spacious, colorful place serves up inventive Nuevo Latino cuisine, variations of Cuban and Puerto Rican classics, in a casual yet efficient manner. Enjoy the house speciality passion-fruit drink at the bar before moving to the adjacent dining room or back courtyard. Appetizers include mouthwatering crab cakes and tamarind-barbecued ribs, while main courses range from seared blackened tuna in a dark rum sauce to *churrasco* (barbecued steak) with tomato chimichurri. The Parrot Club's presence on the east end of Calle Fortaleza has prompted other restaurants to open around it, a testament to its well-deserved popularity. ✉ *363 Calle Fortaleza,* ☎ *787/725–7370. Reservations not accepted. AE, DC, MC, V.*

$$–$$$ ✕ **La Mallorquina.** The food here is good basic Puerto Rican and Spanish fare (such as asopao and paella), but it's the atmosphere that recommends the place. It's said to date from 1848, and is thus considered to be Puerto Rico's oldest restaurant. The decor consists of peach walls and whirring ceiling fans, and the staff is nattily attired and friendly. ✉ *207 Calle San Justo,* ☎ *787/722–3261. AE, MC, V. Closed Sun.*

★ $ ✕ **La Fonda del Jibarito.** This family-run restaurant, serving freshly prepared Puerto Rican specialties in a casual setting, has been a favorite with *sanjuaneros* for years. On the walls are fanciful depictions of Calle Sol (the street outside), and there is a back porch filled with plants and fresh fruit. The conch ceviche and chicken fricasse are two house specialties. ✉ *280 Calle Sol,* ☎ *787/725–8375. Reservations not accepted. No credit cards.*

Spanish

★ $$–$$$ ✕ **El Picoteo.** This chic tapas bar is one of the best spots in Old San Juan for a drink, but many patrons make a meal out of the appetizers that predominate on the menu, including delectable shrimp, roast pork, and brick-oven pizza. Entrées such as paella are also well worthwhile. There's a long, lively bar inside, and one dining area overlooks Hotel El Convento's courtyard, while the other has a view of the action on Calle Cristo. Even if you have dinner plans elsewhere, consider stopping here for a cocktail and appetizer or a nightcap. ✉ *El Convento Hotel, 100 Calle Cristo,* ☎ *787/723–9621. AE, D, DC, MC, V.*

Greater San Juan

Argentine

$$ ✕ **Che's.** Juicy *churrasco* (barbecued steak), lemon chicken, and grilled sweetbreads are specialties at this casual Argentine restaurant. The hamburgers are huge, and the french fries are fresh. The Chilean and Argentine wine list is also good. ✉ *35 Calle Caoba, Punta Las Marías,* ☎ *787/726–7202. AE, D, DC, MC, V.*

Asian

$$–$$$ ✕ **Great Taste Chinese Restaurant.** This is the favored restaurant of the local Chinese, and with good reason. A tasty dim sum menu is available daily from noon to 5 PM; everything else on the menu is served until 2 AM. It's located in a faded condominium, and canned disco music plays through cheap speakers. But the view over the Condado Lagoon is beautiful, and the Chinese food is New York City's Chinatown quality. ✉ *1018 Av. Ashford,* ☎ *787/721–8111. AE, D, DC, MC, V.*

Cafés

$–$$ ✕ **Kasalta Bakery, Inc.** Make your selection from rows of display cases full of tempting treats. Walk up to the counter and order from an assortment of sandwiches (try the Cubano), meltingly tender octopus salad, savory *caldo gallego* (a soup of fresh vegetables, sausage,

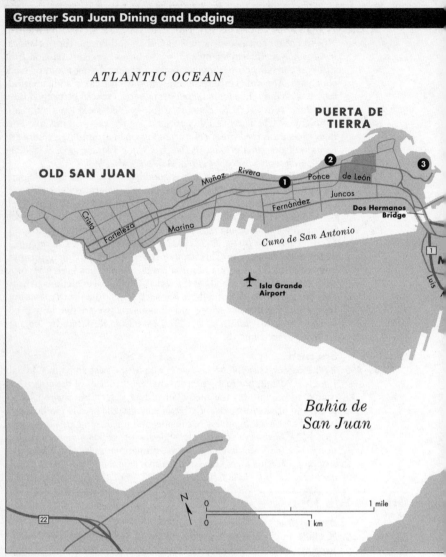

Lodging

El Canario by the Sea **10**	Excelsior **5**	San Juan Grand Beach Resort and Casino **35**
Caribe Hilton San Juan **3**	L'Habitation Beach Guest House **26**	
Colonial San Juan Beach Hotel **33**	Hostería del Mar . . . **27**	San Juan Marriott Resort and Stellaris Casino **16**
Condado Plaza Hotel and Casino **6**	Hotel La Playa **34**	
El Consulado **9**	Numero Uno **24**	Wyndham El San Juan Hotel and Casino . . . **32**
	Ritz-Carlton San Juan Hotel and Casino . . . **31**	

and potatoes), cold drinks, strong café con leche, and luscious pastries. ⊠ *1966 Calle McLeary, Ocean Park,* ☎ *787/727–7340. AE, MC, V.*

$ ✕ **La Patisserie.** This French café is a popular spot looking over a quiet stretch of the Condado strip. Everything here, from the pastries to the pastas, is delicious. For breakfast there are wonderful omelettes stuffed with fresh vegetables and imported cheeses. For lunch and dinner there are sandwiches—from pastrami to king crab, on croissants, baguettes, or other breads—and pasta and salads. Crepes and tarts are other specialities, and the pecan pie is the best in San Juan. ⊠ *1504 Av. Ashford, Condado,* ☎ *787/728–5508. AE, MC, V.*

Caribbean/Creole

★ $$$ ✕ **Ajili Mojili.** The traditional Puerto Rican food served here is prepared with a flourish and served in an attractive plantation-style setting. Sample the fried cheese and yautía dumplings with the house sauce, a tomato, herb, garlic, and shaved almond concoction. The *mofongo,* a mashed plantain casserole with seafood or meat, is wonderful, as are the plantain-crusted shrimp in a white-wine herb sauce. ⊠ *1052 Av. Ashford, Condado,* ☎ *787/725–9195. AE, DC, MC, V.*

$$–$$$ ✕ **Havana's Café.** This Cuban restaurant in the heart of Santurce, just off Avenida Ponce de León, has photos of Old Havana lining its walls, and it successfully retains the feeling of a 1950s café. Crowds pack in for lunch and dinner because the food here, down to the *moros y cristianos* (black beans and rice), is fresh and lovingly prepared. ⊠ *409 Calle Del Parque, Santurce,* ☎ *787/725–0888. No credit cards. Closed Mon.*

$–$$ ✕ **Casa Dante.** The self-proclaimed *casa del mofongo* is a good place to try this Puerto Rican specialty of plantains mashed with garlic and other ingredients. You can get mofongo filled with seafood, chicken, or beef in a red sauce, or as a side dish to a churrasco or sautéed red snapper. The bright dining room has tourist photos of Puerto Rico covering the walls and is a favorite of families. ⊠ *39 Calle Loíza, Punta Las Marias,* ☎ *787/726–7310. No credit cards. Closed Mon.*

Continental

$$$–$$$$ ✕ **Augusto's Cuisine.** Austrian-born chef Augusto Schreiner, a graduate of Salzburg Culinary School, regularly wins awards for his classic European cuisine. The menu changes seasonally; some of the dishes commonly found are veal carpaccio, steak au poivre, and seared tuna or shrimp in a mango curry. The bright dining room is decorated with floral prints and large bouquets. ⊠ *801 Av. Ponce de León, Hotel Excelsior,* ☎ *787/725–7700. AE, MC, V. Closed Sun., Mon.*

$$$ ✕ **Dumas Restaurant.** The back porch overlooks the Atlantic crashing against the rugged Puerta de Tierra coastline at this, one of the few oceanfront restaurants in San Juan. There's usually a fine breeze, and sunsets behind the Old City skyline are especially breathtaking. While the highlight at Dumas may be the view, the food is solid: seafood is a specialty, and the steaks and poultry are also rewarding. Some recommended dishes are clams casino, roast sirloin with mushroom sauce, and the seafood marinara. ⊠ *Av. Muñoz Rivera, Parada 7½,* ☎ *787/721–3550. AE, MC, V.*

$$$ ✕ **The Palm Restaurant.** The same great steak, seafood, and Italian dishes are found here as at the Palm's sister restaurant in New York. The caricatures of local and international celebrities that adorn the walls set the atmosphere. ⊠ *Wyndham El San Juan Hotel and Casino, Av. Isla Verde, Isla Verde,* ☎ *787/791–1000. AE, D, DC, MC, V. Closed Mon.*

Eclectic

$$$–$$$$ ✕ **Chayote.** Slightly off the beaten path, this chic eatery done in earth tones and decorated with contemporary Puerto Rican art is an "in" spot to eat. The chef blends haute international cuisine with tropical

panache. Starters include *sopa del día* (soup of the day) made with local produce, chayote stuffed with prosciutto, and corn tamales with shrimp in a coconut sauce. Half the menu's entrées are seafood dishes, including the excellent pan-seared tuna with Asian ginger sauce. The ginger flan and the almond floating island in rum custard sauce are musts for dessert. ☒ *Hotel Olimpo Court, 603 Av. Miramar, Miramar,* ☎ *787/722–9385. AE, MC, V. Closed Sun. No lunch Sat.*

$$$–$$$$ ✕ **Pikayo.** At the restaurant in the Museo de Arte de Puerto Rico, Chef Wilo Benet artfully fuses classic French, Caribbean creole, and California nouvelle cuisine with definite Puerto Rican flair. The beautifully presented dishes from the changing menu are a feast for the eye as well as the palate. Your meal might consist of tostones stuffed with oven-dried tomatoes, followed by mofongo topped with saffron shrimp, or a hearty land-crab stew. ☒ *Museo de Arte de Puerto Rico, 300 Av. de Diego, Santurce,* ☎ *787/721–6194. AE, MC, V.*

$$$–$$$$ ✕ **Zabor Creative Cuisine.** This inventive restaurant is housed in a restored turn-of-the-20th-century plantation set back off bustling Avenida Ashford. The pastoral front yard is enough to make you feel far from San Juan. Grazing—sharing appetizers with your dinner companions—is one of the main pastimes here, with popular choices including breaded calamari in a tomato-basil sauce, and lobster and apio pancakes in beurre blanc. Notable main courses include veal chops stuffed with provolone, pancetta, and herbs, served with a garlic-merlot sauce, and the catch of the day over yellow-raisin couscous in a mango-rosemary curry. ☒ *14 Calle Candida, Condado,* ☎ *787/725–9494. AE, D, DC, MC, V. No lunch.*

$$$ ✕ **Caribbean Grill Restaurant.** This restaurant in Isla Verde's Ritz-Carlton takes the elegance associated with the Ritz name and gives it a Caribbean twist. The menu emphasizes a variety of grilled seafood; there's a mix of Caribbean and North American fare. Overall, it has some of the most consistently first-rate cuisine in San Juan. ☒ *Ritz-Carlton Hotel,* ☎ *787/253–1700. AE, D, DC, MC, V.*

$$–$$$ ✕ **The Greenhouse.** This popular, casual restaurant in the heart of the Condado serves a steady flow of diners from 11:30 AM to 4:30 AM, and has been doing so for over 20 years now. The wide-ranging menu offers such standards as burgers, French onion soup, and grilled chicken sandwiches, but also has more ambitious choices, such as sophisticated omelets, lobster tail, and baked salmon. Everything is consistently well prepared and available at all hours of the day. The desserts are also a smash, from rich chocolate cake to light fruit sorbets. The late-night hours draw a lively crowd. ☒ *1200 Av. Ashford, Condado,* ☎ *787/725–4036. AE, D, MC, V.*

Italian

$$$ ✕ **Martino.** Located beneath a glass atrium on the top floor of the Black Diamond Hotel, Martino is a San Juan favorite for its classic northern Italian cuisine and its spectacular view of the Condado beach district. Start off with clams *posilolipo* or hot seafood antipasto, followed by osso buco *alla milanese* or one of the several fine pasta dishes, which are meals in themselves. Chef Martin Acosta's creations taste like they've come direct from the mother country to your table. ☒ *55 Av. Condado, Condado,* ☎ *787/722–5356. AE, DC, MC, V.*

Latin

$$–$$$ ✕ **Las Vistas Restaurant & Ocean Terrace.** You can choose from a wide-ranging menu while enjoying an ocean view at this 24-hour restaurant at the San Juan Marriott in the Condado. There are Mexican, seafood, Puerto Rican, Caribbean, and Argentinian specials on different nights of the week. The regular menu includes such appetizers as crab cakes and seafood *arepa* salad, and for an entrée try shrimp with garlic, pa-

paya, and cilantro. ⊠ *San Juan Marriott Resort and Stellaris Casino, 1309 Av. Ashford, Condado,* ☎ *787/722–7000. AE, MC, V.*

Middle Eastern

$$ ✕ **Jerusalem.** San Juan has a number of Middle Eastern restaurants; Jerusalem is one of the oldest and one of the best. Like many of its competitors, it's decorated in "Arabian tent" style, with hypnotic desert music piped in over the sound system. The ambience may feel a bit contrived, but the belly dancers are among the most sensual in town. The baba ghanouj makes a good starter, as does the tabbouleh. The grilled chicken kebabs are quite tasty, and specials include baked lamb. All entrées are served with Arabian rice, mixed with parsley and almonds, and a cucumber tomato salad. For dessert, the baklava is unrivaled. ⊠ *G-#1 Calle O'Neill,* ☎ *787/764–3265. AE, D, MC, V.*

$$ ✕ **Tierra Santa.** The small community of Middle Eastern immigrants in San Juan is not numerous enough to explain the local affection for that region's cuisine—or the popularity of belly dancing, which has become something of a craze. You can contemplate this mystery as you dine at Tierra Santa, one of several such restaurants found throughout the Hato Rey financial district. Everything is good here, from the classic hommus and falafel to the roasted halibut in almond, lime, and garlic and the lamb curry with oranges and onions. Dancers do their gyrations on Friday and Saturday nights. ⊠ *284 Av. Roosevelt, Hato Rey,* ☎ *787/754–6865. AE, MC, V.*

Seafood

$$–$$$ ✕ **Marisquería La Dorada.** This fine seafood establishment on Condado's restaurant row is surprisingly affordable. The grilled seafood platter is the specialty, but there are also excellent pastas and other fish dinners, including mahimahi in caper sauce and codfish in green sauce. Local cuisine, from seafood-stuffed mofongo to pork chops, is tasty. The friendly service creates an atmosphere where diners feel genuinely welcome. ⊠ *1105 Av. Magdalena, Condado,* ☎ *787/722–9583. AE, D, MC, V.*

$$ ✕ **Marisquería Atlántica.** At this combination restaurant–retail store, the seafood is fresh and reasonably priced. Stop in for a cool drink at the bar and a side dish of calamari, served lightly breaded and in a spicy sauce. Specialties include fresh Maine lobster, grilled red snapper in a garlic sauce, and paella loaded with scallops, clams, shrimp, squid, and fish. ⊠ *2475 Calle Loíza, Punta Las Marías,* ☎ *787/728–5444. AE, MC, V. Closed Sun.;* ⊠ *Calle Lugo Viñas at Punta de Tierra,* ☎ *787/ 722–0890. AE, MC, V. Closed Mon.*

Spanish

$$$$ ✕ **Compostela.** Contemporary Spanish food and a 10,000-bottle wine cellar are the draws here. The dining room is pleasant, with bright colors and many plants, and the kitchen is honored yearly in local competitions for specialties such as mushroom pâté, port *pastelillo* (wild mushroom turnover), grouper fillet with scallops in salsa verde, rack of lamb, duck with orange and ginger sauce, and paella. ⊠ *106 Av. Condado, Santurce,* ☎ *787/724–6088. AE, DC, MC, V. Closed Sun.*

★ **$$$–$$$$** ✕ **Ramiro's.** Step into a sea-green dining room, where you'll discover imaginative Castilian cuisine. Chef-owner Jesus Ramiro is known for his artistic presentation: flower-shape peppers filled with fish mousse, a mix of seafood caught under a vegetable net, roast duckling with sugarcane honey, and, if you can stand more, a kiwi dessert sculpted to resemble twin palms. ⊠ *1106 Av. Magdalena, Condado,* ☎ *787/721– 9049. AE, DC, MC, V. No lunch Sat.*

$$$ ✕ **La Casona.** San Juan's moneyed class comes here for power lunches and dinners, but it's also a nice spot for an intimate, romantic meal. The setting is a restored Spanish colonial residence, with elegantly appointed rooms and blooming gardens. The menu is based solidly in Spain, but has many creative flourishes—start with the duck pâté or smoked salmon and move on to the rack of lamb, which is first baked and then sautéed with brandy and fruit, or the duck breast in a raspberry sauce. ⊠ *609 San Jorge, Santurce,* ☎ *787/727–2717. AE, D, DC, MC, V. Closed Sun.*

$$$ ✕ **Urdin.** The owners, who include Julián Gil, a well-known Puerto Rican model and actor, describe the menu here as Spanish with a Caribbean touch. The soup and seafood appetizers are particularly good, and a highly recommended entrée is *chillo urdin de lujo,* red snapper sautéed with clams, mussels, and shrimp in a tomato, herb, and wine sauce. The name of the restaurant comes from the Basque word for blue, which is the dominant color in the dining room. ⊠ *1105 Av. Magdalena, Condado,* ☎ *787/724–0420. AE, MC, V.*

$$–$$$ ✕ **Miró Marisquería Catalana.** This small restaurant is nestled beside the lobby of Hotel El Portal and has large windows looking out on a bustling corner in the Condado. Like its namesake, painter Joan Miró, it draws its inspiration from the Catalan region of Spain, where the cuisine is heavy on seafood and hearty tapas. Prints by the artist hang on the walls, and the overall design, dominated by bright hues and brass, also shows Miró's influence. Start off with braised chorizo and peppers or steamed clams with garlic. Main courses include lamb chops and grilled tuna or codfish in a red-pepper and eggplant sauce. ⊠ *76 Av. Condado, Condado,* ☎ *787/721–9593. AE, MC, V.*

LODGING

In San Juan the hotels tend to be situated near beaches. Large hotels and resorts line the Condado and Isla Verde strands to create a sort of miniature Miami Beach, and it is here that most of the city's visitors end up. There are several outstanding smaller hotels interspersed among the resorts, and the neighborhood of Ocean Park, wedged between Isla Verde and Condado, has no high-rises at all. Here the norm is small and homey inns on a fine beach.

Other small inns and hotels are found in the near-the-beach suburbs of Miramar and Santurce, on the south sides of Condado and Ocean Park. These cater primarily to business travelers, but can be good bargains and are comfortable and clean in their own right.

Casinos are found in many of the major Condado and Isla Verde resorts. In Old San Juan, there are four hotels of note (reviewed below), only one of which has a casino. The island's small country inns, called *paradores,* are sponsored by the government and are great bargains (prices range from $60 to $125 for a double room), but are found *en la isla* (out on the island), not in San Juan.

Most hotels in Puerto Rico operate on the EP, although larger establishments often offer other meal plans or even all-inclusive packages.

When looking for small hotels in the San Juan area, try **Small Inns of Puerto Rico** (⊠ 954 Av. Ponce de León, Suite 702, San Juan 00907, ☎ 787/725–2901, FAX 787/725–2913). The organization, a branch of the Puerto Rico Hotel and Tourism Association, is a marketing arm for some 25 small hotels island-wide. Those they recommend in San Juan are clean, affordable, and among the best the city has to offer in that category. The organization occasionally offers package deals including casino coupons and LeLoLai tickets (☞ The Arts, *below*).

Staying in a self-catering apartment or condo has advantages over a resort hotel, especially for families—you cook when and what you want and enjoy a bit more autonomy than at a hotel. When booking, ask about maid service and other amenities on the property, such as swimming pools. Investigate rates at higher-end properties in San Juan's Isla Verde area through **Condo World** (✉ 4230 Orchard Lake Rd., Ste. 5, Orchard Lake, MI 48323, ☎ 800/521–2980, 𝐅𝐀𝐗 248/683–5076). **Puerto Rico Vacation Apartments** (✉ Marabella del Caribe Oeste S-5, Isla Verde, San Juan 00979, ☎ 787/727–1591 or 800/266–3639, 𝐅𝐀𝐗 787/268–3604) represents some 200 properties in the Condado and Isla Verde areas.

Old San Juan

★ $$$$ 🏨 **El Convento Hotel.** Once a Carmelite convent, this 350-year-old, caramel-color building is Old San Juan's premier example of Old World gentility enhanced by modern luxury. Much of its original architecture is intact, including a colonial interior courtyard. Rooms have a Spanish-deco look, with dark woods, wrought-iron lamps, ornate furniture, and unusual antique details; walls are ocean blue or mustard yellow. Complimentary evening wine and hors d'oeuvres are served before dinner, and the third-floor honor bar, just steps away from a terrace plunge pool, is open until 4 AM. Shaded by a giant nispero tree, the courtyard's Café de Nispero has a popular Sunday brunch. At night, locals and visitors crowd the second-floor terrace restaurant, El Picoteo, as much for the tapas as for the sangria. The street-side Café Bohemio is a great spot for lunch or a quick coffee. ✉ *100 Calle Cristo (Box 1048), 00902,* ☎ *787/723–9020 or 800/468–2779 (direct to hotel),* 𝐅𝐀𝐗 *787/721–2877. 54 rooms, 4 suites. 3 restaurants, 2 bars, air-conditioning, in-room safes, minibars, pool, exercise room, shops, library, meeting room, parking (fee). AE, D, DC, MC, V. CP.* 🍃

$$$$ 🏨 **Wyndham Old San Juan Hotel & Casino.** The gleaming, modern Wyndham has a triangular structure that subtly echoes the cruise ships docked nearby, yet also has classic neo–Spanish colonial lines. The lobby, adjacent to the casino, shines with multihue tiles and mahogany. Each standard room—decorated with honey-color rugs, floral prints, and light woods—has a two-line phone, cable TV, a coffeemaker, and a hair dryer. Spacious suites also have sitting rooms, extra TVs, and minibars. On the ninth floor you'll find a small patio swimming pool and whirlpool bath; the seventh-floor concierge level provides hassle-free check-ins, Continental breakfasts, and evening hors d'oeuvres. In the second-floor Dársena restaurant, spices from around the world are blended into Caribbean and Puerto Rican dishes. ✉ *100 Calle Brumbaugh, 00901,* ☎ *787/721–5100 or 800/996–3426,* 𝐅𝐀𝐗 *787/721–1111. 185 rooms, 55 suites. Restaurant, 2 bars, pool, hot tub, massage, exercise room, casino, concierge floor, business services, meeting rooms, parking (fee). AE, D, DC, MC, V. EP.* 🍃

★ $$–$$$$ 🏨 **Gallery Inn.** Owners Jan D'Esopo and Manuco Gandia transformed this rambling, classically Spanish house—one of the city's oldest residences—into an inn of "bohemian opulence," as some describe it. It's full of comforts and quirky details: winding, uneven stairs; balconies; a music room with a Steinway grand piano; and lots of public areas in which to curl up with a good book. The lush courtyard gardens, where Jan's pet macaws and cockatoos hang out, reach for the sunlight. Each room has a decor all its own as well as a phone and air-conditioning. Several have whirlpool baths, but not one room has a TV. From the rooftop deck there's a spectacular view of the El Morro and San Cristóbal forts and the Atlantic. Galería San Juan, a small gallery and studio on the first floor, displays various pieces by Jan D'Esopo,

Bruno Lucchesi, and others. There's no restaurant, but meals for groups can be prepared upon request. (They're served in the small dining room.) The inn has no sign in front, so tell your taxi driver it's on the corner of Calles Norzagaray and San Justo. ⊠ *204–206 Calle Norzagaray, 00901,* ☎ *787/722–1808,* ℻ *787/724–7360. 13 rooms, 10 suites. Dining room, piano. AE, DC, MC, V. CP.* ✑

$$ ⊞ **Hotel Milano.** This modest, clean, and affordable hotel has been a welcome addition to the Old San Juan lodging scene since opening in 1999. It's central to the Old City, just steps from its plazas, shops, and museums, and the rooftop restaurant, aptly called Panorama, provides expansive views of the city and pier area. The rooms, on four floors accessed by an elevator, are not spartan, but they're not laden with amenities either. All come with cable TV, phone, and private bath, while about half have small refrigerators. Some, such as number 410, are Lilliputian—but cheap. The decor is standard Caribbean florals, and more rooms have two double beds than kings or queens. Streetside rooms might be a bit noisy, but in Old San Juan noisy is a way of life—get a room at the back for less clamor. Continental breakfast is served at the rooftop grill. ⊠ *307 Calle Fortaleza, 00901,* ☎ *787/729–9050 or 877/729–9050,* ℻ *787/722–3379. 30 rooms. Restaurant, bar, air-conditioning, refrigerators (some). AE, MC, V. CP.* ✑

San Juan

$$$$ ⊞ **Caribe Hilton San Juan.** After being closed for eight months to undergo $50 million in renovations, the Caribe Hilton reopened in late 1999 with a new face. The rooms and halls are vibrant with new paint and furniture all around; the three-level pool has gentle cascades as well as an attached wading pool and (cold water) whirlpool tubs, and the beach, the only private one in San Juan, has been expanded with imported sand. Room balconies feature ocean or lagoon views; the higher the floor, the better the view. The executive floor provides business travelers with services such as private check-in and checkout, complimentary evening cocktails, and complimentary Continental breakfast. The spacious open-air lobby, with a sunken bar looking out over the pool, is decorated with beige marble and regal columns. New restaurants include the steak house Morton's of Chicago and the informal Atlantico grill. Originally built in 1949, this property occupies 17 acres on Puerta de Tierra. ⊠ *Calle Los Rosales, San Gerónimo Grounds, Puerta de Tierra, 00901,* ☎ *787/721–0303 or 800/468–8585,* ℻ *787/ 725–8849. 602 rooms, 44 suites. 3 restaurants, 2 bars, air-conditioning, pool, wading pool, spa, 3 tennis courts, beach, shops, children's programs, parking (fee). AE, D, DC, MC, V. EP, MAP.* ✑

$$$$ ⊞ **Condado Plaza Hotel and Casino.** The Atlantic and the Condado Lagoon border this large high-rise hotel. Two wings, fittingly named Ocean and Lagoon, are connected by an enclosed, elevated walkway. Standard rooms have walk-in closets and separate dressing areas. There's a variety of suites, including spa suites with oversize hot tubs. The Plaza Club floor has 24-hour concierge service and a private lounge; if you stay on this floor you'll receive complimentary Continental breakfast and refreshments all day long. The Ocean wing sits on a small strip of a public beach called La Playita la Condado, and there are four pools to chose from. Children can find plenty to do at their own activity center, Camp Taíno. Dining options include Tony Roma's (a branch of the American chain), an informal poolside restaurant, and Max's Grill, open 24 hours for late-night noshing. ⊠ *999 Av. Ashford, Condado, 00902,* ☎ *787/721–1000, 800/468–8588, or 800/624–0420 (direct to hotel),* ℻ *787/722–7955. 570 rooms, 62*

suites. 7 restaurants, 2 bars, 2 lounges, air-conditioning, 3 pools, wading pool, 3 hot tubs, 2 tennis courts, health club, beach, dock, boating, casino, children's programs, concierge floor, business services. AE, D, DC, MC, V. CP, EP, MAP. ✍

$$$$ 🏨 **Ritz-Carlton San Juan Hotel and Casino.** San Juan has been "puttin' on the Ritz" since this resort opened in late 1997. The high-rise hotel on Isla Verde beach is just about everything you think a Ritz should be—with some qualifications. The wide, beige-tint lobby, with imported Italian marble and columns dominating the decor, is elegant but perhaps a bit precious in its understatement. The standard rooms are decorated in light Caribbean florals, with muted carpets, dark wood armoires, marble sinks, and bathrooms that feel small for a luxury hotel. They all come with cable TV, in-room movies, phones with data ports, and terry-cloth robes. The windows on most floors are not geared for the pleasant sea breeze—they're sealed shut, for hurricane protection and to muffle noise from the nearby international airport. But the beach is lovely, as is the large free-form pool, and the hotel spa, one of the island's largest, begs to pamper. A Ritz Kids room and a well-equipped business center fulfill their purposes ably. ✉ *6961 State Rd. 187, Isla Verde, 00979,* ☎ *787/253–1700 or 800/241–3333,* ℻ *787/253–0700. 403 rooms, 11 suites. 3 restaurants, 3 bars, sushi bar, air-conditioning, minibars, no-smoking floor, pool, hot tub, beauty salon, spa, 2 tennis courts, exercise room, casino, nightclub, concierge floor. AE, D, DC, MC, V. EP.* ✍

$$$$ 🏨 **San Juan Grand Beach Resort and Casino.** In the place of the former Sands Hotel stands the sparkling San Juan Grand, open since late 1998. The 16-story monolith sits on one of the city's most popular beaches, and the theme of understated luxury carries through from the large cream- and brown-tile lobby, with its blue-sky ceiling motif, to the spacious rooms, decorated in somber brown and green hues. Suites of the upscale Plaza Club, which has 24-hour snacks on hand and a private concierge, overlook the pool area, but the views from the standard rooms—either over the ocean or toward the city and the San José Lagoon—are pleasant. Off the lobby is the jangling casino, and on-site restaurants include the steak emporium Ruth's Chris Steak House; Momoyama for Japanese cuisine; and the Grand Market Café, with deli favorites you can eat on the spot or have packed for a beach picnic. ✉ *187 Av. Isla Verde (Box 6676), Isla Verde, 00914,* ☎ *787/791–6100, 800/544–3008, or 800/443–2009,* ℻ *787/253–2510. 381 rooms, 19 suites. 6 restaurants, 3 bars, air-conditioning, in-room safes, no-smoking rooms, pool, hot tub, exercise room, spa, boating, beach, shops, casino, nightclub, video games, children's programs, concierge floor, business services, meeting rooms. AE, D, MC, V. EP.* ✍

$$$$ 🏨 **San Juan Marriott Resort and Stellaris Casino.** The red neon sign atop this hotel is a beacon to its excellent Condado location. Rooms have soothing pastel carpeting, floral spreads, attractive tropical artwork on the walls, and balconies that overlook the ocean, the pool, or both. Restaurants include the Tuscany, for northern Italian cuisine, and the more casual La Vista, which is open 24 hours and popular for dining alfresco. On weekends, there's live entertainment in the enormous lobby, which, combined with the ringing of slot machines from the adjoining casino, makes the area quite noisy. (Rooms are soundproof.) Gorgeous Condado Beach is right outside, as is a large pool area. ✉ *1309 Av. Ashford, Condado, 00907,* ☎ *787/722–7000 or 800/228–9290,* ℻ *787/722–6800. 512 rooms, 17 suites. 3 restaurants, 2 lounges, air-conditioning, no-smoking rooms, pool, beauty salon, hot tub, 2 tennis courts, health club, beach, casino, children's programs, business services, meeting rooms. AE, D, DC, MC, V. EP, FAP, MAP.* ✍

★ **$$$$** ▦ **Wyndham El San Juan Hotel and Casino.** An immense antique chandelier illuminates the hand-carved mahogany paneling, Italian rose marble, and 250-year-old French tapestries in the 13,000-square-ft lobby of this resort on the Isla Verde beach. You'll be hard pressed to decide whether you want a main tower suite with a whirlpool bath and wet bar; a garden room with a patio and whirlpool bath; or a casita with a sunken Roman bath. All guest quarters have such amenities as CD players, VCRs, and walk-in closets with irons and ironing boards. Dark rattan furnishings are complemented by rich carpets and tropical-print spreads and drapes throughout. Relax at the lobby's Cigar Bar and sample some of Puerto Rico's finest cigars, selected from one of 100 humidors, or take dinner at the Ranch, a rooftop country-western bar and grill complete with juicy ribs, horseshoe tossing lanes, and, yes, a mechanical bull. ⊠ *Av. Isla Verde (Box 2872), Isla Verde, 00902,* ☎ *787/791–1000, 800/468–2818, or 800/996–3426,* ℻ *787/791–0390. 332 rooms, 57 suites. 8 restaurants, 14 bars, air-conditioning, in-room data ports, minibars, no-smoking rooms, 2 pools, wading pool, 5 hot tubs, 3 tennis courts, health club, beach, shops, casino, nightclub, children's programs, business services. AE, DC, MC, V. EP, MAP.* ❧

$$$ ▦ **Colonial San Juan Beach Hotel.** On the dead-end street that serves as the public entrance to Isla Verde beach, the medium-size Colonial is a good bet for those who want to be in the thick of the beach scene. Rooms are simple and sunny, many with balconies or wide bay windows for full or partial ocean views. Be aware, however, that the hotel's advertised oceanfront rooms are not precisely that—they look over the road separating the hotel from the beach. Standard in the rooms are cable TV, phone, one king or two full size beds, and fresh tropical flowers delivered daily. For days when the beach is just too much, the roof with its pool, hot tub, and Bella Vista Bar and Grill is a great spot to cool off, enjoying tremendous views of the Isla Verde area. The hotel restaurant, Basilico, serves northern Italian fare. ⊠ *2 Calle José M. Tartak, Isla Verde, 00979,* ☎ *787/253–0100 or 888/265–6699,* ℻ *787/253–0220. 82 rooms, 2 suites. Restaurant, bar, outdoor café, air-conditioning, room service, pool, exercise room, parking (fee). AE, D, MC, V. EP.* ❧

$$–$$$ ▦ **Numero Uno.** Former New Yorker Esther Feliciano bought this three-story, red-roof guest house on the beach, spruced it up, and made it a very pleasant place to stay. It's in a quiet residential area in the middle of San Juan's nicest beach, Ocean Park. The simple but clean rooms offer double, queen-, or king-size beds, and all are air-conditioned and have ceiling fans and phones. Three rooms have ocean views, and the two apartments come with kitchenettes. A walled-in patio provides privacy for sunning or hanging out by the small pool, the bar, and Pamela's restaurant (which serves international cuisine with an emphasis on seafood). Beyond the wall, the wide, sandy beach beckons; if you're a guest here you're provided with beach chairs and towels. ⊠ *1 Calle Santa Ana, Ocean Park, 00911,* ☎ *787/726–5010,* ℻ *787/ 727–5482. 11 rooms, 2 apartments. Restaurant, bar, air-conditioning, fans, pool, beach. AE, MC, V. CP.*

$$ ▦ **El Canario by the Sea.** This three-story, hunter-green hotel, wedged between a couple of blocky condo complexes, is just 50 ft from the beach, and that's it's main attraction. The rooms are decorated in a comfortable style of mostly matching furniture, with a double or two twin beds, phone, cable TV, desk, and private bath. A simple Continental breakfast of fruit punch, coffee, pastries, and bread is offered in the small enclosed patio, and there are soda machines on the property. The luxury here is not in the accommodations, but in the access to the wide and expansive Condado Beach. The water fronting the hotel is often so rough that swimming is not allowed, but you can walk either way along the beach for a calmer spot. ⊠ *4 Av. Condado, Con-*

dado, 00907, ☎ 787/722–8640 or 800/742–4276, FAX 787/725–4921. 25 rooms. Breakfast room, air-conditioning. AE, DC, MC, V. CP. ✺

$$ 🏨 **El Consulado.** This pretty Spanish colonial building, white with terra-cotta roof tiles, sits on the main drag in Condado, a couple of blocks from the sea. Primarily a business hotel, it's low on frills but a comfortable, clean, safe spot. Rooms are sedate; the wood trim, paneling, rugs, and furniture tend to be dark, and all rooms come with air-conditioning, private baths, phones, and cable TV. Some rooms have small refrigerators, and all come with one queen or two double beds. Continental breakfast is served in a small brick patio on the side of the hotel, and, although there is no hotel restaurant or bar, the restaurant Hermes is next door, and numerous eateries are within walking distance on Avenida Ashford. The hotel's name refers to its days as the Spanish Consulate, from 1957 to 1974. ✉ 1110 Av. Ashford, Condado 00907, ☎ 787/289–9191 or 888/300–8002, FAX 787/723–8665. 29 rooms. Air-conditioning, refrigerators (some). AE, D, DC, MC, V. CP. ✺

$$ 🏨 **Excelsior.** Across the Condado Lagoon in a commercial area of Miramar (a 15-minute walk or two-minute shuttle from the beach), the family-run Excelsior has been popular with business travelers for more than 30 years. Room decor here is standard hotel fare, but each room has a phone with modem port, a refrigerator, cable TV with in-room movies and video game hookups, coffeemaker, and a private bath with a hair dryer; some have kitchenettes. Fine carpets adorn the corridors, and sculptures decorate the glass-laden lobby. Augusto's, one of the hotel's restaurants, is highly respected for its international cuisine. Complimentary coffee, newspaper, and shoe shine are available each morning. ✉ 801 Av. Ponce de León, Miramar, 00907, ☎ 787/721–7400; 800/289–4274 (direct to hotel), FAX 787/723–0068. 130 rooms, 10 suites. 2 restaurants, bar, air-conditioning, refrigerators, pool, exercise room, free parking. AE, D, DC, MC, V. EP.

$$ 🏨 **Hotel La Playa.** Small, unassuming, and almost hidden, Hotel La Playa sits over the glistening green waters of Isla Verde beach. It bills itself as a quiet, gentle retreat, and, particularly in contrast to the towering glitz of neighboring Isla Verde resorts, it lives up to its claim. The rooms are simple, each with a double or a double and single bed, cable TV, private bath, and phone, and the upper floors have views of the water. The floors are tiled and clean, and the small lobby bar area is reached through a plant-filled courtyard. On a deck over the water is La Playita Lounge and Restaurant, famous for its burgers. The clientele is mostly a mature crowd—there's no band, no disco, little noise. The vast beach is steps to the west. And the price is a bargain, particularly for the area. ✉ 6 Calle Amapola, Isla Verde, 00979, ☎ 787/791–1115 or 800/791–9626, FAX 787/791–4650. 15 rooms. Restaurant, bar, air-conditioning, free parking. AE, MC, V. CP. ✺

$–$$ 🏨 **L'Habitation Beach Guest House.** On the beach in Ocean Park is this guest house with a definite French atmosphere and a primarily gay clientele. Owner Alain Tasca is from Paris by way of Guadalupe and Key West. He has established a very relaxed ambience in this 10-room accommodation. Rooms are simple and comfortable; numbers 8 and 9 are the largest and have ocean views. A combined bar–snack bar sits in a corner of a palm-shaded patio between the guest house and the beach. Beach chairs and towels are provided: get your beach gear together before you have one of Alain's margaritas, which will knock your sandals off. ✉ 1957 Calle Italia, Ocean Park, 00911, ☎ 787/727–2499, FAX 787/727–2599. 10 rooms. Bar, snack bar, air-conditioning, fans, beach, free parking. AE, D, MC, V. CP. ✺

★ $–$$ 🏨 **Hosteria del Mar.** This small, white inn's location on the beach in Ocean Park, a residential neighborhood, is a wonderful alternative to the hustle and bustle of the Condado or Old San Juan—you have to go down to the beach and look west to see the high-rises of the Condado looming in the distance. Rooms here are attractive and simple, with tropical prints and rattan furniture, and many have ocean views. Four apartments have kitchenettes with microwaves and two-burner stoves. The staff is courteous and helpful. The ground-floor restaurant, which serves many vegetarian dishes as well as seafood and steaks, faces the trade winds, offering fabulous views of the wide beach. ⊠ *1 Calle Tapia, Ocean Park, 00911, ☎ 787/727–3302 or 800/742–4276, ℻ 787/268–0772. 8 rooms, 4 apartments, 1 minisuite. Restaurant, air-conditioning, beach, free parking. AE, D, DC, MC, V. EP.* ⊗

NIGHTLIFE AND THE ARTS

There are several resources at your disposal if you want to find out what's going on culturally in San Juan. *Qué Pasa,* the official visitor's guide, has current listings of events in the city as well as out on the island. For more up-to-the-minute information, pick up a copy of the *San Juan Star,* the island's oldest daily, and it's only in English. The Thursday edition's weekend section is especially useful. *Bienvenidos* and *Places,* two publications of the Puerto Rico Hotel and Tourism Association, can also be of help. The English-language *San Juan City Magazine* has extensive lists of events and restaurants, as well as reviews and articles of a cultural bent. And you can always consult with the local tourist offices and the concierge at your hotel to find out what's doing.

The Arts

Puerto Rico's lively arts scene is centered in San Juan, and on most nights of the week there's likely to be music, dance, ballet, a play, an art opening, or a pop music concert. This is the land that gave us Ricky Martin as well as Chita Rivera, and music is food for the soul of Puerto Rico. Music performances are often held at local hotels and at the **Centro de Bellas Artes Luis A. Ferré** (☞ Performing Arts *below*) in Santurce.

Art galleries and museums abound throughout the city, particularly in Old San Juan, and one way to see the best in local art is to take advantage of Old San Juan's **Gallery Night** (☎ 787/723–6286). Galleries and select museums open their doors after hours for viewing, accompanied by refreshments and music. Gallery Night is held the first Tuesday of the month, September–December and February–May, 6–9.

Island Culture

LeLoLai is a year-round festival that celebrates Puerto Rico's Indian, Spanish, and African heritage. Performances take place each week, moving from hotel to hotel, showcasing the island's music, folklore, and culture. Because it's sponsored by the Puerto Rico Tourism Company and major San Juan hotels, passes to the festivities are included in some packages offered by participating hotels. You can also purchase tickets to a weekly series of events for $15. For information, contact the LeLoLai office (☎ 787/723–3135 weekdays; 787/791–1014 weekends and evenings).

Performing Arts

Centro de Bellas Artes Luis A. Ferré (Luis A. Ferré Center for the Performing Arts; ⊠ Corner of Av. José De Diego and Av. Ponce De León, Santurce, ☎ 787/725–7334) is the largest venue of its kind in the Caribbean, and is one of San Juan's cultural hubs. There's something going on nearly every night, from pop concerts to plays to opera to ballet to jazz. It's also the home of the San Juan Symphony Orchestra. Luciano Pavoratti held his annual competition Operalia here in 1999, and Cuban musicians reunited as the Buena Vista Social Club played sold-out shows here in 2000.

Nightlife

From Thursday through Sunday, it can feel like there's a celebration going on nearly everywhere in San Juan. Friday and Saturday are the big nights—if you're planning on going out, dress to party. Bars are usually casual, but if you have on jeans, sneakers, and a T-shirt, you'll probably be refused entry at most nightclubs and discos, unless you look like a model. You're likely to be impressed by the stylish flair of Puerto Ricans: men and women love getting dressed up to go out, and they do it well.

During the evening in any large hotel lobby you'll see well-dressed locals and tourists mingling and making the scene. There's usually live music near the lobby bar, and you'll find shows charging admissions of $10 or more at the clubs within the hotels. Of late, Condado's San Juan Marriott and Isla Verde's El San Juan Hotel and Casino have had the liveliest lobby scenes, but such things are subject to shifting trends. Casino rules have been relaxed in recent years, injecting life into the conservative hotel gaming scene. The range of games has expanded, and such standard gambling perks as free drinks and live music in the casinos are now allowed.

Lively bars and restaurants, often featuring live music, are found throughout the beach districts of Condado and Isla Verde. Even rustic Piñones, the mostly undeveloped beachfront east of the airport, has nightlife: merengue combos play at open-air beach bars, while some establishments have live Brazilian jazz trios or reggae bands.

Old San Juan's Calle San Sebastián has been a hub of nightlife for decades now. Bars and restaurants, intermingled with three-story apartment buildings dating from the first half of the 20th century, line the street, from Aqui se Puede, on the corner of Calle San Justo, to Nono's, on the corner of Calle Cristo—right across the street from Plaza San José, where the young and beautiful gather to flaunt and socialize. Cut-rate poolhalls blaring salsa from jukeboxes compete for space with top-flight restaurants and night spots presenting live jazz and tropical music. In late January you'll find here the Fiestas de la Calle San Sebastián, one of the best street parties and art fairs in the Caribbean.

Bars

El Batey (✉ 101 Calle Cristo, Old San Juan, ☎ 787/725–1787) is a hole-in-the-wall run by crusty New Yorker Davydd Gwilym Jones III; it looks like a military bunker, complete with a pool table and graffiti covering the walls and ceiling (grab a marker and add your own message). But it has the best oldies jukebox in the city and is wildly popular.

Dunbar's (✉ 1954 Calle McCleary, Ocean Park, ☎ 787/728–2920) is popular with young professionals who want to get casual by the beach. You'll find good food, sports on TV, a back pool room, and live music Thursday–Saturday.

El Patio de Sam (✉ 102 Calle San Sebastián, Old San Juan, ☎ 787/723–1149) is an Old San Juan institution whose clientele claims it serves the best burgers on the island. Potted plants and strategically placed canopies create the illusion of an outdoor patio.

Hard Rock Café (✉ 253 Recinto Sur, Old San Juan, ☎ 787/724–7625), almost as common as McDonald's these days, has a location in Old San Juan.

The Reef Bar & Grill (⊠ first turn after bridge when you enter Piñones, ☎ 787/791–1374) is in rustic Piñones, the undeveloped beachfront east of the airport. It has stunning sunsets and a priceless view, from the gleaming hotels of Isla Verde to the distant fortresses of Old San Juan, all from its outside terrace. The piña coladas, served in plastic cups, are tasty. You can also order fried fish fritters and other local snacks, listen to the jukebox, and shoot pool. At night, there's often live music, from salsa to reggae.

Rumba (⊠ 152 Calle San Sebastián, Old San Juan, ☎ 787/725–4407) has live salsa and Afro-Cuban music performances Wednesday through Saturday, plus special engagements. It's an attractive place, with locally produced art on the walls. There's a large stage and dance area, with the main bar set apart in a front room. The air-conditioning blasts, the crowd is always hip, and the house bands smoke. It's often the best party in town.

Casinos

By law, all casinos are in hotels. Among the San Juan hotels (☞ Lodging, *above*) that have casinos are: the Ritz-Carlton San Juan Hotel, Condado Plaza Hotel, San Juan Grand Beach Resort, San Juan Marriott Resort and Stellaris Casino, Wyndham El San Juan Hotel, and Wyndham Old San Juan Hotel. The government keeps a close eye on them. Dress for the larger casinos tends to be on the more formal side, and the atmosphere is refined. The law permits casinos to operate noon–4 AM, but within those parameters individual casinos set their own hours. In addition to slot machines, typical games include blackjack, roulette, craps, Caribbean stud poker (a five-card stud game), and *pai gow* poker (a combination of American poker and the ancient Chinese game of pai gow, which employs cards and dice). Hotels that house casinos have live entertainment most weekends, restaurants, and bars; drinks are usually served in the casino to players. The minimum age is 18.

Dance and Music Clubs

Nightclubs have a short shelf life; they come and go with the whims of the hip crowd. Currently, many are heading to **The Stargate** (⊠ Av. Robert Todd, Santurce, ☎ 787/725–4664 or 787/725–4675) for live music and dancing. Wednesday is casual night and Thursday–Saturday are dressy dancing nights. Upstairs is a cigar bar.

Café Bohemio (⊠ El Convento Hotel, 100 Calle Cristo, Old San Juan, ☎ 787/723–9200), a Latin restaurant, turns into a live jazz club from 11 to 2 each night (after the kitchen closes); Tuesday night is best. **Café Matisse** (⊠ Av. Ashford, Condado, San Juan, ☎ 787/723–7910) offers live jazz and blues, classic rock and roll, and poetry readings Tuesday–Sunday. The multilevel **Club Lazer** (⊠ 251 Calle Cruz, ☎ 787/725–7581) has a landscaped roof deck overlooking San Juan and attracts different crowds on different nights; Saturday is ladies' night.

Eros (⊠ 1257 Av. Ponce de León, Santurce, ☎ 787/722–1390) plays terrific dance music and is popular with the gay community. **La Fiesta Lounge** (⊠ Condado Plaza Hotel and Casino, 999 Av. Ashford, Condado, ☎ 787/721–1000) sizzles with steamy Latin shows. **Houlihan's** (⊠ Av. Ashford, Condado, ☎ 787/723–8600) is a restaurant with an upstairs nightclub popular with the local party crowd. On weekends, revelers line up on the sidewalk, waiting to get in. A dressy crowd heads for the dance music, live performances, record parties, and fashion shows

at **Martini's** (✉ 187 Av. Isla Verde, San Juan Grand, Isla Verde, ☎ 787/
791–6100, ext. 356) Thursday, Friday, and Saturday nights.

OUTDOOR ACTIVITIES AND SPORTS

Not surprisingly, many of San Juan's most enjoyable outdoor activities take place in and around the water. With miles of beach stretching across Isla Verde, Ocean Park, and Condado, there's a full range
of water sports, including scuba diving, deep-sea fishing, waterskiing,
jet-skiing, parasailing, windsurfing, sailing, and paddle-boating, as
well as cruising to outlying areas on sunset and party boats.

Options for land-based activities include tennis and walking or jogging at local parks. With a bit of effort—meaning a short drive out of
the city—you'll find a world of golf, horseback riding, and rain-forest
trekking available to you. Baseball is big in Puerto Rico, and the games
are worth seeing for true fans. The players are world class; many are
recruited from local teams to play in the U.S. major leagues (think of
Hall-of-Famers Roberto Clemente and Tony Perez, among many
others). The season runs October–February. Games are played in San
Juan as well as other venues around the island.

Beaches

In the San Juan area you have at your disposal several of the finest beaches
on the island. **Balneario de Carolina,** a government-maintained, gated
beach, is about 9½ km (6 mi) east of Isla Verde on Avenida Los Gob-
ernadores (Rte. 187), and so close to the airport the trees rustle when
planes take off. The long stretch of beach is shaded by palms and almond trees, with an often rough surf. There's plenty of sand and space
to spread out, as well as lifeguards, bathhouses, picnic gazebos (seats
and a barbecue grill, bring your own fuel), and loads of parking ($2).
The gates are open daily 8 AM–4:30 PM, and city buses (50¢ from San
Juan) stop at the beach.

★ **Isla Verde Beach,** a white-sand beach bordered by high-rise resort hotels, has good snorkeling, with water-sports equipment and chair
rentals, as well as restaurants and bars, along the beach. Set near San
Juan, it's a lively beach popular with city folk, and it's always open,
always free. There are no lifeguards here. The best entrance is from
the dead-end Calle José M. Tartak off Avenida Isla Verde, where some
street parking is available. As an alternative to parking on the street,
use the valet parking at the Colonial Hotel on Calle Tartak, where fees
start at $5 for the first two hours.

Ocean Park, a residential neighborhood just east of the Condado, is
home to one of San Juan's prettiest beaches. The waters off this wide,
1½-km-long (1-mi-long) stretch of fine golden sand are often choppy
but very swimmable—take care, however, as no lifeguards are on duty.
On weekends it fills up with local college students; it's also one of the
two city beaches popular with the gay community. (The other is in front
of the Atlantic Beach Hotel.) There are public rest rooms, a playground, and a small police station at Parque Barbosa on the south side
of the beach road, Calle Park Boulevard. (Take Calle McLeary to Calle
Soldado Serrano and Calle Park Boulevard.) Several parking spots
line the road.

Just west of Ocean Park is the city's popular Condado area, where the
long and wide **Condado Beach** is the attraction for the numerous resorts that tower over the sand. The beach here is open and free, and
you'll find beach bars, water-sports rentals, chair rentals, and plenty

of space (but no lifeguards). The beach can be reached by several side roads off Avenida Ashford, where you'll have to park on the street. Among the access roads are Calles Vendin, Earle, and Court. Children will like **Playita Condado,** marked "Condado Public Beach" on its sign. The tiny beach has a gentle surf (due to outlying rocks that temper the waves), lifeguards, and some shade from trees. It's adjacent to the Condado Plaza Hotel off busy Avenida Ashford.

After $22 million in refurbishments, the Parque de Tercer Milenio (Third Millennium Park) opened in late 1999. The park, off Avenida Muñoz Rivera on the Puerta de Tierra stretch at the entrance to Old San Juan, encompasses **Balneario Escambrón,** a patch of honey-color beach with shade from coconut palms and a mostly gentle surf, and with lifeguards, shower taps, and bathrooms, as well as several restaurants; parking is $2, and the park is open daily 7 AM–7 PM.

Participant Sports

Boating and Sailing

Many of the resort hotels on San Juan's Condado and Isla Verde strips have water-sports centers, or recommend water-sports centers on the beach. Their activities (with approximate prices) include: small Sunfish ($30/hour), Windsurfers ($25/hour, including lesson), Jet Skis ($45/half-hour or $60/two riders per half hour), single kayaks ($25/hour), double kayaks ($35/hour), and Wave Runners ($65/half-hour). The waves can be strong and the surf choppy, but the constant wind makes for good sailing. In San Juan, contact **Sun Riders Watersports** (⊠ Condado Plaza Hotel and Casino, 999 Av. Ashford, Condado, ☎ 787/721–1000, ext. 2699) or **San Juan Water Fun** (⊠ Wyndham El San Juan Hotel and Casino, Av. Isla Verde, Isla Verde, ☎ 787/643–4510). Boating and sailing trips of all kinds are offered by **Caribe Aquatic Adventures** (⊠ Radisson Normandie Hotel, corner of Av. Rosales and Av. Muñoz Rivera, Puerta de Tierra, ☎ 787/724–1882 or 787/281–8858), **Caribbean School of Aquatics** (⊠ 1 Calle Taft, Suite 10F, Condado, ☎ 787/728–6606), and **Castillo Watersports** (⊠ ESJ Towers, Isla Verde, ☎ 787/791–6195 or 787/725–7970).

Fishing

Puerto Rico's waters are home to large game fish such as marlin, snook, wahoo, dorado, tuna, and barracuda; as many as 30 world records for catches have been set off the island's shores. Prices for fishing expeditions vary, but inevitably include all your bait and tackle, as well as refreshments, and start at $450 (for a boat of as many as six people) for a half-day trip to $750 for a full day of fishing. Other boats charge by the person, starting at $150 for a full day. Half-day, full-day, split charter, and big- and small-game fishing can be arranged through **Benitez Deep-Sea Fishing** (⊠ Club Náutico de San Juan, Miramar, ☎ 787/723–2292). Other options include **Caribe Aquatic Adventures** (☞ Boating and Sailing, *above*) and **Castillo Watersports** (☞ Boating and Sailing, *above*).

Golf

For aficionados worldwide, Puerto Rico is known as the birthplace of golf legend and raconteur Chi Chi Rodriguez—and he had to hone his craft somewhere. Currently, you'll find more than a dozen courses on the island, including some of championship caliber. Several are close enough to San Juan for easy day trips. Be sure to call ahead for details on reserving tee times; hours vary and several hotel courses allow only guests to play or give preference to them. Greens fees start at about $25 and go as high as $115. There are four attractive Robert Trent Jones–designed 18-hole courses shared by the **Hyatt Dorado Beach and**

the Hyatt Regency Cerromar Beach hotels (⊠ Rte. 693, Km 10.8 and Km 11.8, Dorado, ☎ 787/796–1234, ext. 3238 or 3016), about an hour west of town. East of San Juan you'll find 18-hole courses at the **Bahia Beach Plantation** (⊠ Rte. 187, Km 4.2, Río Grande, ☎ 787/256–5600), the **Berwind Country Club** (⊠ Rte. 187, Km 4.7, Río Grande, ☎ 787/876–3056), and the **Westin Río Mar Beach Resort and Country Club** (⊠ 6000 Río Mar Blvd., Río Grande, ☎ 787/888–6000).

Hiking

Thirteen hiking trails totaling some 24 mi loop past giant ferns, exotic orchids, sibilant streams and waterfalls, and broad trees reaching for the sun at **El Yunque** (⊠ El Portal Tropical Forest Center, Rte. 191, Palmer, ☎ 787/888–1810 or 787/888–1880). The park, officially the Caribbean National Forest, is about an hour's drive along Route 3 east of San Juan.

Scuba Diving and Snorkeling

The San Juan area's diving is not the best on the island, but several outfitters conduct short excursions to where tropical fish, coral, and sea horses are visible at depths ranging from 30 ft to 60 ft. Some outfitters offer package deals combining accommodations with daily diving trips. Escorted half-day dives range from $45 to $90 for one or two tanks, including all equipment. Packages including lunch and other extras start at $100. Night dives are often available at close to double the price. Snorkeling excursions, which include transportation (most often a sailboat filled with snorkelers), equipment rental, and sometimes lunch, start at $50. Snorkel equipment rents at beaches for about $5–$7. (Caution: coral-reef waters and mangrove areas can be dangerous to novices. Unless you're an expert or have an experienced guide, avoid unsupervised areas and confine your snorkeling to the watersports centers of hotels.)

Contact the dive outfitters **Caribe Aquatic Adventures** (☞ Boating and Sailing, *above*), **Caribbean School of Aquatics** (☞ Boating and Sailing, *above*), and **Mundo Submarino** (⊠ Laguna Garden Shopping Center, Av. Baldorioty de Castro, Carolina, ☎ 787/791–5764).

Tennis

If you'd like to use the tennis courts at a property where you aren't a guest, call in advance for information about reservations and fees. Your best bet for playing tennis in the San Juan area is the 17 lighted courts at **San Juan Central Municipal Park** (⊠ Calle Cerra, exit on Rte. 2, Santurce, ☎ 787/722–1646). Fees run $3 per hour 8 AM–6 PM and $4 per hour 6 PM–10 PM. The four lighted tennis courts of the **Isla Verde Tennis Club** (⊠ Calles Ema and Delta Rodriguez, Isla Verde, ☎ 787/727–6490) are open for non-member use at $4 per hour, daily 8 AM–10 PM. There are also two tennis courts at the **Condado Plaza Hotel and Casino** (⊠ 999 Av. Ashford, Condado, ☎ 787/721–1000). Fees for nonguests range from $10 to $20 per hour.

Spectator Sports

Baseball

Does the name Roberto Clemente ring a bell? The late, great star of the Pittsburgh Pirates, who died in a 1972 plane crash delivering supplies to Nicaraguan earthquake victims, was born near San Juan and got his start in the Puerto Rican pro leagues. Many other Puerto Rican stars have played in the U.S. major leagues, including the brothers Roberto Alomar and Sandy Alomar Jr.; their father, Sandy Alomar; and recent Hall of Fame inductees Tony Perez and Orlando Cepeda. The island's season runs October–February. Stadiums are in San Juan (Esatadio Hiram Bithorn), Santurce, Ponce, Caguas, Arecibo, and Mayagüez;

the teams also play once or twice in Aguadilla. General admission seats run about $5, while the most expensive box seats range $6–$7. Contact the tourist office (☞ Visitor Information *in* Smart Travel Tips) for details or call **Professional Baseball of Puerto Rico** (☎ 787/765–6285).

Horse Racing

Thoroughbred races are run year-round at **Hípodromo El Comandante,** a racetrack about 20 minutes east of San Juan. On race days the dining rooms open at 12:30 PM. Post time is 2:30 PM. ⊠ *Av. 65th Infantry (Rte. 3), Km 15.3, Canóvanas,* ☎ *787/724–6060.* ☉ *Mon., Wed., and Fri.–Sun. 12:30–6.*

SHOPPING

San Juan isn't a duty-free port, so you won't find bargains on electronics and perfumes. You can, however, find excellent prices on china, crystal, fashions, designer items, and jewelry. Look to the streets of Old San Juan for the city's largest collection of shops. In Condado, Avenida Ashford is a good bet for artisans shops, designer clothing boutiques, and art galleries, as well as T-shirt and curio stores.

Shopping for local crafts can also be gratifying: you'll run across a lot of tacky items, but you can also find some treasures, and in many cases you can watch the artisans at work. For guidance, contact the Puerto Rico Tourism Company's **Asuntos Culturales** (Cultural Affairs Office, ☎ 787/723–0692). Popular items include *santos* (small hand-carved figures of saints or religious scenes); hand-rolled cigars; Panama hats; handmade *mundillo* lace from Aguadilla; *veijigantes* (colorful masks made of papier-mâché and coconut husks and used during Carnival and local festivals) from Loíza (east of San Juan); and fancy men's shirts called guayaberas. Also, some folks swear that Puerto Rican rum is the best in the world.

Shopping in San Juan differs little from shopping in North America— cash of course is always accepted, and in most cases traveler's checks and major credit cards are fine. Vendors who sell crafts and other items on the streets, primarily in Old San Juan, are likely to accept cash only, and are likely to bargain. Bargaining for items in shops and boutiques is not as common—while you are always welcome to suggest a reasonable price, don't be surprised if the store owner's marked price is the final one.

Areas and Markets

Old San Juan is full of shops, especially on Calles Cristo, Fortaleza, and San Francisco. The Old City is perhaps the best single destination for the serious shopper in San Juan—the stores are all within walking distance of each other and trolleys are at your beck and call. On Old San Juan's streets you'll find everything from T-shirt emporiums to selective crafts stores, bookshops to art galleries, jewelry boutiques to shops that make Panama hats to order. Since Old San Juan is also one of the premier cruise-ship stops in the Caribbean, you'll often find yourself among groups of shoppers, which of course makes bargains harder to find.

Look for vendors selling crafts at the small **Artesania Puertorriqueña** (Puerto Rican Artisans) tables at the Tourism Company's La Casita at Plaza Dársenas near Pier 1 in Old San Juan (☎ 787/722–1709). Several vendors also set up shop to sell items such as belts, handbags, and toys along Calle San Justo in front of Plaza Dársenas.

Old San Juan Shopping

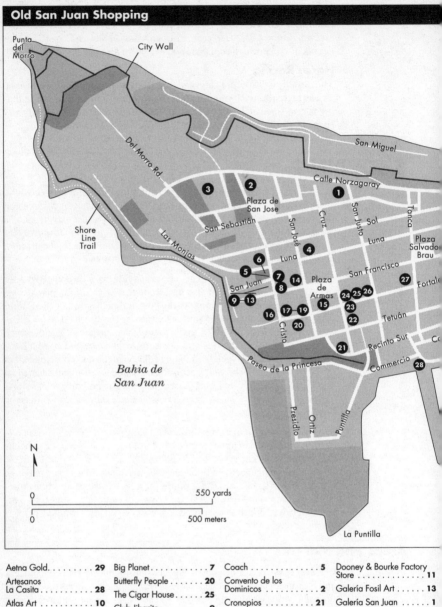

Punta del Morro

City Wall

Del Morro Rd.

San Miguel

Calle Norzagaray

Plaza de San Jose

San Sebastián

Shore Line Trail

Las Monjas

San José

Cruz

San Justo

Sol

Tanca

Luna

Plaza Salvador Brau

③

②

①

④

Luna

⑥

⑤

San Juan

⑦ ⑭

⑧

San Francisco

⑨ ⑬

Plaza de Armas

⑮

㉔ ㉕ ㉖

㉗

Fortale

⑯

⑰ ⑲

㉓

㉒

Tetuán

⑳

Cristo

Recinto Sur

㉑

Co

Paseo de la Princesa

Commercio

㉘

Bahia de San Juan

Presidio

Ortiz

Puntilla

La Puntilla

N

| 0 | 550 yards |
| 0 | 500 meters |

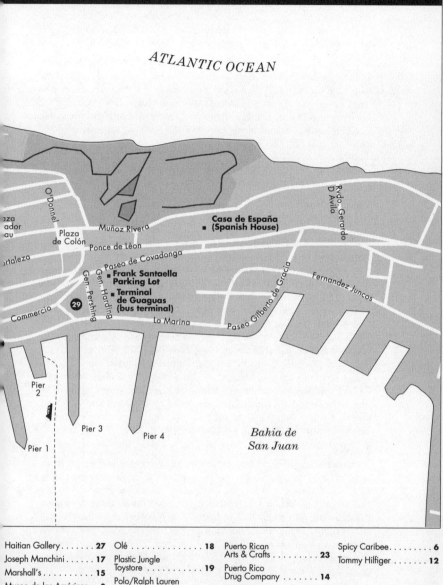

ATLANTIC OCEAN

O'Donnel

aza
ador
au

Plaza
de Colón

Muñoz Rivera

Casa de España
(Spanish House)

Rvdo. Gerardo
D'Ávila

Ponce de Léon

rtaleza

Paseo de Covadonga

Gen. Harding

Gen. Pershing

Frank Santaella
Parking Lot

Terminal
de Guaguas
(bus terminal)

29

Commercio

La Marina

Paseo Gilberto de Gracia

Fernandez Juncos

Pier
2

Pier 3

Pier 4

Bahia de
San Juan

Pier 1

In Carolina, a few minutes east of San Juan, you'll find a **Mercado Arte-sanal** (Artisan Market) and cultural fair every Sunday 1–5 PM at the Julia de Burgos Memorial Park on Avenida Roberto Clemente (corner of Paseo de los Gigantes). In addition to craft and food booths, live bands perform and there's often entertainment for the kids.

San Juan area malls include **Plaza Las Américas** (✉ 525 Av. Franklin Delano Roosevelt, Hato Rey, ☎ 787/767–1525), which has 200 shops including the largest JC Penney store in the world, the Gap, Sears, Banana Republic, Macy's, Borders Books and Music, Godiva, and Old Navy, as well as restaurants and movie theaters. About 10 minutes east of San Juan you'll find **Plaza Carolina** (✉ Av. Fragosa (exit off Rte. 26), Carolina, ☎ 787/768–0514).

Specialty Shops

Art

Galería W. Labiosa (✉ 200 Calle Tetuán, Old San Juan, ☎ 787/721–2848) features work by Wilfredo Labiosa and other contemporary Latin American painters. **DMR Gallery** (✉ 204 Calle Luna, Old San Juan, ☎ 787/722–4181) has handmade furniture by artist Nick Quijano. **Galería Fosil Arte** (✉ 200 Calle Cristo, Old San Juan, ☎ 787/725–4252) features art pieces by Radames Rivera made from coral and limestone more than 30 million years old, as well as original paintings by Yolanda Velasquez. **Atlas Art** (✉ 208 Calle Cristo, Old San Juan, ☎ 787/723–9987) carries contemporary paintings and prints, and sculptures in glass and bronze. **Galería Botello** (✉ 314 Av. Franklin Delano Roosevelt, Hato Rey, San Juan, ☎ 787/250–8274) exhibits and sells antique santos. **Galería San Juan** (✉ Gallery Inn, 204–206 Calle Norzagaray, Old San Juan, ☎ 787/722–1808) has the sculptures of artist Jan D'Esopo. Don't forget to take advantage of Old San Juan's **Gallery Night** (☎ 787/723–6286), when the galleries and select museums open their doors after hours for viewing, accompanied by live music and wine and cheese. Gallery Night is held the first Tuesday of the month September–December and February–May, 6 PM–9 PM.

Books

Borders Books (✉ Plaza Las Américas, 525 Av. Franklin Delano Roosevelt, Hato Rey, ☎ 787/777–0916), part of the U.S. superstore chain, fills 28,000 square ft in San Juan's biggest mall with an extensive selection of popular titles. Among the city's finest bookshops is **Cronopios** (✉ 255 Calle San José, Old San Juan, ☎ 787/724–1815), which carries a full range of fiction and nonfiction in both English and Spanish, as well as music CDs. **Thekes** (✉ Plaza Las Américas, 525 Av. Franklin Delano Roosevelt, Hato Rey, ☎ 787/765–1539) sells contemporary fiction, magazines, and travel books in English and Spanish.

Cigars

Club Jibarito (✉ 202 Calle Cristo, Old San Juan, ☎ 787/724–7797), with its large walk-in humidor, is the place to stop for the best in Puerto Rican and imported cigars, as well as such smoking paraphernalia as designer lighters, personal humidors, pipes, and pipe tobacco. Also on hand are silk ties, cuff links, and designer pens from Alfred Dunhill. **The Cigar House** (✉ 255 Calle Fortaleza, Old San Juan, ☎ 787/723–5223) has a small, eclectic selection of local and imported cigars.

Clothing

You can buy high-end men's and women's original designs at **Nono Maldonado** (✉ 1051 Av. Ashford, Condado, ☎ 787/721–0456). **Kation Boutique** (✉ 1016 Av. Franklin Delano Roosevelt, Hato Rey, ☎

787/749–0235) sells unique designer items from Fendi, Moschino, Gianni Versace, and Dolce and Gabbana.

In Old San Juan, discounts on Ralph Lauren apparel are found at the **Polo/Ralph Lauren Factory Store** (⊠ 201 Calle Cristo, Old San Juan, ☎ 787/722–2136). At **Tommy Hilfiger** (206 Calle Cristo, Old San Juan, ☎ 787/721–4888) you can buy some of the Hilfiger-emblazoned items that have become so ubiquitous. **Big Planet** (⊠ 205 Calle Cristo, Old San Juan, ☎ 787/725–1204) sells shorts, knit shirts, and active-wear clothing. **Speedo Authentic Fitness** (⊠ 65 Calle Fortaleza at Calle Cristo, ☎ 787/724–3089) sells swimsuits for men and women, warm-up jackets, sandals, and swimming goggles. Aficionados of the famous lightweight Panama hat, made from delicately hand-woven straw, should stop at **Olé** (⊠ 105 Calle Fortaleza, Old San Juan, ☎ 787/724–2445). The shop sells top-of-the-line hats for as much as $1,000, as well as antiques, santos, sandals, and delicately crafted marionettes. People line up to enter **Marshall's** (⊠ Plaza de Armas, Old San Juan, ☎ 787/722–0874) for basic clothing and department-store items.

Handicrafts

The **Haitian Gallery** (⊠ 367 Calle Fortaleza, Old San Juan, ☎ 787/725–0986) carries Puerto Rican crafts and a selection of folksy, often inexpensive paintings from around the Caribbean. At the **Convento de los Dominicos** (⊠ 98 Calle Norzagaray, Old San Juan, ☎ 787/721–6866), the Dominican Convent on the north side of the old city that houses offices of the Instituto de Cultura Puertorriqueña, you'll find baskets, masks, the famous *cuatro* guitars, santos, books and tapes, and Indian artifacts. The small shop at the **Museo de las Américas** (⊠ Cuartel de Ballajá Old San Juan, ☎ 787/724–5052) sells authentic folk crafts from around Latin America. For one-of-a-kind buys in santos, art, and festival masks, head for **Puerto Rican Arts & Crafts** (⊠ 204 Calle Fortaleza, Old San Juan, ☎ 787/725–5596). You should pay a visit to the **Artesanos La Casita,** an artisans market at the Tourism Company's La Casita at Plaza Dársenas near Pier 1 in Old San Juan (☎ 787/722–1709). The small crafts tables set up outside the offices will, on a given day, contain leather wallets or handbags, belts, handmade dolls, and souvenir items, some tacky, some worth checking out.

Jewelry

Diamonds and gold galore are found at **Joseph Manchini** (⊠ 101 Calle Fortaleza, Old San Juan, ☎ 787/722–7698). For a wide array of watches and jewelry, visit the two floors of **Bared** (⊠ Calles Fortaleza and San Justo, Old San Juan, ☎ 787/724–4811). **N. Barquet Joyers** (⊠ 201 Calle Fortaleza, Old San Juan, ☎ 787/721–3366), one of the bigger stores in Old San Juan, has on hand Fabergé jewelry, pearls, and gold, as well as crystal and watches. **Aetna Gold** (⊠ Plaza del Hotel Wyndham, 111 Calle Gilberto Concepción de Gracia, Old San Juan, ☎ 787/721–4756), adjacent to the Wyndham Old San Juan Hotel, sells exquisite gold jewelry designed in Greece.

Leather

The **Coach outlet** (⊠ 158 Calle Cristo, Old San Juan, ☎ 787/722–6830) sells high-end leather handbags, briefcases, and luggage. The **Dooney & Bourke Factory Store** (⊠ 200 Calle Cristo, Old San Juan, ☎ 787/289–0075) specializes in seconds and irregular leather bags, luggage, and other items. **Louis Vuitton** (⊠ 1054 Av. Ashford, Condado, ☎ 787/722–2543) carries designer luggage and leather items, as well as scarves and business accessories.

Toiletries

If you've run out of toothpaste, you'll find it and other standard drug-store items at **Puerto Rico Drug Company** (⊠ 157 Calle San Francisco, Old San Juan, ☎ 787/725–2202) or the 24-hour **Walgreens** (⊠ 1130 Av. Ashford, Condado, San Juan, ☎ 787/725–1510). Walgreens also operates more than 30 pharmacies on the island, including a 24-hour store at Plaza Carolina on Avenida Fragosa in Carolina.

Unique Items

Plastic Jungle Toystore (⊠ 101 Calle Fortaleza, Old San Juan, ☎ 787/723–1076) sells creative toys, games, puzzles, and fun masks for children. You can find a world of unique spices and sauces from around the Caribbean, kitchen items, and cookbooks at **Spicy Caribbee** (⊠ 154 Calle Cristo, Old San Juan, ☎ 787/625–4690). Exotic butterflies mounted in clear cases line the walls of **Butterfly People** (⊠ 152 Calle Fortaleza, Old San Juan, ☎ 787/732–2432); there's also a gift shop featuring books on butterfly collecting, and a café.

SAN JUAN A TO Z

Arriving and Departing

By Airplane

The **Luis Muñoz Marín International Airport** (☎ 787/791–4670), in Isla Verde east of downtown San Juan, is one of the easiest and cheapest destinations to reach in the Caribbean. Luis Muñoz Marín is the Caribbean hub for **American Airlines** (☎ 787/749–1747), which controls some 70% of all air traffic from North America to the Caribbean. American operates nonstop flights from New York, Boston, Newark, Miami, and many other North American cities. **American Trans Air (ATA)** (☎ 787/791–3135) operates nonstop from New York, Orlando, Fort Lauderdale, Indianapolis, and Chicago. **Continental** (☎ 787/793–7373) has daily nonstop service from Newark, Houston, and Cleveland. **Delta** (☎ 787/754–3333) operates nonstop service from Atlanta. **Northwest** (☎ 787/253–0206) has daily nonstop flights from Detroit, Memphis, and Minneapolis. **TWA** (☎ 787/253–0440) flies nonstop from New York, Boston, Orlando, Fort Lauderdale, Los Angeles, and St. Louis. **United** (☎ 787/253–2776) flies daily nonstop from Chicago and weekends from New York and Washington, D.C. **US Airways** (☎ 800/428–4322) offers daily nonstop flights from Pittsburgh, Philadelphia, and Charlotte.

International carriers include **Air Canada** (☎ 800/776–3000), **Air France** (☎ 800/237–2747), **British Airways** (☎ 787/723–4327), **BWIA** (☎ 800/538–2942), **Canadian Airlines** (☎ 800/426–7000), **LACSA** (☎ 787/724–3444 or 800/225–2272), and Lufthansa's **Condor** (☎ 800/645–3880).

Connections between Caribbean islands can be made through **American Eagle** (☎ 787/749–1747), **Air Jamaica** (☎ 800/523–5585), **Cape Air** (☎ 800/352–0714), **KLM** (☎ 800/374–7747), **LIAT** (☎ 787/791–0800), and **Martin Air** (☎ 787/723–7474).

FROM THE AIRPORT

Many area hotels provide transport, free or for a fee, for their guests arriving at the airport. Before you pay for transportation, call your hotel to see what arrangements can be made. Otherwise, **Taxis Turísticos** (☞ Getting Around, *below*) charge set rates based on zones, so the fare depends on the destination. Uniformed and badged officials help you find a cab at the airport (look for the Tourism Company booth) and hand you a slip with your fare, which you can present to your driver.

To Isla Verde, the fare is $8; to Condado, it's $12; to Old San Juan, it's $16. If you don't hail one of these cabs, you're at the mercy of the meter and the driver.

Another option is the **Airport Limousine Service** (☎ 787/791–4745), which provides minibuses to hotels in the Isla Verde, Condado, and Old San Juan areas at basic fares of $2.50, $3, and $3.50, respectively; the fares do vary, depending on the time of day and number of passengers, and you may have to wait until the van fills before leaving the airport. Limousines of **Dorado Transport Co-op** (☎ 787/796–1214) serve hotels and villas in the Dorado area for $20 per person. **Wheelchair Getaway** (☎ 787/883–0131) runs wheelchair transport from the airport to metro San Juan hotels for $90 round-trip.

By Boat

You are only likely to enter San Juan via boat if you are on a cruise (☞ Cruises *in* Smart Travel Tips).

FROM THE DOCKS

Cruise ships pull into the city piers on Calle Gilberto Concepción de Gracia in Old San Juan. Most cruise passengers who have tours of the island planned will have made those arrangements with the cruise line ahead of time, and transportation will be waiting on their arrival. For those who want to wing it, the metro bus terminal is next to Plaza de Colón in Old San Juan, and taxis line the street next to Pier 2.

Getting Around

Old San Juan is definitely a walking city. If you have a rental car, your best option is to park it in any of the municipal lots and go it on foot. In Old San Juan, park at La Puntilla, at the head of Paseo de la Princesa, an outdoor lot where the rates start at 50¢ per hour. This is the cheapest lot in the old city. Other garages are the Felisa Rincón de Gautier lot, also called Dona Fela, on Calle Gilberto Concepción de Gracia (also called Calle la Marina), and the Frank Santaella lot, also called the Covadonga lot, between Paseo de Covadonga and Calle Gilberto Concepción de Gracia, across from cruise-ship Pier 4. This is also the main bus terminus in Old San Juan, and the spot where the Old San Juan trolleys originate. Parking starts at $1.25 for the first hour. The lots are open until 10 PM weekdays and as late as 2 AM on weekends.

The best way to get around "new" San Juan is by taxi—while the streets are generally well marked, there are several confusing one-way streets and the inevitable construction detours that are best navigated by someone knowledgeable. And parking is usually not an easy proposition. By the time you drive, get lost, and hunt down a parking space, you might have wished you'd left the driving to a pro. Taxi fares are calculated by zones ($6–$16 in the city), or you can opt to hire a taxi by the hour. The going hourly rate for city touring is $30, often negotiable for excursions of more than a couple of hours.

Note that San Juan has embarked on construction of a $1.6-billion elevated train system that will connect major suburbs of the city. The first phase of the system, due for completion in 2002, will connect Bayamón, Guaynabo, and Santurce. The second phase, due to be completed in 2004, will connect Río Pedras to the municipality of Carolina, and later to Luis Muñoz Marín International Airport. The system will eventually connect an estimated 16 city stops.

By Bus

The **Metropolitan Bus Authority** (AMA; ☎ 787/767–7979) operates *guaguas* (buses) that thread through San Juan, connecting the areas of

Old San Juan, Santurce, Ocean Park, Isla Verde, Carolina, and the southern and western suburbs. The fare is 25¢ or 50¢, depending on the route,
and the buses run in exclusive lanes on major thoroughfares, stopping
at signs reading PARADA. The main terminals are Covadonga parking
lot and Plaza de Colón, in Old San Juan, and Capetillo Terminal in
Río Piedras, next to the central business district, but you can get on
or off at any stop on the route. The fare is paid upon entering the bus
(try to have some quarters on hand). Buses marked A5 and B21 cover
the popular beach and hotel areas of Isla Verde, Condado, and Old
San Juan. Buses are comfortable—most are air-conditioned—but the
schedules are not always adhered to or even evident. Count on a bus
passing your stop every 15–30 minutes, less frequently on Sunday and
holidays. Buses start their morning runs between 5 AM and 6 AM, and
the last run for most city buses is between 9 PM and 10 PM.

By Car

A valid driver's license from your country of origin can be used in Puerto
Rico for three months. Rental rates can start as low as $30 a day (plus
insurance), most often with unlimited mileage. Discounts are offered
for long-term rentals, and insurance can be waived for those who rent
with American Express or certain gold credit cards (be sure to check
with your credit-card company before renting). Some discounts are offered for AAA members or for booking more than 72 hours in advance.
Most car-rental agencies have shuttle service to or from the airport and
the pickup point. Speed limits are posted in miles, distances in kilometers; gas prices are per liter, averaging 35¢ when this book went to
press. Gas is readily available in stations all over San Juan, although
there are no stations in Old San Juan, and numerous metro area stations are open 24 hours.

All major U.S. car-rental agencies are represented on the island, including
Avis (☎ 787/721–4499), **Budget** (☎ 787/791–3685), **Hertz** (☎ 787/
791–0840), **National** (☎ 787/791–1805), and **Thrifty** (☎ 787/253–2525).
Local rental companies, sometimes less expensive, include **Charlie Car
Rental** (☎ 787/791–1101 or 800/289–1227), **L & M Car Rental** (☎ 787/
791–1160 or 800/666–0807), and **Target** (☎ 787/728–1447 or 800/
934–6457).

By Ferry

The **ferry** (☎ 787/788–1155) between Old San Juan (Pier 2 on Calle
Marina) and Cataño costs a mere 50¢ one-way. It runs daily every half
hour from 6 AM to 10 PM.

By Taxi

The Puerto Rico Tourism Company oversees a well-organized taxi program. Taxis painted white and sporting the *garita* (sentry box) logo
and **Taxi Turistico** label charge set rates depending on the destination
zone; they run from the airport or the cruise-ship piers to Isla Verde,
Condado/Ocean Park, and Old San Juan, with rates ranging from $6
to $16 per car. They also can be hailed in the same manner as metered
cabs. City tours start at $30 per hour.

Metered cabs authorized by the **Public Service Commission** (☎ 787/
751–5050) start at $1 and charge 10¢ for every additional ⅓ mi, 50¢
for every suitcase. Waiting time is 10¢ for each 45 seconds. The minimum charge is $3. Be sure the driver starts the meter.

Virtually every hotel in San Juan has cabs waiting outside to transport
guests to points around the city; if there is no taxi, the bellman or front
desk can call one for you. If you'd like to bypass them, call **Major Taxi-
cabs** (☎ 787/723–2460) or **Atlantic City Taxi** (☎ 787/268–5050).
Called taxis might charge an extra $1 for the pickup.

Contacts and Resources

Embassies and Consulates

Since Puerto Rico is a U.S. commonwealth, Americans will not need to visit any embassies in times of trouble. Other consulate contacts include: **United Kingdom** (☎ 787/721–5193), **Canada** (☎ 787/790–2210). **Australia** and **New Zealand** have no consulates in Puerto Rico.

Emergencies

Puerto Rico's emergency system follows that of the North American mainland.

Ambulance, police, and fire: ☎ 911.

Hospitals and Clinics: Ashford Presbyterian Memorial Community Hospital (✉ 1451 Av. Ashford, Condado, San Juan, ☎ 787/721–2160), **Clínica Las Américas** (✉ 400 Av. Franklin Delano Roosevelt, Hato Rey, San Juan, ☎ 787/765–1919), **San Juan Health Centre** (✉ 200 Av. de Diego, San Juan, ☎ 787/725–0202).

Pharmacies: Contact **Puerto Rico Drug Company** (✉ 157 Calle San Francisco, Old San Juan, ☎ 787/725–2202) or the 24-hour **Walgreens** (✉ 1130 Av. Ashford, Condado, San Juan, ☎ 787/725–1510). Walgreens operates more than 30 pharmacies on the island.

Festivals and Holidays

Puerto Rico's festivals are colorful and inclined toward lots of music and feasting. Every year each of the island's 78 municipalities celebrates *fiestas patronales* (patron saints' festivals). In San Juan in June, the **San Juan Bautista Day** honors city patron St. John the Baptist with a week of parades, music, dance, and, ultimately, a traditional backward walk into the ocean to bring good luck in the ensuing year.

In addition to the patron saint festival, Old San Juan holds an annual **San Sebastián Street Festival** in January, with several nights of live music in the plazas, food festivals, and *cabezudos* parades featuring folk legends in oversize masks. The **Casals Festival,** held at the Luis A. Ferré Performing Arts Center in San Juan in early June, honors the late, great cellist with 10 days of classical music.

In mid-November you can attend the annual **Festival of Puerto Rican Music** in San Juan and other venues, celebrating the vibrancy of Puerto Rico's plena y bomba folk music and dance, highlighted by a contest featuring the cuatro, a traditional guitar. Sport anglers will want to keep the annual **International Billfishing Tournament** in mind; held in August and September, this gamefishing tournament sponsored by San Juan's Club Náutico attracts anglers from the world over competing for prizes for the biggest marlin and other billfish.

Public holidays in Puerto Rico include all U.S. federal holidays as well as local holidays: New Year's Day, Three Kings Day (Jan. 6), Eugenio María de Hostos Day (Jan. 8), Dr. Martin Luther King Jr. Day (third Mon. in Jan.), Presidents' Day (third Mon. in Feb.), Palm Sunday, Good Friday, Easter Sunday, Memorial Day (last Mon. in June), Independence Day (July 4), Luis Muñoz Rivera Day (July 16), Constitution Day (July 25), José Celso Barbosa Day (July 27), Labor Day (first Mon. in Sept.), Columbus Day (second Mon. in Oct.), Veteran's Day (Nov. 11), Puerto Rico Discovery Day (Nov. 19), Thanksgiving Day (Nov. 25), and Christmas.

Health and Safety

San Juan, like any other big city, has its share of crime, so guard your wallet or purse on the city streets. Puerto Rico's beaches are open to the public, and muggings can occur at night even on the beaches of the posh Condado and Isla Verde tourist hotels. Although you certainly can, and should, explore the city and its beaches, use common sense. Don't leave anything unattended on the beach. Leave your valuables in the hotel safe, and stick to the fenced-in beach areas of your hotel. Always lock your car and stash valuables and luggage out of sight. Avoid deserted beaches at night.

Tap water is generally fine on the island; just avoid drinking it after storms (when the drinking-water supply might become mixed with sewage). Thoroughly wash or peel produce you buy in markets and grocery stores before eating it. When on the streets shopping, avoid pulling out large wads of cash to make transactions—it can mark you as a target for criminals. Women should avoid open basket-type hand-bags, which make the task of a pickpocket all too easy.

San Juan is a cosmopolitan and sophisticated city, and gays and les-bians will find it an easy city in which to mingle. There are gay-friendly hotels and clubs throughout the suburbs, and the beach at Ocean Park tends to attract a gay crowd. However, normal precautions regarding overt behavior stand; Puerto Ricans are often conservative about mat-ters of sexuality and dress.

Telephones and Mail

Puerto Rico's area code is 787—for North Americans, dialing Puerto Rico is the same as dialing another state or Canadian province: sim-ply dial 1 plus 787, and the number. Calling many other Caribbean is-lands follows the same routine. When calling from Puerto Rico to other regions of the United States or Canada, dial 1 plus the area code and number. For spots that use international country codes, dial 011, the country code (plus city code, if applicable), and the number. Prepaid phone cards, used in many public phones, are common. There are plenty of phones and lines in the country, but these days, as is the case throughout the northern hemisphere, everyone seems to be toting a cel-lular phone. There are plans to put a second area code, 939, into ser-vice in August 2001.

The island uses U.S. postage stamps and has the same mail rates as the mainland United States: 20¢ for a postcard, 33¢ for a first-class letter to the United States; 40¢ for a postcard and 46¢ for a letter to Canada; 35¢ and 40¢, respectively, to Mexico; and 50¢ for a postcard and 60¢ for a letter to other international destinations. Post offices in major Puerto Rican cities offer Express Mail next-day service to the U.S. mainland and to Puerto Rican destinations. San Juan postal areas and all of Puerto Rico's towns carry Zip codes; letters addressed to San Juan should carry the name, street or post box address, and "San Juan, PR," plus the five-digit Zip code. Post offices are open weekdays 7:30–4:30 and Satur-day 8–noon. Major **post office branches** are at 153 Calle Fortaleza (☎ 787/723–1277) in Old San Juan and 163 Avenida Fernandez Juncos (☎ 787/722–4134) in San Juan.

Guided Tours

You can see Old San Juan from the free trolley, or on a self-guided walk-ing tour (look for tours in a copy of *Qué Pasa*, available at all tourist offices and hotels). The **Caribbean Carriage Company** (☎ 787/797–8063) gives tours of the Old City in open horse-drawn carriages. It's a bit hokey, but it gets you off your feet. Call them or find them at Plaza Dársenas near Pier 1 in Old San Juan. They give three tours of differing lengths; the cost is $30–$60 per couple.

Most San Juan hotels have a tour desk that can make arrangements for you. The three standard half-day tours ($20–$35) are of Old and "new" San Juan; Old San Juan and the Bacardi Rum Plant; and Playa

Luquillo and El Yunque rain forest. All-day tours ($25–$45) can include a trip to Ponce, a day at El Comandante Racetrack, or a combined tour of the city and El Yunque rain forest.

Leading tour operators include **Normandie Tours, Inc.** (☎ 787/722–6308), **Rico Suntours** (☎ 787/722–2080 or 787/722–6090), **Tropix Wellness Outings** (☎ 787/268–2173), and **United Tour Guides** (☎ 787/725–7605 or 787/723–5578). **Cordero Caribbean Tours** (☎ 787/786–9114; 787/780–2442 evenings) runs tours in air-conditioned limousines for an hourly rate. **Wheelchair Getaway** (☎ 787/883–0131) offers city sightseeing trips as well as wheelchair transport from airports and cruise-ship docks to San Juan hotels.

Visitor Information

Before you go, contact the **Puerto Rico Tourism Company** (✉ Box 902-3960, Old San Juan Station, San Juan, PR 00902-3960, ☎ 787/721–2400). The office, open 9–5 weekdays (U.S. eastern time), can help with information on upcoming events, contacts for hotels and paradores, and recommendations for side trips from San Juan. The Tourism Company, however, is not a booking agency, and cannot make hotel reservations for you. The Tourism Company's main office is at the old city jail, La Princesa, in Old San Juan. It operates a branch office in a pretty pink colonial building called La Casita at Plaza Dársenas near Pier 1 in Old San Juan (✉ ☎ 787/722–1709), open Monday–Wednesday 8:30–8, Thursday and Friday 8:30–5:30, weekends 9–8. Here you can find brochures and walking maps of the city, and you can get further information by speaking to someone at the reception desk. (They also have rum samples.) Be sure to pick up a free copy of *Qué Pasa*, the official visitors' guide, which covers hotels, restaurants, tours, and general island information. Helpful information officers, identified by their caps and shirts with the Tourism Company patch, are posted around Old San Juan (look for them at the cruise-ship piers and at the Catedral de San Juan) during the day to help visitors.

Tourism Company information officers are also found at Luis Muñoz Marín International Airport in Isla Verde (☎ 787/791–1014 or 787/791–2551), often at the lower levels (near the baggage claim areas). The three offices are at the American Airlines terminal and terminals B and C. The offices are open for most incoming flights, daily 9–10 in high season, 9–8 in the slow season.

Other tourist information offices affiliated with the municipality of San Juan are located in the city hall, Alcaldía (✉ ☎ 787/724–7171 ext. 2391), on the Plaza de Armas in Old San Juan, and in a small booth at Playita Condado (✉ ☎ 787/740–9270), in front of the Condado Plaza Hotel on Avenida Ashford in Condado. Both offices are open weekdays 8–4.

From North America, you can call the Puerto Rico Tourism Company in New York toll-free at ☎ 800/223–6530. Other branches: ✉ 3575 West Cahuenga Boulevard, Suite 560, Los Angeles, CA 90068, ☎ 213/874–5991 and 901 Ponce de León Boulevard, Suite 601, Coral Gables, FL 33134, ☎ 305/445–9112.

3 EASTERN PUERTO RICO, VIEQUES, AND CULEBRA

To slide out of metropolitan San Juan and head east is to enter a Puerto Rico of the past, before the island boasted high-rises and glittery casinos. The cities of eastern Puerto Rico are, of course, developed; some are thriving industrial centers. But the scenery between them is timeless. Windswept bluffs, shallow surfless beaches, a verdant tropical rain forest, rocky shorelines, and lush groves of swaying coconut palms are just some of the delights. Offshore, on the quiet islands of Vieques and Culebra, are a bay illuminated by sea organisms that sparkle at night and some of the region's loveliest beaches, solitary strands of powdery white sand lapped by crystalline water.

By Mary A.
Dempsey

T HE EASTERN SIDE OF PUERTO RICO is filled with superlatives. From 28,000-acre El Yunque, the only tropical rain forest in the U.S. National Forest system, to Las Cabezas de San Juan Nature Reserve with its seven ecosystems, to the rare and amazing Bioluminescent Bay in Vieques, this region presents you with an abundance of natural beauty. Even the area's towns share in it: Loíza is tucked among lush coconut groves, Río Grande sits on the island's only navigable river, and Naguabo overlooks what used to be huge expanses of sugarcane fields. Along the eastern coast, rolling green hills cascade down to the ocean.

Eastern Puerto Rico also beckons sun and sea worshippers. Culebra's stunning beaches are isolated havens, as are those of nearby Vieques. Perched on the edge of the Atlantic, Fajardo serves as a jumping-off point for diving, fishing, and catamaran excursions. Luquillo offers a fully equipped family beach with special facilities that allow wheelchair users to enter the sea.

You can golf, go horseback riding, hike marked trails, plunge into water sports, and rent bikes throughout the area. And those interested in the history and culture of Puerto Rico can explore the island's African heritage—particularly strongly felt in Loíza—the impact of fishing on the culture of oceanside communities such as Fajardo, and the sugar-plantation legacy of the outer islands, including the influence of French settlers.

Finally, if you're looking to get away from it all and want a trip that's neatly packaged, eastern Puerto Rico has three of the island's top resorts: Wyndham El Conquistador, Rio Mar, and Palmas del Mar. These large and largely self-contained complexes have extensive facilities and many luxury services. They succeed in fulfilling many people's definition of "the good life."

Pleasures and Pastimes

Beaches

Puerto Rico's Atlantic east coast is edged with sandy, palm-lined shores as well as some dramatic rugged stretches of beach. Some of these beaches are quiet, isolated escapes. Others, such as Luquillo and the Hucares beach, are jammed with water-loving families, especially on weekends and during the Easter holidays. Some of the most attractive strands in all of Puerto Rico are found on the outer islands of Culebra and Vieques.

Golf

There's something to be said for standing on the tee with a rolling, palm-tree-lined fairway in front of you and a view of the ocean at your back. And then there are the ducks, iguanas, and pelicans that congregate among the mangroves near some holes. That's what you get in eastern Puerto Rico, where a majority of the island's golf courses are found (at press time, another was on the drawing board in Vieques). The Arthur Hills–designed course at El Conquistador Resort and Country Club is one of the top ranked in the region. The Palmas del Mar resort's Flamboyan course, designed by Rees Jones and built in 1983, also gets rave reviews. An old-time favorite is the Bahia Beach Plantation course, developed on the beachfront property that once was home to a coconut plantation.

Nature

Tree frogs, the rare Puerto Rican parrot, wild horses roaming the beaches of Culebra, tiny sea creatures that appear to light up in the water, and coral reefs rife with tropical fish are just the beginning of the list of nature's offerings in eastern Puerto Rico. A lush and varied landscape, which includes bluffs, rain forest, bays, and even arid terrain, proves a dramatic backdrop for encounters with exotic flora and fauna.

Dining

Puerto Ricans are lovers of sybaritic pleasures, and that includes food. On the eastern edge of the island you'll find the same international and Continental cuisine as in the San Juan area, but you'll also find more authentically native food. That includes savory seafood, the deep-fried snacks (often stuffed with meat or fish) known collectively as *frituras,* and numerous dishes laced with coconut. That's not to say that the Italian and Chinese cuisine found at the resorts or the Nuevo Latino fare or even the pub grub available in the area isn't all worthwhile. But if you're eager to try the unusual blend of European, Native American, and African traditions that forms the basis of traditional Puerto Rican food, you should try it here. Plantains appear as the starring ingredient in hearty *mofongo,* a seafood-stuffed dish, or as *tostones* (fried plantain chips). Fresh fish is commonly prepared with tomatoes, onions, garlic, or some combination of the three. Desserts explode with exotic fruit flavors, including coconut, passion fruit, mango, guava, and tamarind.

Puerto Ricans' eating habits are the same as those of mainland U.S. residents: they have breakfast, lunch, and dinner. The most notable difference is in their coffee-drinking routine. Rather than down coffee all day long, like many of their counterparts in the rest of the United States, islanders like a steaming, high-test cup of coffee in the morning and another between 2 and 4 PM. They may finish a meal with coffee, but they never drink coffee *during* a meal.

Tipping is expected in restaurants and service is most often not included in the bill. The standard tip is 15%–20%.

CATEGORY	COST*
$$$$	over $35
$$$	$25–$35
$$	$15–$25
$	under $15

*per person for an appetizer, entrée, and dessert, excluding tax, tip, and beverages

✍ *following the text of a review is your signal that the property has a Web site, where you will find details and, usually, images; for a link, visit www.fodors.com/urls.*

Lodging

The eastern side of the island was undergoing a hotel-development boom as this book went to press. Several new luxury properties were in the works on the outer islands, where once only modest guest houses (and camping) were the primary options. At the same time, the construction is expected to boost the mid-range accommodations on the mainland, where lodging has been either one extreme or the other: lavish resorts or modest inns. Currently, the east coast boasts a few government-approved *paradores,* some of the island's largest and most lavish resort hotel developments, and a few "theme" properties, including an eco-lodge.

CATEGORY	COST*
$$$$	over $150
$$$	$100–$150
$$	$50–$100
$	under $50
*All prices are for a double room in high season, excluding taxes.	

Exploring Eastern Puerto Rico

As the ocean bends around the northeastern coast of Puerto Rico, it carves high bluffs that gaze out over pounding surf, turns the coast into beaches of soft sand and palm trees, and almost magically creates a roster of ecosystems that run the range from rain forest to mangrove swamp. Lush green hills flow down toward plains that once held expanses of coconut groves (groves still encircle the town of Loíza) or were used for sugarcane plantations such as those near Naguabo and Humacao. Beautiful, gentle beaches found at Luquillo and the outer islands of Culebra and Vieques are complemented by the more rugged shores of the southeastern section of the island. The protected bay at Fajardo has become a hub of deep-sea activity. Most notable about this side of the island, however, is its precipitation-fed landscape: green is the dominant color, and not just at El Yunque rain forest.

Numbers in the text correspond to numbers in the margin and on the Eastern Puerto Rico, Vieques, and Culebra and the El Yunque maps.

Great Itineraries

IF YOU HAVE 3 DAYS

If you have just three days to explore the eastern side of the island, combine a trip to **El Yunque rain forest** ②–⑥ with a swim at nearby **Luquillo Beach** ⑧ for your first day. Then head farther east to **Reserva Natural Las Cabezas de San Juan** ⑩ with its historic lighthouse and check out Seven Seas Beach outside **Fajardo** ⑨. Don't leave without a cold drink and snack or a meal at the seafood kiosks near the beach. If there's no moon, sign up for a late-night excursion from Fajardo to the phosphorescent **Mosquito Bay** ⑫ at the outer island of **Vieques** ⑪– ⑬. Use your third day for a catamaran trip so you can snorkel among the coral reefs just off the east coast.

IF YOU HAVE 5 DAYS

Spend your first day hiking and picnicking at **El Yunque rain forest** ②– ⑥; take binoculars and you may be lucky enough to spot a rare Puerto Rican green parrot. On your second day, hit the sand and seas at **Luquillo Beach** ⑧ if you have children in tow, or the Seven Seas Beach near **Fajardo** ⑨ if you don't. At night, get a taste of salsa or Latin rock— along with some Nuevo Latino cuisine—at Caribbean Blues restaurant in Fajardo. Use your third day to hop a ferry to **Vieques** ⑪–⑬, where you can lounge on a nearly deserted beach and drink rum cocktails at sunset. In the evening, visit **Mosquito Bay** ⑫—also known as Phosphorescent Bay or Bioluminescent Bay—aboard a nonpolluting boat and swim with the sparkling dinoflagellates. On the fourth day, rent a bike and pedal around Vieques to visit the old Spanish fort, the shops, or even the lighthouse. Watch for the so-called "green flash" as the sun goes down, then head to Bananas to join the rest of the evening crowd for a cold beer and conversation. Take the ferry back to Fajardo on your fifth day.

IF YOU HAVE 7 DAYS

Head straight to **Fajardo** ⑨ and begin your exploring on the outer islands. On the first day, hop the ferry to **Vieques** ⑪–⑬, lounge at one of its gorgeous beaches, and use the evening to visit **Mosquito Bay** ⑫ and the glittery sea creatures that seem to light up when the water is moved. Use your second day to get a good look at the island, which has an old fort dating from the Spanish conquest and a restored lighthouse. Indulge in a savory meal at Café Blu and finish the evening under the stars with a snifter of aged Puerto Rican rum. On the third day, jump on the ferry to sister island **Culebra** and visit stunning **Flamenco Beach.** (Walk down the beach until you spot the abandoned military tank.) On the fourth day, go snorkeling or diving. Head back to Fajardo on the ferry the next day; if there's time, visit **Las Cabezas de San Juan Nature Reserve** ⑩. Use your sixth day to make an early trip to **El Yunque** ②–⑥, then drive farther south along the coast to **Naguabo** ⑮ and explore the waterside development at **Hucares** (a good place to grab a fresh-from-the-ocean lunch). Finish your trip at the posh Palmas del Mar resort outside **Humacao** ⑯.

When to Tour

Puerto Rico's high season begins December 15 and runs through April 15, but the east coast tends to be less in demand than the metropolitan San Juan area, so anytime is fine for a visit. (Keep in mind, however, that hurricane season runs from June to October.) Prices go down somewhat after high season.

The east coast of Puerto Rico and the off-islands are perfect for travelers who prefer abandoned beaches and nature reserves over casinos and crowds—except at Easter time. During the Easter holiday, Puerto Ricans traditionally flock to the seaside. The beaches of Vieques and Culebra become crowded with sun lovers, merrymakers, and campers. Luquillo Beach also is jammed.

To get a real feel for the history and culture of the coastal communities on the east side of Puerto Rico, try to plan your visit around at least one local festival. While festivals mean bigger crowds, they also offer a peek at the lively side of Puerto Rican life. Make reservations well in advance if you're visiting a community during any of its festival days.

THE NORTHEAST AND EL YUNQUE

It takes less than an hour, traveling east from San Juan, to escape from the urban hubbub on peaceful palm-lined roads interrupted at intervals by dramatic views of the ocean. The northeastern corner of the island may have an "away from it all" flavor, but it is not off the beaten track: Puerto Ricans flock here, especially on weekends, for the beaches, the rain forest, and the ferries from Fajardo. This is also a region especially rich in both ecological and cultural assets.

The first major town you'll encounter east of San Juan is Loíza, where residents proudly claim their African heritage and where one of the island's most renowned mask-makers lives. Farther southeast and inland is bustling Río Grande, a community that grew by virtue of its location beside the island's only navigable river. The river rises within El Yunque, the local name for the Caribbean National Forest, a sprawling blanket of green covering a mountainous region south of Río Grande. In the rain forest you'll find an explosion of flora and fauna, including the endangered Puerto Rican green parrot. Back on the coast, Luquillo maintains one of the most unusual public beaches on the island. Not only does the Luquillo Beach offer a full range of services—from cocktails and snacks sold at little kiosks to dressing rooms and showers—but the lovely palm-lined stretch of sand has facilities that permit wheelchair users to play in the ocean.

Southeast of Luquillo sits Las Cabezas de San Juan Nature Reserve, with its restored lighthouse and variety of ecosystems. Anchoring the east coast of the island is Fajardo, a fishing town that has grown into a lively port city with the island's largest marina, a ferry service to the outer islands, and a string of offshore cays. Fajardo is the jumping-off point for deep-sea water sports: catamarans take tourists on day trips to snorkel, other craft chug out of the marinas ready for a day of fishing, and lovely yachts of Caribbean explorers move in and out of the bay to refuel and stock up on supplies.

Loíza

❶ *31 km (19 mi) east of San Juan.*

Loíza, a coastal town of 30,000 set amid stunning coconut groves, is known for its colorful festivals and its respect for tradition. Early on the area was largely undeveloped because the marshy land bred mosquitoes, but it became a haven for the descendants of blacks who had been brought to the island under bondage. Today it's a community steeped in its African heritage.

The drive from San Juan to this seaside town is lovely. Leaving the island's capital, the urban highway suddenly becomes a curving road banked by swaying palms and lush foliage. (Part of the area is designated as the Piñones State Forest.) Occasionally the ocean pops into view, white surf slapping against the shore. You'll see locals strolling along the shoulder of the road with strings of coconuts dangling from their hands, and you'll often encounter outdoor kiosks serving cold coconut juice and fried snacks. Clusters of small pastel-color wooden houses, sometimes elevated on short stilts, appear at intervals along the drive.

After slavery brought Africans to the Caribbean, Loíza emerged as a center for the *bomba,* a dance traced to the Kongo people of West Africa. Sometimes wearing a flouncy white dress, the woman in a dancing couple moves in a relatively fixed pattern of steps while her partner improvises to the drumbeat. The music is provided by a lead singer, a choir, and group of musicians playing maracas, two wooden sticks called *fua* that are smacked against a hard surface, two low-sounding barrel-shape drums called *buleadores,* and a higher-pitched drum called a *subidor.* The singer and the choir engage in a call-and-response song recounting a local story or event as the dancers sway to the music.

Bomba is one element of the revelries you'll find at the annual Festival de Santiago Apóstol (St. James the Apostle Festival), held every July. During the exuberant celebrations, which go on for 10 days late in the month, masked and costumed Loizanos combine religious processions—to a spot where a statue of the Virgin Mary is said to have been found under a tree many generations ago—with parades, fireworks, and other secular merrymaking. Each year, a family in the community is selected to "host" the festival. Family members erect an elaborate home altar for the Mary statue and provide refreshments for the townspeople who gather at their home on festival days.

Despite the festivities, St. James is not the patron saint of Loíza. St. Patrick holds that distinction, and the cathedral is dedicated to him. Lively St. Patrick's Day festivities occur if the holiday falls on a weekend. Otherwise, local residents save their energy for the bigger Santiago Apóstol fiesta.

Loíza is not a tourist-oriented community, although its small downtown has been renovated and is pleasant (albeit slowly filling with the

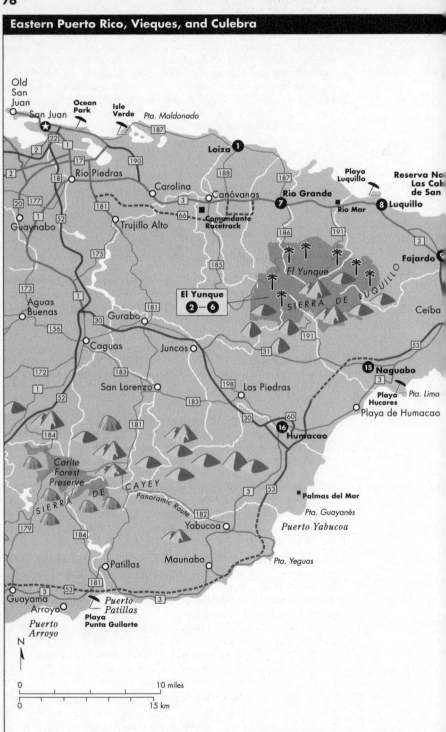

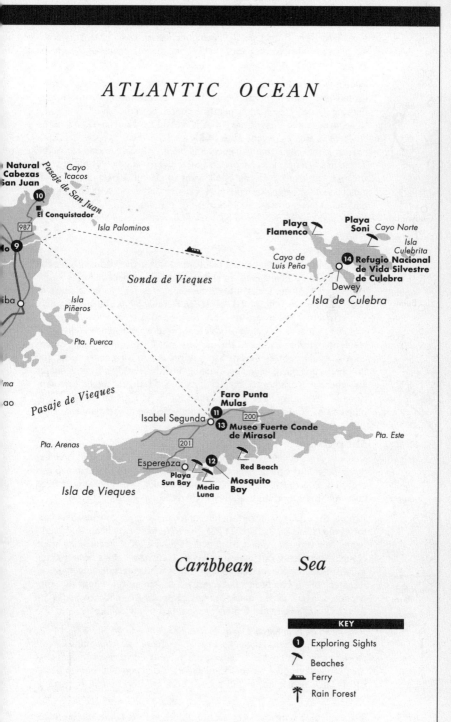

ATLANTIC OCEAN

Natural
Cabezas
San Juan

Cayo
Icacos

10

El Conquistador

987

9

Isla Palominos

Sonda de Vieques

Isla
Piñeros

Pta. Puerca

ma

ao

Pasaje de Vieques

Pasaje de San Juan

iba

ba

Playa
Flamenco

Playa
Soni

Cayo Norte

Isla
Culebrita

Cayo de
Luis Peña

14 Refugio Nacional
de Vida Silvestre
de Culebra

Dewey

Isla de Culebra

Faro Punta
Mulas

Isabel Segunda

11

13 Museo Fuerte Conde
de Mirasol

200

Pta. Este

Pta. Arenas

201

Esperanza

12

Red Beach

Playa
Sun Bay

Media
Luna

Mosquito
Bay

Isla de Vieques

Caribbean   Sea

KEY

1 Exploring Sights

Beaches

Ferry

Rain Forest

fast-food restaurants and chain-store outlets ubiquitous to Puerto Rico). Still, even when it's not festival time, the area is worth a stop for the scenery and to see the crafts, including museum-quality festival masks made from coconut shells. Loizanos are proud of their town and welcome visitors.

Iglésia de San Patricio (St. Patrick's Church) is a national historic monument, with some portions of the structure dating from 1645—making it one of the oldest operating churches on the island. It is home to a statue of the Virgin Mary that is worshipped during the Santiago Apóstol festivities. A side altar holds a statue of St. Patrick, the city's patron saint. Note that the church is open only on Sunday for mass. There are brief periods before and after the mass when you can walk through the church (if you don't want to attend the service), but regardless of whether you take part, be sure to behave with the respect and discretion appropriate to a place of worship. ⊠ *10 Calle Espíritu Santo, Loiza,* ☎ *787/876–2229.* 🎟 *Free.* ☉ *Open to the public only during 10 AM Sunday mass.*

The Arts
While Loizanos fiercely cling to old traditions, they do not have the facilities—such as museums or cultural centers—where visitors can get an overview of the community's customs. One way to get a sense of the culture is through **Ballet Folklórico Hermanos Ayala.** Bomba may be entrenched in Loíza today, but its modern renaissance dates only to 1961, when a television producer showed up in town searching for residents who remembered the dance form. In response, mask-maker Castor Ayala put together this folk music group (originally called the Bomberos de Loíza), which performs around the island and, occasionally, elsewhere in Latin America. After Ayala's death, succeeding generations of his family have taken up the torch. The group has no headquarters or studio, but you can get its schedule at **Artesanías Castor Ayala** (☞ Shopping, *below*).

Shopping
Loíza is not known as a shopping haven by any means, but it offers you a peek at the often African-linked crafts that are particular to this region of Puerto Rico. Detailed coconut masks, craft items made from coconut shells, and high-quality artwork are available.

Among the offerings at the fabulous mask-makers' shop **Artesanías Castor Ayala** (⊠ Rte. 187, Km 6.6, ☎ 787/876–1130) are beautifully elaborate coconut-shell masks dubbed "Mona Lisas" because of their elongated smiles. Craftsman Raul Ayala Carrasquillo has been making museum-quality festival masks for more than 40 years, following in the footsteps of his late father, the esteemed craftsman for whom the store is named. Many of the masks, ranging in price from $50 to $350, are used in Loíza's festivals. Others are snapped up by collectors.

At **Estúdio de Arte Samuel Lind** (⊠ Rte. 187, Km 6.6, ☎ 787/876–1494), down a short, dusty lane across the street from the Artesanías Castor Ayala, artist Samuel Lind sculpts, paints, and silk-screens images that are quintessentially Loizano. Lind's work is displayed in the two floors of his latticework studio. Of special note are his colorful folk-tradition posters.

En Route   Try your luck with the exactas and quinielas at **El Comandante Racetrack,** the largest thoroughbred horse-racing track in the Caribbean. Following Route 951 south of Loíza to Route 3, then west, brings you to the racetrack in Canóvanas (Rte. 3, Km 15.3; 787/724–6060). Post time is 2:15 PM on Monday, Wednesday through Friday, Sunday, and holidays. The last race (there are seven or eight daily, up to nine on

Sunday) is usually before 6 PM. A restaurant and air-conditioned club-house are part of the facilities. Parking and admission to the grand-stand are free; admission to the clubhouse is $3.

El Yunque (the Caribbean National Forest)

11 km (7 mi) southeast of Río Grande; 43 km (26 mi) southeast of San Juan.

Tucked in an inland spot between Río Grande and Luquillo, on Route 191, are the 28,000 acres of verdant foliage and often rare wildlife that make up El Yunque, the only rain forest within the U.S. National Forest system. Formally known as the Caribbean National Forest, El Yunque's local name is believed to be a derivative of the Taíno word for the good spirit Yukiyu, although some people say it comes from the Spanish word for "anvil" because some of the rain forest's peaks have snub shapes. Either way, this green refuge is a must-see stop for anyone visiting Puerto Rico.

In 1903, the United States officially designated part of what is now El Yunque as the Luquillo Forest Reserve. In 1907 it was renamed Luquillo National Forest and, 28 years later, it was given its current name.

Rising up to 3,500 ft above sea level, this protected area did not gain its "rain forest" designation for nothing: more than 100 billion gallons of precipitation fall over it annually, spawning fields of oversized wild impatiens and ferns, 240 tree species, orchids, vines, rushing streams, and cascading waterfalls such as La Coca and La Mina. Although plant life seems to dominate, the forest bursts with fauna as well. In the evening, the trees erupt in song as millions of inch-long *coquís* (tree frogs) begin their calls. El Yunque is also home to the cotorra, the endangered green parrot of Puerto Rico, and 67 other types of birds.

Tucked among the abundance of nature are 13 hiking trails, many of them easy to walk and less than a mile long; the trails of El Yunque are well maintained but designed for foot travel only. Although overnight camping is not permitted, there are picnic areas with tables under covered shelters, bathrooms, and a touring road for if you want to see the sights from your car. You can wander through the interactive exhibits at El Portal Visitors Center, climb the observation tower at Yokahu, take a refreshing dip in the natural pool at La Mina Falls, and hike to one of many quiet, peaceful areas.

Many of the trailheads, observation points, marked waterfalls, and other highlights of El Yunque lie along Route 191. Las Cabezas Observation Point sits at Km 7.8, La Coca Falls lies just past Km 8.1, and Yokahu Tower sits at Km 8.9. When weather (including hurricanes and mudslides) has not closed portions of the road, you can drive straight from the rain forest entrance to Km 13, the base of El Yunque Peak.

There is plenty to discover at El Yunque, so arrive early and plan to stay the entire day if your schedule permits. (The recreation areas are open from 7:30 AM to 6 PM daily except at Christmas.) Bring water, sunscreen, and bug spray; wear comfortable clothes, a hat or visor for the sun, and good walking shoes. Remember that this is a rain forest, so be prepared for rain. And binoculars are always a good idea: you may be one of the lucky visitors who spots a rare green parrot.

You'll be charged an admission fee for El Portal Information Center ☞ *below*, but the rest of the park, including the other information centers, is free.

El Yunque (Caribbean National Forest)

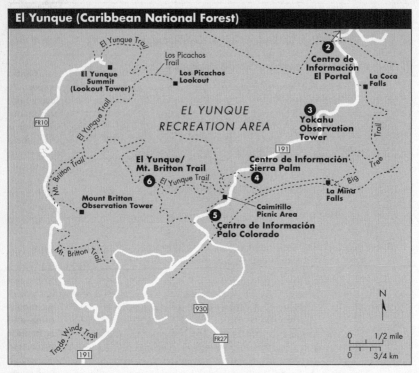

★ ❷ A lizard's tongue darts across three video screens, a beautiful forest erupts in flames, a tiny seedling pushes from the ground and begins to flourish in the lush tropical rain forest. Before you begin driving or hiking through El Yunque, stop at **Centro de Información El Portal,** a marvelous information center near the northern park entrance along Route 191, and take a look at its high-tech interactive displays. The airy complex is made up of three pavilions with exhibits and films explaining forests in general and El Yunque in particular. Test your sense of smell at an exhibit on forest products, then see the beautiful multiscreen video identifying the threats to rain forests around the globe. Listen to actor Jimmy Smits (who is part Puerto Rican) narrate a movie on El Yunque, then see how much you've learned at a question-and-answer display. Although El Yunque has no handicapped-accessible trails as yet (a braille trail with wheelchair access is on the drawing board), El Portal is fully accessible. This multimillion-dollar information center is also a good place to find out if there are special ranger-sponsored activities the day you visit, to obtain maps and conditions on hiking trails, and to buy souvenirs. If you've forgotten film for your camera, soft drinks, or snacks, you can also get these at the center. All exhibits and materials are bilingual (English and Spanish). ⊠ *Rte. 191, Km 4.3 (just off Hwy. 3),* ☎ *787/888–1880.* ☜ *$3 (to entire park for full day).* ⊙ *Daily 9–5; closed Christmas Day.*

❸ Take your camera with you as you begin climbing the circular stairway that goes to the top of **Yokahu Observation Tower,** which looks like a castle turret rising from a little hill along the roadside. Even if you peek out the windows on your way up for a view of the rain forest from different directions, you won't be prepared for the magnificence of the panoramic vista awaiting you at the top of the tower. You'll see thousand-year-old trees, exotic flowers in brilliant blues and reds and pinks, and birds in flight overhead. Postcards and books on El

Yunque are sold in the small kiosk at the base of the tower. The parking lot beside the tower has rest rooms. ⊠ *Rte. 191, Km 8.9,* ☎ *no phone.* ▣ *No additional admission (other than vehicle entrance tag).* ⊙ *Daily 7:30–6.*

❹ Just past the halfway point along Route 191 in the rain forest, **Centro de Información Sierra Palm** makes a good stopping place—especially for trail updates. El Yunque's steep slopes, unstable wet soil, heavy rainfall, and exuberant plant life result in the need for intensive trail maintenance; some trails must be cleared and cleaned at least twice a year to keep them open. Forest rangers at this site staff a little office where they provide information on trail closures, the condition of open trails, what flora and fauna you should be on the lookout for, and any special activities planned that day. There are rest rooms and water fountains by the parking lot. This is a good area to leave the car to hike or to pull out your cooler and amble down a wide path where you'll find picnic tables. ⊠ *Rte. 191, Km 11.6,* ☎ *no phone.* ▣ *No additional admission (other than vehicle entrance tag).* ⊙ *Daily 7:30–6.*

❺ **Centro de Información Palo Colorado** is home to Forest Adventure Tours, a program that gives you the opportunity to hike a short trail with a guide. (Reservations for the guided tours are required, and there is a fee.) This is also the gateway to some of the more challenging trails in the forest, including the Mt. Britton trail to the peak of El Yunque mountain. There is a picnic area near the center, as well as rest rooms and parking. The trails that lead off from this information center include the easy Baño del Oro Trail that starts at a swimming pool constructed in the 1930s (swimming is not permitted) and loops 1½ km (1 mi) through an area dubbed Palm Forest. The even shorter El Caimitillo Trail starts at the same place and runs for about 1 km (½ mi). Palo Colorado, the red-barked tree for which the center is named and in which the endangered green parrot nests, dominates the forest here. ⊠ *Rte. 191, Km 11.9,* ☎ *787/888–5646.* ▣ *Guided trail hike $5.* ⊙ *Daily 8–5.*

❻ **El Yunque/Mt. Britton Trail.** Beginning at the Palo Colorado Visitor Center, this asphalt trail (which later turns to gravel) leads to El Yunque Peak, 3,496 ft above sea level. Just after the start of the trail is the Palo Colorado Stream, followed by a left-hand detour to the old concrete pool at the end of the Baño del Oro Trail. Also on El Yunque Trail, another branch-off leads to the Caimitillo Picnic Area. The trails here are edged by giant ferns, bamboo, and oversize pink impatiens. At a higher elevation of the trail is the Mt. Britton spur to an observation tower, a Civilian Conservation Corps project from the 1930s that resembles a castle turret. Climb the tower for a spectacular view of the rain forest. There are no poisonous snakes in the forest (or on the island as a whole), but bugs can be ferocious, so be sure to wear repellent. The El Yunque path includes some mild ascents and generally takes about three hours round-trip (unless you detour onto the side trails). Signs clearly mark each turnoff along the path, so it's virtually impossible to lose your way. ⊠ *Rte. 191, Km 12,* ☎ *no phone.* ▣ *Free.* ⊙ *Daily 7:30–6.*

Shopping

Buy a recording of the tree frog's song or a video about the endangered green parrot, pick up a coffee-table book about the rain forest, try on El Yunque T-shirts, and check out the books for eco-minded children at the large and lovely **Caribbean National Forest Gift Shop** (⊠ Rte. 191, Km 4.3, ☎ 787/888–1880). Tucked among the rain-forest gifts are other Puerto Rican items, including note cards, maps, soaps, jams, and coffee.

IN SEARCH OF THE PUERTO RICAN GREEN PARROT

THE TAÍNO INDIANS called it the *Iguaca,* Spanish speakers refer to it as the *cotorra,* and scientists know it as *Amazona Vittata.* Whatever moniker it takes, the Puerto Rican green parrot is a bird that keeps surprising scientists by its refusal to die off.

The parrot—the only one native to the island—figures on the list of the world's 10 rarest birds. Its decline has much to do with humans: development in Puerto Rico has destroyed much of its natural habitat, and there was once trafficking in the live birds and their feathers. But man is not the only factor affecting the tiny creature. Hurricanes have repeatedly obliterated its nests and habitat. The parrot is currently known to nest only in the upper levels of El Yunque and in nearby Sierra de Luquillo (Luquillo Mountain). Occasionally, lucky and observant visitors to the rain forest will spot a green parrot flying overhead or foraging in the picnicking areas.

Almost entirely green (with blue touches on the wing visible when the bird is in flight), it has a white ring around its eyes and a red band just above its beak. It's usually only about 12 inches long, and its call—a raucous squawk—does not match its delicate appearance. Green parrots, which mate for life, reproduce in February, the time of least rain in the rain forest, and build nests within tree hollows. They usually lay three or four eggs; the young are fed by both parents.

When the Spanish arrived in Puerto Rico, it is estimated that a million of the birds populated the island, as well as Vieques and Culebra. But colonization meant deforestation, and by the middle of the 19th century there was already a recorded decline in the number of birds. That heightened after the Spanish-American War, when the United States began even more development, clearing forest lands for agriculture and urban development. Parasites and rats also affected the parrot population. And until outlawed in 1940, parrot hunting was common.

The Puerto Rican green parrot was declared in danger of extinction in 1967; four years later, the population was only 19. Still, a program to breed the birds in captivity and then release them has shown marked success. Presently, more than 100 of the parrots are believed to live in El Yunque. Scientists with the U.S. Forest Service, the Puerto Rico Department of Natural Resources, the U.S. Fish and Wildlife Service, and The World Wildlife Fund continue to monitor the flock.

Río Grande

❼ *13 km (8 mi) along Rte. 187 east and south of Loíza on Rte. 3; 35 km (21 mi) east of San Juan on Rte. 3.*

This urban cluster of about 50,000 residents (at the crossroads of Routes 187 and 3) proudly calls itself "The City of El Yunque," as it's the closest community to the rain forest (and most of the rain forest reserve falls within its district borders). Two images of the rare green parrot, which makes its home in El Yunque, are found on the city's coat of arms; another parrot peeks from the town's flag.

The Río Espíritu Santo, which runs through the city, begins in the highest levels of El Yunque and carries the distinction of being the only navigable river on the island. It was the waterway used to transport lumber, sugar, and coffee from plantations in generations past, when the community was part of Loíza and home to coffee workers, sugar-plantation laborers, and lumbermen. Immigrants flocked here to take advantage of the opportunities; many of today's residents trace their families to Spain, Austria, Corsica, and Italy. In 1940, Río Grande became an independent municipality with its own name.

Tourists most often visit the city because it is the closest community to the posh Westin Río Mar resort, known for its seaside golf courses, lovely beach, and first-class restaurants.

If you have any interest in horses, family-run **Hacienda Carabali** ranch is a good place to see Puerto Rico's Paso Fino horses in action. You can even jump in the saddle yourself. Riding excursions include a one-hour jaunt along the Mameyes River, galloping along the beach or a two-hour journey into the foothills of El Yunque. When the weather is steaming, a swimming break at the river is incorporated into the itinerary. Shuttle transportation from San Juan can be arranged through the ranch. Sometimes outdoor concerts are held here. ⊠ *Rte. 992, Km 4 (at Mameyes River Bridge), Barrio Mameyes, Río Grande,* ☎ *787/ 889–5820 and 787/889–4954.* ⊠ *$45/hr to ride.* ☼ *Daily 8–5.*

Dining and Lodging

$$$ ✕ **Palio.** You'll find northern Italian cuisine at this beautifully decorated restaurant at the Westin Río Mar. Executive chef Marcus Rodriguez enlivens his dishes with aromatic spices. Try one of the seafood items. ⊠ *6000 Río Mar Blvd.,* ☎ *787/888–6000, ext. 4808. AE, MC, V. Closed Tues. No lunch.*

$$ ✕ **Café Carnival.** This lively, casual eatery is dominated by colorful carnival decor and food with a Caribbean flair. The à la carte menu offers a multitude of options, from generous salads to creole seafood dishes to one of the items for which the restaurant is best known: steak. If you've come with an big appetite, try the buffet. The restaurant is one of seven at the Westin Río Mar. ⊠ *6000 Río Mar Blvd.,* ☎ *787/888– 6000, ext. 4821. AE, MC, V. Closed Mon. No lunch.*

$$ ✕ **Las Vegas.** Puerto Rican food is the specialty at this *meson gastronómico* (a designation the government tourism company gives to restaurants that specialize in typical island food). Here that means chicken marinated in local spices, served with rice and *gandules* (pigeon peas). There is also a selection of delicious seafood dishes. ⊠ *Rte. 191, Km 1.3,* ☎ *787/887–2526. AE, MC, V.*

$$ ✕ **Villa Pesquera.** The lovely view of the Espíritu Santo River is what brings diners into this restaurant overlooking the waterway. The savory seafood is what keeps them coming back. Try the catch of the day—whatever it is, it's always a winner. This is also a sweet spot for a cocktail and an appetizer as the sun sets. ⊠ *Rte. 877, Km 6.6,* ☎ *787/887–0140. MC, V.*

$$$$ ⊞ **Westin Río Mar Beach Resort.** Opened in 1995, this $178-million complex meanders beside the ocean. The long, seven-story hotel anchors one of the island's top resorts; much of the fun is focused on the mile-long beach, lined with palm trees, which the hotel overlooks. Every room has a balcony, facing either the sea or the lush championship golf courses and the mountains. The tropical-color rooms are spacious and have luxury touches, including natural wood, Italian tile, and marble accents. The activities—from golf and water sports to biking and tennis—are a big attraction. A new collection of 59 one- and two-bedroom villas was slated to open in late 2000 to expand the facility. ⊠ *6000 Río Mar Blvd.; Box 2006, Barrio Palmer 00721,* ☎ *787/888–6000,* FAX *787/888–6204. 600 rooms, 72 suites. 7 restaurants, 4 lounges, air-conditioning, in-room data ports, in-room safes, in-room VCRs, no-smoking rooms, 3 outdoor pools, 2 golf courses, 13 tennis courts, spa, exercise room, beach, dive shop, windsurfing, boating, fishing, bicycles, shops, casino, dance club, children's programs, dry cleaning, laundry service, concierge, business services, meeting rooms, tours, car rental, airport shuttle, parking. AE, MC, V. FAP.* ✥

$$$ ⊞ **Río Grande Plantation Eco Resort.** A portion of what was a 200-acre sugarcane plantation dating from the late 1700s has been transformed into this lovely resort in the foothills of El Yunque. Two walking paths wind among the fruit trees and tropical flowers. The accommodations are primarily two-story villas with numerous amenities, including Jacuzzis, color TVs, VCRs, refrigerators, and microwaves. This is a peaceful property, often used for corporate retreats, and it prides itself on the extra attention it offers guests. ⊠ *Rte. 956, Km 4, Guzman Abajo (Box 6526, Loíza Station, Santurce, 00914),* ☎ *787/887–2779,* FAX *787/888–3239. 4 rooms, 19 villas, 1 cottage. Air-conditioning, in-room VCRs, kitchenettes, pool, hot tub, basketball, billiards, free parking. AE, MC, V. FAP.* ✥

Nightlife

The Río Grande area does not have the large numbers of nightclubs found in San Juan. However, you'll find cocktails and friendly crowds in the lounges at the Westin Río Mar and plenty of action around the gaming tables at its casino. From Caribbean stud poker and 14 blackjack tables to video poker and 150 slot machines, the Las Vegas–style **Westin Río Mar Resort Casino** (⊠ 6000 Río Mar Blvd., ☎ 787/888–6000) is hopping; if the wagers work up a thirst, the Players Bar is connected to the gaming room.

Outdoor Activities and Sports

There are a couple of notable beaches in this area—particularly Las Picúas—and local residents sometimes kayak on the Espíritu Santo River, but most of the outdoor activity here focuses on golf and the watersports center at the Westin Río Mar.

BEACHES

Las Picúas beach (Rte. 187, 2 km/1 mi north of Rte. 3), northeast of Río Grande, sits in a bay close to where the Espíritu Santo River meets the Atlantic ocean. There are no facilities here, but the water is lovely and local residents are likely to turn up on weekends. The beach borders the Berwind Country Club.

BIKING

You can rent bikes from **Iguana Watersports** (☞ Water Sports, *below*).

GOLF

The 18-hole **Bahia Beach Plantation Course** (⊠ Rte. 187, Km 4.2, ☎ 787/256–5600) skirts the north coast beaches in Río Grande. A public course, it was carved out of a long-abandoned beachfront coconut grove.

The **Berwind Country Club** (⊠ Rte. 187, Km 4.7, ☎ 787/876–3056) has an 18-hole course known for its tight fairways and demanding greens.

Part of the Westin Río Mar Beach Resort (☞ Lodging, *above*), the **Westin Río Mar Country Club** (⊠ 6000 Río Mar Blvd., Barrio Palmer, ☎ 787/888–1401) has two courses offering vistas of both El Yunque rain forest and the Atlantic Ocean. The newer River Course, designed by pro golfer Greg Norman, has challenging fairways and bunkers. The Ocean Course, with slightly wider fairways than its sister, was renovated in 1996; ducks, iguanas, and pelicans congregate in the mangroves near its fourth hole.

HORSEBACK RIDING

Hacienda Carabali, (☞ *above*) has one- and two-hour riding excursions.

TENNIS

The **Westin Río Mar Country Club** (⊠ 6000 Río Mar Blvd., Barrio Palmer, ☎ 787/888–7066) has 13 courts available, four of them lighted.

WATER SPORTS

Iguana Watersports (⊠ 6000 Río Mar Blvd., Barrio Palmer, ☎ 787/888–6000) at the Westin Río Mar rents out windsurfing equipment and sea kayaks, and can direct you to the resort's catamaran excursions desk.

Shopping

Shopping isn't a primary attraction in Río Grande, but there are opportunities to pick up local crafts or artwork.

Puerto Rican pottery, with some lovely designs inspired by the Taíno Indians, fill the shelves of **Cerámicas Los Bohio** (⊠ 65th Infantry, Km 21.7, ☎ 787/887–2620).

The picturesque **Treehouse Studio** (⊠ unmarked road off Rte. 3, ☎ 787/888–8062), not far from the rain forest, sells vibrant watercolors by Monica Laird, who also gives workshops. Call for an appointment and directions.

En Route   Puerto Ricans rarely drive from El Yunque or Río Grande to Luquillo without a stop at the seafood kiosks (known locally as *friquitines*) lining Highway 3 just west of the turnoff for the beach. These rustic dining spots aren't much to look at, but they're fun and funky places to stop for a plate of fresh fried fish (head and tail still attached) and a cold drink. Finger foods include conch salad and fritters (usually codfish or corn). All the kiosks offer pretty much the same fare—some have larger seating areas than others. A local favorite is **Monelly #55.** You'll find the kiosks busy all day, serving passing truckers, suited businessmen from the area, and sand-covered families back from a morning or afternoon at the beach in Luquillo.

Luquillo

❽ *13 km (8 mi) northeast of Río Grande; 45 km (28 mi) east of San Juan.*

Known as the "Sun Capital" of Puerto Rico, Luquillo has one of the prettiest, best-equipped family beaches on the island. It is also a community where old-time fishing traditions are respected. On the east end of Luquillo Beach, past the guarded swimming area, you can watch fishermen launch small boats and drop nets in the open stretches between coral reefs.

Like many other Puerto Rican towns, Luquillo has its signature festival, in this case the Festival de Platos Tipicos (Festival of Typical Dishes), a late-November culinary event that revolves around one main ingredient: coconut. During the festivities, many of the 18,000 residents of the community—along with other islanders and tourists—gather at the lovely main square to try a range of taste treats rich with coconut or coconut milk. There's also plenty of free entertainment, including folk shows, troubadour contests, and live salsa music.

Dining and Lodging

Gastronomy is an important part of Luquillo culture, but the best of it is usually found at the dinner tables of private homes rather than in restaurants. Some local restaurants, however, deftly employ the area's favorite ingredient, coconut, offering everything from chilled coconut water to coconut pastries and sweets. Seafood is also likely to be a winner.

$$$ ✕ **Chef Wayne.** Chef Wayne Michaelson, who has worked in kitchens across the island, has put together an eclectic menu for his own establishment, featuring such entrées as Cajun-style chicken breast, grilled Caribbean lobster, and filet mignon. Set in a large white house surrounded by rain forest, the restaurant's main dining room is decorated in a Western theme. You can also eat outside, at one of a few tables on a front balcony that looks out toward the ocean, or on a back balcony facing the forest. Note that Chef Wayne is located on a winding, unmarked road off Route 992. You should call ahead for directions or consult with someone at your hotel who knows the way. ⊠ *Rte. 992,* ☎ *787/889–1962 or 787/889–2911. MC, V. Closed Tues. No lunch Fri.*

$$ ✕ **Brass Cactus Bar & Grill.** This cantina offers pub grub with a southwestern flair. The ribs and burgers melt in your mouth, and the crispy fries come in generous helpings. Buffalo wings, poppers (stuffed hot peppers), chicken, and steak are also mainstays. Nearly everything is washed down with beer. The multiple televisions broadcast the latest sporting events, and on the weekend live music usually replaces the jukebox. ⊠ *Rte. 3, Complejo Turistico Condominio,* ☎ *787/889–5735. AE, MC, V.*

$ ✕ **Victor's Place.** Housed in a small blue building right on the main downtown plaza, this local institution has been serving up Puerto Rican specialties for more than six decades. Main dishes such as traditionally prepared seafood and steaks come with generous servings of beans, rice, and tostones. The atmosphere is casual. ⊠ *2 Jesús T. Piñero,* ☎ *787/889–5705. Reservations not accepted. MC, V.*

$$$ ⊡ **Luquillo Beach Inn.** This five-story, white-and-pink hotel was built in 1991 and renovated in 1999. It's within walking distance of the public beach and caters to families—children stay free with their parents. The one- or two-bedroom suites have sofa beds, kitchenettes, and living rooms equipped with televisions and stereos; the largest sleep up to six people. It's a good jumping off point for visits to El Yunque. Transportation (for about $45) can be arranged from San Juan. ⊠ *701 Calle Ocean Dr., 00773,* ☎ *787/889–1063,* FAX *787/889–1966. 30 suites. Bar, room service, air-conditioning, fans, in-room VCRs, kitchenettes, pool, outdoor hot tub, dry cleaning, laundry service, business services, free parking. AE, MC, V. FAP.*

$$ ⊡ **Grateful Bed & Breakfast.** This simple, funky guest house sits in the foothills of the Luquillo mountains and offers an unusual formula for determining the cost of overnight stays: the rooms are "officially" free of charge, but you pay for your meals (breakfast is complimentary) and the activities you do. That means anything from canoe trips to horseback outings to nature hikes. (Most guests end up with bills in the range of $50–$90 per night.) A vague Grateful Dead theme runs through the establishment, mostly in the music room jammed with Dead collectibles and tapes. ⊠ *Off Rte. 3, down unmarked road beside El Rancho bar,*

ONE LAST TRAVEL TIP:

Pack an easy way to reach the world.

Wherever you travel, the MCI WorldCom Card℠ is the easiest way to stay in touch. You can use it to call to and from more than 125 countries worldwide. And you can earn bonus miles every time you use your card. So go ahead, travel the world. MCI WorldCom℠ makes it even more rewarding. For additional access codes, visit **www.wcom.com/worldphone**.

MCI WORLDCOM.

EASY TO CALL WORLDWIDE

1. Just dial the WorldPhone® access number of the country you're calling from.

2. Dial or give the operator your MCI WorldCom Card number.

3. Dial or give the number you're calling.

Aruba (A) ⁙	800-888-8
Australia ◆	1-800-881-100
Bahamas ⁙	1-800-888-8000
Barbados (A) ⁙	1-800-888-8000
Bermuda ⁙	1-800-888-8000
British Virgin Islands (A) ⁙	1-800-888-8000
Canada	1-800-888-8000
Costa Rica (A) ◆	0800-012-2222
New Zealand	000-912
Puerto Rico	1-800-888-8000
United States	1-800-888-8000
U.S. Virgin Islands	1-800-888-8000

(A) Calls back to U.S. only.   ⁙ Limited availability.   ◆ Public phones may require deposit of coin or phone card for dial tone.

EARN FREQUENT FLIER MILES

Limit of one bonus program per customer. All airline program rules and conditions apply. © 2000 WorldCom, Inc. All Rights Reserved. The names, logos, and taglines identifying WorldCom's products and services are proprietary marks of WorldCom, Inc. or its subsidiaries. All third party marks are the proprietary marks of their respective owners.

© 2000 Visa U.S.A. Inc.

Paris, France.

Paris, Texas.

When it Comes to Getting
Cash at an ATM,

Same Thing.

Whether you're in Yosemite or Yemen, using your Visa® card or ATM card with the PLUS symbol is the easiest and most convenient way to get cash. Even if your bank is in Minneapolis and you're in Miami, Visa/PLUS ATMs make getting cash so easy, you'll feel right at home. After all, Visa/PLUS ATMs are open 24 hours a day, 7 days a week, rain or shine. And if you need help finding one of Visa's 627,000 ATMs in 127 countries worldwide, visit **visa.com/pd/atm**. We'll make finding an ATM as easy as finding the Eiffel Tower, the Pyramids or even the Grand Canyon.

It's Everywhere You Want To Be.®

then to the left, 00773, ☎ 787/889–4919, 6 rooms. Dining room, hiking, horseback riding, free parking. MC, V. FAP.

Outdoor Activities and Sports

Outdoor activity in Luquillo is dominated by the beach; this is a great area for water sports.

BEACHES

★ Gentle, shallow waters lap the edges of **Balneario de Luquillo** (✉ Rte. 3, Km 35.4, ☎ 787/889–4329 or 787/889–5871), a full-service public beach open daily 9–5. It's a magnet for families and reportedly one of the most-photographed stretches of palm-lined sand on the island. Dressing rooms and rest rooms, staffed lifeguard stations, guarded parking, food stands, picnic areas, and even cocktail kiosks make this Puerto Rico's best-equipped spot for a day at the beach. But the most distinctive aspect of the beach is its *Mar Sin Barreras* (Sea Without Barriers) facility. A low-sloped ramp leading directly into the water allows wheelchair users to take a dip in the ocean. Admission is $2 per car.

Playa La Pared (✉ Luquillo Beach Blvd.), literally "The Wall Beach," is a surfer haunt. Numerous local surfing competitions are held here throughout the year, and several surfing shops are close by just in case you need a wet suit or a wax for your board. The waves here are medium-range.

Waving palm trees and fishing boats add charm to the smaller, less crowded **Playa Costa Azul** (✉ Luquillo Beach Blvd. at Ocean Dr., Luquillo), although the ugly residential buildings along the beach make an unattractive backdrop. The water here is good for swimming, but there are no facilities.

WATER SPORTS

Divers' Outlet (✉ 38 Fernández Garcia, ☎ 787/889–5721 or 888/746–3483) is a full-service dive shop. It offers PADI certification, rents equipment, and can arrange scuba outings.

Shopping

La Selva Surf (✉ 250 Fernández Garcia, ☎ 787/889–6205), two blocks from La Pared Beach, has anything a surfer could need, including news about current surfing conditions; it also sells sunglasses, T-shirts, skateboards, sandals, watches, bathing suits, and other necessities for those who want to spend a day on the beach.

Fajardo

 11 km (7 mi) southeast of Luquillo; 55 km (34 mi) southeast of San Juan.

Fajardo, founded in 1772, has historical notoriety as a port where pirates stocked up on supplies. It later developed into a fishing community and an area where sugarcane flourished. (There are still some cane fields on the fringes of the city.) In recent times it has become a jumping-off point for the yachts that use its marinas, the divers who explore its offshore islets, and for the visitors who take day excursions on catamarans or travel—by ferry or plane—to the peaceful off-islands of Culebra and Vieques. With the most significant docking facilities on the east side of the island, Fajardo is a bustling city of 37,000—so bustling, in fact, that the downtown is often congested and difficult to navigate.

⑩ **Reserva Natural Las Cabezas de San Juan,** north of Fajardo, is a 316-acre nature reserve, situated on a headland and owned and managed by the nonprofit Conservation Trust of Puerto Rico. You ride in open-air trolleys and wander down boardwalks through seven separate ecosystems, including lagoons, mangrove swamps, and dry-forest areas. Green iguanas skitter across paths and nature guides identify other endangered species. You can take a half-hour hike down a wooden walkway around the mangrove-lined Laguna Grande, where bioluminescent microorganisms glow at night. The beautifully restored Fajardo lighthouse sits within the reserve. Its Spanish colonial tower has been in operation since 1882, making it the second-oldest lighthouse in Puerto Rico, and it's currently used for scientific research. The first floor houses ecological displays; a winding staircase leads to its observation deck and a spectacular view of the rain forest and the offshore islands. The lighthouse is the final stop on the reserve's mandatory tour—reservations are required. There is only limited wheelchair access. ⊠ *Rte. 987 near Las Croabas*, ☎ *787/722–5882, 787/860–2560.* ➳ *$5.* ☉ *Fri.–Sun.; groups only Wed. and Thurs. Guided tours are required: tours in Spanish at 9:30, 10, and 2; English tours at 2.*

Puerto del Rey Marina, home to 750 ships, is the largest marina in the Caribbean as well as one of the newest in Puerto Rico. It's the place to catch a catamaran, hook up with a scuba-diving group, or charter a fishing boat. The marina has several restaurants and boating-supply stores. Boat trips to Vieques's Bioluminescent Bay can be arranged here. ⊠ *Rte. 3, Km 51.2,* ☎ *787/860–1000.* ➳ *Free.* ☉ *Daily.*

Dining and Lodging

Much of the best food in Fajardo comes from the sea. Just a few miles past the Reserva Las Cabezas de San Juan is the fishing area known as Las Croabas, where people go for seafood snacks sold along the waterfront, including fish empanadillas (deep-fried turnovers).

$$$$ ✕ **Cassave.** This elegant restaurant at El Conquistador Resort specializes in Caribbean Rim foods. That means pork and chicken combined with hints of tropical-fruit flavors, seafood laced with ginger and coconut, and presentation that makes each dish a work of art. ⊠ *Rte. 987, Km 3.4,* ☎ *787/863–1000. Reservations essential. AE, MC, V. No lunch.*

$$$ ✕ **La Fontanella.** The heaven-kissed Portobello mushroom appetizer
★ sautéed in oil and garlic may seem like the highlight of the menu, but once you move on to other courses you'll realize it's just the beginning. This Sicilian restaurant has a marvelous eggplant parmigiana and a rich *risotto con pesce,* along with with a number of savory pasta and chicken dishes. Make sure to leave room for dessert: the chocolate-amaretto cake is to die for. ⊠ *Rte. 987, Km 2.4,* ☎ *787/860–2480. Reservations essential. AE, MC, V. Closed Mon. No lunch.*

$$$ ✕ **Ristorante Otello.** You can dine inside, enveloped in the romance of soft light, or slide outside to the terrace for a breezy meal under the stars at this northern Italian restaurant, one of the many eateries at Wyndham El Conquistador Resort and Country Club. Start with the minestrone—it's a guaranteed winner—and follow it with one of the pasta dishes. ⊠ *Rte. 987, Km 3.4,* ☎ *787/860–0555. AE, MC, V. No lunch.*

$$ ✕ **A La Banda.** At this waterside eatery you can sit in a dining room with nautical decor or on a terrace overlooking the marina. Steaks and poultry figure on the menu, but the seafood is where the kitchen excels. ⊠ *Puerto del Rey Marina, Rte. 3, Km 51.2,* ☎ *787/860–9162. MC, V.*

$$ ✕ **Anchor's Inn.** Seafood is the specialty at this spot, one of the government-designated *mesones gastronómicos.* Clever maritime decor and superb cooking have made it a local favorite; the convenient location just down the road from El Conquistador Resort makes it a lure for tourists. Try the *chillo entero* (fried whole red snapper) or the paella. ⊠ *Rte. 987, Km 2.7, Villas Las Croabas,* ☎ *787/863–7200. Reservations not accepted.. AE, MC, V. Closed Tues.*

$$ ✕ **Rosa's Sea Food.** A meson gastronómico, this restaurant—despite its name—is a good spot for steak and chicken prepared with traditional Puerto Rican spices. The seafood is always a safe bet, too. ⊠ *Rte. 195, Tablazo 536,* ☎ *787/863-0213. Reservations not accepted. AE, MC, V.*

$ ✕ **Sardinera.** If you've worked up a hunger at Seven Seas Beach, head over to neighboring Calle Croabas. This little eatery sits among the collection of seafood kiosks lining the road and offers a rich selection of Puerto Rican *pastelitos,* deep-fried turnovers stuffed with crab, shrimp, or lobster. You can also order a range of other seafood dishes, including crab stew and grilled red snapper. Best of all, the experience is gentle on your wallet. The place closes at around 7 PM daily. ⊠ *Calle Croabas, Km 5.5, Las Croabas,* ☎ *787/863–0320. Reservations not accepted. No credit cards. Closed Thurs.*

$$$$ 🏨 **Wyndham El Conquistador Resort and Country Club.** Many travel-
★ ers consider this Puerto Rico's loveliest resort, although some may find its massive size too isolating—it's virtually its own self-contained community. Four separate hotels form the complex, dramatically perched on a bluff above the ocean. They incorporate touches of Moorish and Spanish colonial architecture, including cobblestone streets, terra-cotta buildings, and fountain-filled plazas. Lovely Palomino Island offshore serves as the hotel's beach; a free shuttle boat takes guests there and back. The staff prides itself on its attentive service. If the place seems familiar, it may be because the James Bond movie *Goldfinger* was filmed here. ⊠ *1000 Av. El Conquistador (Box 70001), 00738,* ☎ *787/863– 1000, 800/996–3426, or 800/468–5228,* ℻ *787/253–0178. 918 rooms and suites. 9 restaurants, 8 bars, air-conditioning, minibars, 6 pools, spa, 18-hole golf course, 6 tennis courts, exercise room, beach, dive shop, dock, snorkeling, windsurfing, boating, jet skiing, shops, casino, nightclub, children's program, airport shuttle. AE, MC, V. FAP.* 🐾

$$ 🏨 **Fajardo Inn.** There are two parts to this 4-acre hilltop property: a hotel and a separate, smaller B&B. The views are lovely from either, offering a sweeping vista of the Atlantic Ocean and the El Yunque rain forest against a backdrop of lush gardens peppered with tropical plants and trees. It's a comfortable inn with reasonable prices. ⊠ *52 Parce-las Beltran, 00740,* ☎ *787/860–6000,* ℻ *787/860–5063. 54 rooms. Restaurant, breakfast room, sports bar, air-conditioning, pool, meeting rooms, free parking. AE, MC, V. EP.* 🐾

$$ 🏨 **Parador La Familia.** This guest house on the list of government-approved paradores could use a face-lift, but it's still a convenient spot to land for the night. The white wooden house that serves as its centerpiece used to be known as the Family Guest House. The view? Right onto the ocean. ⊠ *Rte. 987, Km 4.1, Las Croabas, 00648,* ☎ *787/863–1193,* ℻ *787/860–5354. 27 rooms. Restaurant, bar, pool, shop, free parking. AE, DC, MC, V. FAP.*

Nightlife

In the evening, locals drink beer at neighborhood bars, but most of the action takes place in the lounges and casino at El Conquistador Resort.

Caribbean Blues (⊠ Marginal road at Puerto del Rey exit off Hwy. 53, ☎ 787/860–0060 and 787/860–1222) is the only place on the east coast where you can hear high-quality live music every weekend. The sounds are mostly blues, rock, and jazz, with occasional Latin favorites tossed in to heat up the crowds. There's a $3 cover when live bands perform; when they aren't on the schedule, the jukebox fills in. The bartender here is first-class and the kitchen serves up some good bar food. The regulars include military men from the nearby U.S. naval base.

You can play slots, blackjack, roulette, and video poker at **El Conquistador Casino** (✉ 1000 Av. El Conquistador, ☎ 787/863–1000), a typical hotel gambling facility set within the resort's lavish grounds.

Outdoor Activities and Sports

Fajardo is a welcoming spot if you want to try your hand aboard a sailboat, get your scuba-diving certification, snorkel over fish-rich reefs, or play a round of golf with the trade winds ruffling your hair.

BEACHES

Balneario Seven Seas (✉ Rte. 987, Km 5), near Las Cabezas de San Juan Nature Reserve, presents a long stretch of powdery white sand, some refreshment kiosks, and a smattering of shade. It also has picnic and camping areas. On weekends, it attracts crowds keen on its calm and clear waters for swimming and water sports.

DIVING AND SNORKELING

Palomino Divers (✉ 1000 Av. El Conquistador, ☎ 787/863–1077), at El Conquistador Resort, focuses on scuba and snorkeling activity on the islets of Palomino, Lobos, and Diablo.

At **Sea Ventures Pro Dive Center** (✉ Puerto del Rey Marina, Rte. 3, Km 51.4, ☎ 787/863–3483) you can get PADI certified if you're a novice or arrange dive trips to 20 offshore sites if you're already experienced.

GOLF

The 18-hole Arthur Hills–designed course at **El Conquistador Country Club** (✉ 1000 Av. El Conquistador, ☎ 787/863–1000) is ranked as one of the best in the Caribbean, famous for its 200-ft changes in elevation. The trade winds make every shot challenging.

SAILING

Learn to Sail (✉ Puerto del Rey Marina, Rte. 3, Km 51.4, ☎ 787/863–7703) offers sailing lessons aboard a 26-ft sailboat; it also rents sea kayaks. Boating and sailing trips are also organized at **Sea Ventures Pro Dive Center** (☞ Diving and Snorkeling, *above*).

Shopping

Sometimes it seems like the only stores in Fajardo are linked to fishing, water sports, and yachting. The city has shopping centers, of course, but they tend toward the same chain stores you can find anywhere.

Chocolate-loving Laurie Humphrey had trouble finding a supplier for her sweet tooth, so she created the **Paradise Store** (✉ Hwy. 194, Km 0.4, ☎ 787/863–8182). Lindt and other gourmet chocolates jam the shop, which also sells flowers and gift items (including Puerto Rican–made soaps).

At El Conquistador Resort, Maria Elba Torres runs the **Galeria Arrecife** (✉ 1000 Av. El Conquistador, ☎ 787/863–3972), hoping to draw attention to island artists; only works by artists living in Puerto Rico and the Caribbean are shown. Her shop also features ceramics by Rafael de Olmo and jewelry made from fish scales.

VIEQUES AND CULEBRA

West from Fajardo, a hop across the water, are the two most important of Puerto Rico's outer islands, Vieques and Culebra. The beauty of both is readily apparent, whether you approach by sea or air. Banana-shape Vieques floats atop azure water, while smaller Culebra is edged by white beaches and encircled by tiny islets. At either, beaches are the primary attraction.

The two islands are where Puerto Ricans—and others in the know—go when they want to escape from civilization. Bereft of traffic lights, casinos, fast-food chains, movie houses, and the other trappings of modern life, these are sleepy outposts where the temperatures hover around 80 degrees, the stunning white beaches are void of crowds, and "casual" is the operative word. Many of the restaurants are open-air, and the simple guest houses that dominate the accommodations rely on overhead fans and trade winds to keep guests comfortable.

There's only one time of the year when the sparsely populated islands transform into a lively, crowded party scene. That's during the Easter holidays, when mainlanders flock to them for camping and partying on the beach. (If you're planning a trip to the islands during Holy Week, make reservations as early in advance as possible. And if you seek peace and tranquility, look elsewhere at that time of year.)

Both islands are accessible from the main island via 90-minute ferry trips that leave Fajardo daily. There is also air service aboard puddle-jumper planes that make the 10-minute trip from Fajardo, or you can catch a flight from San Juan. Both outer islands are also the subjects of increasing interest from the tourism industry, with new hotel projects planned and a golf course under discussion for Vieques.

Vieques

13 km (8 mi) southeast of Fajardo by sea.

Local lore has it that Captain Kidd once visited Vieques when it was a haven for pirates. Through the early 1900s, sugarcane dominated the economy—until the United States used its control of the island to transform it into a naval training ground.

Although a referendum was in the works to allow Vieques residents to decide whether they want the navy to stay, at the time this book went to press the military still controlled two-thirds of the island, including some of the best beaches. Some say the navy's presence is what has kept the island pristine—there is little land to develop megahotel projects on, and military exercises with live ammunition are off-putting for some visitors.

In truth, even when the exercises are underway, the bombing sounds mostly like distant rolling thunder. And when they aren't in progress, the navy allows civilians to visit the isolated beaches it controls. The navy's presence is also what has blessed Vieques with roadways, water service, and an airport that's better maintained than might otherwise be expected on an island this size.

Some 9,300 civilians call Vieques home, many of them expatriate artists and guest-house owners from the mainland United States. They were drawn here by the same thing that lures tourists: the quiet days, the small-town friendliness, and the natural beauty. Just 4 mi across at its widest point, the 21-mi-long island is packed with stunning beaches (so many that some aren't even named) and marvelous scuba and snorkeling opportunities.

There are only two communities on Vieques: Isabel II, where the ferries dock, and the smaller Esperanza. Many of the islanders fish for a living or work in the tourism-related fields. Some of the homes are part-year vacation villas for mainland Puerto Ricans or other Americans.

Just because Vieques is sleepy doesn't mean there's nothing to do besides hit the beach. The island is home to the astonishing Mosquito Bay, where

VIEQUES: PLACID BEACHES AND A POLITICAL HOTBED

FOR NEARLY SIX DECADES the U.S. Navy has set the course of Vieques's development, claiming two thirds of the island as military property and conducting live-fire exercises on the outer island. In late 1999, controversy over the navy's claim promised to move toward an end as the island's governor signed an agreement calling for Vieques residents to vote on whether the Navy should stay or go.

The navy once also owned most of Culebra. In 1901 the tiny outer island was placed under U.S. Navy jurisdiction. The navy's interest in it solidified during World War II. As Hitler's armies raced across Europe, U.S. policy makers launched a plan to develop a huge naval complex in Puerto Rico. They envisioned two concrete piers, each 7,000 ft long. But the bombing of Pearl Harbor showed the danger of concentrating military vessels in one location. Protesters in 1971 forced the military to stop using its range on Culebra; four years later President Richard Nixon ordered the navy to leave and much of the military land was turned into a nature preserve.

On Vieques the navy owns both the eastern and western sections of the island, with a civilian area sandwiched in between. In 1999, Puerto Rico's Secretary of State Norma Burgos began compiling the information necessary to nominate the residents of Vieques for the Nobel Peace Prize in 2000 because of the "years of suffering which they have endured" with a navy presence on the off-island. Fishermen have protested the military maneuvers for years, and since a bomb dropped off target killed a civilian on navy land on April 19, 1999, opposition to the military presence has increased.

Since the military holdings include some of the best beaches, tourism development has been slow (although a new hotel boom may be on the horizon). However, the navy's presence has also provided the island with an outstanding infrastructure that includes good roads, an airport, and a water pipeline. Tourism industry observers predict that while the navy's departure, if the Viequenses vote to oust the military, could open the door to new attractions and hotels, much of the navy terrain will probably become park land.

The isolation and dearth of crowds that have made Vieques so appealing will not disappear.

undersea creatures seem to illuminate at night, a lovely fort built by the early Spanish governors, and a number of good restaurants.

⑪ **Faro Punta Mulas,** a Spanish-built lighthouse, dates from the late 1800s. In 1992 it was carefully restored and now houses a maritime museum that traces much of the island's history, including the time South American liberation leader Simon Bolivar visited the island. The lighthouse is located beside a ferry dock. ⊠ *At the end of Rte. 200,* ☎ *787/741–0060.* ⊡ *Free.* ⊙ *Wed.–Sun. 10–4.*

★ ⑫ **Mosquito Bay,** more commonly known as Bioluminescent Bay or Phosphorescent Bay, this is one of the best spots in the world to have a glow-in-the-dark experience with undersea dinoflagellates. Travel operators offer kayak trips or excursions on special nonpolluting boats to see the bay's tiny microorganisms that appear to light up when their water is agitated. Dive into the bay and you'll emerge covered in sparkling water. Look behind your boat and you'll see a twinkling wake. Even the fish that jump from the water will bear an eerie glow. The high concentration of dinoflagellates sets Vieques's Mosquito Bay apart from the other spots (including others in Puerto Rico) that are home to these tiny organisms. The bay is at its best when there is little or no moonlight; rainy nights are beautiful, too, because the raindrops splashing in the water produce ricochet sparkles. Some of the best excursions to the bay are offered by Sharon Grasso of Island Adventures (☞ Outdoor Activities and Sports, *below*). ⊠ *South central side of the island, on unpaved roads off Rte. 997,* ☎ *no phone.* ⊡ *Free.* ⊙ *Daily.*

⑬ **Museo Fuerte Conde de Mirasol** (Count of Mirasol Fort) was the last military structure begun by the Spaniards in the New World. Erected on Vieques's northern coast in 1840 at the order of Count Mirasol, then governor of Puerto Rico, this small defensive fortification was designed to insure Spain's claim on the island. Now it houses a museum of changing local art exhibits. The museum also chronicles Vieques's past, using Taíno Indian relics, flags of the European powers that hoped to lay claim to the island, and a bust of one of Vieques's most famous visitors, Venezuelan Simon Bolivar, known as "the George Washington of South America." A map collection shows how early cartographers saw the island. ⊠ *471 Calle Magnolia, Isabel II,* ☎ *787/741–1717.* ⊡ *$1.* ⊙ *Wed.–Sun. 10–4.*

Dining and Lodging

For an island so small and so isolated, Vieques has a surprisingly wide array of restaurants. Most are casual, but that doesn't mean the cooking is taken lightly. Local kitchens are proud of what they prepare, whether it be fresh fried fish served at a seaside café or a Nuevo Latino delicacy from an upscale restaurant.

$$$$ ✕ **Café Blu.** The most elegant restaurant on the island sits beside the ★ posh Inn on the Blue Horizon guest house, right on the coast. Start with a drink at the popular bar, then move to a table for an unforgettable meal of pan-blackened tuna, fresh trout marinated with tropical spices, or Asian barbecued lamb. After the meal, if you're a cigar smoker, seek out the "Cigar Tree," where stogie lovers congregate to light one up and savor a snifter of port. ⊠ *Rte. 966 outside Esperanza,* ☎ *787/741–3318. AE, MC, V. Closed Sun. and Mon. No lunch.*

$$$$ ✕ **La Casa del Frances.** Think of a tropical ingredient and you'll find it in one of the dishes that emerge from the kitchen here. That means avocado, pineapple, mango, banana, and plantain woven into the seafood-focused lunch and dinner specials. You can opt to eat in the more formal dining room or on the terrace overlooking a pool. ⊠ *Rte. 996, Esperanza,* ☎ *787/741–3751. AE, MC, V.*

$$ ✕ **Cafe Media Luna.** You'll have a hard time figuring out what type of food is the specialty here; the menu runs the gamut from Vietnamese spring rolls to tandoori chicken to seafood cooked in wine. Fortunately, all of the options are good ones. Tucked into an old building in Isabel II, this eatery has become a local favorite. ✉ *351 Calle Antonio G. Mellado, Isabel II,* ☎ *787/741–2594. Reservations not accepted. AE, MC, V.*

$$ ✕ **Trapper John's.** This restaurant at the Crow's Nest guest house is popular for its happy hour (from 5 to 7 with complimentary appetizers) and its "theme" nights. On Friday and Saturday, for example, prime rib is the special. But the real treats are the Caribbean lobster and veal scallopini. ✉ *Rte. 201, Km 1.6, Barrio Florida,* ☎ *787/741–0033. AE, MC, V.*

$$$$ 🏨 **Inn on the Blue Horizon.** Currently the most expensive hotel on the
★ island, this gorgeous inn is composed of four villas built near the sea on what used to be a plantation. The 20-acre complex allows great privacy. In accord with the owners' vow to take their guests "away from it all," there are no televisions or telephones in the rooms. Even air-conditioning is rare (only two of the rooms have it), but with the breezy location you won't notice the absence. A hearty country breakfast comes with the room rate. At press time, owner James Weis was working with investors on a new project that would add at least two boutique hotels on 100 acres of property near the inn. ✉ *Rte. 996 outside Esperanza (Box 1556), 00765,* ☎ *787/741–3318,* 🖷 *787/741–0522. 9 rooms. Restaurant, bar, air-conditioning, fans, pool, massage, bicycles, free parking. AE, MC, V. BP.*

$$$ 🏨 **Hacienda Tamarindo.** Commercial interior designer Linda Vail and
★ her husband Burr are the charming hosts at this guest house named after a venerable old tamarind tree rising three stories tall in the lobby. Situated on a hilltop with a panoramic view and boasting a stunning swimming pool, this is an exceptional property landscaped with coconut palms, mahogany trees, and tropical flowers. Half the guest rooms—which combine terra-cotta floors, light pastel colors, and antiques—have air-conditioning. The rest are cooled by overhead fans and trade winds. ✉ *Rte. 996, Km 4.5, outside Esperanza (Box 1569), 00765,* ☎ *787/741–8525,* 🖷 *787/741–3215. 16 rooms. Breakfast room, air-conditioning, fans, pool. AE, MC, V. BP.* ✍

$$ 🏨 **The Crow's Nest.** At the center of the island, this 12-room guest house is spread over 5 acres of land. It's quiet, has lovely grounds, and boasts an outdoor deck with a marvelous view. Although it's not on the water, its central location makes it an easy jumping-off point for visits to beaches on either coast. It's just a few minutes drive from Esperanza (and its restaurants). ✉ *Rte. 201, Km 1.6, Barrio Florida, 00765,* ☎ *787/741–8525,* 🖷 *787/741–0033. Breakfast room, air conditioning, fans, pool, restaurant. AE, MC, V. BP.*

Nightlife

If you're looking for nightlife, you're in the wrong place. It's usually quiet here after sunset, and most Viequenses' idea of a night on the town is dinner or a cocktail out.

Amapola Tavern (✉ 144 Calle Flamboyán, Esperanza, ☎ 787/741–1382) has salsa music coming from the sound system, the biggest TV screen on the island (making this *the* place to go on sports nights), and a bartender who turns out exquisite tropical concoctions.

Bananas (✉ 142 Calle Flamboyán, Esperanza, ☎ 787/741–8700) equals burgers, beer, and booze. If you're looking for crowds, you'll find them here at the most lively of the island bars. There's sometimes live music and dancing.

Outdoor Activities and Sports

The ocean is the focus of most activities on Vieques.

BEACHES

Of Vieques's more than three dozen beaches, **Sun Bay Public Beach** (✉ Rte. 997) is one of the most popular. That's because it's one of the most beautiful, with white sand skirting a 1-mi-long, crescent-shape bay. There are picnic tables, camping areas, and a bathhouse. Despite its popularity, it's not unusual to find few people there on weekdays. Wild horses graze among the palm trees in the shady area facing the sea. Food kiosks are located across the street from the beach.

An unpaved road from Sun Bay leads to **Playa Media Luna** (✉ east of Sun Bay, off Rte. 997), a pretty little beach that is ideal for families because the water is calm and below your knees for yards as you wade out. This is a good spot to try your hand at snorkeling. Take note, though, that there are no facilities here.

Situated within navy territory, **Red Beach** (✉ down a series of unpaved, unnamed roads; ask for directions at your hotel or from the locals) is the primo spot for power sunbathing. It's a charming beach with crystal-clear water, but its strong surf is best avoided by uncertain swimmers. However, it's a beautiful spot to stretch out with sunscreen and a good book. There are no facilities here, so bring plenty of drinking water.

BOATING

Former schoolteacher Sharon Grasso's **Island Adventures** (✉ Rte. 996, Esperanza, ☎ 787/741–0720) offers Mosquito Bay visitors an unusual option: she takes them to the glowing bay aboard nonpolluting, electrically powered pontoon boats for about $20 apiece.

Agua Frenzy Kayaks (✉ at dock area below Calle Flamboyán, Esperanza, ☎ 787/741-0913) has kayak tours of Mosquito Bay, as well as kayak rental. Reservations for the excursions, which cost $20, must be made at least 24 hours in advance.

SCUBA DIVING AND SNORKELING

Blue Caribe Dive Center (✉ Calle Flamboyán, Esperanza, ☎ 787/741–2522) offers scuba excursions to several sites; night dives in Mosquito Bay can also be arranged.

Environmentalist Richard Barone's **Get Snorkeled! with Captain Richard** (✉ no office; trips are launched from the shore at Esperanza, ☎ 787/741–1980) is a program of shallow-water, from-the-shore snorkeling expeditions especially geared toward children. As you snorkel, he stops to point out the habits of sea creatures.

Shopping

While Vieques has never been a shopping mecca, the situation for shoppers may be on the upswing. Some of the potters, artists, and other creative people who are enamored of the island are showing an interest in setting up shop there.

Casa Vieja Gallery (✉ Rte. 996 outside Esperanza, ☎ 787/741–3078), located in a Caribbean-style building at the entrance to the grounds of Inn on the Blue Horizon, offers a space for artists to show their work.

For tropical swimsuits and sun dresses, try **The Mall** (✉ Rte. 996, Esperanza, ☎ 787/741–3751), which isn't a mall in the conventional sense, but rather a bright boutique.

Culebra

28 km (17 mi) east of Fajardo by sea.

As far as inhabited areas of Puerto Rico go, Culebra is one of the most idyllic. There is archaeological evidence that small groups of pre-

Columbian people lived here, and certainly pirates landed on the island from time to time, but Puerto Rico's Spanish rulers didn't bother laying claim to it until 1886; its dearth of freshwater made it unattractive for settlement. Although it now has modern conveniences, its pace seems little changed from a century ago.

Seven miles long, 3 mi wide, and mostly unspoiled, Culebra is actually more of an islet than an island. At one point it was controlled, like its neighbor Vieques, by the U.S. Navy. When the navy withdrew, it turned much of the land into a wildlife reserve. There is only one town, Dewey, named after U.S. admiral George Dewey.

The whole of the island operates like a small town: people know each other, people respect each other, and no one wants noise or drama. For that reason, this is *not* the spot for nightlife. When the sun goes down, Culebra winds down as well. But during the day it's a delightful place to stake out a spot on the beach and read or swim or search for shells.

So what causes stress on the island? Nothing.

🔼 Commissioned by President Theodore Roosevelt in 1909, **Refugio Nacional de Vida Silvestre de Culebra** is one of the oldest national wildlife refuges in the United States. Some 1,500 acres of the island make up a protected area popular with hikers and nature lovers. It is also a lure for bird-watchers; Culebra teems with seabirds, from laughing gulls and roseate terns to red-billed tropic birds and a colossal colony of sooty terns. Maps and trails of the refuge are difficult to locate, but you can stop by the U.S. Fish and Wildlife Service office near the airport (and close to the cemetery) to see about trail conditions and whether you're headed to an area that requires a permit. The office also can tell you whether the leatherback turtles are nesting. From mid-April to mid-July, tourists join the volunteers helping to monitor and tag the giant turtles that nest on Culebra's beaches, especially Resaca Beach and Brava Beach. Volunteers must agree to help out for at least three nights. ⊠ *Between Rte. 250 and Rte. 251, near Monte Resaca, north of Dewey,* ☎ *787/742–0115; for information about leatherback monitoring, 787/254–3456.* 🎟 *Free.* ☉ *Daily.*

Dining and Lodging
On Culebra you won't find anything remotely resembling the dining and lodging facilities on the main island or even on Vieques, but that lack of development is a big part of the island's appeal. You will find restaurants and guest houses that are perfectly pleasant and that suit the laid-back atmosphere.

$$ ✕ **Dinghy Dock.** You'll notice Culebra's version of traffic around the dock where this restaurant sits, including the thatch-covered water taxi, Muff the Magic Fun Boat, coming in to tie up. That's because Dinghy Dock is more than just a restaurant, it's a pulse point for Dewey. The long and varied menu includes vegetarian specialties. For carnivores, there's always a good T-bone steak. The daily specials often concentrate on the restaurant's forte: creole-style seafood. ⊠ *Carretera Fulladoza, Dewey,* ☎ *787/742–0581. Reservations not accepted. AE, MC, V.*

$$ ✕🏠 **Mamacitas.** At the restaurant here, start with a cool tropical drink and then move on to well-made pasta dishes and seafood plucked fresh from the ocean. Diners sit at plastic tables on a breezy dock overlooking a canal. It's the kind of place where you strike up a conversation with the folks at the next table—and end up making fast friendships. The adjoining guest house has only three rooms, but every one is lovely. One has a kitchenette, and each has a balcony. Best of all is the location, within walking distance of the "downtown" retail district of Culebra's only settlement. ⊠ *66 Calle Castelar, Dewey 00775,* ☎

787/742–0090. *3 rooms. Restaurant, air-conditioning, fans, dock. AE, MC, V. FAP.*

$$ ⊞ **Posada La Hamaca.** Functional rather than cozy, this little guest house is located in a concrete building on a canal at the edge of Culebra's only town. It's within walking distance of restaurants, shops, and grocery stores. Ice, coolers, and towels for the beach are provided free of charge. Guests can hang out at the back dock, which sits on a canal separating Culebra's harbor from the Caribbean. ⊠ *68 Calle Castelar (Box 388), Dewey 00775,* ☎ *787/742–3516,* FAX *787–7420. 9 rooms, 1 suite, 2 apartments with kitchens. Air-conditioning, fans, kitchenettes, dock. AE, MC, V. EP.* ⊛

Outdoor Activities and Sports
BEACHES
Take a dive boat or water taxi to the north shore of Culebra's offshore islet, Culebrita, where you'll find **Playa Culebrita** and its fabulous coral reef. The beach is gorgeous, and there is a series of rocks that form natural pools. Snuggling into one of them is like taking a warm bath. This is a superb spot for snorkeling right from the shore, and if you want to go exploring, you'll find an old lighthouse on this teeny cay.

★ On Culebra's north coast, **Playa Flamenco** (⊠ off Rte. 250) has the reputation of being the most stunning beach in Puerto Rico. It's an amazingly long stretch of white sand. During the week it is pleasantly uncrowded; on the weekend, though, it fills up. As you stroll along the beach, don't be surprised if you come upon a rusting tank or two—they're left over from when the area was used by the U.S. Navy. (To get there, you should ask for directions from a local; the nearest roads are unnamed and unnumbered.)

As you head down the rugged roads to **Playa Zoni** (⊠ at the end of Rte. 250, northeast of Dewey), you'll wonder whether it's worth the tortuous journey. It is. Perched on the northeastern end of the island, about 7 mi from Dewey, it is far more isolated—precisely because of the hassle getting here—than Flamenco Beach, and many believe it's just as beautiful. If you want to feel like the beach is all yours, you've found the perfect place. It's also a good spot for snorkeling.

BIKING
Biking is a good way to explore the island on your own. You can rent bikes by the hour or by the day at **Culebra Bike Shop** (⊠ 138 Calle Escudero, Dewey, ☎ 787/742–2209).

BOATING
At **Flamenco Resort & Fishing Club** (⊠ 10 Pedro Nárquez, Flamenco Beach, ☎ 787/742–3144) you can charter sailboats for offshore exploring. **Reef Link Divers** (☞ Scuba Diving and Snorkeling, *below*) rents kayaks for about $8 an hour.

SCUBA DIVING AND SNORKELING
Travelers have recounted some spectacular dives as a result of being hooked up with **Culebra Dive Shop** (⊠ 317 Calle Escudero, Dewey, ☎ 787/742–3335), which charges about $45 for a dive with one oxygen tank. Day-long snorkeling trips, for about $45 per person, can also be arranged.

Reef Link Divers (⊠ Carretera Fulladoza, inside the Dinghy Dock restaurant, Dewey, ☎ 787/742–0581) caters to everyone—from beginners to the most experience scuba experts—and specializes in coral-reef sites near Culebra. A day package starts at $55; a full-week package that includes a night dive runs about $350. Reef Link also arranges snorkel trips for about $45 per person, including lunch.

Shopping

People visit Culebra to get away from it all—and that includes the frenzy of shopping malls and consumer hype. That said, the island is slowly seeing some interesting boutiques pop up.

Loma Gift Shop (⊠ Calle Escudero, Dewey, ☎ 787/742–3565) is a good spot for T-shirts, jewelry, island photographs and watercolors, and other souvenirs. The tiny gift shop at **Mamacitas** guest house (☞ Dining and Lodging, *above*) has exceptional hand-painted T-shirts and other original-design Culebra gift items.

THE SOUTHEASTERN COAST

From Fajardo, a good way to explore the southeast is to travel along the old coastal Route 3 as it weaves on and off the shoreline and passes through small towns. The route takes a while to travel but offers lovely beach and mountain scenery.

Naguabo

⑮ *18 km (11 mi) southwest of Fajardo.*

This fast-growing municipality is working hard to boost its appeal to tourists. Mostly it wants to capitalize on its lovely beaches; it recently opened a food and shopping pedestrian mall along a boardwalk close to Hucares Beach. Downtown, blue and pink paint gives the main plaza a bit of the look of a child's nursery (and local leaders should consider sprucing up the landscaping), but the plaza is a good spot to sit and people-watch until the heat drives you to the beach. The bright-yellow church sits on one side of the plaza, facing the bright-yellow city hall. A pink-and-blue amphitheater anchors a corner of the square.

More than just a beach, **Playa Hucares** is *the* place to spend the day in Naguabo. Casual outdoor eateries and funky little shops, including some selling souvenirs, compete with the water for your attention. A boardwalk lets you stroll along the palm-lined strand. And the beach itself offers great swimming (the waves aren't too rough), a bit of shade, and rest rooms and changing houses. ⊠ *Off Rte. 3 outside Naguabo,* ☎ *no phone.* ⌨ *Free.* ⊙ *Daily.*

Lodging

$$$ ⊡ **Casa Cubuy Ecolodge.** Rebuilt in 1997, this isolated retreat at the edge of El Yunque is for nature lovers who truly want to forget about the world. The lodge rises amid lush scenery (there are lots of stairs to climb to the upper rooms), and the rooms are simple but comfortable— tile floors, rattan furniture, white bedspreads, and one wall of windows in each room, including a sliding glass door that opens onto a balcony. The main common area is an outdoor tile-floor veranda where guests gather to eat meals or relax in hammocks; plastic patio chairs and tables make up the furniture. The proprietor believes healthy eating translates into healthy living and offers her guests a tasty menu of wholesome meals. There are no televisions, and the rooms are exceedingly quiet. Hiking trails from the lodge lead to a waterfall. ⊠ *Rte. 191, Km 22, Barrio Río Blanco, 00744,* ☎ *787/874–6221. 10 rooms. Fans, free parking. AE, MC, V. FAP.*

Humacao

⑯ *15 km (9 mi) southwest of Naguabo; 55 km (34 mi) from San Juan.*

Humacao, a city of 52,000, is a powerhouse in the southeast. It's an educational center and has a growing industrial sector that's slowly replacing the agriculture-based economy. Although it's not considered a tourist destination in and of itself, it's the city associated with the sprawling Palmas del Mar resort, which is outside town. Downtown Humacao, with its narrow, heavily trafficked streets, contains some interesting neo-colonial architecture.

Offshore, Cayo Santiago—also known as Monkey Island—is the site of some of the world's most important rhesus monkey research. A small colony of monkeys was introduced to the island in the late 1930s, and since then scientists have been studying their habits and health, especially as they pertain to the study of diabetes and arthritis. You aren't allowed to visit Cayo Santiago, but the Palmas del Mar resort offers a boat trip that circles the island.

Museo Casa Roig, the former residence of sugarcane plantation owner and banker Antonio Roig Torruellas, was built in 1919. Czech architect Antonio Nechodoma designed an unusual facade, distinctive for its wide eaves, mosaic work, and beautiful stained-glass windows with geometric patterns. This was the first 20th-century building in Puerto Rico to go on the register of Historic National Monuments. The Roig family lived in the home until 1956, and it was then abandoned for several years before being turned over to the University of Puerto Rico in 1977. It's currently a museum and cultural center, with historical photos and furniture and rotating exhibits by contemporary Puerto Rican artists. ⊠ *66 Calle Antonio López,* ☎ *787/852–8380.* ⊠ *Free.* ☉ *Wed.– Fri. and Sun. 10–4.*

Plaza de Humacao, the downtown square, is Humacao's pulse point. The broad plaza is anchored by the pale pink **Catedral Dulce Nombre de Jesús** (Sweet Name of Jesus Cathedral), which dates from 1869. Even when the cathedral's grille door is locked, you can peek through to see its sleek altar, polished floors, and stained-glass windows dominated by blues. The church has an unusual castlelike facade. Across the plaza, four fountains splash under the shade of old trees, and park benches offer respite from the heat. People pass through the plaza feeding pigeons, children race down the promenade, and retirees congregate to chat. Look for the little monument with the globe on top; it's a tribute to city sons who died in wars. ⊠ *Av. Font Martel at Calle Ulises Martinez.*

Swamps, lagoons, and forested areas are all found in the **Refugio de Vida Silvestre de Humacao** nature reserve, which has recreational areas, an information office, rest rooms, children's activities, and camping sites. Hunting, fishing, and hiking are allowed in some parts of the reserve; check in advance to see what permits are required. ⊠ *Rte. 3, Km 74.3,* ☎ *787/852–6088 and 787/724–2500.* ⊠ *Free.* ☉ *Weekdays 7:30–3:30.*

Dining and Lodging

For dining, your best bets are at one extreme or the other: the casual seafood eateries where locals congregate or the creative, upscale restaurants at the Palmas del Mar resort.

$$$$ ✕ **Hermes Creative Cuisine.** Chef Hermes Vargas, from the Condado restaurant that also bears his name, has come up with a distinctive menu for this elegant restaurant at the Palmas del Mar Country Club. After a day on the golf course, this is *the* spot to celebrate (or forget about) your score. The kitchen here likes to experiment with game, including wild boar and venison. Diners can eat al fresco on the lovely terrace or by candlelight in the dining room. (There's a private area of the dining room for country club members and their guests.) ⊠ *Rte. 906, Pal-*

mas del Mar, ☎ *787/285–2277 or 787/285–2266. Reservations essential. AE, MC, V. No dinner Mon.*

$$$ ✕ **Chez Daniel.** The dockside setting and casual atmosphere belie the elegance of the meals that Chef Daniel Vasse turns out here. French country-style cuisine is a prize winner, and the Catalan-style bouilli-nade, bursting with fresh fish and steeped in a white garlic sauce, is exceptional. When the stars are out and the candles are lit, this sea-side spot is 100% romantic. ✉ *Rte. 906, Palmas del Mar,* ☎ *787/852–6000. Reservations essential. AE, MC, V. Closed Tues. No lunch.*

$ ✕ **El Chinchorro.** Past the Palmas del Mar Marina is a spot where local fishing boats come in. A clever entrepreneur with a penchant for cook-ing has set up picnic tables and a little kitchen where the seafood dishes can't get any fresher. Fried fish is the mainstay—the selection gives new meaning to the term "catch of the day." The setting is ultra-casual. ✉ *Off Rte. 906, past the Palmas del Mar Marina,* ☎ *no phone. Reservations not accepted. No credit cards.*

$ ✕ **La Pesqueria.** It's difficult to find this rustic waterside restaurant. It has no sign, so you have to look for the telltale picnic tables outside and busy parking lot. Order the fresh catch, which comes from the kitchen whole. The menu varies from day to day—red snapper is es-pecially good, and there are always lighter snacks available, including octopus salsa. ✉ *Off Rte. 906, near the Palmas del Mar Marina,* ☎ *no phone. Reservations not accepted. No credit cards.*

$$$$ ▥ **Palmas del Mar Resort & Villas.** This sprawling resort of nearly 3,000 acres seems never to stop growing. Construction activity is primarily concentrated on condo-villas that are sprouting up throughout the com-plex. The rooms and public spaces of the hotel are open and airy, and there is no shortage of activity, from water sports to golf to tennis to boating. Many of the rooms have balconies, so you can catch the east-coast breezes or sit out and watch the sunset. For those who want larger accommodations, some of the villas can be rented by the day, the week, or longer. The unwieldy size of the resort can be a drawback, although parking attendants and other personnel are deft about giv-ing directions around the seemingly unending grounds. Shuttle buses scoot guests from place to place, including to and from the many restaurants. ✉ *Rte. 906 (Box 2020), 00792,* ☎ *787/852–6000,* ℻ *787/852–6320. 100 rooms, 135 villas. 14 restaurants, 15 bars, air-condi-tioning, minibars, room service, pool, 2 18-hole golf courses, 20 ten-nis courts, exercise room, horseback riding, beach, dive shop, dock, windsurfing, snorkeling, jet skiing, fishing, shops, casino, children's pro-grams, airport shuttle. AE, MC, V. MAP.* ✍

Nightlife

Palmas del Mar Casino (✉ Rte. 906, ☎ 787/852–6000) offers every-thing from blackjack to slot machines. The action is liveliest on week-ends.

Outdoor Activities and Sports

FISHING

Shiraz Charters (✉ Rte. 906, Palmas del Mar Resort, Site 6, ☎ 787/285–5718) specializes in deep-sea fishing charters, especially those in search of tuna and mahimahi. Four-hour outings start at about $90 per person.

GOLF

Palmas del Mar Resort (✉ Rte. 906, ☎ 787/285–2256) has two courses: the Rees Jones–designed Flamboyan course, opened in 1983, is named for the nearly six dozen flamboyant trees that pepper the fair-way. (They're easy to spot: they turn flaming red in late spring and sum-mer.) The course winds around a lake, over a river, and to the sea before turning toward sand dunes and wetlands. The older, Gary Player–designed Palmas course has a challenging par 5 that scoots around wetlands.

SCUBA DIVING AND SNORKELING

Coral Head Divers (✉ Rte. 906, Palmas del Mar Resort, ☎ 787/850–7208 or 800/635–4529) has excursions to more than two dozen dive sites famous for their coral. It also offers PADI certification and rents snorkeling equipment and sea kayaks.

EASTERN PUERTO RICO, VIEQUES, AND CULEBRA A TO Z

Arriving and Departing

By Airplane

Commuter flights from the **Isla Grande Airport** in San Juan and nine-passenger shuttle planes from Fajardo's small **Diego Jiménez Torres Airport** represent the principal air connections to Vieques and Culebra. The Culebra air service is available aboard **Flamenco Airways** (☎ 787/723–8110 in San Juan; 787/863–3366 in Fajardo; and 787/742–3885 in Culebra) as well as **CaribAir** (☎ 800/981–0212). The route to Vieques is covered by **Vieques Air Link** (☎ 787/722–8736 in San Juan; 787/863–3020 in Fajardo; and 787/741–8311 in Vieques).

Isla Nena Air Service (☎ 787/791–5110 or 888/263–6213) flies from San Juan's **Luis Muñoz International Airport** to the outer islands.

Flights to Culebra land at **Benjamin Rivera Noriega Airport** at the end of Calle Escudero, which runs right into the heart of downtown Dewey. From the airport in Vieques, it is a short cab ride to Isabel II.

By Car

From San Juan, the east coast of Puerto Rico is accessible by following Route 3 (or Route 187 if you want to visit Loíza). At Fajardo, the road intersects with Highway 53—a fast toll road—which continues down the coast. However, Route 3 also continues, running parallel, and provides a more scenic, if slower, trip. All of the main roads are in good shape, but take note that many highway signs (including those on the turnpike) have been blown down by hurricanes and may or may not have been replaced by the time you make your trip.

Getting Around

By Boat

The maritime route for reaching Culebra and Vieques is via the ferry that leaves many times a day from Fajardo. The **Fajardo Port Authority** (☎ 787/863–0705, 787/863–4560, or 787/863–0852) is in charge of the service between Fajardo and Culebra, Fajardo and Vieques, and Culebra and Vieques. In Fajardo, the ferries leave from the dock in the Puerto Real district; in Culebra, the ferry (☎ 787/742–3161) pulls right into downtown Dewey. In Vieques, the ferry dock (☎ 787/741–4761) is on the edge of downtown Isabel II (and within walking distance of the commercial district).

By Bus

Puerto Rico's bus system is inefficient and difficult to use if you don't know the island well and/or don't speak Spanish fluently. Minivans offer service from San Juan to Fajardo. (They'll stop anywhere they're flagged down, but it's best to catch them outside bus terminals.) Within the cities and towns there are local buses. Vieques and Culebra are the easiest destinations to manage aboard the inexpensive *públicos* (public vans), because many of the drivers speak English and are used to tourists.

By Car

Driving in Puerto Rico can be trying; drivers often forget to use turn signals, pass in the right-hand lane, and make illegal U-turns. Most highways are in good condition, but in 1999 Hurricane Georges knocked down highway exit signs and their replacement has been slow, so buy a good road map before you start out and allow yourself time to get lost. Puerto Ricans are helpful about giving directions—even when you ask in makeshift Spanish. Note that speed-limit signs are in miles but distance signs are in kilometers.

Car rental agencies in Fajardo include **L & M** (Rte. 3 Marginal, ☎ 787/860–6868), **Leaseway of Puerto Rico** (Rte. 3, Km 44.4, ☎ 787/860–5000), and **Thrifty** (Puerto del Rey Marina, ☎ 787/860–2030). On Vieques, you can rent cars from **Island Car Rentals** (Rte. 201, Barrio Florida, ☎ 787/741–1666) and **Vias Car Rental** (Calle 65th Infantry, ☎ 787/796–6404). On Culebra, you can rent cars from **Prestige Car Rental** (Culebra airport, ☎ 787/742–3242) and **Culebra Car Rental** (Culebra airport, ☎ 787/7442–3277).

By Taxi

You can flag a cab down, but if the circumstances permit it's often better to have your hotel call one for you. Either way, make sure the driver is clear on whether he or she will charge a flat rate or use a meter to determine the fare.

Contacts and Resources

Emergencies

Puerto Rico's emergency system follows that of the North American mainland. **Ambulance, police, and fire:** ☎ 911.

If 911 should for any reason fail to bring immediate results, you can also try the following numbers: **Loíza:** ☎ 787/876–2042 for medical emergencies, ☎ 787/876–2429 for police. **Río Grande:** ☎ 787/823–2550 for medical emergencies, ☎ 787/887–2020 for police. **Luquillo:** ☎ 787/889–2620 for medical emergencies, ☎ 787/889–2020 for police. **Fajardo:** ☎ 787/863–2550 for medical emergencies, ☎ 787/863–2020 for police. **Naguabo:** ☎ 787/874–7440 for medical emergencies, ☎ 787/874–2020 for police.

Festivals

For three days near the end of November each year, Luquillo hosts the **Festival de Platos Tipicos** (Festival of Typical Dishes; ☎ 787/889–2851, 787/889–0404, or 787/889–2525), which focuses on foods made with coconut. Music, dance, and revelry accompany the festival. For 10 days in early December, **Humacao's patron saint festival** celebrates the Virgin of the Immaculate Conception; the festival coincides with the city's sprucing up for Christmas. **Naguabo's patron saint festival** honors Our Lady of the Rosary the first 10 days of October.

In Fajardo, the **Festival de Chiringas** (Kite Festival) is held every April, the same month as the annual **Regata de Veleros Copa Kelly** (Kelly Cup Sailboat Regatta). In May, the same town's **Festival de Bomba y Plena** turns the spotlight on Puerto Rico's lively Afro-influenced music and dance. Río Grande celebrates a **Carnival** during the first and second week of July and a **marathon** in June.

Health and Safety

Tap water is generally fine on the island; just avoid drinking it after storms (when the drinking-water supply might become mixed with sewage). Thoroughly wash or peel produce you buy in markets and grocery stores before eating it. There are few food-related difficulties for travelers, but bugs can be a problem. Mosquitoes carrying Dengue Fever are not uncommon; wear repellent if you notice mosquitoes or are traveling during the rainy season. Wear trousers and long-sleeved shirts while hiking in wildlife reserves. And do not swim in water where you see signs indicating unsafe conditions (because of either undertow or pollution).

Crime can be a problem in San Juan, but is less so outside of the metropolitan area. However, use prudence. And if in doubt about another motorist's behavior (or you suspect a fender bender is part of a scam), drive to a populated area, a gas station, or highway toll booth rather than stopping.

Tour Operators and Travel Agencies
Blackbeard West Indies Charter (Captain James Smith) (✉ HC-01 Box 13025, Río Grande 00745, ☎ 787/887–4818).

Fajardo Tours Traveler (✉ Carretera 987, Km 1.3, Villa Marina, Fajardo, ☎ 787/863–2821 or 787/863–1646).

Palomino Divers (David Black/Leo Black) (✉ 1000 Av. del Conquistador, Fajardo, ☎ FAX 787/863–1077).

Sea Ventures Pro Dive Center (Peter Seusert) (✉ Hwy. 3, Km 51.2, Puerto del Rey, Fajardo, ☎ 787/863–3483, 800/739–3483, FAX 787/863–0199).

Visitor Information
Río Grande Office of Tourism and Culture (☎ 787/887–2370). **Luquillo Tourism Office** (☎ 787/889–2851). **Fajardo Tourism Office** (☎ 787/863–4013). **Vieques Tourism Office** (☎ 787/741–5000). **Culebra Tourism Office** (☎ 787/742–3291). **Naguabo Tourism Office** (☎ 787/874–0389). A tourism desk in the city hall of Vieques's Isabel II (449 Calle Carlos Lebrón, Isabel II, ☎ 787/742–3521) has information on bike rental (about $5 for a half day) as well as maps and brochures on what to do on the island—and how to get to each of the beaches. The routes to many are complicated (though locals know the way) because some roads are unmarked.

4 PONCE AND SOUTHERN PUERTO RICO

The Maunabo Lighthouse in the east and El Faro Lighthouse in the west serve as bookends to Puerto Rico's "other side," the less tourist-trafficked area to the south of the central mountain range. Here you can lunch on a balcony overlooking lush inland valleys, sun and swim on tiny uninhabited off-shore cays, stroll around city plazas rich with Spanish colonial architecture, or hike through a rare dry tropical forest filled with twisted cacti and over 130 species of birds.

By Delinda
Karle

F IRST INHABITED BY TAÍNO INDIANS and then scouted by Spanish explorers, southern Puerto Rico has long held an identity distinct from the rest of the island. While San Juan to the north was becoming a fortified center of colonial power and conflict, in the south development focused on agriculture, as enterprising planters put the rich soil to use—having particular success with sugarcane. The many seaside coves and off-shore cays also attracted pirates and smugglers. San Germán, Puerto Rico's second-oldest city, was a hub for both farmers and outlaws; now it is one of the island's historical treasures, a town that feels as if it still lives in its 19th-century heyday.

The urban center of the region throughout the 20th century and into the 21st has been Ponce, which rises elegantly from the middle of the southern coastal plain. In the early 1900s the city went through a period of architectural development unparalleled on the island, and in the 1990s it devoted great effort toward restoring and preserving the distinctive older buildings of its downtown district. Elsewhere, smaller south-central towns such as Aibonito and Barranquitas have quaint plazas and are surrounded by dramatic mountain peaks and valleys. Coamo, like San Germán, was once an important Spanish colonial center and retains much of its historical charm. The coastal areas draw a casual and fun-loving crowd to the many beaches skirting the rugged, dry coast. The Cabo Rojo and La Parguera areas have become especially popular with local families looking to get away from the hustle and bustle of urban life. The region also draws divers and hikers from around the world to explore teaming underwater life and unique forest reserves.

Governors, patriots, and poets have hailed from southern Puerto Rico, and this rich history is a source of pride for present-day residents. Throughout the region you'll find meticulously maintained historic homes, and museums large and small dot the land. When traveling the usually well-maintained network of roads, it's wise to carry a good map—but don't hesitate to ask for directions from the locals. As often as not you'll get a history lesson thrown into the bargain.

Pleasures and Pastimes

Beaches
Southern Puerto Rico is a sun lover's dream. There are plenty of sunny days, and plenty of beaches to spend them on. You'll find surfing beaches in both southwestern and southeastern Puerto Rico—check out Inches near Patillas—as well as beaches with calm water conducive to swimming, such as Boquerón Beach. U-shape bays, including the Ballena Bay near Guánica, hide stretches of sand that are often deserted, and numerous boat operators make trips to uninhabited off-shore cays ringed with sand, such as Guilligan Island off the coast of Guánica and Caja de Muertos off Ponce.

Dining
In the south, much like elsewhere on the island, the more ambitious restaurants are experimenting with their own versions of "nouvelle cuisine," which means you'll find typical Puerto Rican and Caribbean dishes given a new twist: fish cooked with a plantain crust, chicken or pork with tamarind or guava sauce. The southern coast—especially the city of Salinas and the Joyuda area in Cabo Rojo—is known for its seafood. Many restaurants will offer a long menu of fresh fish done in a variety of ways. Along the stretch of Route 184 near Cayey, look for slow-roasted *lechón* (pork), a local delicacy cooked outdoors over coals.

Reservations aren't as crucial here as they can be in San Juan, but it's always better to be safe than sorry, particularly on weekends in the more touristy areas. A 15%–20% tip is customary; most restaurants will not include it in the bill, but it's wise to check rather than assume that this is the case.

CATEGORY	COST*
$$$$	over $35
$$$	$25–$35
$$	$15–$25
$	under $15

*per person for an appetizer, entrée, and dessert, excluding tax, tip, and beverages

✎ *following the text of a review is your signal that the property has a Web site, where you will find details and, usually, images; for a link, visit www.fodors.com/urls.*

Lodging

Southern Puerto Rico doesn't have the abundance of luxury hotels and resorts found to the north and east, although Ponce boasts the Ponce Hilton, and the Copamarina Beach Resort in Guánica has developed into a self-contained complex with a breadth of the facilities and services comparable to those found elsewhere on the island. Because many Puerto Ricans take their vacations here, especially on the southwestern part of the island, there's a good number of modest, family-oriented establishments that are conveniently located near the water or in the heart of town.

CATEGORY	COST*
$$$$	over $150
$$$	$100–$150
$$	$50–$100
$	under $50

*All prices are for a double room in high season, excluding taxes.

Outdoor Activities and Sports

HIKING

There are two major draws here for hiking: the lush, tropical Bosque Estatal Carite (Carite Forest Reserve) between Cayey and Patillas; and the distinctive dry forest near Guánica, where you'll find vegetation with the stunted, twisted look of Japanese bonsai, as well as excellent bird-watching. There's also plenty of good hiking outside the forests. The walk to the Cabo Rojo Lighthouse (known as El Faro) along the rugged cliffs at the southwesternmost tip of the island is breathtaking.

SCUBA DIVING AND SNORKELING

Diving in southern Puerto Rico is coming into its own. The dramatic 20-mi-long wall several miles off the southern coast between Cabo Rojo and Guánica is a marvel, where you can still see black coral along with an astonishing array of sea life. Cays off Ponce and Salinas also hold a variety of corals and fish.

Exploring Southern Puerto Rico

Traveling down the Luis A. Ferré Expressway (Rte. 52) south of San Juan, you encounter some of Puerto Rico's highest elevations, part of the mountainous backbone of the island. Towns such as Cayey, Aibonito, and Barranquitas are blessed with cool breezes, especially at night. (In the winter, overnight temperatures can drop into the 40s.) Stretching along the Caribbean Sea, southern Puerto Rico is drier than the north or east—while El Yunque in the east gets an average of 200 inches or rain yearly, the southwestern town of Guánica averages 30 inches. The southeastern part of the island—which includes a section of the scenic *Ruta Panorámica* (Panoramic Route)—has a rugged shoreline where cliffs seem to drop right into the water. Covered with dry vegetation, the southwest's ragged coast has wonderful inlets and bays and jagged peninsulas that make for breathtaking views.

Numbers in the text correspond to numbers in the margin and on the Southern Puerto Rico, Downtown Ponce, Greater Ponce, and San Germán maps.

Great Itineraries

IF YOU HAVE 3 DAYS

Head south from San Juan to **Ponce** via the Luis A. Ferré Expressway, stopping for a seafood lunch in **Salinas** ⑨. Spend the afternoon touring historic **downtown Ponce** ⑫–⑱. On the following day, visit some of the other notable cultural attractions in and around the city, including the **Museo de Arte de Ponce** ⑲, **Castillo Serrallés** ㉒, **Centro Ceremonial Indígena de Tibes** ㉓, and **Hacienda Buena Vista** ㉔ (which requires a reservation). Dedicate your final day to **Guánica** ㉕, where you'll find wonderful beaches and the **Bosque Estatal de Guánica** ㉗, one of the best examples of a dry tropical forest in the world.

IF YOU HAVE 5 DAYS

Make a leisurely trip south from San Juan on the Luis A. Ferré Expressway, spending a night in one of the mountain towns and taking the thermal waters of **Coamo** ⑩ (thought by some to be Ponce de León's Fountain of Youth) or, if you're a serious hiker, seeking out the seldom-explored **Cañon de San Cristóbal** ④. Then continue on to **Ponce** ⑫–㉔ for two days of exploring the city's historic buildings and first-class museums. For your final two days, travel west along the coast and settle at a waterfront hotel near either **Guánica** ㉕ or **Cabo Rojo** ㊶, from which you can venture out to enjoy the region's beaches and hike the **Bosque Estatal de Guánica** ㉗.

IF YOU HAVE 7 DAYS

Hit the road, taking three days to drive the La Ruta Panorámica (☞ Close-Up box *below*), which encompasses much of inland Puerto Rico's most beautiful scenery. Traveling east to west you'll reach the end of the route in Mayagüez (☞ Chapter 5), from which it's a short trip south to **Cabo Rojo** ㊶. Make that area your base for two days of relaxing on the region's beaches, snorkeling among the reefs, hiking in the **Bosque Estatal de Guánica** ㉗, and exploring the historic town of **San Germán** ㉛–㊵. Set aside a night for dinner at one of the many fine seafood restaurants in nearby **Joyuda,** and, if your trip falls during a new moon, take a nighttime excursion to the **Bahía Fosforescente** ㉚ to see the shining dinoflagellates. Finish up with two days of seeing the sights in **Ponce** ⑫–㉔—or, if the relaxed pace of life *en la isla* has gotten in your blood, just kick back for two more days on the beach.

When to Tour

With its cool breezes, the mountainous central zone is a pleasure to visit year-round. Locals especially like to head up to this area during the hot summer months for the refreshing air, and some of the towns hold their biggest festivals at this time of year. (Aibonito's Flower Festival is in late June or July, and the Barranquitas Artisans Fair is in July.) With fewer clouds, southern Puerto Rico can feel hot any time of the year, but there are plenty of beaches where you can cool off. Ponce's yearly pre-Lenten Carnival, held the week before Ash Wednesday, draws many visitors—if you're planning to go, it's best to book several months in advance. The resort towns of Cabo Rojo, Guánica, and

La Parguera are popular with residents during the summer when children are out of school and many families take their vacations. Cabo Rojo is especially crowded over Easter weekend, when it has become a tradition to go to beaches in the area. Note that during busy times, some *paradores* and hotels require a minimum two- or three-night stay on weekends.

CENTRAL SOUTHERN PUERTO RICO

The mountainous stretch between San Juan and the Caribbean coast of Puerto Rico provides some dramatic scenery: church steeples loom above picturesque towns nestled in valleys, trees form arches over roads that twist and turn up the sides of mountains, flaming red *flamboyán* trees cover hillsides in the spring. More than likely, drivers will have to slow down several times for cows leisurely crossing narrow mountain roads. Many *sanjuaneros* start feeling like they've escaped the urban hustle and bustle and are en la isla, or "out on the island," once the Luis A. Ferré Expressway hits the city of Cayey, known for its scenic restaurants nestled in nearby hillsides. Aibonito, at some 2,000 ft above sea level, is the highest town in Puerto Rico and is known as "The Queen of Flowers" because of the abundant flora that thrive in its cool breezes. Barranquitas, while more isolated, nevertheless has historically been a cradle of political and intellectual thought, and the quaint town is still revered as being the home of island patriot Luis Muñoz Rivera.

When you cross over to the southern side of the Central Mountain Range, the scenery becomes drier and more rugged. The Caribbean Sea makes its appearance, and the flat landscape between the sea and the mountains, once the heart of the sugarcane industry, is now dotted with cattle grazing in open fields. Nestled in the foothills, Coamo, an important center in Spanish times and a popular resort in the early 1900s because of its thermal springs, still has many historic buildings. Ponce, known as "The Pearl of the South," retains much of its eclectic colonial charm in the downtown area, while its outskirts take on the modern-day trappings of strip malls and shopping centers.

Cayey

❶ *50 km (30 mi) south of San Juan via the Luis A. Ferré Expressway (Rte. 52).*

Cool mountain breezes have drawn islanders to the town of Cayey, located in a fertile valley at the foot of the Cayey Mountain Range, since it was founded in 1773. The Spanish soon realized the climate here was perfect for growing crops, and it became a center of coffee and tobacco production. Today, Cayey is a bustling town with a permanent population of more than 46,000. Mainland-style strip malls have gone up on the outskirts of town, but the surrounding hills and valleys retain a rural feeling. On weekends, sanjuaneros visit the numerous restaurants perched on nearby mountain roads or picnic in Bosque Estatal Carite just east of town.

❷ You can reach **Bosque Estatal Carite** (Carite National Forest, also known as the Guavate Forest) by taking the Route 184 exit off the Luis A. Ferré Expressway just north of Cayey. The forest covers more than 7,000 acres between Cayey and Patillas. Some 25 mi of hiking trails go through lush vegetation that includes prickly palms, royal palms, Honduras mahogany, and Spanish cedar, as well as many species of orchids. One trail leads to Charco Azul (Blue Pond), which is known for its deep blue color and cool water that lures bathers. Picnic tables and campgrounds are nearby. There's also the man-made Carite Lake:

it's stocked with bass and other fish, and you'll often see people fishing from the bank. (If you want to join them you'll need to bring your own equipment.) The forest has two campsites; camping permits must be obtained in advance at the Puerto Rico Department of Natural Resources near the Club Náutico on Avenida Fernández Juncos in San Juan. Picnic tables and bathroom facilities are available. Information on hiking trails can be obtained at the park manager's office near the entrance on Route 184. ⊠ *Rte. 184, Km 20, Guavate Sector,* ☎ *787/ 747–4545; for camping permits in San Juan, 787/724–3724.* 🖼 *Free.* ⊘ *Manager's office open weekdays 9–5.*

NEED A BREAK? The smell of fresh vegetation isn't the only thing in the air near the Carite National Forest. Just before the entrance on Route 184 is a string of eateries offering **lechón** (pork), marinated and slow-roasted over open pits for ultimate tenderness. The rustic restaurants—where you can often see the pigs roasting—also serve slow-roasted chicken and traditional side dishes such as rice and beans, yucca, and plantains. On weekends, day-trippers flock to the area, and many of the restaurants feature salsa or merengue bands. The greatest concentration of *lechoneras* is around kilometer 27.

Dining and Lodging

$ ✕ **Martin's BBQ.** This unpretentious spot at the Cayey exit off the Luis A. Ferré Expressway is often filled with locals wanting a quick fix of authentic *arroz con pollo, habichuelas* (red beans), and other Puerto Rican dishes. Diners order their food at the counter, choosing precisely what meats and side dishes they want. You can eat inside, outside at picnic tables, or take your food with you. ⊠ *Rte. 1 at Cayey exit off the Luis A. Ferré Expressway,* ☎ *787/738–1144. MC, V.*

$$ ✕🖬 **The Sand and the Sea.** Nestled on a mountainside near Cayey, this
★ establishment is best known for its open-air dining room, which has a breathtaking view of the island's south coast and refreshing cool breezes (its fireplace is often lit in the winter). Open for lunch and dinner ~~Friday through Sunday~~, it has a changing menu that's written on a blackboard and brought to your table. Regular features are charcoal-grilled steaks and fish dishes, and you'll also often find "Russian tostones," traditional deep-fried plantains topped with sour cream and caviar. There's piano music nightly, and diners often start singing along to old Broadway tunes or Puerto Rican ballads. Overnight guests are welcome to stay in four rooms available on the second floor, which are decorated like a New England–style bed-and-breakfast. It's a very convenient place to stay if you're driving the Panoramic Route. Reservations should be made at least a week in advance by calling the restaurant on the days it is open. ⊠ *Rte. 714, Km 5.2, Cercadillo Sector, 00736,* ☎ *787/738–9086. 4 rooms. Restaurant. AE, D, MC, V. Restaurant closed Mon.–Thurs. CP*

Aibonito

❸ *20 km (12 mi) northwest of Cayey via Rte. 7722, Rte. 772, and Rte. 162.*

One legend has it that Aibonito, the highest city in Puerto Rico at some 2,000 ft above sea level, got its name when a Spaniard exclaimed *"Ay, que bonito"* ("Oh, how pretty") upon seeing the high valley where the town now stands. The cool climate allows many colorful blooming plants to thrive, and as a result Aibonito has come to be known as "The Queen of Flowers." Greenhouses are scattered throughout the area, and the city hosts an extremely popular flower festival every year, usually in late June or July. The family-oriented affair gives awards for flowers and garden design and features live music and crafts. A double-steepled

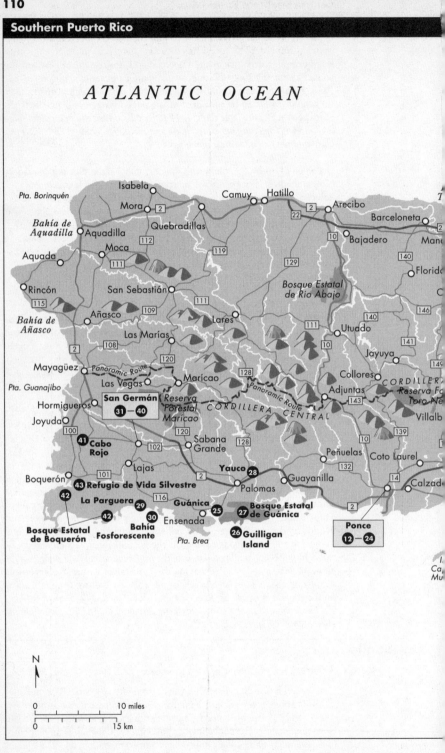

ATLANTIC OCEAN

Pta. Borinquén

Isabela

Mora

Camuy

Hatillo

Arecibo

Barceloneta

2

Bahía de Aquadilla

Aquadilla

Quebradillas

22

2

10

Bajadero

Man

Moca

112

119

129

140

Aquada

111

Florid

Rincón

San Sebastián

Bosque Estatal de Río Abajo

115

109

146

Bahía de Añasco

Añasco

Lares

Utuado

140

141

Las Marías

111

Jayuya

149

Mayagüez

108

120

Maricao

128

Colores

CORDILLER

Pta. Guanajibo

Las Vegas

Panoramic Route

Adjuntas

Reserva F Toro Ne

San Germán

Reserva Forestal Maricao

CORDILLERA CENTRAL

143

Hormigueros

31 — 40

Panoramic Route

Villalb

Joyuda

120

10

139

100

Sabana Grande

128

Peñuelas

Coto Laurel

41 Cabo Rojo

102

Lajas

Yauco

132

Boquerón

101

2

Guayanilla

14

Calzad

43 Refugio de Vida Silvestre

Palomas

28

2

42

La Parguera

116

Guánica

29

25

27

Bosque Estatal de Guánica

Ponce

42

30

Ensenada

12 — 24

Bosque Estatal de Boquerón

Bahía Fosforescente

Pta. Brea

26 **Guilligan Island**

I Ca Mu

N

0   10 miles

0   15 km

cathedral graces the pretty town square, and nearby streets are dotted with small businesses and a few shops. Restaurants have also taken advantage of the scenic location, and adventure groups organize outings to the nearby San Cristóbal Canyon.

Mirador Piedra Degetau (Degetau Lookout Rock) is a scenic point near Aibonito from which you can view the surrounding mountains. It's named after Federico Degetau y González, the island's first resident commissioner in Washington, D.C., and it's equipped with a lookout tower with a telescope, as well as picnic tables under gazebos and a children's playground. Route 7718, where Mirador Piedra Degetau is located, intersects Route 7722 just before Aibonito's city center. ⊠ *Rte. 7718, Km 0.7,* ☎ *787/735–3880.* ⌑ *Free.* ⊙ *Wed.–Sun. 9–6.*

★ ❹ One of Puerto Rico's best-kept secrets, **El Cañon de San Cristóbal,** lies north of Route 725 between Aibonito and Barranquitas. This canyon— almost impossible to find without local help—is more than 5 mi long and some 500 ft deep. It's filled with lush vegetation and has a breathtaking waterfall. The canyon is under the management of the Conservation Trust of Puerto Rico, and there's been some talk of developing it for eco-tourism, but for now only a few hearty souls find their way in to view its beauty. Félix Rivera, a local guide (☎ 787/735–5188, 787/612–0338, or 787/735–8721), leads expeditions starting from La Piedra restaurant (☞ Dining, *below*). The fee is $20 per person; call for reservations.

Dining

$$ ✕ **La Piedra.** This popular restaurant on the outskirts of Aibonito has a gorgeous mountain view. It's known for its fresh ingredients—many of the herbs and vegetables used are from its own garden. The Sunday buffet featuring gourmet Puerto Rican cuisine draws many repeat visitors. The menu features arroz con pollo, lechón, tostones, yucca, and rice and *grandules* (chickpeas). ⊠ *Rte. 7718, Km 0.8,* ☎ *787/735–1034. AE, D, MC, V. Closed Mon.–Tues.*

Barranquitas

❺ *15 km (9 mi) northwest of Aibonito via Rte. 162 to Rte. 719.*

Founded in 1804, the small mountain city of Barranquitas is best known for its famous natives, particularly Luis Muñoz Rivera, a politician and newspaperman. Today, a mausoleum in the city honors Muñoz Rivera and his son, Luis Muñoz Marín, the island's first elected governor, and Muñoz Rivera's birthplace has been turned into a museum. Barranquitas's city center has hilly streets and a quaint plaza with a yesteryear feel. Like other cities in the mountains, it has been a popular location for summer homes. One of the most beautiful, El Cortijo on Route 162 at Km 9.9, was built in 1938 and is said to be haunted by a former servant dismissed abruptly by his boss. The home is currently closed to the public, but there are plans to allow visitors. In July, craftspeople from all over Puerto Rico gather in Barranquitas for its annual Artisans Fair, one of the most popular such events on the island.

Museo Luis Muñoz Rivera, one block west of the main square on Calle Muñoz Rivera, occupies the house where Luis Muñoz Rivera, a politician, poet, and journalist known for his support of Puerto Rican autonomy, was born in 1859. Many original manuscripts of his political writings and poems are housed here, as well as his desk, other personal belongings, and even his car. ⊠ *Calle Muñoz Rivera and Calle Manuel Torres,* ☎ *787/857–0230 or 787/857–2065, ext. 227.* ⌑ *Free.* ⊙ *Mon.–Sat. 8:30–5.*

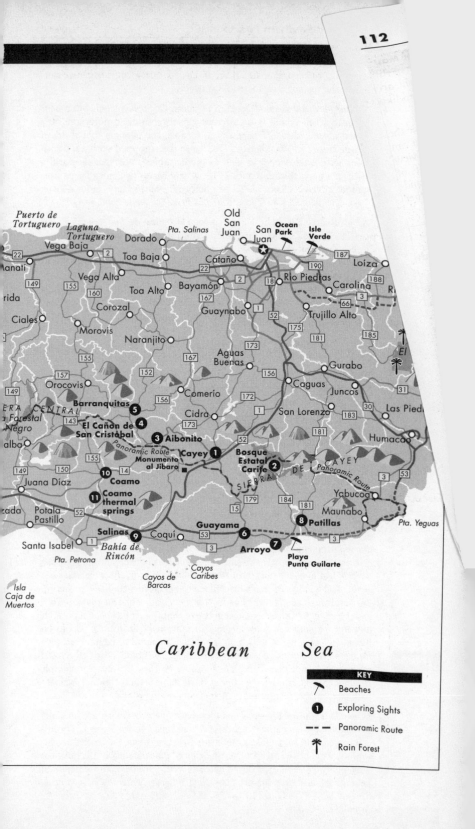

Steps away from Luis Muñoz Rivera's birthplace you'll find the **Mausoleo de la Familia Muñoz** (Calle Padre Berríos, two blocks west of the main plaza), where Muñoz Rivera and his son, Luis Muñoz Marín, are buried with other members of their family. There's a small, parklike area and a memorial to the two island politicians.

En Route Heading south again on the Luis A. Ferré Expressway, you'll see the tall, white **Monumento al Jíbaro Puertorriqueño** at Km 49. You can pull over—there's no parking or rest rooms, but there's a great view of the expressway curving around the rugged mountains and lots of photo opportunities. The monument itself makes a dramatic sight, standing amid green and brown mountain peaks. It depicts a mother, father, and child, and honors Puerto Rican *jíbaros*, or rural workers.

Guayama

6 *28 km (17 mi) southeast of Cayey via the Luis A. Ferré Expressway (Rte. 52) to Rte. 53 going east.*

To explore a bit of southeastern Puerto Rico, pick up Route 53 east off the Luis A. Ferré Expressway, which will lead you into Guayama, a city that has maintained much of its Spanish colonial charm. It was founded in 1736, but a mysterious fire destroyed much of it in the early 1800s; most of the existing buildings date from the mid-1800s onward. Guayama thrived in the 19th century as the sugarcane industry grew and merchants built Spanish colonial and Puerto Rican–creole style buildings, examples of both of which can still be seen throughout the city. One of the finest 19th-century creole homes is the Casa Cautiño on the main plaza, now a museum.

Guayama's 40,000-plus residents are proud of the city's claim to being the cleanest urban area in Puerto Rico. On Sunday, a trolley gives tours of the city starting at the Casa Cautiño museum, and often the mayor takes the wheel. The nearby countryside is known for its Paso Fino horses. Each March at the Marcelino Blondet Stadium you can watch these high-stepping show horses strut their stuff at the Dulce Sueño Paso Fino Fair. Folk music and crafts are also part of the festivities.

★ **Casa Cautiño,** on Guayama's main square, is an elegant home built in 1887 for sugar, cattle, and coffee baron Genaro Cautiño Vázquez and his wife, Genoveva Insúa. Outside there's a sweeping balcony with ornate grillwork, and the interiors are decorated in mahogany Victorian and art deco furniture. Things are so well preserved that you suspect the former owners could walk in and not find a thing out of place. Don't miss the modern-for-its-time bathroom, complete with a standing shower. ⊠ *1 Calle Palmer at Calle Vicente Palé Matos,* ☎ *787/864–9083.* ☐ *$1.* ⊙ *Tues.–Sat. 9:30–4:30, Sun. 10–5:30.*

Dining and Lodging

$ ✕ **El Balcó Café.** This charming wooden house with a long balcony provides a great setting for enjoying a sandwich, a natural juice, or a cup of *café con leche.* Mainly a breakfast and lunch spot, it stays open later on Friday and Saturday, when it takes on the feel of a bohemian bar—locals stopping in to share a drink often take out guitars and provide their own entertainment. ⊠ *47 Calle Hostos,* ☎ *787/864–7272. No credit cards. Closed Sun. No dinner Mon.–Thurs.*

$ ✕ **El Suarito.** Surround yourself with history in this restaurant housed in Guayama's second-oldest building, dating from 1862. The site has been used as a repair shop for horse-drawn buggies, a gas station, and, since the mid-1900s, a restaurant. The place is always hopping with townspeople who stop by at all hours of the day for a meal or something to drink. The dinner menu includes Puerto Rican favorites such as roasted chicken and pork chops. You can also get eggs and toast for breakfast, and sandwiches are served throughout the day. ✉ *6 Calle Derkes, at Calle Hostos,* ☎ *787/864–1820. MC, V. Closed Sun.*

$$ ✕▯ **Molino Inn.** This tidy hotel is often used by business travelers in
★ the area, but it's also a great, undiscovered spot for families—it doesn't get overrun with locals on weekends and holidays the way some paradores do. It's located on the outskirts of Guayama, near the ruins of an old Spanish *molino* (sugar mill), and has comfortable, rattan-decorated rooms with air-conditioning, cable television, and small writing desks. The 9 acres of grounds surrounding the hotel's two buildings contain colorful flower beds and a large pool. The cozy restaurant—popular with the local business crowd—offers a mix of international and Caribbean cuisines, including filet mignon, grilled chicken, and a wide selection of seafood. There's often live music on weekends. ✉ *Av. Albizu Campos at Rte. 54 (Box 2393), 00785-2393,* ☎ *787/866–1515,* ℻ *787/866–1510. 20 rooms. Restaurant, lounge, air-conditioning, cable TV, pool, tennis court, basketball court, laundry service. AE, MC, V. EP.*

Outdoor Activities and Sports

GOLF

Duffers can get in nine holes at the **Aguirre Golf Club** (✉ Rte. 705, Km 3, Aguirre, ☎ 787/853–4025), built in 1925 for the executives of a sugar mill. Open daily, it's known as a short but tough course.

Arroyo

❼ *6 km (4 mi) east of Guayama via Rte. 3.*

This sleepy seaside town of mostly single-story buildings was founded in 1855 and has long been tied to sugar. Cane fields still surround it, and what was once one of the island's largest sugar-processing factories, Central Lafayette (now closed), used to handle much of the sugar in the region. Today, a refurbished sugarcane train takes visitors along an old sugar railway between Guayama and Arroyo on weekends and holidays.

Despite its out-of-the-way location, Arroyo was at the forefront in the development of modern communications. Samuel F. B. Morse placed a telegraph machine in his son-in-law's farm on the outskirts of Arroyo in 1858 and connected it up to the center of town, creating what is believed to be the first telegraph line in Latin America. The town's main street is named after Morse, and there's a monument to the inventor in the city's main plaza.

Arroyo is best known for the nearby beaches, especially Punta Guilarte, and for its many festivals. Its patron saint festival—honoring the Virgin of Carmen, patron saint of fishermen—is held every July, and its fish festival is in October. Most of the festivities take place on the boardwalk along the *malecón* (sea wall), officially known as El Paseo de Las Américas.

Housed in an ornate pink building next to the city hall, the **Museo Antigua Aduana de Arroyo** (Museum of the Old Customs House of Arroyo) traces the history of the town and tells about some of its well-known inhabitants, including Samuel F. B. Morse. ✉ *65 Calle Morse,* ☎ *787/839–8096.* ▣ *Free.* ☉ *Wed.–Sun. 9–4:30.*

🅒 **El Tren del Sur** (The Train of the South) takes passengers for a one-hour round trip along an old sugarcane railroad line between Arroyo and Guayama. The train carried sugarcane from the fields to the mills from 1915 to 1958; today it's one of the few active trains on the is-

TRAVELING LA RUTA PANORÁMICA

ONE WAY TO CAPTURE the flavor of lush, untamed Puerto Rico is to take the Caribbean's most beautiful drive. Twisting and turning on mountain roads brightened by flamboyáns and flowers, La Ruta Panorámica (the Panoramic Route) lives up to the promise of its name. If you choose to start from the east, you'll find yourself on the southeastern tip of Puerto Rico at the town of Yabucoa. From there you'll loop around toward the Caribbean Sea, then head inland as the route crosses the mountainous spine of Puerto Rico. You'll ride high above valleys and pass through small rural towns, until you reach the west coast terminus, the city of Mayagüez. In some areas along the way, the scenery and climate can change dramatically in less than an hour, as you travel up a mountainside or descend into a valley.

La Ruta is not one straight, continuous highway, but a collection of some 40 interconnecting country roads. (It's highlighted on maps that can be purchased at gift shops and gasoline stations.) Sometimes intersections are clearly marked, other times they're not, but finding the way is part of the adventure. Veterans of the route suggest taking at least three days to make the journey from end to end. The trip requires some flexibility—there are small *colmados* (country stores) and restaurants along the way, but they might not come along at the exact time you want them; gas stations are found throughout the countryside, but you may have to go a mile or two out of your way to refuel. You usually have to pull off the route to find lodging, though some of the island's paradores are very close by, especially Hacienda Juanita and Hacienda Gripiñas on the west coast, and Baños de Coamo farther east.

As with everything in Puerto Rico, you're rewarded if you take your time along La Ruta. Some of the most interesting sights on the island can be reached with only a minor detour: Hacienda Buena Vista is south of the route near Ponce off Rte. 10; the Río Camuy Cave Park is north via Rtes. 128 and 129; the Arecibo Observatory is near the caves on Rte. 625; and the Caguana Indian Ceremonial Center is in the same vicinity on Rte. 111. While the Panoramic Route itself is 264 km (165 mi) long, you'll probably drive at least 480 km (300 mi) if you really want to get the most out of the journey.

If you're not up to a drive of three days, you can seek out one of the highlights of the route. At the east end, Rte. 901 loops around to hug the Caribbean Sea, and you'll encounter huge boulders along the roadside on Rte. 3. Heading to the island's mountain spine on Rte. 143 past Aibonito, you'll get a bird's-eye view in spots of both the Atlantic to the north and the Caribbean to the south. The western portion of the route winds through a rural coffee-growing region and rustic small towns where impatiens and fruit trees grow wild along the road.

land. The trip is particularly popular with children and history buffs. Afterward, a trolley makes a scenic tour of the town, including stops at the **Museo Antigua Aduana de Arroyo** and the malecón. ⊠ *Rte. 3 near the former Central Lafayette factory,* ☎ *787/271-1574.* 🖾 *$3.* ⊙ *Trains on weekends and holidays hourly 9:30–4:30.*

Dining and Lodging

$–$$ ✕ **La Llave del Mar.** This casual, air-conditioned restaurant across from Arroyo's malecón on the Caribbean Sea is a convenient place to cool off and have a satisfying meal. It's popular with the townsfolk for its wide variety of seafood, and the menu also includes grilled steaks. ⊠ *Paseo de Las Américas,* ☎ *787/839–6395. AE, MC, V. Closed Mon.–Tues.*

$$ ▦ **Centro Vacacional Punta Guilarte.** Twenty-eight rustic cabins and 32 newer "villas" are located on the Punta Guilarte beach and run by the government. Geared primarily toward Puerto Rican families, this very casual vacation center can be a good choice if you're on a budget and traveling with children or looking for a no-frills beachside destination. The cabins and villas have refrigerators and stoves, but you need to supply your own bed linen and kitchen utensils. (In a pinch you can find inexpensive supplies at the Wal-Mart 15 minutes west on Route 3 at the Guayama exit.) Some pillows and blankets are available, but you should make arrangements for them at the same time you make your reservation. Also state in advance the number of beds you need. Most units have two bedrooms that can be arranged to accommodate up to six people in the cabins, up to seven in the villas. The newer villas have air-conditioning. ⊠ *Balneario Punta Guilarte, Rte. 3, Km 128.5, 00714,* ☎ *787/722–1771 or 787/839–3565,* 🖷 *787/722–0090. Refrigerators, stoves, air-conditioning (villas), 2 pools. MC, V. EP.*

Beaches

Balneario Punta Guilarte (Rte. 3, Km 128.5), just east of Arroyo's city center, is one of the largest and best-known beaches on the south coast. There are palm trees for shade, changing facilities, picnic tables, and barbecue grills. During the summer the beach can become crowded with locals, especially on weekends and holidays, but in winter you may be one of just a handful of people enjoying the sand.

Patillas

❽ *6 km (4 mi) east of Arroyo via Rte. 3.*

This tranquil city of about 20,000 was founded in 1811 and is known as the "Emerald of the South." The city itself has a small plaza and hilly, narrow streets, but the best sightseeing is along the coast east of town, where Route 3 skirts the Caribbean then starts curving northward and rugged cliffs drop sharply to the water. The stretch of road passes some beautiful beaches, many of which have not yet been discovered by the tourist crowd.

Dining and Lodging

$$ ✕▦ **Caribe Playa Beach Resort.** This casual resort offers a good base from which to explore the southeast coast or just lie back and chill out. The rooms border a crescent-shape beach (a little rocky, but good for a refreshing dip) and come with air-conditioning, cable television, refrigerators, coffeemakers, and either a patio or a balcony; they're clean and comfortable and have nice touches such as wind chimes hanging outside the doors. You'll find lots of areas where you can relax—by the pool, in a hammock swung between coconut trees, or in the informal library. There are barbecue grills, a children's playground, and beach chairs, and you can arrange for boat trips, fishing, scuba div-

ing, and massages. The Seaview Terrace is open for breakfast, lunch, cocktails, and dinner. ✉ *Rte. 3, Km 112.1 (HC 764, Box 8490), 00723,* ☎ *787/839–7719 or 787/839–6339,* ℻ *787/839–1817. 32 rooms. Air-conditioning, refrigerators, cable TV, pool, playground. AE, MC, V. EP.* ✍

Beaches

There's a beach for everyone along Route 3 heading east from Patillas. **El Bajo de Patillas** south of Patillas offers tranquil sunning and good swimming. **Channel,** in front of Caribe Playa, is good for bodysurfing and swimming, although the bottom can be rocky. **Inches,** a few miles to the east of Patillas, is known as a surfing beach.

OFF THE
BEATEN PATH

Panoramic Route East and the Maunabo Lighthouse – Route 3 going eastward intersects with Route 901, the eastern portion of the cross-island Panoramic Route. This loop provides attractive views of cliffs, the ocean, and animals grazing in fields. Turn off on Route 760 and take it to the end for a dramatic view of the Maunabo Lighthouse at Punta Tuna. (The lighthouse isn't open to the public, but it's pleasant to view from a distance.)

Salinas

❾ *29 km (18 mi) west of Guayama, off the Luis A. Ferré Expressway.*

Most tourists are familiar with this town only from seeing its name on an exit sign along the Luis A. Ferré Expressway. Islanders, however, know that the exit leads to some of the best seafood restaurants in Puerto Rico. Most of them are scattered along the seafront in the Playa de Salinas area, reached by heading south on Rte. 701.

Dining

$$ ✕ **Costa Marina Restaurant.** This family-friendly, second-story restaurant in the Marina de Salinas has nautical-theme decor and a view of the water. The menu, naturally, emphasizes fish, featuring halibut, lobster, and stuffed red snapper. You can also get good steaks and *asopao.* ✉ *G-8 Calle Chapin,* ☎ *787/824–6647. AE, D, MC, V.*

$$ ✕ **Puerta la Bahía.** You'll find a spacious, air-conditioned dining area here with huge windows looking out on the water and an extensive menu of fresh seafood. For a lighter meal, try one of the fish soups or fish croquettes stuffed with crab. Heartier dishes include salmon fillets, grouper, lobster, and mofongo stuffed with octopus or conch. If you're not in the mood for fish, you can try one of the staple Puerto Rican chicken or beef dishes, served with rice and beans. ✉ *End of Calle Principal, Sector Playita Final,* ☎ *787/824–7117. AE, MC, V.*

Coamo

❿ *33 km (20 mi) southwest of Cayey, via the Luis A. Ferré Expressway and Rte. 153.*

Founded by Spanish settlers in 1579, Coamo was the third city established in Puerto Rico. It dominated the south of the island until the mid 1880s, when political power moved to Ponce. The town, however, remained an important Spanish outpost, and several decisive battles were fought here during the Spanish-American War in 1898.

Coamo has long been known for its thermal springs—Indians are said to have bathed in the warm waters just outside of the city and, according to legend this area was the Fountain of Youth the Indians described to Ponce de León. In the mid-1800s a fashionable resort was built near the waters, and Coamo began drawing the elite from around the island for restful getaways. Today the waters continue to be a draw—the resort is now a country inn popular with Puerto Rican families.

Coamo is also known for its San Blas Half-Marathon, which draws competitors, and spectators, from around the world every February. The city's quaint plaza is dominated by a white 18th-century church, and the hilly streets have many buildings dating from the 19th century—you'll find car mechanics, hair salons, and pharmacies still operating out of them. New on the scene is the 18-hole Coamo Springs Golf Course near Parador Baños de Coamo.

Just off the main square, the **Museo Histórico de Coamo** is appropriately housed in the former residence of one of the city's illustrious citizens, Clotilde Santiago, a wealthy farmer and merchant born in 1826. The museum is located on the second floor of this sprawling, tangerine-color building dating from 1863. Several rooms are decorated with colonial-style furnishings, and old photos capture the town's history. ⊠ *29 Calle José I. Quintón,* ☎ *787/825–1150.* ☞ *Free.* ☼ *Weekdays 8–noon and 1–4:30.*

⑪ You can bathe in the famous **thermal springs,** said to have curative powers, located just outside Coamo on Route 546. The Baños de Coamo parador allows day-trippers to bathe in its warm pool for $5. (The parador's guests enjoy the pool for free.) A small public bathing area reached by a path behind the parador is free. ⊠ *Rte. 546, Km 1,* ☎ *Baños de Coamo: 787/825–2186.* ☼ *Both daily 10–5:30.*

Dining and Lodging

$–$$ ✕ **Chicken Burger.** Don't let the name fool you—there's more than chicken burgers at this popular spot at the entrance to Coamo. While known for its grilled chicken, the menu also features steaks, hamburgers, fish, mofongo with lobster, and more. You can sit indoors in air-conditioning or outside on a spacious patio. ⊠ *Rte. 153 near Coamo entrance,* ☎ *787/825–4761. MC, V.*

$–$$ ✕🏨 **Parador Baños de Coamo.** Located at the hot springs that are said
★   to be the Fountain of Youth of Ponce de León's dreams, this rustic country inn consists of four two-story buildings surrounding a pretty interior patio where you'll find trees, flowers, benches, and a bar. Local groups often play traditional Puerto Rican music there on weekends. Rooms have a lodgelike feel and come with air-conditioning, televisions, and balconies. The thermal water flows into a swimming pool located a few steps away from a cool-water pool where you can still see walls dating from 1843, when the inn first opened. The dining room has its own building decorated with photos of the inn dating back from the early 1900s. The portions of traditional Puerto Rican food such as *churrasco* (steak) with rice and beans and fried chicken are generous and delicious. ⊠ *Rte. 546, Km 1 (Box 540), 99769,* ☎ *787/825–2186 or 787/825–2239,* ℻ *787/825–4739. 48 rooms. Air conditioning, pool. AE, D, MC, V. EP.*

Outdoor Activities and Sports

GOLF

The **Coamo Springs Golf Course** (⊠ Rte. 546 just before Baños de Coamo parador, ☎ 787/825–1370) opened in 1998 and is gaining popularity for its rugged beauty. Sanjuaneros are known to drive down for a day of play on the drier southern coast when it is raining in the capital. The course, designed by Ferdinand Garbin, is open daily.

PONCE

34 km (21 mi) southwest of Coamo via Rte. 153 and the Luis A. Ferré Expressway. The mountainous Rte. 14 also runs between Coamo and Ponce. 112 km (70 mi) from San Juan via the Luis A. Ferré Expressway.

The port city of Ponce, nestled between the Caribbean Sea and the foothills of the central mountain range, spent the 19th century developing into a center of international commerce, luring immigrants from around the world. The money and cultural sophistication that trade brought with it manifested themselves in architecture: elegant, ornate homes and public buildings are the city's hallmark. They are in striking contrast to the fortresslike structures of the more military-minded Old San Juan.

Now the second-largest urban area in Puerto Rico (population 210,000), Ponce, known as the "Pearl of the South," still retains much of its historical charm. The *Ponce en March* (Ponce on the Move) program of the early 1990s brought about the refurbishment of many older buildings, leaving the city dotted with pastel mansions, some of which now house museums. Ponce is also the hometown of former governor Luis A. Ferré, who endowed it with what has become the best art museum in Puerto Rico and possibly the best in all of the Caribbean—the Museo de Arte de Ponce.

The city is also home to one of the island's most celebrated pre-Lenten carnivals. The colorful costumes and signature *vejigante* (roughly meaning "troublemaker") masks worn during the festivities are famous all over the island. *Poceños* have fierce pride in their city, and are known as warm and gracious hosts. The city runs free trolleys and *chu chu* trains from Plaza las Delicias, the main square, to major tourists attractions, and free horse-and-carriage rides are available around the plaza on weekends.

Downtown Ponce

Downtown Ponce is a wonderful blend of neoclassical, art deco, and ornate *criollo* architecture. At its heart is the Plaza las Delicias (Plaza of Delights), arguably the prettiest central square on the island. It's dominated by the huge Catedral Nuestra Señora de Guadalupe and accentuated with trees, benches, and a huge fountain. Many historic buildings, including the fanciful Parque de Bombas and the stately Teatro La Perla, are found on the main plaza or on streets branching off it, making the area ideal for a leisurely morning or afternoon walking tour.

A Good Walk

Start your walk on the tree-lined Plaza las Delicias; you'll find nearby parking on Calle Luna, Calle Concordia, and Calle Mayor. Looming over the plaza is the **Catedral Nuestra Señora de Guadalupe** ⑫, dating from 1835, and across the street on the west side of the plaza is the ornate **Casa Armstrong-Poventud** ⑬, home of the Puerto Rican Institute of Culture's Ponce branch. Leaving Armstrong-Poventud, cross back over onto the plaza, circle south by the Alcaldía (City Hall), with its clock brought to Ponce in 1877, and continue to the east side of the plaza to visit the red-and-black-stripe **Parque de Bombas** ⑭.

Cross the street to the intersection of Calles Marina and Cristina, and take Calle Cristina a block east to see one of the city's first restoration projects, **Teatro La Perla** ⑮, at the corner of Cristina and Mayor. One block north of the theater, at Calles Mayor and Isabel, is the historic home that now houses the **Museo de la Historia de Ponce** ⑯. A block east, at the corner of Calles Salud and Isabel, is another historic home,

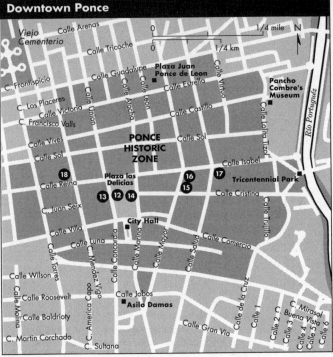

Downtown Ponce

PONCE HISTORIC ZONE

now the **Museo de la Música Puertorriqueña** ⑰. Four blocks west from
there (you will go by Plaza las Delicias again, and Calle Isabel will turn
into Calle Reina) is the 1911 architectural masterpiece **Casa Wiechers-Villaronga** ⑱. If you want to take in even more turn-of-the-20th-
century architecture, continue west on Calle Reina, and shortly you
will see some beautiful examples of *casas criollas*, wooden homes with
sweeping balconies popular in the Caribbean during the early 1900s.

TIMING

To get the most out of downtown Ponce you should devote a full day
to it (and an evening as well, to stroll the plaza with the townspeople
and see it beautifully lit up). But, if you keep an eye on your watch,
you can see the area in a morning or an afternoon.

Sights to See

⑬ **Casa Armstrong-Poventud.** Inaugurated in 1901 as the residence of
banker and industrialist Carlos Armstrong and his wife, Eulalia Pou,
this neoclassical home was built by Manuel V. Domenech and is known
for the ornate embellishments on its French-influenced facade. Today
it houses the Ponce offices of Institute of Puerto Rican Culture and has
several rooms decorated in colonial furnishings that visitors can walk
through. ⊠ *Calle Union across from Catedral,* ☎ *787/844–8240 or
787/840–7667.* 🎟 *Free.* ⊙ *Weekdays 8–4:30.*

⑱ **Casa Wiechers-Villaronga.** Alfredo B. Wiechers, a Ponce native, studied in Paris and then returned home to become one of the city's premier architects. He designed this house, which was built in 1911, and
then lived here until 1918, when he sold it to the Villaronga-Mercado
family. The arches and columns found throughout the interior are
Wiechers trademarks, creating many nooks and niches. The facade has
a chamferred corner, a common site on turn-of-the-20th-century buildings in Ponce, and the ornamentation and stained-glass windows are

also noteworthy; be sure to look for the gazebo on the rooftop. Inside, you'll find original furnishings on display and information on Wiechers and other Ponce architects of his era. ⊠ *Calle Reina at Calle Meléndez Vigo,* ☎ 787/843–3363. ☑ *Free.* ⊘ *Wed.–Sun. 8–4:30.*

⑫ **Catedral Nuestra Señora de Guadalupe.** This gigantic cathedral dedicated to the Virgin of Guadalupe sits on the site of a 1670 chapel that was destroyed by several earthquakes. Parts of the current structure, where mass continues to be held daily, date from 1835, but after a 1918 earthquake new steeples were erected, a new roof was put on, and neoclassical embellishments were added to the facade. Inside you'll see stained-glass windows, chandeliers, and two alabaster altars. ⊠ *Plaza las Delicias,* ☎ 787/284–3338. ⊘ *Services daily at 6 AM and 11 AM.*

⑯ **Museo de la Historia de Ponce.** Housed in two neoclassical buildings, this museum has 10 exhibition halls that cover Ponce's development from the days of the the Taíno Indians to the present. Guided tours in English and Spanish last 50 minutes and give a thorough overview of Ponce's past. ⊠ *51–53 Calle Isabel,* ☎ 787/844–7071 or 787/843–4322. ☑ *$3.* ⊘ *Wed.–Mon. 10–6:30.*

⑰ **Museo de la Música Puertorriqueña.** At this museum you'll learn how Puerto Rican music has been influenced by African, Spanish, and Indian cultures. On display are instruments such as the triple (a small string instrument resembling a banjo) and memorabilia of local composers and musicians. The small museum takes up several rooms in a neoclassical former residence. ⊠ *Calle Isabel at Calle Salud,* ☎ 787/848–7016. ☑ *Free.* ⊘ *Wed.–Sun. 9–4.*

⑭ **Parque de Bombas.** Built in 1882 as a pavilion for an agricultural fair and then used as a firehouse, this distinctive red-and-black-stripe building is now a firefighting museum, complete with antique fire trucks. Half-hour tours in English and Spanish are given on the half hour. ⊠ *Plaza las Delicias,* ☎ 787/284–4141, ext. 342. ☑ *Free.* ⊘ *Wed.–Mon. 9:30–6.*

NEED A
BREAK?

An institution for 40 years, **King's** (787/843–8520), across from Plaza las Delicias at 9223 Calle Marina, is *the* spot for ice cream in Ponce. It serves 12 varieties, from tamarind and passion-fruit to the classic chocolate and vanilla, and is open daily from 8 AM to midnight. A bench in the tiny storefront seats three, but most ice-cream lovers take their cups and cones across the street and stake out shady benches on the plaza.

---

⑮ **Teatro La Perla.** This theater was lovingly restored in 1941 after an earthquake and then a fire damaged the original structure built in 1864. The striking interior seats 1,047 and boasts wonderful acoustics. It's generally open for the public to tour on weekdays, but visits are suspended when there are rehearsals. ⊠ *Calle Mayor at Calle Cristina,* ☎ 787/843–4322 (administration), 787/843–4080 (ticket office). ☑ *Free.* ⊘ *Weekdays 8–4:30.*

Greater Ponce

The city center is not the only part of Ponce with sights to see. In fact, the greater Ponce area has some of Puerto Rico's most notable cultural attractions, including the island's finest art museum and its most important archeological site.

A Good Tour

The **Museo de Arte de Ponce** ⑲ stands on Avenida Las Américas, south of Plaza las Delicias and not far from the Luis A. Ferré Expressway. Anyone with a taste for European art can happily while away a morning in its galleries. East of the museum you can pick up Route 14 south

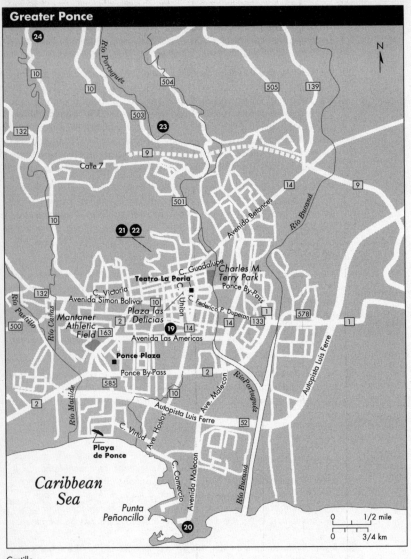

Greater Ponce

to the Caribbean and **La Guancha** ⑳, a boardwalk area with food kiosks, a playground, and a small, child-friendly public beach; it's a good place to relax and let younger members of your group work off some energy. From there, if you retrace your path north past downtown you can find your way to Calle Bertoly and Vigía Hill, where the **Cruceta El Vigía** ㉑ towers over the city and the **Castillo Serrallés** ㉒, a former sugar baron's villa, is a popular attraction.

Farther north on Route 503 is the **Centro Ceremonial Indígena de Tibes** ㉓, where you'll find remnants of native culture dating back over 1,500 years. You'll have to backtrack a bit to reach Rte. 10, then head north to **Hacienda Buena Vista** ㉔, a former coffee plantation that's been carefully restored by the Puerto Rican Conservation Trust. Call ahead to arrange for a tour.

While you can drive to the sights of greater Ponce, you also have the option of using the free trolleys and chu chu trains that run from Plaza las Delicias to the museum, La Guancha, and El Vigía Hill. You'll need a car or a cab to get to Tibes and Hacienda Buena Vista.

TIMING
The sights of greater Ponce aren't numerous, but they require some time to get the most out of them. To follow the full tour above, you should plan on spending 1½ or 2 days. If you don't want to devote that much time, you should choose the sights you find most appealing.

Sights to See

★ ㉒ **Castillo Serrallés.** This lovely Spanish-style villa overlooking the city and the sea was built in the 1930s for Ponce's wealthiest family, the makers of Don Q rum. Now a museum, it's a favorite tourist attraction. A guided tour offers a look at the area's history as a center for sugar production and at the lifestyles of the sugar barons. ⊠ *17 El Vigía,* ☎ *787/259–1774.* ⊡ *$3.* ⊙ *Tues.–Sun. 9:30–5.* ✎

㉓ **Centro Ceremonial Indígena de Tibes.** The Tibes Indian Ceremonial Center, discovered after flooding from a tropical storm in 1975, is considered the most important archaeological find on the island. Pre-Taíno ruins and burial grounds here date from AD 300 to AD 700. Be sure to explore the small museum before taking a walking tour of the site, which includes ceremonial playing fields bordered by smooth stones, some containing petroglyphs. Several thatch huts have been reconstructed in a village setting. ⊠ *Rte. 503, Km 2.2,* ☎ *787/840–2255 or 787/840–5685.* ⊡ *$2.* ⊙ *Tues.–Sun. 9–4.*

㉑ **Cruceta El Vigía.** At the top of Vigía Hill is a colossal concrete cross that is said to mark the spot where an Old Spanish observation post once stood. Generations ago, the Spanish used this vantage point to watch for offshore ships, including marauding pirates. You can climb the stairs or take an elevator to the top of the 100-ft cross, where you'll find a lovely panoramic view of the city and beyond. ⊠ *Across from Castillo Serrallés, El Vigía Hill,* ☎ *787/259–3816.* ⊡ *$1.* ⊙ *Tues.–Sun. 10–5.*

★ ㉔ **Hacienda Buena Vista.** Built in 1838 by Salvador Vives as a fruit farm, Hacienda Buena Vista later became a corn-flour mill and finally a coffee plantation. The plantation house was restored by the Puerto Rican Conservation Trust in 1987, which also preserved the original waterwheel, hydraulic systems, and other machinery from the coffee-processing past. Inside the two-story house, furniture, documents, and other memorabilia give a sense of what it was like to live on a coffee plantation nearly 150 years ago. The two-hour tour, given four times a day (once in English), is by reservation only. You can buy coffee beans and souvenirs at the gift shop. Allow yourself half an hour to travel the winding Route 10 from Ponce up to the Hacienda. ⊠ *Rte. 10, Km 16.8,* ☎ *787/722–5882.* 🖵 *$5.* ☉ *Wed.–Sun. (tour groups only Wed.– Thurs.).* 🕾

♨ ⑳ **La Guancha.** Stretching around a cove in a working harbor, this seaside boardwalk/park is a gem. There are kiosks where local food and drink are served, and where on weekends you'll hear live music. A large children's area is filled with playground equipment, while the nearby public beach has rest rooms, changing areas, and a medical post. There's plenty of free parking. ⊠ *End of Rte. 14,* ☎ *no phone.*

★ ⑲ **Museo de Arte de Ponce.** A lovely building designed by Edward Durrell Stone, who was also the architect for New York's Museum of Modern Art, houses one of the finest art collections in the Caribbean, containing more than 1,500 paintings, sculptures, and prints including works by Rubens, Rodin, and Gainsborough. The highlight is the selection of pre-Raphealite paintings, particularly *Flaming June* by Frederick Leighton, which has become an unofficial symbol of the museum. It also presents special exhibits and occasional concerts. ⊠ *2525 Av. Las Américas,* ☎ *787/848–0505.* 🖵 *$4.* ☉ *Daily 10–5.* 🕾

Dining and Lodging

$$–$$$ ✕ **Pito's.** Dine indoors or on a waterfront balcony at this popular seafood restaurant near the entrance to Ponce on Route 2. The menu includes lots of seafood—to indulge, try the shrimp wrapped in bacon, one of the house specialties. There are also chicken and steak dishes and an extensive selection of wines from the cellar. On Friday and Saturday there are often musicians playing romantic music. ⊠ *Rte. 2, Sector Las Cucharas,* ☎ *787/841–4977. AE, MC, V.*

$–$$$ ✕ **El Ancla.** A local favorite, especially for families, this restaurant sits perched on the edge of the ocean. The kitchen serves up generous— and affordable—plates of fish, crab, and other fresh seafood. Try the shrimp in garlic or the delectable mofongo, a plantain mash stuffed with treats from the sea. There are two dining rooms; the one where smoking is allowed has large windows overlooking the sea. ⊠ *9 Av. Hostos Final, Ponce Playa,* ☎ *787/840–2450. AE, MC, V.*

$$ ✕ **Puerto Santiago.** Most of the eateries along La Guancha boardwalk are casual food stands serving up such snacks as tacos and icy Medalla beer. This nautical-theme bar and grill offering sit-down service is an exception. Families flock here on weekends for seafood just plucked from the water. Steaks and lighter meals also figure on the menu. The restaurant's first-floor dining room is air-conditioned; upstairs there are outdoor tables on a balcony overlooking the marina. ⊠ *Local #27, La Guancha,* ☎ *787/840–7313. AE, MC, V. No dinner Mon.*

$–$$ ✕ **Lupita's.** Mariachis and margaritas are the perfect accompaniment to the savory Mexican-American food at this downtown restaurant. Heaping portions are the rule, whether you eat indoors in the dining room or outside in the casual courtyard. Mariachis usually perform on weekends; on weeknights there are dinner specials. ⊠ *60 Calle Isabel,* ☎ *787/848–8808. MC, V.*

$$$$ ✕🖽 **Ponce Hilton.** The biggest resort on the south coast—a cream-and-turquoise complex on 80 acres of landscaped gardens—is completely self-contained and caters primarily to a corporate clientele. You'll find a casino, a shopping arcade, a pool, access to a public beach, a disco, a children's program, a playground, and two restaurants. The ro-
★ mantic, dark-paneled **La Cava** has a menu that gracefully melds international cuisines—try the grilled beef tenderloin with goose liver or the vegetable spring rolls. A wine cellar can be reserved for private din-

ners. La Terraza is more casual, serving buffet breakfasts and lunches and often presenting theme dinners, such as steak night or paella night. Although the lobby has all the warmth of an airline terminal, the large guest rooms are attractive enough; they're decorated in sky-blue, teal, and peach, with modern rattan furniture and balconies. ⊠ *1150 Av. Caribe (Box 7419), 00732,* ☎ *787/259–7676 or 800/445–8667,* ℻ *787/259–7674. 145 rooms, 8 suites. 2 restaurants, 3 bars, in-room safes, minibars, pool, 4 tennis courts, fitness center, spa, sauna, driving range, bicycles, baby-sitting, children's program, playground, business center, meeting rooms. AE, DC, MC, V. EP.* ✺

$$ ✕▥ **Hotel Meliá.** Set in the heart of Ponce, near the Plaza las Delicias, ★ this family-owned hotel provides a good, low-key base for exploring the turn-of-the-20th-century architecture, museums, and landmarks of the downtown area. The lobby has an Old World feel with high ceilings, blue-and-beige tile floors, and well-worn but charming decor. Room furnishings are standard and somewhat dated. Breakfast is served on the rooftop terrace, which offers pretty views of the city and mountains. Mark's, the award-winning hotel restaurant owned by Mark French, former executive chef at the Ponce Hilton, offers some of the finest dining on the south coast. The eclectic menu includes teriyaki tuna, corn-encrusted snapper, and Long Island duck breast. ⊠ *2 Calle Cristina (Box 1431), 00753,* ☎ *787/841–3602 or 800/742–4276,* ℻ *787/841–3602. 75 rooms. Restaurant, bar, air-conditioning. AE, MC, V. CP.* ✺

$$$ ▥ **Holiday Inn Ponce.** Popular with both families and a business clientele, this recently renovated member of the Holiday Inn chain has 116 spacious rooms, decorated in tropical colors and each with a private balcony. You'll find an Olympic-size swimming pool and a children's pool, a casino, and an exercise room. The Tanama Restaurant serves Spanish, Puerto Rican, and nouvelle cuisine, and Holly's disco is popular on the weekends. ⊠ *3315 Ponce By-pass, 00731,* ☎ *787/844–1200 or 800/ 465–4329,* ℻ *787/841–8683. 116 rooms. Restaurant, bar, 2 pools, exercise room, dance club, meeting rooms. AE, MC, V. EP.* ✺

Nightlife and the Arts

The Arts

You can check for local theater productions and primarily classical concert performances at the **Teatro La Perla** (⊠ Calle Mayor at Calle Cristina, ☎ 787/843–4322 for administration; 787/843–4080 for ticket office). The **Museo de Arte de Ponce** (⊠ 2525 Av. Las Américas, ☎ 787/848–0505) occasionally sponsors concerts by small classical ensembles and recitals by members of the Puerto Rico Symphony Orchestra.

Nightlife

In **downtown Ponce,** people continue the Spanish tradition of strolling around the main plaza, which is perhaps even prettier at night with its old-fashioned street lamps glowing and the fountain lit. **La Guancha** is normally a lively scene at night, with couples walking and families out for a bite to eat. On weekends, there are often live bands playing.

The **Ponce Hilton** (⊠ Rte. 14, 1150 Av. Caribe, ☎ 787/259–7676) has several options for nightlife: a casino stays open nightly until 4 AM, and on Friday and Saturday you can dance at the Pavilion disco and listen to merengue or salsa at La Bohemia lounge. At the **Holiday Inn Ponce** (⊠ 3315 Ponce By-pass, ☎ 787/844–1200) you'll find Holly's disco open on Friday and Saturday nights and a casino open nightly until 4 AM.

Outdoor Activities and Sports

Beaches

The public beach by **La Guancha** (☞ Sights to See, *above*) at the end of Route 14 is small, but the shallow water makes it a nice beach for children. There's some shade under thatched umbrellas, but bring suntan lotion.

The offshore island of **Caja de Muertos** (Coffin Island) has lovely beaches with picnic shelters. **Rafy Vega's Island Venture** (☎ 787/842–8546) leaves from La Guancha and takes day-trippers to the island—a 45-minute ride—for $20 per person, which includes a light lunch. He goes on weekends, holidays, and during the week when there are 10 people or more.

Diving and Snorkeling

You'll see coral, parrotfish, angelfish, grouper, and more off the island of **Caja de Muertos** (☞ Beaches, *above*). **Rafy Vega's Island Venture** (☞ Beaches, *above*) offers two-tank dives and snorkeling trips.

Shopping

Souvenir and gift shops dot Plaza las Delicias. **Utopia** (⊠ 78 Calle Isabel, ☎ 787/848–8742) has a nice selection of carnival masks and crafts. There are also shops along the **Paseo Atocha**, a pedestrian mall running north of Plaza las Delicias. On holidays and during town festivals, artisans sell wares in booths on the plaza.

Just outside town, **Plaza del Caribe Mall** (⊠ Rte. 2, Km 227.9, ☎ 787/259–8989), one of the largest malls on the island, has stores such as Sears, JC Penney, and Gap.

SOUTHWEST PUERTO RICO

With sandy shores nestled between twists and turns of the coastline, southwestern Puerto Rico will feel like paradise if you love miles of palm-lined beaches—many of which are nearly deserted, especially on weekdays. The area has become popular with local vacationers and nature lovers, who dive, hike, and relax on the sands. Offshore cays such as Guilligan (a.k.a. Gilligan's) Island are popular getaways, and you'll find dozens of alluring diving sites in the area. Towns and villages along the way are often picturesque places where oysters and fresh fish are sold at the roadside stands. On the southwesternmost peninsula, the rugged stretch leading to the Cabo Rojo Lighthouse (also called El Faro) is trimmed with pink-sand beaches, making for a breathtaking hike, especially at sunset.

Guánica

㉕ *38 km (24 mi) southwest of Ponce via Rte. 2 to Rte. 116.*

Juan Ponce de León first explored this area in 1508 when looking for the elusive Fountain of Youth (☞ Coamo, *above*). Nearly 400 years later, U.S. troops were coming ashore at Guánica, their first landing point in Puerto Rico during the Spanish-American War in 1898. The event is marked by an engraved stone on the city's malecón. Despite its somewhat tumultuous past, Guánica today is a small, laid-back town with a shady plaza. What action there is takes place on the city's outskirts, where you can enjoy fine turquoise beaches, explore rugged shorelines and uninhabited offshore cays, or head to the Bosque Estatal de Guánica, a dry tropical forest designated an International Biosphere Reserve by the United Nations.

㉖ **Guilligan Island,** affectionately called Gilligan's Island by locals, is an offshore cay surrounded by coral reefs and skirted by gorgeous beaches. There are picnic tables and rest rooms, but beyond that no signs of civilization. Major hotels have boats to the island or can make arrangements. Boats leave from the dock by San Jacinto Restaurant & Bar, making trips during the week every hour, on the hour, from 10 to 5; on the weekend they leave every half hour from 8:30 to 5. Round-trip passage is $4. (To get to San Jacinto, take the first right after the Copamarina Beach Resort on Route 333 and go to the end of the road.) The island is often busy on weekends and around holidays, but during the week it's usually quiet. On Monday it's closed for cleaning.

★ ㉗ Unique hiking and birdwatching opportunities abound in the 9,200-acre **Bosque Estatal de Guánica** (Guánica State Forest), a United Nations Biosphere Reserve. Dramatically different from the lush tropical forests elsewhere on the island, this reserve is considered one of the best examples of a tropical dry coastal forest in the world, with some 700 species of plants and over 100 different species of birds. There are 12 major hiking trails on and around the sun-bleached hills from which you'll see many unusual and striking forms of cacti. Enter on Route 333, which skirts the southwestern portion of the forest, or on Route 334, where the forest office is located at the end of the road. ⊠ *Rte. 333 or 334,* ☎ *787/821–5706.* 🎟 *Free.* ⊙ *Daily 9–5.*

Dining and Lodging

$$ ✕ **La Concha.** Enjoy lunch or dinner at this popular restaurant, which is part of the government's *mesones gastronómicos* program. The menu includes typical Puerto Rican dishes and fish, including lobster. ⊠ *C-4 Calle Principal, Playa Santa, Ensenada,* ☎ *787/821–5522. AE, MC, V.*

$$$$ ✕🛏 **Copamarina Beach Resort.** This resort is on 16 acres between the
★ sea and the Guánica Dry Forest. The pool sits on the edge of the sea and is surrounded by the open-air reception area, manicured lawns, Las Palmas Café, and the building wings. It has its own beach and is minutes away from some of best beaches in the Guánica area. The spotless rooms have small terraces with water views and one queen-size or two double beds. Try the red snapper in the Coastal Cuisine restaurant, and stop in Las Palmas for the bartender's straight-up margarita. There are scuba-diving packages available, and you can arrange a day at the beach or snorkeling excursion to Guilligan Island. ⊠ *Rte. 333, Km 6.5 (Box 805), 00653,* ☎ *787/821–0505 or 800/468–4553,* 𝖥𝖠𝖷 *787/ 821–0070. 106 rooms. 2 restaurants, 2 bars, air-conditioning, 2 pools, wading pools, hot tubs, 2 tennis courts, playground, meeting rooms. AE, MC, V. EP.* ✎

$$$ 🛏 **Mary Lee's by the Sea.** Known as a place to get away from it all,
★ this meandering complex of apartments and suites looks out on the water from a quiet cul-de-sac full of bright flowers. The distinctive layout is the result of a hodgepodge of colorful additions to the original building. The eight units have fully equipped kitchens, air-conditioned bedrooms with colorful bedspreads, and sea-theme decorations. Fresh towels and linens are supplied daily, and maid service is available upon request. Seven of the units have a sea view; the eighth has a partial view of sea as well as of the Guánica Dry Forest. Near many of Guánica's beaches, Mary Lee's also has its own boat that makes trips to Guilligan Island. ⊠ *Rte. 333, Km 6.7 (Box 394), 00635,* ☎ *787/821–3600,* 𝖥𝖠𝖷 *787/821–0744. 8 units. Air-conditioning, kitchenettes. No credit cards. EP.*

Outdoor Activities and Sports

BEACHES

The calm water at **Balneario Caña Gorda** (⊠ Rte. 333, Km 5.9) is complemented by a wide beach accentuated with palm trees and picnic tables. There are bathrooms, showers, and changing facilities. Rugged cliffs make for dramatic backdrops while sunning on the sand around **Punta Jacinto** (⊠ Rte. 333 heading to Ballena Bay), but the water can
★ be rough. U-shape **Ballena Bay** (⊠ end of Rte. 333) combines a beautiful beach with calm water. The uninhabited **Guilligan Island** (☞ Sights to See, *above*) has gorgeous beaches that can be nearly empty on weekdays.

HIKING

★ The **Bosque Estatal de Guánica** (☞ Sights to See, *above*) has 12 major trails. The forest office on Route 334 has maps.

SCUBA DIVING AND SNORKELING

Dramatic walls created by the continental shelf provide exquisite div-
★ ing off the **Guánica coast.** There are also shallow gardens around **Guilligan Island** and **Cayo de Caña Gorda** (off Balneario Caña Gorda) that attract snorkelers and beginning divers. **Dive Copamarina** (☎ 821–6009, ext. 771 or 719) at the Copamarina Beach Resort offers instruction and trips.

Yauco

28 *8 km (5 mi) north of Guánica.*

The picturesque town of Yauco in the southern foothills of the Cordillera Central is known for its coffee (there's a yearly festival in February celebrating the end of harvest) and horse ranches. Less known, however, are Yauco's *chuletas can can* (twice-cooked pork chops), said to have been invented here (and called *can can* because their resemblance the edges of dancing girls' skirts).

Dining

$–$$ ✕ **La Guardarraya.** At this restaurant outside of Yauco (take Route 127 toward Gauyanilla) you'll find some of the best chuletas can can anywhere. You'll dine in an old-fashioned, country-style house with open windows looking out on the surrounding gardens. In addition to pork chops, the menu includes traditional Puerto Rican dishes such as stewed rice and pork, steak with onions, and fried chicken. The vanilla flan is especially tasty. ⊠ *Rte. 127, Km 6.0,* ☎ *787/856–4222. MC, V. Closed Mon.*

Outdoor Activities and Sports

HORSEBACK RIDING

Campo Allegre (⊠ Rte. 127, Km 5.1, ☎ 787/856–2609) is a 204-acre horse ranch that conducts ½-hour, 1-hour, and 2-hour rides through the hills surrounding Yauco. There are also pony rides for children.

La Parguera

29 *13 km (8 mi) west of Guánica via Rte. 116 to Rte. 304.*

This seaside fishing village is part of the municipality of Lajas, known for its fertile soil. (February through April, keep your eyes open for roadside vendors just outside town selling the area's famous pineapples.) La Parguera has long drawn tourists to its bioluminescent bay, a beautiful sight on a moonless night (though it doesn't glow as brightly as Vieques's Mosquito Bay). Of late the town has taken on new vitality, with the opening of a number of new restaurants, small hotels, and souvenir shops. A pedestrian walkway on the shore (in front of where the glass-bottom boats leave for trips into the bay) has a Coney Island feeling, with booths selling candy and tropical drinks. The town fills up with Puerto Rican vacationers on long holiday weekends and in the summer. In addition to nighttime boat rides, good diving and fishing attract the sports-minded, and bathers can take boats to offshore cays or go to beaches in nearby Guánica or Cabo Rojo.

30 At night, boats line up along the pedestrian mall in La Parguera to take visitors out to view the **Bahía Fosforescente.** In the bay, microscopic bioluminescent dinoflagellates shine like Christmas-tree lights when disturbed by any kind of movement. The phenomenon can best be seen on moonless nights; it's not as spectacular as the phosphorescent Mosquito Bay off Vieques, but it's still an impressive sight. ✉ *On the pedestrian mall.* 🎫 *Boat ride $5.* ⏲ *Nightly 7:30–midnight; trips take about 45 minutes.*

Dining and Lodging

$$ ✕ **Los Balcones.** The second-floor balcony here is a great place to enjoy a meal while observing the evening activity below on the main street in La Parguera. You can get generous portions of regional dishes such as red snapper, grouper, shrimp, steak, and mofongo stuffed with seafood. There's also an air-conditioned dining room downstairs. ✉ *Rte. 304, directly across from entrance to pedestrian walkway,* ☎ *787/899–2145. AE, MC, V. Closed Tues.*

$$ ✕ **Parguera Blues Café.** Off the main street of La Parguera, this restaurant has a cozy, publike atmosphere with indoor and outdoor seating. Plates include the Blues Burger (made with blue cheese), filet mignon, chicken or shrimp with pasta, and a fish of the day. There's live music on Friday and Saturday nights. ✉ *Centro Commercial El Muelle, Av. Los Pescadores,* ☎ *787/899–4742. MC, V.*

$$ ★ ✕🏨 **Parador Villa Parguera.** This stylish parador on the Bahía Fosforescente is popular with Puerto Rican vacationers. Large, colorfully decorated rooms each have a balcony or terrace. A spacious dining room, overlooking the small swimming pool and the bay beyond, serves excellent native and international dishes, and on the weekend the dance club features live music and a floor show. Honeymoon packages are available, and children under 10 stay free when sharing a room with a parent. ✉ *Rte. 304, Km 3.3 (Box 273, Lajas), 00667,* ☎ *787/899–7777 or 787/899–3975,* FAX *787/899–6040. 70 rooms. Restaurant, lounge, air-conditioning, pool, dance club. AE, D, DC, MC, V. EP.*

$$ 🏨 **Parador Villa del Mar.** On a hill overlooking La Parguera, this parador provides a relaxing alternative to the hustle and bustle of nighttime activity downtown. Rooms are comfortable and spanking clean, but don't have spectacular views. (Catch those on the way up the hill.) You'll find a small lounge by the registration area and a small pool tucked between the administrative building and the guest accommodations. An open-air restaurant serves breakfast to guests for an additional $5 per person. ✉ *3 Calle Albizu Campos (Box 1297, San Germán), 00683,* ☎ *787/899–4265,* FAX *787/899–4832. 25 rooms. Restaurant for breakfast, air-conditioning, pool. AE, MC, V. EP.*

Nightlife and the Arts

The **pedestrian mall** heats up at sunset, with people strolling by outdoor vendors near the sea. There's a live floor show at **Parador Villa Parguera** (☞ Dining and Lodging, *above*) on the weekend. On Friday and Saturday, **Parguera Blues Café** (☞ Dining and Lodging, *above*) has a rock or blues band starting at 9 PM or 10 PM.

Outdoor Activities and Sports

BOAT TOURS

In addition to trips to see the **Bahía Fosforescente** (☞ *above*) at night, boats offer daily one-hour tours of the mangrove areas near the offshore

cays, usually charging $25 per person. You can also find boats that will
drop you off on one of the islands and pick you up again—most popular are **Isla Mata de la Gata** and **Cayo Caracoles**—for a day of swimming
and snorkeling for $5 per person. Check with the numerous informa-
tion stands on the pedestrian walkway where the boats dock.

FISHING

You can spend a day or half-day fishing for blue marlin, tuna, or reef
fish with Captain Mickey Amador at **Parguera Fishing Charters** (⊠
Rte. 304, Km 3.8, ☎ 787/382–4698).

SCUBA AND SNORKELING

There are more than 50 dive sites off La Parguera that will appeal to
beginners as well as advanced divers. Some of the most popular are
Fallen Rock, Old Buoy, Black Wall, the Aquarium, and **the Pinnacles.**
Paradise Scuba (⊠ Rte. 304 in the center of town, ☎ 787/899–7611)
offers classes and trips. **Parguera Divers** (⊠ Posada Porlamar, Rte. 304
at the sea, ☎ 787/899–4171) is a good resource for expeditions and
basic training.

Shopping

Outdoor stands near the bay sell all kinds of souvenirs, from T-shirts
to beaded necklaces. There are also small souvenir shops in town, including **Nautilus** (⊠ Rte. 304 in the center of town, ☎ 787/899–
4565), that sell T-shirts, posters, mugs, and trinkets made from shells.

San Germán

10 km (6 mi) north of La Parguera, via Rtes. 304, 305, 116, and 101;
166 km (104 mi) southwest of San Juan via the Luis A. Ferré Expressway
and Rte. 2.

The oldest settlement in southwestern Puerto Rico and the second-oldest on the island, San Germán, a city of about 39,000, has managed to
keep its Old World atmosphere in spite of the U.S.-style strip malls that
surround it and the bustling seaside vacation spots to its south and west.
Walking down its streets is like visiting a living, breathing architectural
museum—there's a striking range of styles, from a simple mission-style
chapel to highly ornate Victorian homes. The 17th-century Capilla de
Porta Coeli is the oldest chapel in Puerto Rico. Much like Ponce, San
Germán experienced a flurry of exceptional building in the early 1900s,
resulting in some of the most beautiful structures on the island.

San Germán was scouted in 1508 by Juan Ponce de León, and about
40 years later Dominican priests took up residence on the hilly site.
During its early years the settlement was easy prey to smugglers, French
pirates, and island natives, all of whom attacked several times. In response to the aggression, the town relocated inland, finally settling in
its current location in 1570. Attacks continued nonetheless, and as a
result tunnels were built under the city—tunnels that are now part of
the water system.

San Germán's position as the administrative center of southern and western Puerto Rico diminished during the 18th and 19th centuries with
the growth of other cities in the region, including Aguada, Ponce, and
Mayagüez. However, it remained a hub of progressive political thought.
One of the town's heroes, Francisco Mariano Quiñones, was an influential fighter for the abolition of slavery.

San Germán is compact, and there isn't nearly the tourist traffic of Old
San Juan or even Ponce, so you can take in the sights in the course of
an afternoon—which is fortunate, because most of the good lodging
options are outside town. The two main plazas, the **Plazuela Santo**

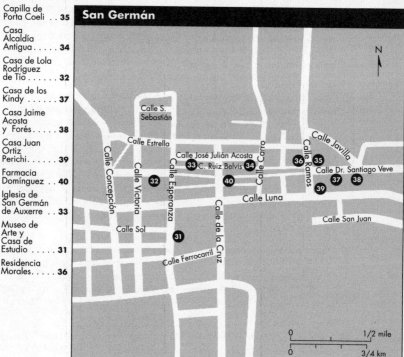

San Germán

Domingo and the **Plaza Francisco Mariano Quiñones,** are only a block apart, and many of the city's historic homes are on the surrounding streets. Only two of the historic buildings are geared toward tourists—the **Capilla de Porta Coeli** and the **Museo de Arte y Casa de Estudio,** both of which contain museums. Most of the noteworthy residences are either private homes or empty, but their delightful facades can be viewed from the street. You can take in the sights on foot, or, Thursday through Sunday, use the free air-conditioned trolley that leaves from the Casa Alcaldía Antigua.

③① The **Museo de Arte y Casa de Estudio,** on Calle Esperanza at the southern edge of the city, is a good place to begin a tour of San Germán. This early-20th-century home has been turned into a museum with one room decorated in colonial style, several others filled with religious art and Taíno artifacts, and additional art exhibits. ✉ *7 Calle Esperanza,* ☎ *787/892–8870.* ▣ *Free.* ☉ *Wed.–Sun. 10–noon and 1–3.*

③② West off Calle Esperanza, at 13 Calle Dr. Santiago Veve, is the **Casa de Lola Rodríguez de Tío,** once home to the sisters of the poet and independence activist whose name it now bears. The two-story building is one of San Germán's notable works of residential architecture. It houses Lola Rodríguez de Tío's desk and papers, and while it's not regularly open to the public, you can check with the Tourism Office (☎ 787/ 892–7345) to arrange for a private appointment to see it.

③③ The central Plaza Francisco Mariano Quiñones is dominated by the **Iglesia de San Germán de Auxerre.** This yellow-and-white church dates from 1739 and was built atop its predecessor. The nave features a carved wood ceiling and an impressive crystal chandelier that was added in 1860. Services are still held here daily. ✉ *Plaza Francisco Mariano Quiñones,* ☎ *787/892–1027.* ☉ *Masses Mon.–Sat. at 7 AM and 7:30 PM, Sun. at 7, 8:30, and 10 AM and 7:30 PM.*

③④ The **Casa Alcaldía Antigua** (Old Municipal Building) is at the eastern end of Plaza Francisco Mariano Quiñones. It was erected between 1839 and 1844 and served as the city hall and municipal prison until 1950. As this book was going to press, the bright-blue building was in the process of being restored, with plans for the San Germán Office of Tourism to make it it's home when work is completed.

★ ③⑤ San Germán's main tourist attraction is the **Capilla de Porta Coeli,** which overlooks the long, rectangular Plazuela de Santo Domingo. Its name translates as "Heaven's Gate," and it's one of the oldest Christian religious structures in the Americas. Built in 1606 as part of a convent, it was also used as a hospice and a primary school. In 1866 the convent, by then in ruins, was demolished, leaving only the chapel and the vestige of the convent's front wall that still stand today. The chapel was restored and reopened for services in 1878. Now it functions as a museum of religious art, displaying primarily painted wooden statuary by Latin American and Spanish artists. ⊠ *Plazuela Santo Domingo,* ☎ *787/892–5845.* ⊡ *$1.* ⊙ *Wed.–Sun. 9–4:45.*

③⑥ The **Residencia Morales** (⊠ 38 Calle Ramos), across the street from the Capilla de Porta Coeli on the Plazuela de Santo Domingo, is perhaps the most admired of the private homes in San Germán. Designed in 1913 by architect Pedro Vivoni for his brother, Tomás Vivoni, it takes up an entire city block and has numerous towers and gables. The current owners have kept it in mint condition.

③⑦ **Casa de los Kindy** (⊠ 64 Calle Dr. Santiago Veve), east of the Plazuela de Santo Domingo, is a 19th-century home known for its eclectic architecture. Note the stained glass-windows and the highly detailed latticework on the balcony.

③⑧ Just down the street from Casa de los Kindy is **Casa Jaime Acosta y Forés** (⊠ 70 Calle Dr. Santiago Veve), a traditional wooden house built in 1917 and 1918. Although its exterior is not as ornate as some in San Germán, it's considered one of the most beautiful homes in Puerto Rico. Inside, the walls are covered floor to ceiling with stenciling, and there's attractive fretwork over the doors. Unfortunately, the house is not open to the public.

You'll find an excellent example of Puerto Rican ornamental architecture ③⑨ in the **Casa Juan Ortiz Perichi** (⊠ 94 Calle Luna), a block to the southeast of the Plazuela de Santo Domingo. This gigantic white home with a sweeping balcony was built in 1920; look for its fine detail work, including many small balusters, stained-glass windows, and wood trim around the doors. It is currently not opened to the public; there are offices on the ground floor.

④⓪ Constructed in 1877, the terra-cotta–color **Farmacia Domínguez** (⊠ Calles Cruz and Dr. Santiago Veve) takes its place among San Germán's notable buildings foremost because of its chamferred corners—a design element popular in the late 1800s and early 1900s. The structure housed a pharmacy (from which it gets its name), and is now home to Cilantro's restaurant (☞ *see* Dining, *below*), which has kept displays of old apothecary jars intact.

Dining

$–$$ ✕ **Cilantro's.** You'll find "nuevo Puerto Rican" cuisine served here in a former pharmacy that's one of San Germán's architectural landmarks. Chef Carlos Rosario's creations include Canadian smoked salmon with caramelized mango and *churrasco* with *chimichurri.* ⊠ *Calle Cruz and Calle Dr. Santiago Veve,* ☎ *787/264–2735. MC, V.*

$–$$ ✕ **Del Mar y Algo Mas.** Chef Eric John has made paella the trademark dish at this restaurant conveniently located near Porta Coeli. The menu includes a variety of typical Puerto Rican dishes, with an emphasis, as the name implies, on seafood. ✉ *Plazuela Santo Domingo at Calle Carro,* ☎ *787/636–4265. MC, V.*

Cabo Rojo

㊶ *11 km (7 mi) west of San Germán via Rte. 102.*

Named Cabo Rojo (Red Headlands) for the pinkish cliffs that surround it, this town was founded in 1771 and in its early years was a well-known port for merchant vessels—and for the smugglers and pirates that inevitably accompanied ocean-going trade. In fact, the famous pirate Roberto Cofresí was born here in 1791; he was to die before a firing squad on the grounds of El Morro. Today, Cabo Rojo is known as a family-oriented resort destination. Small hotels dot the many nooks and crannies of its shoreline, and Puerto Ricans from all over flock to the area in the summer and on holiday weekends. It seems like most of the island goes to the beaches here, particularly Balnerario Boquerón, over Easter weekend—so if you're looking for peace and quiet, this isn't the time to visit.

Cabo Rojo has a town square and a slightly weathered look about it; some visitors to the area never bother to go into town at all. The biggest attractions are on its outskirts, particularly the beautiful beaches, including Boquerón, Combate, and Buyé. Seaside settlements such as Puerto Real and Joyuda—the latter has a strip of more than 30 seafood restaurants overlooking the water—are found up and down the shoreline, and you can hike in wildlife refuges or out to the Cabo Rojo Lighthouse, known as El Faro, at the southwestern tip of the island.

★ **㊷** The **Bosque Estatal de Boquerón** (Boquerón National Forest) encompasses three separate tracts of land on the southern tip of the island, including the rugged peninsula where the **Cabo Rojo Lighthouse** stands watch. (The lighthouse, known as El Faro, is at the end of Rte. 301. You can hike up to it, but it's not open to the public.) The forest also includes the **Refugio de Aves,** a bird sanctuary on Route 301 at Km 1.2, and an **interpretive center** on Rte. 101 in the village of Boquerón; both are open weekdays. ✉ *Rte. 301 and Rte. 101,* ☎ *787/851–7260 (interpretive center).* ▨ *Free.* ☉ *Weekdays 9–5.*

㊸ **Refugio de Vida Silvestre,** run by the U.S. Fish and Wildlife Service, this refuge has an interpretive center that includes exhibits of live freshwater fish and sea turtles. Bird lovers are drawn to the hiking trails, where if you're patient you might spot the elusive yellow-shouldered blackbird or any of a number of other native species. Like the surrounding area, the 500-plus-acre refuge is normally hot and dry, so bring plenty of water and suntan lotion with you. ✉ *Rte. 301, Km 5.1,* ☎ *787/ 851–7070.* ▨ *Free.* ☉ *Weekdays 7–3:30.*

Dining and Lodging

$–$$$ ✕ **El Bohio.** A local favorite, this informal restaurant specializes in fish
★ and also serves steaks, chicken, and mofongo. The long list of seafood is prepared in a wide variety of ways—shrimp comes breaded, stewed, or in a salad; conch is served as a salad or cooked in a butter and garlic sauce. You can dine on the large, enclosed wooden deck that juts out over the sea—where you can watch tarpon play in the water—or in the dining room inside. ✉ *Rte. 102, Km 9.7, Playa Joyuda,* ☎ *787/ 851–2755. AE, DC, MC, V.*

$$ ✕ **Tino's.** This cozy restaurant is a longtime area favorite. It serves family recipes for regional seafood—the lobster turnovers and seafood mofongo are standouts. ⊠ *Rte. 102, Km 13.6, Playa Joyuda,* ☎ *787/851–2976. AE, MC, V.*

$–$$ ✕ **Cafetería del Chopín.** This rustic seaside shack abutting El Combate beach has cold drinks, snacks, and fish and chicken dishes. Try the house specialty, a sandwich using plantains as bread. ⊠ *Calle 3, Playa Combate,* ☎ *787/254–4005. MC, V.*

$$–$$$ ✕⛱ **Bahía Salinas Beach Hotel.** At the southwesternmost tip of the is-
★ land, this airy resortlike property has a private feel about it—its closest neighbors are the Cabo Rojo Lighthouse and the surrounding
natural salt flats and beaches. The modern, spacious rooms are decorated in light tropical colors, and the complex is next to a beach and
has its own boardwalk, pool, Jacuzzi, gym, kayak rental, and children's
play area. Scuba diving and snorkeling can be arranged. Agua al Cuelo
restaurant is known for its seafood and giant tostones, and on weekends there's live music, such as traditional Puerto Rican *trios* and
merengue. Honeymoon packages, family packages, and packages with
different kinds of meal plans are all available. ⊠ *End of Rte. 301 (HC-
01 Box 2356), 00622,* ☎ *787/254–1212,* ℻ *787/254–1215. 24 rooms.
Restaurant, lounge, air-conditioning, pool, hot tub, exercise room,
dive shop, playground. MC, V. BP, CP, EP, MAP.* 🐾

$$ ✕⛱ **Parador Boquemar.** You can walk to the Boquerón public beach
from this parador. The rooms are comfortable, each decorated in the is-
land uniform of tropical prints and rattan. Ask for a third-floor room
with a balcony overlooking the water. La Cascada restaurant is well known
for its traditional Puerto Rican cuisine. On weekends the lounge is filled
with live music. ⊠ *Calle Gill Buyé (Box 133), 00622* ☎ *787/851–2158
or 888/634–4343,* ℻ *787/851–7600. Restaurant, lounge, air-condi-
tioning, minibars, refrigerators, pool. AE, D, DC, MC, V. EP.*

$$ ✕⛱ **Parador Perichi's.** This fanciful multilevel hotel has balconies jutting out from each window. It's centrally located, near many of the area's
beaches as well as the seafood restaurants of Joyuda, though it boasts
an award-winning restaurant of its own. The modern, clean rooms are
air-conditioned and have televisions and balconies, and there is a large
central terrace with a pool. ⊠ *Rte. 102, Km 14.3 (Box 16310, Joyuda),
00623,* ☎ *787/851–0590 or 800/435–7197,* ℻ *787/851–0560. 49
rooms. Restaurant, air-conditioning, pool. AE, D, MC, V. EP.*

$$ ⛱ **Parador Joyuda Beach.** Right on the beach and near Joyuda's
restaurant row, this friendly parador has a large lobby and spacious rooms
with tropical-color bedspreads, air-conditioning, and televisions. Ask for
one of the sunset suites, which have ocean views. You'll find a bar and
snack bar by the pool. ⊠ *Rte. 102, Km 11.7 (HC-01 Box 18410,
Joyuda), 00623,* ☎ *787/851–5650 or 800/981–5464,* ℻ *787/255–
3750. 41 rooms. Snack bar, air-conditioning, pool. AE, MC, V. EP.*

Nightlife and the Arts

Nighttime activity is spread out in the region. Some hotels, such as **Bahía
Salinas Beach Hotel** (☞ Dining and Lodging, *above*), often host live
music. **El Combate beach** has become the popular spot for summer-
time concerts and festivals; call **Caribbean Connection Guest House &
Café** (☎ 787/254–7053) to see if any are scheduled. Visitors often go
to neighboring **La Parguera's** waterfront (☞ *above*).

Outdoor Activities and Sports

BEACHES

The long stretch of sand at **Balneario Boquerón** (⊠ just off Rte. 101)
is a favorite with locals. There are changing facilities, cabins, show-
ers, rest rooms, and picnic tables; it costs $2 to enter with a car. **El Com-
bate** (⊠ at the end of Rte. 3301) draws college students and has some
rustic waterfront eateries; it's also popular with jet-skiers on weekends
and holidays. The white-sand **Buyé Beach** (⊠ Rte. 301, Km 4.8) boasts

★ crystal-clear water and is dotted with palm trees. Crescent-shaped **La Playuela** (⊠ Rte. 301, near the salt flats) is the most secluded of all.

FISHING

Tour Marine (⊠ Rte. 101, Km 14.1, ☎ 787/851–9259) takes anglers into the waters off Cabo Rojo's coast.

GOLF

Get in nine holes at the **Club Deportivo del Oeste** (⊠ Rte. 102, Km 15.4, Joyuda Sector, ☎ 787/254–3748). The hilly course, designed by Jack Bender, is open daily and has panoramic views.

HIKING

The **Refugio de Vida Silvestre** (☞ *above*) and the Bosque Estatal de Boquerón's **Refugio de Aves** (☞ *above*) have hiking trails. You can also hike up to the **Cabo Rojo Lighthouse** (☞ *above*).

SCUBA AND SNORKELING

Several reef-bordered cays lie off the Cabo Rojo area near walls that
★ drop to 100 ft. A mile-long reef along **Las Coronas,** better known as Cayo Ron, displays a variety of hard and soft coral, reef fish, and lobster. Take trips with **Caribbean Reef Divers** (⊠ 1158 Calle Principal, Puerto Real, ☎ 787/254–4006).

SOUTHERN PUERTO RICO A TO Z

Arriving and Departing

By Airplane

Aeropuerto Mercedita (⊠ Rte. 506 off Rte. 52, ☎ 787/842–6292) is about 8 km (5 mi) east of Ponce's downtown. It handles private planes and two daily American Eagle flights from San Juan (☎ 787/844–2099 or 787/844–2020 in Ponce; ☎ 787/749–1747 in San Juan). Taxis at the airport operate under a meter system; it costs about $6 to get to downtown.

By Bus

There is no easy network of buses linking the towns in Puerto Rico with the capital of San Juan. Some municipalities and private companies operate buses and large vans *(públicos)* from one city to another, but the schedules are very loose.

By Car

Renting a car is perhaps the best way to see southern Puerto Rico, especially if you are making several stops. Cars can be rented at the Luis Muñoz Marín International Airport in San Juan, at other locations in San Juan, and in some of the larger cities along the south coast (☞ Smart Travel Tips A to Z). From San Juan, a taxi trip to Ponce costs about $100.

Getting Around

By Bus

Buses and públicos from town to town operate sporadically, so it's not a wise idea to count on them as your primary means of transportation. Some tour operators (☞ *below*) and hotels offer van transportation to major sights.

By Car

Driving between points in southern Puerto Rico allows you to see most sights, but plan on extra time for wrong turns (some roads, especially in rural areas, are not plainly marked). Take note that any trip on mountain roads may take twice as long as you would expect from looking at a map, due to the twists and turns. A road map is essential. Get the best one you can find from a gas station, bookstore, hotel, or tourist information office. The free maps provided by rental car agencies usually won't provide the kind of detail you want.

The largest and quickest road through the region is the Luis Ferré Expressway (Rte. 52). It's a toll road that runs from San Juan to Ponce, crossing the island's central mountain range.

By Taxi

In Ponce, taxis can easily be hailed in tourist areas and at hotels. In smaller towns, hotels and restaurants will call one for you. To call for service in Ponce, try **Borinquen Taxi** (☎ 787/843–6100), **Ponce Taxi** (☎ 787/842–3370), or **Union Taxi** (☎ 787/259–7676). You can also hire a car service—it's best to make arrangements through your hotel. Often you can arrange a rate that's lower than what you would pay for a taxi. In Ponce, car service is available through **Ponce Limousine Service** (☎ 787/848–0469).

By Trolley and Train

Ponce offers free transportation to major tourist sites on trolleys and chu chu trains. They both run daily from 9 AM to about 9:30 PM, and leave from Plaza las Delicias. Other cities, including Guayama and Arroyo, offer free trolleys on weekends to major tourist sites in the downtown area.

Contacts and Resources

Emergencies

Ambulance, fire, police (☎ 911).

Hospital Damas, Ponce (✉ 2213 Ponce By-Pass Rd., ☎ 787/840–8686). **Hospital Bella Vista del Suroeste, Yauco** (✉ Rte. 128, Km 1.0, ☎ 787/856–1000). **Hospital de la Concepción, San Germán** (✉ 41 Calle Luna, ☎ 787/892–1860). **Hospital de Area Alejandro Buitrago, Guayama** (✉ Av. Central at Calle Principal, ☎ 787/864–4300 or 787/892–1860).

Festivals

Towns throughout Puerto Rico celebrate *fiestas patronales,* or patron saint festivals, which feature lots of music and dancing. Ponce, for example, honors Nuestra Señora de la Guadalupe the first week of December. Ponce also hosts one of the island's most colorful Carnival celebrations the week before Ash Wednesday. Aibonito holds its annual Flower Festival in late June or July. Barranquitas hosts an annual artisans' fair in July. The Dulce Sueño Paso Fino Fair is held in Guayama in March. Arroyo has its fish festival in October, and Yauco celebrates the coffee harvest in February.

Health and Safety

The island's tap water is generally safe to drink. Fruits should be well washed before eating if bought from a roadside stand or in a market. Remember that the sun is strong and shines most of the time on the south coast, so be sure to have sunscreen and drinking water with you.

Tour Operators and Travel Agencies

For guided excursions to the historical sights in Ponce, call **Turisla** (☎ 787/835–6788) or check with the **Museo de la Historia de Ponce** (☎ 787/844–7071) to arrange for a tour with one of its staff. **Alelí Tours** (✉ La Parguera, ☎ 787/899–6086) offers ecological tours in the southwestern part of the island.

For help with ticketing or travel information in Ponce check with **Arjes Travel** (✉ 83 Calle Union, ☎ 787/844–0740) or **Bonnin Travel** (✉ 16 Paseo Atocha, ☎ 787/842–0084). In Cabo Rojo: **Boquerón Travel** (✉ 60 Muñoz Rivera, ☎ 787/851–4751). In Coamo: **Coamo Travel Agency** (✉ 28 Calle Baldorioty, ☎ 787/825–7522). In San Germán: **Convenient Travel Agency** (✉ Calle 7 Local G-15, ☎ 787/892–6161). In Guayama: **Guayama Travel Agency** (✉ Calle Vicente Pales, ☎ 787/ 864–5405).

Visitor Information

The **City of Ponce tourist office** (✉ 2nd floor of Citibank, Plaza las Delicias [Box 1709], 00733, ☎ 787/841–8160 or 787/841–8044) is open Monday through Saturday. The Commonwealth's **Puerto Rico Tourism Company** (✉ 291 Vallas Torres, ☎ 787/843–0465) is open Monday through Saturday. On the west coast, there's a Cabo Rojo office of the **Puerto Rico Tourism Company** (✉ Rte. 101, Km 13.7, ☎ 787/851–7070) open daily.

5 NORTHWESTERN PUERTO RICO AND THE CENTRAL MOUNTAINS

You can find everything from underground rivers to high mountain peaks in northwestern Puerto Rico. The expansive area stretching west of San Juan to the west coast also has world-class surfing and swimming beaches; championship golf courses; and, inland, some of the best mountain scenery in the Caribbean.

by Delinda
Karle

L ESS THAN A CENTURY AGO, northwestern Puerto Rico and the central mountains were overwhelmingly rural and largely undeveloped. Some large fruit plantations dotted the coast, while further inland coffee was grown on hillside *fincas* (farms). A few ports, notably the west-coast city of Mayagüez, took on a somewhat cosmopolitan air, drawing immigrants from around the world to work in commerce and trade.

The generally slow pace of the area began to change during the mid-20th century. The government's Operation Bootstrap program drew more manufacturing into the area, new roads brought once-isolated towns into the mainstream, and tourists began to discover the gold sand of the Atlantic coast and the mighty waves near the west-coast town of Rincón.

Stretching west of San Juan to Mayagüez and south into rugged mountain terrain, the northwestern region of Puerto Rico today holds an abundance of attractions for all kinds of travelers. Perched on the Atlantic coast, Dorado was one of the first areas to develop luxury resorts, and it now offers top-notch hotels, golf courses, and almost every kind of water sport imaginable. Inland, the more remote mountain areas still produce coffee; they also lure more adventurous travelers to their narrow, winding roads. It's here, in several large forest reserves and around the Río Camuy cave network, that Puerto Rico has its greatest eco-tourism potential, but today you'll still find yourself far from tourist crowds.

On the west coast, the waves around Aguadilla and Rincón are as popular as ever. Visitors of all kinds come here to surf or just enjoy the beaches and sunsets. Many have decided not to return home.

Pleasures and Pastimes

Dining

Throughout northwestern Puerto Rico you'll find restaurants serving top-notch *criollo* cuisine, interspersed with international offerings ranging from French to Japanese. You can enjoy five-course gourmet meals in elegant surroundings at night, then sip morning coffee on an outdoor balcony the next morning. The north central mountains are a good place to sample down-home Puerto Rican cooking; many restaurants here are proud of their *mofongo relleno* (stuffed mashed plantains) as well as their seasoned chicken, pork chops, and rice and beans.

Tips, normally 15%–20%, are usually not included in the bill, but it's always wise to double-check.

CATEGORY	COST*
$$$$	over $35
$$$	$25–$35
$$	$15–$25
$	under $15

*per person for an appetizer, entrée, and dessert, excluding tax, tip, and beverages

Lodging

Lodging in the area runs the gamut from posh resorts offering windsurfing lessons and championship golf courses to rustic cabins in the middle of a forest reserve. The Dorado area has a concentration of sleek resorts; the western part of the island near Rincón has a variety of hotels, from luxurious getaways to furnished apartments geared toward families to basic yet colorful small hotels. In the central mountains, a few old plantation homes have been turned into wonderful country inns that transport you back to slower and quieter times.

CATEGORY	COST*
$$$$	over $150
$$$	$100–$150
$$	$50–$100
$	under $50

All prices are for a double room in high season, excluding taxes.

✎ *following the text of a review is your signal that the property has a Web site, where you will find details and, usually, images; for a link, visit www.fodors.com/urls.*

Surfing

The beaches near Rincón, which hosted the World Surfing Championship in 1968, have some of the best waves in the world, especially during winter months. Other areas on the north coast, such as Aguadilla and Isabela, boast impressive waves as well.

Hiking

Northwestern Puerto Rico has a number of forest reserves that rival the better-known El Yunque to the east in beauty. The Bosque Estatal de Río Abajo has trails in the island's "karst country." The lush, cloud-covered Bosque Estatal de Toro Negro has a number of trails to waterfalls, natural pools, and the island's tallest mountain peak, Cerro de Punta, which rises to 4,398 ft. The drier Bosque Estatal de Maricao is known for its numerous species of birds, including many on the endangered list.

Exploring the Northwest and the Central Mountains

Highway 22 heads west from San Juan, skirting the beaches of the northern coast. Large tracts of coconut palms still stand in the area, and there are expansive fields with grazing cattle. At Arecibo, the island's limestone karst country begins, filled with strangely shaped hills, cliffs, and sinkholes. You can delve into the area by taking Route 10 south, which leads to the Río Abajo Forest Reserve and the mountain town of Utuado, or by taking Route 129, which leads to the karst country's premier attraction, Las Cavernas del Río Camuy.

Numerous small, narrow roads traverse the rugged Cordillera Central, the island's central mountain range. Forest reserves here rival El Yunque in their beauty, and the island's highest peaks loom over small towns in mountain valleys. Much of the Ruta Panoramica (☞ Chapter 4), a network of small roads running horizontally across the island, passes through this area.

Highway 22, which turns into Route 2 just after Arecibo, swings around the northwestern part of the island, where rugged cliffs meet the Atlantic Ocean. On the west coast, the ragged shoreline holds some of the island's best surfing beaches, as well as calmer ones, and a steady contingent of surfers gives the area a laid-back atmosphere.

Numbers in the text correspond to numbers in the margin and on the Northwestern Puerto Rico and the Central Mountains and the Mayagüez map.

Great Itineraries

IF YOU HAVE 3 DAYS

If you feel like indulging yourself, plan on three days at one of the **Dorado** ① resorts, where you can spend your time at windsurfing school, in the spa, at the beach, or on championship-caliber golf courses. Set aside a day to visit one of Puerto Rico's greatest natural wonders, **Par-**

que de las Cavernas del Río Camuy ③, and one of its greatest man-made ones, **Observatorio de Arecibo** ④.

If you want a more relaxed, secluded environment, try **Isabela** ⑤, a quiet town with a gorgeous shoreline and perfect get-away-from-it-all inns. Spend your first day on the beach, capping it off with a sunset horse ride along the shore. For day two, head to **Parque de las Cavernas del Río Camuy** ③ and **Observatorio de Arecibo** ④, and on day three visit the friendly beachfront town of **Rincón** ㉑.

IF YOU HAVE 5 DAYS

Take up residence for three days at one of the former coffee plantations that have been converted into mountain inns near **Utuado** ⑦ and **Jayuya** ⑪. Spend your days visiting the area's sights, such as **Parque de las Cavernas del Río Camuy** ③, **Observatorio de Arecibo** ④, **Bosque Estatal de Toro Negro** ⑫ (where you'll find beautiful waterfalls and the island's highest peak), **Parque Ceremonial Indígena de Caguana** ⑩, and **Lago Dos Bocas** ⑨; at night, let the chirp of the *coquís* (the island's native tree frogs) lull you to sleep. Then make your way to the west coast and **Rincón** ㉑ for two days of great waves, beautiful sunsets, and laidback good times.

IF YOU HAVE 7 DAYS

Seven days will give you a chance to sample a variety of the region's pleasures. Start out with two days at a **Dorado** ① resort, spend three days exploring the inlands and staying at a former coffee plantation in the mountains near **Utuado** ⑦ or **Jayuya** ⑪, and finish up with two days at **Rincón** ㉑ on the west coast. Or . . . forget about variety and dedicate your entire week to one of those three locations. Each will reward you in different ways for your extended stay. With your more leisurely schedule you'll get a better sense of place, and regardless whether you spend your time in the mountains or on the water, by the end of the week you'll be relaxed and reinvigorated. (But don't get so relaxed that you miss **Parque de las Cavernas del Río Camuy** ③, which is a highlight of any trip to this region.)

When to Tour

As elsewhere in the Caribbean, winter is the high season; the weather is at its mild best, but you'll have to compete with other visitors for hotel rooms, so be sure to book well in advance. Winter is also the height of the surfing season on the west coast. In summer many family-oriented hotels fill up with *sanjuaneros* escaping the city for the weekend—some hotels require a two-night stay. Larger resorts normally drop their rates during the summer by at least 10%. The weather gets hot, especially in August and September, but the plentiful beaches help keep everyone cooled off.

THE NORTH COAST, RÍO CAMUY, AND ARECIBO OBSERVATORY

Stretching along the Atlantic Ocean from San Juan to the west coast, northwestern Puerto Rico is a mecca of pristine beaches, scenic roads, and some of the best natural attractions on the island. Just west of San Juan, large tracts of coconut palms silhouette Dorado and its environs, the scenic remnants of large coconut and fruit plantations. Today, the picturesque landscape is home to luxury vacation resorts offering varied water sports and several fine golf courses. Farther west, near Arecibo, the island's limestone "karst country" is distinguished by haystack-shape hills (called *mogotes* by locals) and underground rivers and caves. One of the island's most fascinating geological wonders is

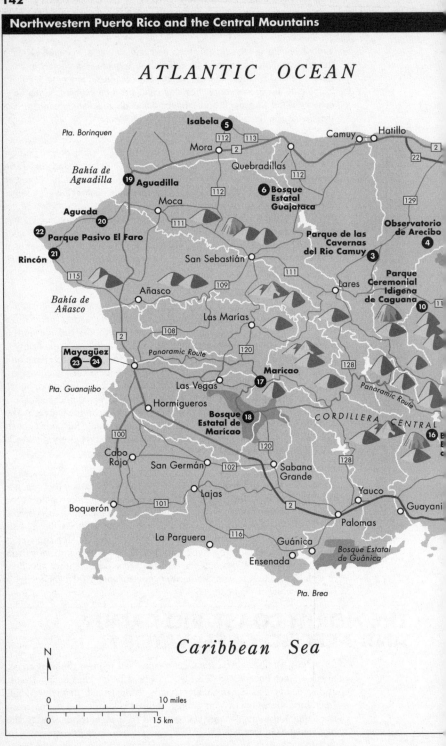

ATLANTIC OCEAN

Pta. Borinquen

Isabela **5**

Mora

Camuy

Hatillo

2

2

22

Quebradillas

112

113

112

Bahía de
Aguadilla

19 Aguadilla

112

Moca

6 Bosque
Estatal
Guajataca

129

Aguada

20

111

**Observatorio
de Arecibo**

22

Parque Pasivo El Faro

**Parque de las
Cavernas
del Río Camuy**

4

Rincón **21**

115

San Sebastián

3

Lares

**Parque
Ceremonial
Idígena
de Caguana**

Añasco

109

111

10

11

Bahía de
Añasco

108

Las Marías

2

120

128

Mayagüez

23 — **24**

Panoramic Route

Maricao **17**

Panoramic Route

CORDILLERA CENTRAL

Pta. Guanajibo

Las Vegas

Hormigueros

**Bosque
Estatal de
Maricao** **18**

16

E

100

120

Cabo
Rojo

San Germán

102

Sabana
Grande

128

Yauco

Lajas

Boquerón

101

2

Palomas

Guayani

La Parguera

116

Guánica

**Bosque Estatal
de Guánica**

Ensenada

Pta. Brea

Caribbean Sea

N

0   10 miles

0   15 km

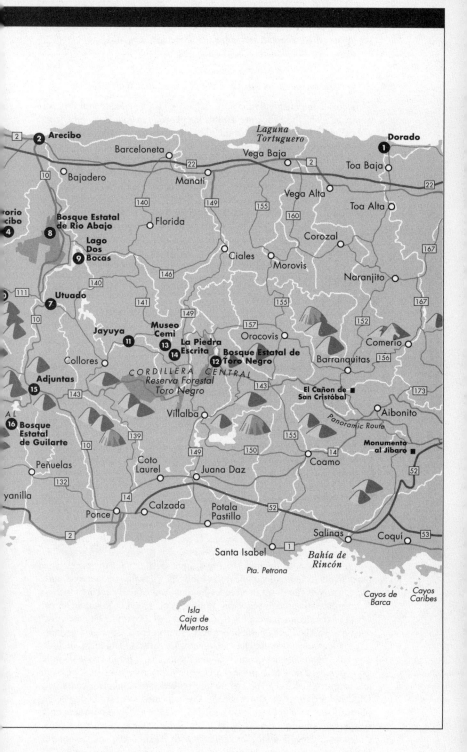

the Río Camuy cave system, one of the largest such systems in the western hemisphere. Nearby, science takes center stage at the Arecibo Observatory, the largest radar/radio telescope in the world.

Dorado

❶ *27 km (17 mi) west of San Juan via Hwy. 22 and Rte. 165.*

This small and tidy town (pop. 30,700) has a definite holiday air about it, even though more and more people who work in San Juan are calling it home. It's one of the oldest resort areas on the island, having gotten a boost in 1955 when Laurance Rockefeller bought the pineapple, coconut, and grapefruit plantation of Dr. Alfred Livingston and his daughter, Clara (one of the first woman pilots in the world), and built a resort on the property. Today, the former plantation is the site of the Hyatt Regency Cerromar Hotel and the Hyatt Dorado Beach Resort & Country Club, two top luxury resorts that include four of the best-known golf courses in Puerto Rico. The town of Dorado itself is fun to visit; its winding road leads across a bridge to a main square, and there are small delis, restaurants, and shops nearby. Most visitors, however, spend the majority of their time on the town's nearby beaches or in its resort complexes.

Dining and Lodging

$$ ✕ **El Ladrillo.** This cozy spot with brick floors and walls (*el ladrillo* translates as "the brick") is known for its grilled steaks, including T-bones and filet mignon. It also has a wide selection of seafood—try the seafood *zarzuela,* a combination of lobster, squid, octopus, clams, and more. ⊠ *334 Calle Méndez Vigo,* ☎ *787/796–2120. AE, MC, V.*

$$ ✕ **Mangére.** You'll find a long menu of Italian cuisine and 86 wines at this spacious restaurant decorated in pastel colors. Entrées include veal medallions with Portabello and porcini mushrooms, smoked Norwegian salmon with capers, and linguine carbonara. ⊠ *Rte. 693, Km 8.5,* ☎ *787/796–4444. AE, D, MC, V.*

$$ ✕ **Yukiyu.** This sleek sushi bar with black tables and Japanese decorations is a good place for lunch, appetizers, or a light dinner. Offerings include sushi, sashimi, seaweed salad, and tuna and avocado salad. ⊠ *Rte. 693, Km 8.5,* ☎ *787/796–4477. AE, D, MC, V. Closed Sun.*

$$$$ ✕⌖ **Hyatt Dorado Beach Resort & Country Club.** The first property built by Laurance Rockefeller on the plantation he acquired from the Livingstons, this resort opened in 1958 and was originally used primarily as a private club for the jet set. It became a Hyatt property along with the neighboring Cerromar Regency Beach Resort in 1985 and today still retains an Old Caribbean atmosphere. The airy lobby has elegant plantation-style furniture, and the lobby bar's walls are covered with old photos of the plantation in its heyday and of early resort visitors. Accommodations are in low-rise buildings on 1,000 landscaped acres. Most of the rooms have a four-poster bed and a patio or balcony, and each has polished terra-cotta floors and a marble bath. Upper-level rooms in the Oceanview Houses have a view of the beach. Amenities include a small spa and fitness center, tennis courts, two pools, two 18-hole golf courses, a new clubhouse, and five restaurants and grills. The large and elegant Surf Room has white linen tablecloths and huge curtained windows looking over the ocean. Su Casa, located in Clara Livingston's plantation house (a National Historic Landmark), serves dinners on a romantic balcony; chef Alfredo Ayala's creative menu includes pork chops with *achiote adobe,* beef fillets with fried yucca, and mahimahi in spicy corn sauce served with corn fritters. You can also use the facilities (including the casino) of Dorado Beach's sister resort, the Regency Cerromar Beach, by hopping one of the free blue-and-white trolleys

that travel between them. ✉ *Rte. 693, Km 10.8 (Box 1351), 00646,* ☎ *787/796–1234 or 800/233–1234,* ℻ *787/796–2022. 298 rooms. 5 restaurants, air-conditioning, 2 pools, 2 18-hole golf courses, 7 tennis courts, spa, jogging, beach, bicycles, children's program. AE, D, DC, MC, V. EP, MAP (MAP compulsory Dec. 15–end of Feb.).* 🐾

$$$$ ✕🏨 **Hyatt Regency Cerromar Beach Resort & Casino.** Right next door to the Hyatt Dorado Beach Resort & Country Club, this hotel has more nightlife than its neighbor, and even during the day it's a livelier place to be. Very sports- and family-oriented, the complex has a 5,000-square-ft health and fitness center, Le Spa; biking and jogging trails; 10 tennis courts; two 18-hole golf courses; and its famous river pool, one of the longest freshwater pools in the world, flowing some 1,776 feet under bridges and over waterfalls and waterslides (including one 187 ft long). The modern seven-story hotel has a newly renovated and very airy lobby. Rooms have tropical decor and balconies, and most have ocean views. The casino and Club Bacchus disco are centers of nightlife, and there are four restaurants on the premises; the Steak Co. is known not only for its steaks but also its pasta and seafood (try the pan-seared swordfish), and Zen Garden serves Japanese and Chinese cuisine and features a sushi bar. You can hop a trolley and go next door if you feel inclined to make use of the facilities at the Dorado Beach. ✉ *Rte. 693, Km 11.8 (Box 1351), 00646,* ☎ *787/796–1234 or 800/233–1234,* ℻ *787/796–4647. 506 rooms. 4 restaurants, bars, air-conditioning, 3 pools, spa, 2 18-hole golf courses, 10 tennis courts, jogging, beach, bicycles, casino, children's program. AE, D, DC, MC, V. EP.* 🐾

Nightlife

Nights are normally quiet in Dorado, but if you are looking for some action, the **Hyatt Regency Cerromar Beach Resort & Casino** (✉ Rte. 693, Km 11.8, ☎ 787/796–1234) is the place to go. The 10,000-square-ft casino is busy at night and at times features live music. The mythology-theme **Club Bacchus** disco is open Thursday through Sunday starting at 8 PM, and the **Flamingo Bar,** overlooking the ocean and the resort's distinctive river pool, has live music in the evenings Wednesday through Sunday.

Outdoor Activities and Sports

BEACHES

Dorado's **Playa Sardinera** (✉ end of Rte. 697) is nice for swimming and has shade trees, changing rooms, and rest rooms. The 2,500-ft-long **Cerro Gordo Beach** (✉ end of Rte. 690) is lined with cliffs and is very popular—it can get crowded on weekends. **Los Tubos Beach** (✉ end of Rte. 687) in Vega Baja is popular for both swimming and surfing. It holds a summer festival with merengue and salsa groups and water-sports competitions, normally the first week of July. **Breñas Beach** (✉ between the two Hyatt resorts in Dorado) is known for its surfing.

FISHING

Dorado Marine Center (✉ 271 Calle Méndez Vigo, ☎ 787/796–4645) has equipment and packages for deep-sea and light-tackle fishing.

GOLF

The four golf courses at the **Dorado Hyatt Resorts** (✉ Rte. 693, Km 10.8 and Km 11.8, ☎ 787/796–1234) were all designed by Robert Trent Jones, Sr. The Hyatt Dorado Beach Resort & Country Club's 18-hole **East Course** underwent a $7-million renovation in 1999. Its 4th hole (13th hole prior to the renovation) has been ranked by Jack Nicklaus as one of the top 10 holes in the world. The Dorado Beach's **West Course** is buffeted by constant breezes off the Atlantic, making it a challenge to negotiate. The **South Course** at the Hyatt Regency Cerromar Beach Resort & Casino has challenging winds and lagoons. The **North Course** has a links-style design; the beautiful 7th hole is surrounded by flowering plants and has a view of the ocean and the resort. All Hyatt courses are open to the public.

The 7,100-yard **Dorado Del Mar** golf course (⊠ Rte. 693 west of Dorado city center, ☎ 787/796–3065) is a Chi Chi Rodríguez signature course with narrow fairways that can be a challenge to hit when the wind picks up.

HORSEBACK RIDING

Tropical Paradise Horse Back Riding (⊠ off Rte. 690, just west of Hyatt Regency Cerromar, ☎ 787/720–5454) offers rides along the Cibuko Beach on beautiful Paso Fino horses.

SNORKELING AND SCUBA DIVING

Puerto Rico's north coast has several good areas for snorkeling and diving, including an underwater "aquarium" full of tropical fish and coral, just a few yards from the shore of the Cerro Gordo Beach (☞ Beaches, *above*). For trips, call **Dorado Marine Center** (⊠ 271 Calle Méndez Vigo, ☎ 787/796–4645).

WINDSURFING

Lisa Penfield, a former windsurfing competitor, gives beginning lessons at her **Watersports Center at the Dorado Beach Resort & Country Club** (⊠ Rte. 693, Km 10.8, ☎ 787/796–2188).

Shopping

For arts and crafts, try **Jorge Cancio Arte y Artesanías** (⊠ Rte. 693, Km 10.8, ☎ 787/796–4025) at the Hyatt Regency Cerromar Beach, where you'll find island-made ceramics; jewelry; spices; jams; and the rare mundillo lace (also called bobbin lace), once commonly made by women of Puerto Rico's northwest coast. Necessities can be purchased in Dorado at **Walgreens** (⊠ 342 Calle Méndez Vigo, ☎ 787/796–1046).

En Route   About 20 minutes from Dorado via Highway 22 at Exit 55 is Puerto Rico's first factory outlet mall. **Prime Outlets Puerto Rico** (⊠ Rte. 2, Km 54.8, Barceloneta, ☎ 787/846–9011) is a pastel village of more than 40 stores selling discounted merchandise from such familiar names as Liz Claiborne, Zales, and Tommy Hilfiger. There's also a food court.

Arecibo

❷ *60 km (38 mi) west of Dorado via Hwy. 22.*

As you approach Arecibo on Highway 22, you see its white buildings glistening in the sun against an ocean backdrop. The town was founded in 1515 and is known as the "Villa of Captain Correa" because of a battle fought here by Captain Antonio Correa and a handful of Spanish soldiers to repel a British sea invasion in 1702. It's a busy manufacturing center today, home to subsidiaries of several *Fortune 500* companies, but travelers know Arecibo best as a junction for visits to two of the island's most fascinating sights—the expansive Parque de las Cavernas del Río Camuy and the Observatorio de Arecibo, both just south of the city—and for heading deeper into the central mountain region.

★ ❸ The 268-acre **Parque de las Cavernas del Rio Camuy** contains one of the world's largest cave networks and the third-longest underground river in the world. A tram takes you down a mountain covered with bamboo and banana trees to the entrance of **Cueva Clara de Empalme**. Hour-long guided tours in English and Spanish lead you on foot through the massive, 180-ft-high cave, which holds such wonders as large stalactites and stalagmites that grow an average of an inch every

300 years and blind fish found only in the region's caves. The visit ends with a tram ride to two large sinkholes. You can't reserve a place on the tour in advance; plan to arrive early on holidays and weekends, when the park is particularly popular both with tourists and local families. In addition to the caves themselves, the park includes a gift shop and a cafeteria.

If you're feeling adventurous, you can also tour **Cueva Catedral,** which you enter by rappelling down a rock wall. Among the highlights inside are petroglyphs left by the Taínos, Puerto Rico's pre-Columbian natives. The cave is open only to groups of eight or more, and you must be over 12 years old to enter. Reservations are required, and they must be made a week in advance. ⊠ *Rte. 129, Km 18.9, ☎ 787/898–3100 or 787/756–5555. ☜ $10; Cueva Catedral $30. ⊘ Wed.–Sun. 8–4, last tour at 3:45.*

★ ❹ Hidden among lush fields and rolling hills is **Observatorio de Arecibo,** the world's largest radar/radio telescope, operated by the National Astronomy and Ionosphere Center of Cornell University. A 20-acre dish, with a 600-ton suspended platform hovering eerily over it, lies in a 563-ft-deep sinkhole in the karst landscape. The observatory has been used to look for extraterrestrial life, and if it looks familiar it may be because scenes from the movie *Contact* were filmed here. You can walk around the platform and view the huge dish (a fantastic photo opportunity), and tour the Angel Ramos Foundation Visitor Center, which has two levels of interactive exhibits on planetary systems, meteors, and weather phenomena. There is also a small gift shop. ⊠ *Rte. 625, Km 3.0, ☎ 787/878–2612. ☜ $3.50. ⊘ Wed.–Fri. noon–4, weekends 9–4.* ✺

OFF THE
BEATEN PATH

LARES – Follow Route 129 south to Rte. 111 and you'll arrive at the small town of Lares, known for a national uprising that took place there in 1868. A rebellious group declared a Republic of Puerto Rico, but the insurgency, now known as "El Grito de Lares," was quickly put down by the Spanish. Today, *independentistas* flock to the town's quaint square, **Plaza de la Revolución,** each September 23 to honor the anniversary of the brief cry for independence. Just across from the square, **Heladería de Lares** (⊠ ☎ 787/897–2062) has been making a more modest, but delicious, nationalistic statement for more than 30 years by serving up ice cream in such flavors as rice, bean, and plantain.

Dining and Lodging

$ ✕ **El Nuevo Olímpico.** A convenient stop when heading west from Arecibo on Highway 22, this restaurant offers fast food Puerto Rican style. You can get snacks such as *empanadillas* (deep fried turnovers); full meals, including chicken or pork with rice and beans; and, in the morning, breakfast, consisting primarily of eggs and sandwiches. There's a small, air-conditioned seating area, or you can join the locals outside at picnic tables on the balcony. The restaurant is open weekdays from 7 AM to midnight and stays open even later on weekends. ⊠ *Rte. 2, Km 93.3, Camuy, ☎ 787/898–4545. MC, V.*

$$ ▥ **Hotel Villa Real.** Conveniently situated at the main entrance to Arecibo, this hotel makes a good spot for an overnight stay if you're heading to the nearby cave park or observatory or are en route to the central mountains or the west coast. The rooms are clean and spacious; some have refrigerators, and others have fully equipped kitchens. A separate building has 13 larger apartments. You'll find both businessmen and families staying here; its restaurant serves criollo food, and there are two pools, one full-size and another for children, on the premises. ⊠ *Rte. 2, Km 67.2 (Box 1241), 00616, ☎ 787/881–4134,*

FAX *787/881–6490. 41 rooms, 13 apartments. Restaurant, air-conditioning, 2 pools. AE, MC, V.*

Outdoor Activities and Sports

KAYAKING AND RAFTING

Locura Arecibeña/Río Grande de Arecibo Kayak Rentals (☎ 787/878–1809) offers kayaking adventure trips, including bird-watching trips using kayaks, around the Barceloneta-Arecibo-Utuado area. Trips go to Caño Tiburones Channel between Barceloneta and Arecibo, the Río Grande south of Arecibo, and the Río Manatí near Ciales. Rafting trips are also available, mainly in the winter months when the rapids are at their best, and mainly on Río Manatí. All trips are on weekends, and reservations must be made three days in advance. (Ask for Jenaro Colón.)

Isabela

⑤ *36 km (23 mi) west of Arecibo via Hwy. 22, Rte. 2, and Rte. 112.*

Founded in 1819 and named for Spain's Queen Isabella, this small, whitewashed town overlooks some of the most breathtaking scenery in Puerto Rico. On the northwesternmost part of the island, it skirts tall cliffs overlooking huge rocks on the shoreline. Locals have long known of the area's natural beauty, and lately more and more off-shore tourists have begun coming to this niche of the island, which offers secluded hotels, fantastic beaches, and, just inland, numerous hiking trails through one of the island's forest reserves.

A forest of 2,357 acres between the towns of Quebradillas and Isabela, **⑥ Bosque Estatal Guajataca** has more than 40 walking trails on which to explore karst topography and subtropical vegetation. The reserve has 186 species of trees, most of which are native, including the royal palm and ironwood, and 45 species of birds—watch for red-tailed hawks and Puerto Rican woodpeckers. At the Route 446 entrance to the forest there is an information office where you can pick up a hiking map, and a little farther down the road is a recreational area with picnic tables and an observation tower. ✉ *Rte. 446, Galateo Alto Sector,* ☎ *787/872–1045.* 🎫 *Free.* ☉ *Information office open weekdays 8–5; access can be limited on Mon. due to cleaning.*

Dining and Lodging

$$$–$$$$ ✕🏨 **Villa Montaña.** This secluded cluster of buildings near the border between Isabela and Aguadilla feels like a community unto itself. The airy one-, two-, and three-bedroom suites have an eclectic and appealing Caribbean decor, with rustic wooden tables and primitive Haitian-style paintings. The grounds abut Shacks Beach and include tennis courts, two pools, a fitness center, and the Eclipse open-air restaurant and bar, which features such fare as shrimp with mushroom sauce and red snapper in coconut-milk sauce. ✉ *Rte. 446, Km 1.2 (Box 530), 00662,* ☎ *787/872–9554 or 888–780–9195,* FAX *787/872–9553. 26 rooms. Restaurant, air-conditioning, 2 pools, 2 tennis courts, exercise room. AE, D, MC, V. EP.* 🍽

$$ ✕🏨 **Villas del Mar Hau.** This fanciful row of pastel cottages overlooking
★   Montones Beach is surrounded by palm and pine trees and wide-open fields. One-, two-, and three-bedroom cottages are linked by a boardwalk that runs in front of the beach. They aren't elaborate or luxurious, but if you're looking for comfortable facilities, a secluded setting, and a relaxed, unpretentious atmosphere, you'll have a hard time doing better. The cottages are simply and tastefully decorated, with balconies looking out on the ocean. Some have TVs; some have air-conditioning in bedrooms and others have fans. Sheets and kitchen

THE ABOMINABLE CHUPACABRA

THE HIMALAYAS have their Yeti, Britain has its crop circles, New Jersey has its legendary Jersey Devil . . . and Puerto Rico has its Chupacabra. This "goat sucker" (as its name translates) has been the subject of numerous reports since the mid-1970s, crediting it with attacks on goats, sheep, rabbits, horses, and chickens that leave the animals devoid of blood, with oddly vampirelike punctures in their necks.

It's the stuff of Puerto Rican legend, but the Chupacabra has also been active in Mexico, southern Texas, and Miami, spots with large Hispanic communities. Eyewitness accounts, on the rise since the 1990s, offer widely differing versions of Chupacabra; it has gray, scraggly hair and resembles a kangaroo or wolf, or walks upright on three-toed feet. Some swear it hops from tree branch to tree branch, and even flies, leaving behind, in the tradition of old Lucifer, the acrid stench of sulphur. It peers through large, oval, sometimes red eyes, and "smells like a wet dog" as its reptilian tongue flicks the night air. It has, according to some, attacked humans, ripped through screen windows, and jumped family dogs at picnics. The brute allegedly strikes most often at night, and vigilante groups, sworn to capturing or destroying the beast, have been organized in some rural communities.

What to make of Chupa? Anthropologists note that legends of blood-sucking creatures permeate history, from the werewolves of France to the human vampires of eastern Europe. Even the ancient Mayans included a vampire deity in their catalogue of gods. And legendary blood-lusters are legion throughout the history of South America and the Caribbean. According to a 1996 article in the *San Juan Star*, Puerto Rico's Pulitzer Prize–winning newspaper, island lore predating the Chupacabra includes a Moca vampire, which also attacked small animals, and the *garadiablo*, a swamp thing that emerged from the ooze at night to wreak havoc on the populace. That these vampire creatures confine themselves to Spanish-speaking countries of Central and South America and the Caribbean has not escaped observers—the Chupacabra hysteria, it seems, has its roots in societies tinged with Roman Catholic and other mystical religions.

Hysteria might be too strong a word. Above the clamor of the fringe elements that believe Chupacabra to be Beelzebub incarnate or part of an advance team of alien invaders, and among those who simply believe in the possibility of weird and yet-undiscovered terrestrial life forms, one hears the more skeptical voice of reason. The government denies (as conspiracy theorists would expect) the existence of the Chupacabra. Zoologists have suggested that the alleged condition of some Chupacabra victims may actually be the result of exaggerated retelling of the work of less mysterious animals, such as a tropical species of bat known to feed on the blood of small mammals. Even some bird species are known to eat warm-blooded animals. This, however, doesn't explain the sightings of the hairy, ravenous beast. Then again, there's no accounting for the Loch Ness Monster either.

–Karl Luntta

equipment are supplied, and maid service is available every two days. In addition to the cottages, larger buildings on the premises contain 16 suites, some with kitchens and some without. The grounds include a swimming pool; barbecue area; tennis, basketball, and sand volleyball courts; and laundry facilities. Horses are also available for riding, and tours can be arranged. The popular on-site restaurant, Olas y Arena, is known for its fish and shellfish; the paella is especially good. ⊠ *Rte. 4466, Km 8.3 (Box 510), 00622,* ☎ *787/872–2045 or 787/872–2627,* ℻ *787/872–0273. 38 rooms. Restaurant, air-conditioning (some), fans, kitchenettes (some), pool, tennis court, basketball, horseback riding. AE, MC, V. Restaurant closed Mon. EP.* 🐾

$$ 🏨 **Parador El Guajataca.** Located between the towns of Quebradillas and Isabela, this small inn, part of the government's paradores program, takes full advantage of the lovely coastal scenery. Perched on a small bluff overlooking the Atlantic, the modern, air-conditioned rooms have ocean views that can be dramatic on days when the waves are breaking hard. Grounds include a palm-lined swimming pool, two tennis courts, a basketball court, a children's playground, paths to the Guajataca Beach, and a restaurant. ⊠ *Rte. 2, Km 103.8 (Box 1558), Quebradillas 00678,* ☎ *787/895–3070,* ℻ *787/895–2204. 38 rooms. Restaurant, air-conditioning, pool, 2 tennis courts, basketball, beach, playground. AE, MC, V. EP.*

Outdoor Activities and Sports

BEACHES

Shacks Beach (⊠ off Rte. 4466) is known for its snorkeling and surfing. On Route 466, **Jobos Beach** is famous for surfing but can have dangerous breaks. **Montones Beach** (⊠ Rte. 466) is a beautiful beach for swimming and frolicking in the sand and has a natural protected pool where children can splash. Toward Quebradillas, **Guajataca Beach** (⊠ off Rte. 113) stretches by what is called El Tunnel, part of an old tunnel used by a passenger and cargo train that ran from San Juan to Ponce from the early to mid-1900s. Today, there is a picnic area around the ruins.

HORSEBACK RIDING

Tropical Trail Rides (☎ 787/872–9256) has two-hour morning and afternoon rides along the beach and through a forest of almond trees. Groups leave from Shacks Beach on Route 4466 at Km 1.8. Horseback riding arrangements can also be made at **Villas del Mar Hau** (⊠ Rte. 466, Km 8.3, ☎ 787/872–2045).

SNORKELING AND SCUBA DIVING

Fantastic underground caves populated with tropical fish lie off Shacks Beach in water no deeper than 40 feet. **La Cueva Submarina Dive Shop** (⊠ Rte. 466, Km 6.3, ☎ 787/872–1390) offers trips to these caves for beginning and advanced divers. It also offers certification courses and snorkeling trips.

OFF THE BEATEN PATH **PALACETE LOS MOREAU –** In the fields south of Isabela toward the town of Moca, a French family settled on a coffee and sugar plantation in the 1800s. In 1905, the original wooden plantation house was rebuilt in concrete and now looms over flat meadows. The grand two-story house, trimmed with gables, columns, and stained-glass windows, was immortalized in the novel *La Llamarada*, written in 1935 by Puerto Rican novelist Enrique A. Laguerre. In Laguerre's novel about conditions in the sugarcane industry, the house was home to his fictional family, the Moreaus. Now known as the Palacete los Moreau, the manor house was acquired by the municipality of Moca in 1993 after it was damaged in a fire. The municipality has renovated it and opened it to the public.

While it doesn't have many furnishings, visitors can walk through the house and also visit Laguerre's personal library, which has been moved to the mansion's basement. The home (✉ Rte. 2 to Rte. 464, then turn left at Ruben's Supermarket, ☎ 787/830–2540) is open free of charge weekdays from 8 to 11 and from 1 to 3:30.

WEST-CENTRAL INLANDS: MOUNTAINS, FORESTS, AND COFFEE

Spanning unruly karst terrain and parts of the Puerto Rico's rugged central mountain range, the west-central inlands is a breathtakingly beautiful mixture of limestone cliffs, man-made lakes, and sprawling forest reserves. It's here, in the Bosque Estatal de Toro Negro, that the island's highest peak, Cerro de Punta, rises 4,398 ft above sea level.

Coffee was once a dominant crop along hillsides between Utuado and Maricao, and it can still be seen growing in small plots today. A few of the old plantation homes have been turned into quaint country inns, all of them stocked with plenty of blankets for cool evenings when temperatures—especially in higher elevations—can drop into the 40s.

Sans large resorts, glitzy casinos, and beaches, this area of Puerto Rico is for those who like to get off the well-traveled roads and spend time exploring small towns, rural areas, and unspoiled nature. Driving here takes patience; some of the roads aren't clearly marked, and others twist and turn for what seems an eternity. But the area's natural beauty has attracted people for centuries, including pre-Columbian Indians, who have left behind remnants of earlier civilizations.

Utuado

❼ *32 km (20 mi) south of Arecibo via Rte. 10; 104 km (65 mi) from San Juan via Hwy. 22 and Rte. 10.*

Surrounded by steep mountains, tall trees, and blue lakes, the town of Utuado sits in the middle of lush natural beauty. Just driving on Route 10 between Arecibo and Utuado is a breathtaking experience—imposing brown limestone cliffs jut out of the earth on either side of the well-paved road, and clouds often hover around the tops of the surrounding hills. Utuado was named after a local Indian chief, Otoao, and today its narrow and sometimes busy streets lead to a double-steepled church on the main plaza. The best sights, however, are outside town along winding side roads.

❽ **Bosque Estatal de Río Abajo,** in the island's limestone karst country, spans some 5,000 acres and includes huge bamboo stands and native lead and silk-cotton trees. It also has several plantations of Asian teaks, Dominican and Honduran mahogany, and Australian pines, which are part of a government tree management program that supplies wood for the local economy (primarily for artisans and fence building). Numerous walking trails wind through the forest, which is one of the wild habitats for the rare Puerto Rican parrot. An information office is near the entrance on Route 621, and a recreation area with picnic tables is farther down the road. ✉ *Rte. 621, Km 4.4,* ☎ *787/817–0984.* ▣ *Free.* ☉ *Daily.*

❾ East of Bosque Estatal de Río Abajo is the U-shape **Lago Dos Bocas,** one of several man-made lakes near Utuado. Government-operated boats take you around the lake from a dock, called El Embarcadero, near the intersection of Routes 123 and 146. Although the boats are used primarily as a means of public transit for residents of the area, the 45-

minute ride around the lake is pleasant and scenic, and gets you to some of the shoreline restaurants. The boats are free of charge and leave daily at 7 AM, 8:30 AM, and every hour on the hour between 10 and 5. The lake is stocked with sunfish, bass, and catfish. You can fish from the shore, but you'll need to bring your own tackle. ⊠ *Off Rte. 10, accessed via Rtes. 621, 123, 146, and 612,* ☎ *787/879–1838 (El Embarcadero).* 🎫 *Free.* ☉ *Daily.*

⑩ West of Utuado on Route 111 is the 13-acre **Parque Ceremonial Indígena de Caguana,** used more than 800 years ago by the Taíno tribes for recreation and worship. According to Spanish historians, the Taínos played a game here—thought to have religious significance—that resembled modern-day soccer. Today you can see 10 *bateyes* (courts) of various sizes, large stone monoliths (some with petroglyphs), and recreations of Taíno gardens. There's also a small museum. ⊠ *Rte. 111, Km 12.3,* ☎ *787/894–7325.* 🎫 *$2.* ☉ *Daily 8:30–4.*

Dining and Lodging

$–$$ ✕ **El Fogón de Abuela.** This rustic restaurant on the edge of Dos Bocas Lake, open only Friday–Sunday, offers food that would make any Puerto Rican grandmother envious. The menu features stews; red snapper (whole or filleted); and several fricassees, including pork chop, goat, and rabbit. The wood-and-tin-roof building is simply decorated and is cooled by fresh breezes off the water. You arrive either by taking the public boat from El Embarcadero on Rte. 612 (☞ Lago Dos Bocas, *above*), by calling the restaurant from a pay phone at the dock and requesting that a boat be sent to pick you up (free of charge), or by driving to the south side of the lake—from Utuado, take Route 111 to Route 140 to Route 612 and follow that to its end. ⊠ *Lago Dos Bocas,* ☎ *787/894–0470. MC, V. Closed Mon.–Thurs.*

$$ ✕🏠 **Hotel La Casa Grande.** It's not hard to imagine Tarzan swinging
★ in for dinner at this quaint country inn surrounded by lakes, lush green vegetation, and mountain peaks. Built in 1947 on a sugar, tobacco, coffee, and cattle plantation, the main house contains a restaurant, bar, and reception area. Five wooden buildings surrounding the main house hold 20 guest rooms with peaked ceilings and fans. The grounds cover 107 acres and include a swimming pool and beautiful gardens lovingly maintained by owner Steven Weingarten. Winner of the 1999 Green Inn Award from the Puerto Rico Hotel & Tourism Association, the hotel makes use of the nearby mountain water supply, recycles its trash, and strives to be as energy efficient as possible. There are no TVs, phones, or radios in the rooms, but a chorus of tiny tree frogs provides symphonies at night. Dining is on an outdoor patio at Jungle Jane's restaurant, which serves breakfast, lunch, and dinner. The menu features mango-glazed salmon, lemon-garlic chicken breast, and Puerto Rican specialties such as *asopao* with shrimp. The inn is near two lakes (including Lago Dos Bocas), the Bosque Estatal de Río Abajo, and the Caguana Indian Ceremonial Park. It is also convenient for day trips to the Arecibo Observatory and the Río Camuy Cave Park. ⊠ *Rte. 612, Km 0.3 (Box 616), 00641,* ☎ *787/894–3939 or 888/894–3532,* 🆎 *787/343–2272. 20 rooms. Restaurant, fans, pool. AE, MC, V. EP.* 🐾

Outdoor Activities and Sports

HIKING
Trails run through the **Bosque Estatal de Río Abajo** (⊠ Rte. 621, Km 4.4, ☎ 787/817–0984).

HORSEBACK RIDING

Rancho de Caballos de Utuado (✉ Rte. 612, across from Hotel La Casa Grande, ☎ 787/894–0240) offers three-to-four-hour horse rides along a river and lake and through mountain forests.

KAYAKING

Kayaks are available for rent at **Rancho Marina** (✉ Rte. 612, Lago Dos Bocas, ☎ 787/894–8035). Jenaro Colón at **Locura Arecibeña/Río Grande de Arecibo Kayak Rentals** (☎ 787/878–1809) can arrange for rentals and weekend guided tours.

Jayuya

⑪ *24 km (15 mi) southeast of Utuado via Rtes. 111, 140, and 144.*

This small town of 15,000 is nestled in the foothills of the Cordillera Central, Puerto Rico's tallest mountain chain. Cerro de Punta, the island's highest peak, looms just to the south of the town's center. Named after the Indian chief Hauyua, Jayuya is known for preserving its Indian heritage and draws people from all over the island for its yearly Indigenous Festival in November, which features crafts, exhibits, parades, music, and dancing. Coffee is still grown in the area—look for the locally produced Tres Picachos, sold mainly in Jayuya.

★ ⑫ The 7,000-acre **Bosque Estatal de Toro Negro** skirts the Cordillera Central and contains the highest peak on the island, 4,398-ft Cerro de Punta. It is also home to the island's highest lake, Lago Guineo; lots of streams, natural ponds, and waterfalls (including the 200-ft Doña Juana Falls); and gigantic bamboo, royal palms, and oak trees. The Doña Juana Recreational Area just off Route 143, and has picnic tables and a campground nearby. Take one of the many hiking trails branching out from the recreational area to watch for exotic birds such as the Guadalupe woodpecker, or drive to a trail on the western edge of the forest that leads to the top of Cerro de Punta (a 30- to 45-minute hike). The reserve also contains a huge but often out-of-service swimming pool built into the side of a mountain. If you're going to camp, be sure to bring blankets, as it can get cold here at night. Camping permits must be obtained at the Department of Natural and Environmental Resources (☎ 787/ 724–3724) on Avenida Fernández Juncos in San Juan, next to the Club Náutico. Permits must be requested at least 15 days in advance. ✉ *Rte. 143, Km 31.8,* ☎ *787/867–3040.* ☜ *Free.* ☉ *Daily.*

⑬ The tiny **Museo Cemí** is housed in a building shaped like a *cemí*, a Taíno artifact believed to possess religious significance. On display is a collection of Taíno pottery and religious and ceremonial objects found on the island. ✉ *Rte. 144, Km 9.3,* ☎ *787/828–1241.* ☜ *Free.* ☉ *Weekdays 8–4:30, weekends 10–3:30.*

⑭ **La Piedra Escrita** ("Written Rock") is a huge boulder with several highly visible Taíno petroglyphs, located in a stream among several other large rocks. It's somewhat hard to find—watch for a sign along the road, then pull over and look for an old stairway that takes you down to the stream. This is also a nice, secluded spot for a picnic lunch. ✉ *Off Rte. 144, near the Museo Cemí.* ☜ *Free.*

Dining and Lodging

$$ ✕🏨 **Parador Hacienda Gripiñas.** Built on the grounds of a coffee plan-
★ tation in 1853 by Spaniard Eusebio Perez del Castillo, this former home was turned into an inn in 1975. Surrounded by beautifully manicured gardens and tall mountain peaks, the inn retains an air of elegance; it has a wide porch, shuttered windows, and lots of polished wood. Rooms are light and airy, with inviting balconies overlooking lush scenery.

COFFEE—PUERTO RICO'S BLACK GOLD

CULTIVATED AT HIGH ALTITUDES in a swirl of cool, moist air and mineral-rich soil, Puerto Rican coffee holds its own among the best coffees of the world.

Introduced in the mid-18th century with shrubs imported from nearby Martinique (after being brought by French farmers to that island from France), coffee started its life in Puerto Rico as a minor cash crop, cultivated mainly for local consumption. By the late 19th century, Puerto Rican coffee had benefited from the labors and experimentation of immigrants experienced in coffee production, and it was highly respected by connoisseurs in Europe and the Americas. Its status grew, yet Puerto Rican coffee, once second only to sugarcane in production, suffered after Spain ceded the island to the United States in 1898, and after several major hurricanes all but wiped out the crop. Today, with chichi coffee bars opening daily throughout the United States and in major urban centers worldwide, Puerto Rican beans have once again taken their place next to the the Jamaica Blue Mountain and Hawaiian Kona varieties as one of the world's premium coffees.

The secret is in the coffee bean itself (called "cherry" when ripe). The island's dominant bean is the *arabica*; it has a more delicate and lower-yielding cherry than the prolific *robusta* bean found on the mega-plantations of Central and South America. The arabica cherry, in the proper conditions, produces an extraordinary coffee. Cloud cover, tree shade, soil composition, and the altitude at which the coffee bushes are grown—higher than 3,000 ft above sea level—combine to produce a slow-ripening bean that stays on the bush at least two months longer than at lower elevations. This lengthy ripening process acts as a sort of "pre-brew," imbuing the bean with a rich flavor and a slightly sweet aftertaste.

Small, family run pulperies are the norm in Puerto Rico. In them the ripened beans are pulped (shelled) and fermented, then dried, roasted, and packed. The main coffee-growing areas of the island lie in the wet, mountainous regions of Yauco, Lares, and Las Marís, where the limited suitable terrain makes large-scale production impossible, and thus makes the coffee all the more precious a commodity.

Throughout Puerto Rico look for the brand Alto Grande Super Premium, which is guaranteed to have been grown at high altitudes. It's best consumed straight up as espresso, or cut with hot milk, the traditional *café con leche*. It also makes a great gift to carry home.

–Karl Luntta

The inn's restaurant serves steaks, lobster, shrimp, and criollo fare such as chicken with rice and beans. For dessert, try the very sweet and very delicious *tembleque*—a custard made from coconut milk and sugar—along with a cup of locally grown coffee. Across from the house are a bar and a swimming pool filled with cool mountain water. One hiking trail near the property leads to Cerro de Punta, about a 2½-hour climb. ⊠ *Rte. 527, Km 2.7 (Box 387), 00664,* ☎ *787/828–1717,* ⅋*787/828–1718. 19 rooms. Restaurant, air-conditioning, pool, hiking. AE, MC, V. MAP.* 🕸

Outdoor Activities and Sports

Trails in the **Bosque Estatal de Toro Negro** (⊠ Rte. 143, Km 31.8, ☎ 787/867–3040) lead to waterfalls and the island's highest peak.

Adjuntas

⑮ *27 km (17 mi) southwest of Jayuya via Rtes. 144, 140, 143, and 10.*

The coffee-growing town of Adjuntas sits just north of Puerto Rico's Panoramic Route (☞ *see* Close-Up box, Chapter 4). While known for its coffee, it is also the world's leading producer of citron, a fruit whose rind is preserved and processed here and then shipped for use in sweets, especially fruitcakes. Surrounded by mountains, lakes, and forests, Adjuntas's main attractions are of the outdoor variety.

⑯ The **Bosque Estatal de Guilarte** is home to 3,900-ft Pico Guilarte, as well as a very scenic picnic area near a eucalyptus grove. Hiking trails, surrounded by wild-growing impatiens, lead up to Pico Guilarte and into other areas of the forest. Bird-watchers have 26 different species to look for, including the carpenter bird. Or if your interest is botany, you can find a wide variety of trees, including candlewood, trumpet, Honduran mahogany, and Honduran pine. ⊠ *Rte. 518 at Rte. 131,* ☎ *787/829–7804.* 🖼 *Free.* ⊙ *Daily.*

Dining and Lodging

$$-$$$ ✕🖬 **Villas de Sotomayor.** Covering 14⅓ acres, this complex of cabins has a camplike atmosphere with a focus on horseback riding. It has its own stable on the premises, from which you can rent horses to ride on your own or with guides. You can also take horse-and-carriage rides around the grounds, which include forest areas. Rooms are in separate, modern cabins and range from one bedroom with a refrigerator to two bedrooms with a kitchenette. All units have air-conditioning, refrigerators, coffeemakers, and TVs; some come with microwaves. There are two pools, tennis and badminton courts, bikes, and barbecue facilities. The on-site restaurant is open daily and serves international and criollo cuisine—it is known for its mofongo relleno. ⊠ *Rte. 10, Km 36.3 (Box 28), 00601,* ☎ *787/829–1717,* ⅋ *787/829–1774. 34 rooms. Restaurant, air-conditioning, kitchenettes (some), 2 pools, 2 tennis courts, badminton, basketball, horseback riding. AE, MC, V. EP.* 🕸

Outdoor Activities and Sports

Hike to the summit of 3,900-ft Pico Guilarte in the **Bosque Estatal de Guilarte** (☞ *above*) or on numerous other trails lined with candlewood, mahogany, and pine trees.

Villas de Sotomayor (☞ Dining and Lodging, *above*) rents horses to guests and nonguests alike. You can explore on your own or take a guide-led ride.

Maricao

⑰ *59 km (37 mi) west of Adjuntas via Rtes. 518, 131, 525, 128, 365, 366, and 120; 43 km (27 mi) east of Mayagüez via Rte. 105.*

Puerto Rico's smallest municipality (pop. 6,200), Maricao is part of the island's coffee country and hosts a well-known Coffee Harvest Festival each February, featuring coffee, coffee pastries, music, and dancing. Although not far from Mayagüez, the third-largest urban area on the island, Maricao has an isolated feeling; driving in the area is more akin to being deep in the central mountain region. The Bosque Estatal de Maricao is well known in birding circles for its numerous endangered species.

★ **⑱** Drier than other forest reserves found near the central mountains, **Bosque Estatal de Maricao** has become known as a bird-watcher's paradise. The 60 species found here—29 of which are endangered—include the Puerto Rican emerald, the Puerto Rican vireos, and the elfin woods warbler. Part of the reserve is the Maricao Fish Hatchery on Route 410 at Km 1.7, which contains a collection of ponds and tanks where fish are raised to stock island lakes. (The hatchery is open weekdays 7:30–noon and 1–4, weekends 8:30–4. Tours are given by appointment—call ☎ 787/838–3710.) You'll find an information center and a stone observation tower about half a mile beyond the forest entrance. The Centro Vacacional Monte de Estado (☞ Dining and Lodging, *below*) has rustic cabins for rent. *Rte. 120 at Rte. 366,* ☎ *787/ 319–4128.* ✉ *Free.* ⊙ *Daily.*

Dining and Lodging

$$ ✕▥ **Parador La Hacienda Juanita.** Part of a coffee plantation in the ★ 1800s, this inn is surrounded by forest and takes on a slower pace of days gone by. The original plantation house holds the reception, dining, and lobby areas, which are decorated with antiques from the heyday of the island's coffee industry. The grounds, which were renovated after Hurricane Georges in 1998, include a pool, a tennis court, and two hiking trails good for bird-watching. (Binoculars are available for guests of the hotel.) Rooms are in four separate buildings on the grounds; about half have TVs, and some are decorated with four-poster beds and antiques. La Casona de Juanita restaurant serves up criollo cuisine, including *sancocho,* a hearty soup made with meat and root vegetables. Meals are served on a beautiful sweeping balcony where you can reach up and pull fruit off the trees. The restaurant also offers vegetarian dishes and has a nice selection of wines. There is traditional Puerto Rican music on Sunday afternoon, and once a month the management brings in a well-known local musician to perform for hotel guests only. ✉ *Rte. 105, Km 23.5 (Box 777), 00606,* ☎ *787/ 838–2550,* ﬁﬂﬃ *787/838–2551. 21 rooms. Restaurant, fans, pool, tennis courts. AE, MC, V. MAP.* ✍

$ ▥ **Centro Vacacional Monte del Estado.** This government-run vacation spot in the Bosque Estatal de Maricao has rustic two-bedroom cabins that can sleep up to six people. It's a place for hearty souls who like the woods and don't mind a bit of cool evening air. The cabins have covered porches, kitchens, bathrooms, and stone fireplaces. You need to supply your own sheets, pillows, blankets, and kitchen utensils; stock up on supplies in San Juan before leaving for the countryside or in Mayagüez at the Mayagüez Mall (☞ *below*). ✉ *Rte. 120, Km 13.1, 00902,* ☎ *787/722–1551, 787/722–1771. 24 cabins. Kitchenettes, fireplaces. MC, V. EP.*

Outdoor Activities and Sports

HIKING

The **Bosque Estatal de Maricao** (⊠ Rte. 120 at Rte. 366) is filled with hiking trails and is a popular spot for bird-watching.

THE WEST COAST

Adventurers since the time of Christopher Columbus have been drawn to the jagged coastline of northwestern Puerto Rico. Columbus made his first stop here on his second voyage to the Americas in 1493. His exact landing point is the subject of ongoing dispute—both Aguadilla on the northernmost tip of the coast and Aguada just to Aguadilla's south claim the historic landing, and both have monuments honoring the explorer.

Five centuries later, people are still discovering the area, lured primarily by the numerous beaches hugging the shoreline. The town of Rincón, which gained notoriety by hosting the World Surfing Championship in 1968, draws surfers from around the globe, especially during winter months when the waves are at their best. Numerous calmer beaches nearby fit the bill if you just want to catch some rays, have a swim, and relax in an area with a laid-back, small-town feel. From December through February, if you keep your eyes on the ocean you may spot one of the humpback whales that spend the winter offshore.

About halfway down the coast is Mayagüez, the island's third-largest urban area, where you'll find an interesting mix of Spanish colonial and eclectic 20th-century architecture. The city makes for an enjoyable day trip, but come nightfall you'll want to make your way to the shore, where you can view some of the most spectacular sunsets anywhere on the island.

Aguadilla

19 *20 km (13 mi) southwest of Isabela via Rtes. 112, 2, and 111; 130 km (81 mi) west of San Juan via Rtes. 22, 2, and 111.*

Weathered but lovely, the faded facades of many of Aguadilla's buildings seem indicative of its long and somewhat turbulent past. It is said Columbus landed here on his second voyage to the Americas in 1493 (though Aguada down the road makes the same claim). Officially incorporated as a town in 1775, Aguadilla subsequently suffered a series of catastrophes, including a devastating earthquake in 1918 and strong hurricanes in 1928 and 1932. Determined to survive, the town rebuilt after each disaster, and by World War II it became known for the huge U.S. Air Force base just north of town, originally called Borinquen Field and renamed Ramey Air Force Base. The base housed such aircraft as the B-17 and B-36 and was an important link in the U.S. defense system throughout World War II and the Cold War.

Downtown Aguadilla has many small wooden homes, and resembles a fishing village. Ramey ceased to be an active U.S. Air Force base in 1973, and today comprises an airport, a golf course, and some small businesses, although many structures stand empty. The natural spring where Columbus is said to have gotten water during his stop is now part of the somewhat rundown **El Parterre Parque** on Avenida Muñoz Rivera. Residents mingle in **Parque Colón** (Columbus Park) at the end of Calle Comercio, but the biggest attractions are swimming, surfing, snorkeling, and diving off Aguadilla's beaches. Modest hotels near town attract budget-conscious travelers; those looking for more luxurious accommodations usually stay in the nearby towns of Isabela or Rincón.

Dining and Lodging

$$ ✕🖬 **Parador El Faro.** Part of the government's parador program, this family-owned inn has modern, roomy, simply decorated rooms and suites with air-conditioning, cable television, and telephones. Well-suited for families, the grounds include a tennis court, basketball court, children's playground, and two swimming pools. The location isn't directly on a beach, but Crashboat and other beaches are just 1½ mi away. There are two restaurants on the premises, including the popular Three Amigos, which features a combination of Italian, Mexican, and criollo cuisines. ✉ *Rte. 107, Km 2.1 (Box 5148), 00605,* ☎ *787/882–8000 or 888/300–8002,* 𝔽𝔸𝕏 *787/882–1030. 70 rooms, 5 suites. 2 restaurants, air-conditioning, cable TV, pool, tennis, basketball. AE, D, DC, MC, V. EP.* 🐾

Outdoor Activities and Sports

BEACHES

★ Aguadilla's **Crashboat Beach** (✉ off Rte. 458) is famous throughout the island for the colorful fishing boats docked on its shores, its long, beautiful stretch of sand, and its clear water, which often has a glasslike look. Named after rescue boats that used to be docked here when Ramey Air Force Base was in operation, the beach is good for swimming and snorkeling when waters are calm, and has picnic huts, showers, and rest rooms. It often hosts music festivals, especially in summer. **Wilderness and Gas Chambers beaches** (✉ just north of Crashboat Beach via Rte. 107) are often frequented by surfers. (Wilderness is recommended only for experienced surfers, as it can have dangerous breaks.) **Playa Borinquen** (✉ Rte. 107) is calmer than the surfing beaches to the south.

SNORKELING AND SCUBA DIVING

Aquatica Underwater Adventures, at the former Ramey Air Force Base (✉ Rte. 110, Km 10, Gate 5, ☎ 787/890–6071), offers scuba diving certification courses and dives off Aguadilla and Isabela beaches. You can also arrange snorkeling trips and rent snorkeling equipment.

GOLF

The 18-hole **Punta Borinquen Golf Course** (✉ Rte. 107, Km 2, ☎ 787/890–2987), on the former Ramey Air Force Base, was built in 1940 for use by the military and is said to have been played by U.S. presidents, including Dwight D. Eisenhower. Now a public course, it is known for its tough sand traps and strong cross winds. It's open daily.

Aguada

⓴ *8 km (5 mi) south of Aguadilla via Rtes. 111 and 115.*

The town of Aguada (pop. 36,000) gleams with modern concrete buildings and has the bustling feel of a large city. It shares with Aguadilla the claim that Christopher Columbus first set foot in Puerto Rico in its vicinity, and it has a statue of the explorer in its main plaza. Regardless of where Columbus actually landed, Aguada seems to be the sentimental favorite; on November 19, crowds descend on the town to celebrate Discovery Day with parades, food, and music. The rest of the year, Puerto Ricans and off-shore visitors find tranquillity on Aguada's beaches.

Lodging

$$ 🖬 **JB Hidden Village.** This whitewashed hotel in a rural area is part of the government's parador program and is known for being family-friendly. The modern rooms and suites all have balconies (some overlook the countryside, others the pool), air-conditioning, and cable

television. Two larger suites have their own Jacuzzis. There's a restaurant on the premises, and fine beaches are close by—Aguada's public beach is 10 minutes away, and it's a 20-minute drive to Rincón. ✉ *Rte. 416, Km 9.5 (Box 937), 00602,* ☎ *787/882–5960,* ℻ *787/888–8701. 45 rooms. Restaurant, air-conditioning, cable TV, pool. MC, V. EP.*

Outdoor Activities and Sports

BEACHES

Balneario Pico de Piedra, also called the Aguada Public Beach (✉ Rte. 441), is a nice swimming beach frequented by families. There are parking facilities, changing rooms, and rest rooms. **Table Rock Beach** (✉ north of Balneario Pico de Piedra on Rte. 441) is known for its snorkeling and surfing.

Rincón

㉑ *9.5 km (6 mi) southwest of Aguada via Rte. 115.*

Jutting out into the ocean along the rugged western coast, Rincón, meaning corner in Spanish, may have gotten its name because of how it is nestled in a "corner" of the coastline. Some, however, trace the town's name to Gonzalo Rincón, a 16th-century landowner who let poor families live on his land. Whatever the history, the name suits the town, which is like a little world unto itself. Rincón remains laid-back and unpretentious even though it jumped into the surfing spotlight after hosting the World Surfing Championship in 1968. It has also become known world-wide for the Horned Dorset Primavera, the only Relais & Chateaux property in Puerto Rico and one of only a handful in the Caribbean. The town caters to all sorts of travelers, from budget-conscious surfers to families to those looking for a romantic getaway. It has long been known for its small hotels and cottages, but recently large, concrete condominiums and larger hotels have begun to spring up, including the 102-room Rincón Del Mar, which is scheduled to open in 2001 on Route 115 next to Corcega Beach.

The beat picks up from October through April, when the waves are the best, but tourists can be found here year-round, and many American mainlanders have settled here. If you visit between December and February, you might get a glimpse of the humpback whales that winter off the coast.

Because of its unusual setting, Rincón's layout can be a little disconcerting. The main road, Route 413, loops around the coast, and many beaches and sights are on dirt roads intersecting with it. Most hotels and restaurants hand out detailed maps of the area.

㉒ Surrounding the Punta Higuera Lighthouse (built in 1892 and rebuilt in 1921, after it was damaged in a 1918 earthquake), **Parque Pasivo El Faro** features small kiosks at the water's edge with telescopes you can use to look for whales. (Have patience, though, even during the "season," from December through February; it could take days to spot one.) You can also glimpse the rusting dome of the defunct Bonus Thermonuclear Energy Plant from here; it has been closed since 1974 but could be resurrected as a nuclear-energy museum. The park is a nice place to watch the beautiful sunsets, and there are also benches, a shop, and a refreshment stand on the grounds. The lighthouse itself is closed to the public, but it's hard to walk away without taking a photo of the stately white structure. ✉ *Calle El Faro off Rte. 413.* 🎟 *Free.* ☉ *Daily 8 AM–midnight.*

Dining and Lodging

$$ ✕ **The Landing.** This spacious restaurant/bar/club has a large, beautiful wooden bar that's often filled with a mix of people, from surfers to retirees. You can dine on pasta, steaks, and burgers inside or on a back terrace overlooking the ocean. There's also a children's menu with junior burgers and chicken fingers. On weekend nights when live bands play, the place often fills with a younger crowd. ✉ *Rte. 413, Km 4.7,* ☎ *787/823–3112. AE, MC, V.*

$$ ✕ **Larry B's.** Tucked next to the bar at Beside the Point Inn is a wooden patio where you can watch the surf crash against the beach while dining on steaks, shrimp, pasta, salads, and fresh fish, all simply prepared and served in generous helpings. Larry himself serves up the food, and he's happy to regale guests with tales of his wave-seeking exploits. ✉ *Rte. 413, Barrio Puntas,* ☎ *787/823–3210. MC, V. Closed Mon.–Wed.*

$$ ✕ **El Molino del Quijote.** Amid beautifully landscaped gardens just off the beach, this restaurant offers Spanish and Puerto Rican cuisine in a charming thatch-roof building with a cozy atmosphere or at tables in the garden overlooking the water. The paella, mofongo, and sangría are superb, and so is the service. ✉ *Rte. 429, Km 3.3,* ☎ *787/823–4010. AE, MC, V. Closed Mon.–Thurs.*

$$$$ ✕▥ **Horned Dorset Primavera.** Nestled in a lush landscape and hardly
★ noticeable from the road, this resort complex overlooking the water and a small, secluded beach is the only Relais & Chateaux property in Puerto Rico. Each room is unique, but all are furnished with antiques, including four-poster beds, dressers, and nightstands. There are no radios, TVs, or phones in the rooms, and no facilities for children— this is a resort targeted to adults looking to get away from it all in luxury. The newer Casa Escondida is designed to resemble a turn-of-the-20th-century Puerto Rican hacienda (note the breathtaking wooden ceiling) and houses eight rooms, four with their own plunge pools. The main house, which contains the lobby, a library, and sitting and dining areas, has elegant West Indian plantation-style furniture and glistening chandeliers. (There are plans to add 22 luxury one-bedroom villas next door to the property, scheduled to open in the fall of 2001.) The hotel's restaurant has an island-wide reputation for excellence. Dinner, served on the second floor of the main house, has tropical touches and a heavy Cordon Bleu influence. The menu changes daily but might include such dishes as crab salad with cilantro and mango, and roasted duck with black cherries. A five-course prix-fixe dinner is $64 per person, and an even more elaborate "chef's tasting" runs $88. You can also order à la carte. Dress is formal by island standards—no shorts are allowed. Breakfast and lunch are more casual than dinner and are served downstairs. ✉ *Rte. 429, Km. 3 (Box 1132), 00677,* ☎ *787/823–4030, 787/823–4050, or 800/633–1857,* ℻ *787/725–6068. 31 rooms. Restaurant, air-conditioning, fans, 2 pools, croquet, exercise room, beach, library. Restaurant reservations required. AE, MC, V. CP, EP, MAP.* ✐

$$$ ▥ **Lemontree Waterfront Cottages.** These large, sparkling-clean apartments sit right on the beach and have staircases leading from their decks to the sand. Each unit has kitchen facilities, cable TV, air-conditioning in the bedrooms, and a deck with a wet bar and a grill. The bright tropical decor includes local artwork. The facility offers one three-bedroom unit with two baths, one two-bedroom unit, two one-bedroom units, and two newer studios with kitchenettes. Maid service doesn't automatically come with the room but can be arranged. The beach here is small, but larger ones are nearby. ✉ *Rte. 429, Km 4.1 (Box 200), 00677,* ☎ *787/823–6452,* ℻ *787/823–5821. 6 apartments. Air-conditioning, cable TV, kitchenettes. AE, MC, V. EP.* ✐

$$ ✕⌾ **Lazy Parrot.** This fanciful hotel built on a mountainside offers rooms decorated in different tropical themes, such as whale and fish motifs. All rooms have air-conditioning, cable TV, phones, and small refrigerators, and a honeymoon suite includes a waterbed and private Jacuzzi. The lush grounds have a pool and a gift shop. The inn's restaurant is popular with surfers (though it draws plenty of nonsurfers as well) and features conch fritters, chicken wings, snapper breaded with almonds and cornflakes, coconut shrimp, and Thai chicken. ⌧ *Rte. 413, Km 4.1, 00677,* ☏ *787823–5654 or 800/294–1752,* ⅨX *787/823–0224. 11 rooms. Restaurant, air-conditioning, refrigerators, pool, hot tub. AE, D, MC, V. Restaurant closed Mon. CP.* ✎

Nightlife

Bars and restaurants are the hubs of nighttime activity in Rincón. On weekends, **Calypso** (⌧ Rte. 413 at Maria's Beach, ☏ 787/823–4151) often has live Spanish or rock 'n' roll bands. **The Landing** (⌧ Rte. 413, Km 4.7, ☏ 787/823–3112) is a popular spot for live music on weekends. For a romantic drink after dinner, try the second-floor dining room of the **Sandy Beach Surf Club** (⌧ Rte. 413 near Sandy Beach, ☏ 787/823–1146), which has a fantastic view of the town's lights at night.

Outdoor Activities and Sports

BEACHES

There's a beach for everyone near Rincón. Surfers swear by the waves at **Tres Palmas, Steps** (named for a concrete set of steps sitting mysteriously at water's edge), **Maria's,** and **Dome's** (named for the nuclear power plant's nearby dome), lined up in a row off Route 413 going north toward the lighthouse. The snorkeling is good at **Tres Palmas Beach.** Swimmers can enjoy the tranquil waters of the **Rincón Public Beach** (⌧ Rte. 115 just before it intersects with Rte. 413), which has parking facilities and rest rooms. The long stretch of yellow sand at **Corcega Beach** (⌧ in front of Parador Villa Antonio and Hotel Villa Cofresí) is considered one of the best swimming beaches in the Rincón area.

BOAT TRIPS

Various operations offer sunset cruises and whale-watching trips in season (Dec.–Feb.). Check with **Desecheo Dive Shop** (⌧ Rte. 413, Km 2.5, ☏ 787/823–0390), **Taíno Divers** (⌧ Black Eagle Marina off Rte. 413, ☏ 787/823–6429), or **Moondog Charters** (⌧ Black Eagle Marina off Rte. 413, ☏ 787/823–7168).

FISHING

Marlin, dorado, wahoo, and kingfish can be hooked in the waters off Rincón. Fishing trips are offered by all of the operators listed under Boat Trips, *above.*

SCUBA AND SNORKELING

For divers, **Desecheo Island,** about 13 mi off the coast of Rincón, has abundant reef and fish life. A rocky bottom sloping to 120 ft rims the island; one formation known as Yellow Reef is distinguished by long tunnels and caverns covered with purple hydrocoral. There are numerous other sites in shallower water off Rincón's shores with plentiful fish and coral. For trips and scuba certification courses, try **Desecheo Dive Shop** (☞ Boat Trips, *above*) or **Taíno Divers** (☞ Boat Trips, *above*).

Shopping

Pick up new and used surfboards, body boards, kayaks, and snorkeling equipment, or rent equipment, at **West Coast Surf Shop** (⌧ 2E Calle Muñoz Rivera, downtown, ☏ 787/823–3935). **HotWavz** (⌧ Rte. 413 at Maria's Beach, ☏ 787/823–3942) rents surfboards and sells beach gear. **Eco-Logic-Co** (⌧ Parque Pasivo El Faro, Calle El Faro, ☏ 787/ 823–1252) has fun and ecologically oriented souvenirs.

Mayagüez

24 km (15 mi) southeast of Rincón via Rtes. 115 and 2.

Known as the "Sultan of the West," Mayagüez was founded in 1760 and is said to have gotten its name from a local Taíno chief called Mayagez, whose name means "place of great waters." The city was a busy port under Spanish rule and was rebuilt after several natural disasters, including a fire in 1841 that devastated the downtown area. Evidence of the influence of diverse immigrants and constant rebuilding is seen in the variety of the city's structures, which run the gamut from neoclassical to Victorian to Baroque. With some 100,000 residents, Mayagüez is now the third-largest urban area on the island, after San Juan and Ponce. Small wooden houses dot the landscape, lending a working-class feel to this port city that became known for its tuna-canning industry in the 20th century. While not a tourist mecca, Mayagüez is nevertheless fun to explore on a morning or afternoon outing. Its pleasant main square, with lots of shade trees and benches, is dominated by a large statue of Christopher Columbus. One block away on McKinley Street is the city's most noteworthy building, the domed Teatro Yagüez, which dates from 1902. Just outside the city center, the U.S. Department of Agriculture runs a research station with acres of beautiful botanical gardens near the University of Puerto Rico's Mayagüez campus. Note that while the city promotes its newly refurbished zoo (the Puerto Rico Zoo) as a tourist attraction, you may find that what the facility has to offer doesn't justify the cost of admission.

㉓ Founded in 1901 on a 235-acre farm on the outskirts of Mayagüez, the **Tropical Agriculture Research Station** is run by the U.S. Department of Agriculture and contains a tropical plant collection that has been nurtured for more than half a century. More than 2,000 plant species from all over the tropical world are found here, including teak, mahogany, cinnamon, nutmeg, rubber, and numerous exotic flowers. Free maps are available for self-guided tours. ⊠ *Rtes. 2 and 108,* ☎ *787/831–3435.* 🎫 *Free.* ☉ *Weekdays 7–4.*

㉔ The **Teatro Yagüez** is an extravagant beige-and-white theater dating from 1902 that's famed throughout the island for its lavish, columned facade and dome roof. The structure is still the main venue for theater in Mayagüez (☞ Nightlife and the Arts *below*). If there aren't rehearsals going on, you can step in for a view of the enormous stage. (Ask at the ticket window whether the theater is open for viewing.) ⊠ *Calle McKinley at Calle Dr. Basora,* ☎ *787/834–0523.* 🎫 *Free.* ☉ *Daily except when rehearsals are scheduled.*

Dining and Lodging

$ ✕ **Ricomini Bakery.** This popular bakery is open daily from 5 AM until midnight and is a good spot to try one of Mayagüez's trademark delicacies, a Brazo Gitano (literally "Gypsy Arm")—a gigantic jellyroll filled with anything from guava to lemon to sweet cheese. You can also find another famous local product here, Fido's Sangría, made from the closely guarded secret recipe of Mayagüez resident Wilfredo Aponte Hernández. There are also other pastries, sandwiches, freshly baked bread, sodas, juices, and coffee available. ⊠ *202 Calle Méndez Vigo,* ☎ *787/832–0565. AE, MC, V.*

$$$–$$$$ ✕🏨 **Mayagüez Resort & Casino.** Formerly the Mayagüez Hilton, this hotel is conveniently located just outside of downtown off Route 2. Catering both to leisure travelers and businesspeople, it offers rooms with such modern amenities as cable TV, phones with voice mail, and coffeemakers; some rooms have private balconies. Big neon signs give the casino a funky feel, but the rest of the hotel has an elegant yesteryear

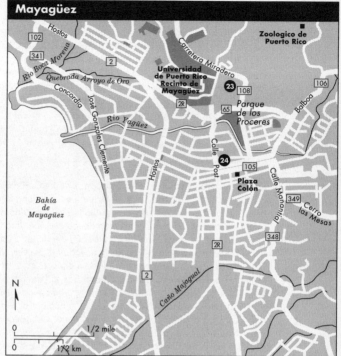

air, especially the Veranda Terrace Bar, a long, sweeping terrace where you can sip a cocktail while watching large tropical plants sway in the breeze and guests frolic in the pool below. The restaurant, El Castillo, combines international cuisine with Caribbean touches and features lots of seafood. At breakfast and lunch you can opt for a buffet or order à la carte. Golf is available at the nine-hole Club Deportivo del Oeste in Cabo Rojo, about 25 minutes to the south, or the 18-hole Punta Borinquen course in Aguadilla, about 30 minutes north. The Añasco Public Beach is some 10 minutes north via Routes 2, 115, and 401. Rincón's beaches are about 25 minutes away. ⊠ *Rte. 104, Km 0.3, off Rte. 2, (Box 3781), 00681,* ☎ *787/832–3030 or 888/689–3030,* FAX *787/265–1430. 140 rooms. Restaurant, bar, lounge, air-conditioning, coffeemakers, pool, 3 tennis courts, exercise room, casino, playground. AE, D, MC, V. EP.* ✆

$$ 🏨 **Hotel El Sol.** Located in the heart of downtown Mayagüez, this small inn, part of the government's parador program, offers clean and modern rooms with rattan furnishings. While the lobby area feels somewhat cramped, the rooms are spacious enough and the hotel also has a bar, a restaurant, and a small swimming pool. ⊠ *9 Calle Santiago Riera Palmer, 00680,* ☎ *787/834–0303 or 888/765–0303,* FAX *787/265–7567. 52 rooms. Restaurant, bar, air-conditioning, pool. AE, D, MC, V. CP.*

Outdoor Activities and Sports

BEACHES

Mayagüez is not famous for its beaches, but the **Añasco Public Beach,** also called Tres Hermanos Beach, is 10 minutes north of town via Routes 2, 115, and 401. The beach, dotted with palm trees, is nice for swimming and has changing facilities and rest rooms. The beaches of Rincón are about 25 minutes to the north.

Nightlife and the Arts

Teatro Yagüez (⊠ Calle McKinley at Calle Dr. Basora, ☎ 787/834–0523) often features plays and comedy revues, mostly in Spanish. The casino at the **Mayagüez Resort & Casino** (⊠ Rte. 104, Km 0.3, ☎ 787/832–3030) is popular with both residents and tourists. **Holiday Inn Mayagüez** (⊠ Rte. 2, Km 149.9, ☎ 787/834–0303) has a busy casino, and its disco is a popular spot for the younger crowd on Friday and Saturday nights.

Shopping

Small stores and pharmacies dot downtown Mayagüez. For heavy-duty shopping, the **Mayagüez Mall** (⊠ Rte. 2, Km 159.4, ☎ 787/834–2760) has local stores, a food court, and stateside chains such as JC Penney.

OFF THE
BEATEN PATH

MONA ISLAND – Known as the Galapagos of the Caribbean, Mona Island, about 48 mi off the coast of Mayagüez, has long been an adventurers' outpost. It's said to have been settled by the Taíno and visited by both Christopher Columbus and Juan Ponce de León. Pirates were known to use the small island as a hideout, and legend has it that there is still buried treasure to be found here. Today, however, Mona's biggest lures are its natural beauty and distinctive ecosystem. Classified as a semi-arid, subtropical climate, the island has 200-ft cliffs filled with caves and is home to a number of endangered species, such as the Mona iguana and leatherback sea turtle. A number of seabirds, including red-footed boobies, also inhabit the island. Off its coast are coral reefs filled with tropical fish, black coral, and underwater caverns. The island is uninhabited except for transient campers and personnel from the Department of Natural and Environmental Resources, which manages the island. Travelers must get there by boat—planes are not permitted to land. Groups such as **AdvenTours** in Mayagüez (⊠ 17 Calle Uroyán, ☎ 787/831–6447), **Desecheo Divers** (⊠ Rte. 413, Km 2.5, ☎ 787/823–0390) and **Moondog Charters** (⊠ Black Eagle Marina, off Rte. 413 before Steps Beach, ☎ 787/823–7168) in Rincón, and **Tour Marine** (Rte. 102, Km. 15.4, ☎ 787/851–9259) in Cabo Rojo offer overnight camping and diving trips to the island. Reservations must be made in advance (AdvenTours requires reservations three months in advance) and trips depend on weather and water conditions in the rough Mona Channel. Generally, the weather conditions are most favorable between July and October.

NORTHWESTERN PUERTO RICO AND THE CENTRAL MOUNTAINS A TO Z

Arriving and Departing

By Air

TWA (☎ 787/253–0400) has daily flights from Newark, NJ, to **Rafael Hernández Airport** (☎ 787/891–2286) on the old Ramey Air Force Base, Aguadilla. **American Eagle** (☎ 787/749–1747) has daily flights to the **Eugenio María de Hostos Airport** (⊠ Rte. 32, Km 148.7, ☎ 787/833–0148) in Mayagüez.

By Bus

There is no easy network of buses linking the towns in Puerto Rico. Some municipalities and private companies operate buses and large vans *(públicos)* from one city to another, but the schedules are very loose.

By Car

Renting a car is perhaps the best way to see northwestern Puerto Rico, especially if you are making several stops. Cars can be rented at the Luis Muñoz Marín International Airport and at other locations in San Juan.

Getting Around

By Bus

Buses and públicos from town to town operate sporadically; it's not a wise idea to count on them as your primary means of transportation. Some tour operators and hotels offer van transportation to major sights in the area, including the Parque de las Cavernas del Río Camuy. Check with tour operators (☞ *below*) or your hotel.

By Car

Driving a car is the best way to see northwestern Puerto Rico, especially the mountain area. The toll road, Highway 22, makes it easy to reach Arecibo from San Juan. Highway 22 turns into Route 2 just after Arecibo, swings by the northwestern tip of the island, then leads south to Mayagüez. The well-maintained and very scenic Route 10, which can be accessed in Arecibo, is a main link to the central mountain region. The Panoramic Route (☞ Close-Up: Traveling La Ruta Panorámica *in* Chapter 4) runs east–west across the island and very near some of the central mountain towns. It is made up of a number of small roads, many of which can be hilly and curving.

CAR RENTAL

Aguadilla: **Avis Rent A Car** (☎ 787/791–2500), **Budget Rent a Car,** (☎ 787/890–1110). Arecibo: **Leaseway of Puerto Rico** (☎ 787/878–1606). Mayagüez: **Hertz** (☎ 787/832–3314 or 787/833–4904)**, L & M Rent a Car** (☎ 787/831–4740).

By Taxi

Taxis can be hailed near the main plaza in Mayagüez, but in the smaller towns they may be hard to come by. Check with your hotel or restaurant. For pickup service in Mayagüez, call **Mr. Special Taxi** (☎ 787/832–1115). For pickup service in Arecibo, call **Arecibo Taxi Cab** (☎ 787/878–2629).

Contacts and Resources

Emergencies

Ambulance, fire, police: ☎ 911 throughout area and the island.

Hospitals: Aguadilla: **Hospital Subregional Dr. Pedro J. Zamora** (✉ Rte. 2, Km 141.1, ☎ 787/791–3000). Arecibo: **Hospital Regional Dr. C. Coll y Toste** (✉ Rte. 129, Km 0.7, ☎ 787/878–7272). Mayagüez: **Hospital Bella Vista** (✉ Rte. 349, Km 2.7, ☎ 787/834–2350) or **General Hospital Dr. Ramón Emeterio Betances** (✉ Rte. 2, Km 157, ☎ 787/834–8686). Utuado: **Centro de Salud** (✉ Calle Isaac González Martínez, ☎ 787/894–2875).

Festivals

Maricao, in the middle of the island's coffee-growing country, celebrates the end of the coffee harvest in February with its **Coffee Harvest Festival.** The mountain town of Jayuya pays tribute to its Indian past with its **Indigenous Festival** in November.

Health and Safety

The water on the island is generally good to drink. Always wash fruit before eating it. For your personal safety, it's best to go to any forest reserve only in daylight hours unless you are camping in a recreational area.

Rental Properties

Rental properties on the west coast (apartments, homes, etc.), for either long or short stays, may be booked through **Island West Properties & Beach Rentals** (✉ Rte. 413, Rincón, ☎ 787/823–2323) or **Gail Taylor at Coconut Palms** (✉ 2734 Calle 8, Rincón, ☎ 787/823–0147).

Telephones and Mail

Public phones are dispersed throughout towns and cities and at toll booths on major highways. Prepaid phone cards, used in many public phones, are common. There are plenty of phones and lines in the country, but these days, as on the mainland, everyone seems to be toting a cellular phone.

The island uses U.S. postage and has the same mail rates as the mainland United States: 20¢ for a postcard, 33¢ for a first-class letter to the U.S.; 40¢ for a postcard and 46¢ for a letter to Canada; 35¢ and 40¢, respectively, to Mexico; and 50¢ for a postcard and 60¢ for a letter to other international destinations. Post offices in major Puerto Rican cities offer Express Mail next-day service to the U.S. mainland and to Puerto Rican destinations. All of Puerto Rico's towns carry Zip codes; letters should carry the name of the recipient, street or post box address, the name of the town or city followed by "PR," and the five-digit Zip code. Post offices are open weekdays 7:30–4:30 and Saturday 8–noon.

Tour Operators

Aguadilla: **Western Tours** (✉ Rafael Hernández Airport, ☎ 787/890–0505). Mayagüez: **AvenTours** (✉ 17 Calle Uroyán, ☎ 787/831–6447). Utuado: **Northwestern Land Tours** (✉ Box 215, Angeles, 00611, ☎ 787/894–7804).

Travel Agencies

Aguadilla: **Liz Travel Agency** (✉ 101 Av. Interamericana, ☎ 787/891–5318). Arecibo: **Manolin Travel Agency** (✉ 360 Av. Rotarios, ☎ 787/879–2245). Mayagüez: **Sultana Travel Agency** (✉ 24 Calle Pablo Casals, ☎ 787/833–5553 or **Travel Network** (✉ 8 Calle Méndez Vigo, ☎ 787/834–3300).

Visitor Information

The **Puerto Rico Tourism Company** has an office at the Rafael Hernández Airport in Aguadilla (☎ 787/890–3315; ☉ daily). The town of Rincón has a **tourism office** on Route 115 (☎ 787/823–5024, ☉ weekdays).

6 PORTRAITS OF PUERTO RICO

PUERTO RICO AT A GLANCE:
A CHRONOLOGY

ca. AD 500   The first human inhabitants arrive in Puerto Rico, apparently on primitive rafts from the Florida mainland. Known today as Arcaicos ("archaics"), these hunter-gatherers live near the shore, where they subsist on fish and fruit.

ca. 1000   The Arcaico are replaced on the island by more advanced Arawak Indians who arrive by canoe from South America. The Taíno (a subgroup of the Arawak) name the island Boriquén, and thrive there in peaceful thatched villages, where they practice basic agriculture.

1493   Christopher Columbus, on his second voyage to the New World, meets a group of Taíno on the island of Guadeloupe. The Taínos guide Columbus to their home island of Boriquén. On November 19, Columbus claims the island for Ferdinand and Isabella of Spain, and christens it "San Juan Bautista."

1508   Caparra, the island's first Spanish settlement, is founded on the south shore of its largest bay.

                   Juan Ponce de León, a soldier who had accompanied Columbus on his second voyage, is appointed governor of the island by the Spanish crown.

1510   The Spanish begin mining and smelting gold on the island.

                   In an effort to Christianize the Taíno, the Spanish institute a program of virtual slavery: the Indians are required to work for Spanish settlers in return for religious instruction.

                   In November, a group of Taíno loyal to a *cacique* (chieftain) named Urayoan set out to determine whether the Spanish are gods. By drowning a young settler in a river, the Taíno prove the Spanish to be mortal.

1511   The Taíno rebel against the conquistadors, but are no match for European armor and firearms. In a brutal act of reprisal, the Spanish hunt down and kill as many as 6,000 Indians on the island.

                   The island is granted a coat of arms by the Spanish crown.

                   The town of Caparra is renamed Puerto Rico ("rich port").

1512   Ferdinand II of Spain issues the Edict of Burgos, intended to protect the surviving Indians of the island from abuse by the settlers.

1513   The first African slaves are introduced to the island.

                   Setting sail from the settlement of San Germán on the west coast of the island, Ponce de León heads north across the Caribbean and discovers Florida.

1521   The island's primary town moves from its original, mosquito-plagued site to a new location across the bay. Also around this time, the names of the island and its capital are switched: The island becomes Puerto Rico, and its seat of government, San Juan.

1523   The first sugarcane processing plant is built.

1532   Puerto Rican gold mines cease to be profitable, and Spanish settlers leave in droves for Peru. Governor Francisco Manuel de Lando declares emigration from the island to be a crime punishable by the amputation of a leg.

1539   To help protect their valuable trade routes in the Caribbean against pirates and competing colonial powers, the Spanish begin construction on the massive fortress of San Felipe del Morro.

1542   The coconut palm is introduced to the island.

1595   English privateer Sir Francis Drake, assigned to disrupt Spanish colonial trade routes, attempts unsuccessfully to capture the town of San Juan.

1598   Another Englishman, George Clifford, 3rd Earl of Cumberland, attacks the island and occupies San Juan with a force of 4,000 men. But Clifford is forced to withdraw a few months later when his troops are decimated by disease.

1625   San Juan is again invaded, this time by Dutch forces under Bowdoin Hendrick. The attack fails when Hendrick is unable to conquer El Morro fortress.

1680   The town of Ponce is founded on the island's south coast.

1736   Coffee is first cultivated in Puerto Rico's central highlands.

1760   The town of Mayagüez is founded on the island's west coast.

1765   The Spanish crown sends Field Marshal Alejandro O'Reilly to inspect military and social conditions. O'Reilly conducts a census and reports that Puerto Rico's races mix "without any repugnance whatsoever."

1776   Coffee is established as a major export item.

1797   When France and Spain declare war on England, 7,000 British troops under Sir Ralph Abercromby invade Puerto Rico. The British are driven back after a two-week campaign.

1806   The first printing press arrives on the island.

1809   After Napoléon Bonaparte deposes the King of Spain, the Spanish Cortes (parliament) permits representatives from Spain's New World colonies to participate in the drafting of a new constitution.

1810   Ramón Power y Giralt is selected as Puerto Rico's first delegate to Spain.

1812   The Cádiz Constitution is adopted, granting Puerto Rico and other Spanish colonies the rank of provinces, and, for the first time, extending Spanish citizenship to colonials.

A brief period of social and economic optimism reigns on the island, and Puerto Rico's first newspaper is founded.

1815   With the fall of Napoléon, the monarchy is restored in Spain, and the Cádiz Constitution is revoked. Puerto Rico reverts to its previous condition as a colony of the Spanish crown.

1825   Notorious Puerto Rican pirate Roberto Cofresi is captured by the United States Navy in the Caribbean and handed over to Spanish authorities, who execute him by firing squad at El Morro fortress.

1843   Puerto Rico's first lighthouse is constructed at El Morro.

The first town is founded on the Puerto Rican island of Vieques.

1868   Inspired by Puerto Rican separatist Ramón Emetrio Betances, several hundred revolutionaries attempt a coup against Spanish rule. The rebels successfully occupy the town of Lares before Spanish authorities crush the revolt. The uprising comes to be known as the Grito de Lares ("cry of Lares").

1873   Slavery is abolished in Puerto Rico by decree of the Spanish king, Amedeo I de Saboya.

1876 The mountain rain forest of El Yunque ("the anvil") is designated as a nature reserve.

1887 Journalist and patriot Luis Muñoz Rivera helps form the Puerto Rican Autonomous Party.

1897 On the verge of the Spanish-American War, Spain approves the Carta Autonómica, granting administrative autonomy to Puerto Rico.

1898 February: Puerto Rico's first autonomous local government is inaugurated.

In April the Spanish-American War breaks out.

In July American troops invade Puerto Rico and conquer the island in 17 days with minimal casualties.

In December, after 405 years of continuous colonial rule, Spain officially cedes Puerto Rico (along with the Philippines and Guam) to the United States. No member of Puerto Rico's autonomous government is consulted.

1899 Hurricane San Ciriaco devastates Puerto Rico, killing 3,000 people and leaving one quarter of the population homeless.

1900 The United States Congress passes the Foraker Act, which declares Puerto Rico to be a U.S. territory. The island's elected civil government remains under the control of a U.S.-appointed governor.

1903 U.S. president Theodore Roosevelt hands over control of Puerto Rico's Culebra Island to the U.S. Navy. The navy later uses this island as a gunnery range.

1904 Luis Muñoz Rivera establishes the Unionist Party of Puerto Rico to combat the widely unpopular colonial regulations imposed by the Foraker Act.

1912 As dissatisfaction with American rule increases, the Independence Party is formed. This is the first political party to claim Puerto Rican independence as its primary goal.

1917 U.S. president Woodrow Wilson signs the Jones Act, which grants U.S. citizenship to Puerto Ricans.

1930 With economic conditions bleak on the island, militant separatist Pedro Albizu Campos forms the Nationalist Party. The party demands immediate independence for Puerto Rico.

1933 Cockfighting is legalized.

1935 After a visit to the island, U.S. president Franklin Roosevelt establishes the Puerto Rican Reconstruction Administration in an effort to rehabilitate Puerto Rico's economy.

1937 A decade of occasional political violence culminates with La Masacre de Ponce (the Ponce massacre). During a Palm Sunday parade of Nationalist Party blackshirts, police open fire on the crowd, killing 19 and injuring some 100 others.

1938 Luis Muñoz Marín, son of Luis Muñoz Rivera, creates the Democratic Popular Party.

1941 The U.S. military establishes bases on the Puerto Rican islands of Vieques and Culebra, relocating a portion of the islands' population to St. Croix, Virgin Islands.

1945 Large numbers of Puerto Ricans begin to emigrate to the mainland United States, particularly to Florida and the New York City area.

1948   The U.S. Congress grants Puerto Ricans the right to elect their own governor.

In November, Luis Muñoz Marín is voted in as the first elected native governor in the island's history. It is a position he will hold for four consecutive terms.

Gambling is legalized in Puerto Rico.

1950   July: U.S. president Harry Truman signs a law permitting Puerto Rico to draft its own constitution as a commonwealth, but radical nationalists are far from satisfied.

In October, political violence breaks out throughout the island, leaving 31 people dead. A few days later, two Puerto Rican nationalists from New York attempt to assassinate Truman in Washington.

1952   Puerto Rican voters approve the new constitution, and the Commonwealth of Puerto Rico is born.

The Puerto Rican flag, based on a patriotic design dating back to the years of Spanish colonialism, is officially adopted.

1953   In this peak year of Puerto Rican emigration to the U.S. mainland, nearly 70,000 people leave the island.

1961   Puerto Rican actress Rita Moreno wins an Academy Award for her performance in the hit film *West Side Story.*

1964   Luis Muñoz Marín steps down as governor after 16 years. His career is remembered as brilliantly successful: under his governorship, the percentage of Puerto Rican children attending school rose from 50% to 90%, and per capita income on the island increased sixfold.

1967   The question of Puerto Rico's political status is put before its voters for the first time. A 60% majority votes to maintain the commonwealth, rather than push for complete independence or U.S. statehood.

1972   Beloved Puerto Rican baseball star Roberto Clemente, an outfielder for the Pittsburgh Pirates, dies in a plane crash. He is inducted into the Baseball Hall of Fame the following year.

1974   A radical nationalist organization called the Fuerzas Armadas Liberación Nacional Puertorriqueña (Armed Forces of Puerto Rican National Liberation, or FALN) claims responsibility for five bombings in New York. Over the next decade, the group commits dozens of acts of terrorism in the United States, causing five deaths and extensive property damage.

1981   Members of the Macheteros, another radical nationalist group similar to the FALN, infiltrate a Puerto Rican Air National Guard base and blow up 11 planes, causing some $45 million in damages.

1993   In a second referendum on Puerto Rico's political status, voters again choose to maintain the commonwealth.

1998   Hurricane Georges strikes Puerto Rico, leaving 24,000 people homeless and causing an estimated $2 billion in damage.

In a third referendum on the political status issue, Puerto Rican voters once more opt to maintain their commonwealth relationship with the U.S., although the pro-statehood vote tops 46%.

1999   Puerto Ricans of all political stripes are unified in protest against the U.S. Navy bombing range on the island of Vieques after a civilian security guard is killed by a stray bomb. Dozens of protesters occupy the bombing range and disrupt naval exercises there.

President Bill Clinton offers clemency to 16 FALN members serving time in federal prisons for a string of bombings in the U.S. during the 1970s and '80s.

2000   In May, 200 protesters encamped on the Vieques naval bombing range are forcibly removed by federal agents.

A GOOD MIX: PUERTO RICO'S BLENDED CULTURE

LONG BEFORE "DIVERSITY" became a household word or "multicultural" a social ideal, Puerto Rico had arrived. Mixing it up for the past five centuries, converging cultures of Spain, Africa, and the Caribbean Indians have melded to create a uniquely Puerto Rican heritage.

Before today's island visitors get out of the airport, or much beyond the gangplank, they have already begun to absorb the basics. They quickly catch on to the Puerto Rican modus vivendi—that the Spanish influence might have been strong enough to leave behind a colonial legacy and a living language, but the islanders who speak it have a broader heritage that also includes clear African and Caribbean Indian roots. Sojourners who have the time to become better acquainted with this lively blend will find ample evidence of its various sources in more than just the faces of the people.

Unfortunately, the influence of the island's Indians is only a subtle element in the cultural mix. Almost wiped out within two decades of their first encounter with Europeans, the Taíno people who greeted Columbus in 1493 nevertheless left their traces. They certainly impressed Columbus, who described the Taíno in his journal as beautiful and tall, with a gentle, laughing language. Although this language was unwritten, it still echoes in some names for places, such as Mayagüez, and everyday objects, such as *casabe* (a kind of bread). Elements of Taíno oral culture—their folktales and myths—have survived through Spanish records.

There's also a slender legacy of surviving art and artifacts created by these peaceful rain-forest dwellers, who called their island Boriquén. The Taíno were especially adept at wood, shell, and stone carving, and the small figures they made of people and animals had great significance. Known as *cemi* (or *zemi*), these diminutive statues were powerfully protective votive objects for families and villages.

WHILE TAÍNO REMNANTS PAINT an intriguing but incomplete picture of a vibrant culture, the admixture of African elements is much easier to point to as a formative influence on modern Puerto Rico. Sabor Africano first came to the island with Ponce de León, who arrived in 1509 accompanied by a black conquistador named Juan Garrido. Other free Africans, *cimarrones* (liberated and escaped slaves), and Ladinos (Christian, Spanish-speaking slaves) followed, joined later by slaves brought to work in the sugarcane fields. Reminders of their collective contributions to the island's cultural heritage turn up daily in artistic expression, from *bomba* music to favorite dishes to the linguistic rhythm of poetry.

Among the customs and beliefs that claim African roots is the colorful Santeria religion, which was brought to Puerto Rico in the 15th century by West African slaves. Forbidden to practice their traditional polytheistic religion, African *santeros*, as Santeria priests are called, disguised their rituals in the trappings of Catholicism. Images and articles important in Santeria, on view today in neighborhood *botánica* shops, bear witness to the island's commingled African, Spanish Christian, and Caribbean Indian culture.

Many of these Santeria images superimpose the familiar symbol of a Catholic saint on the persona of a Santeria deity, often taking the saint's name. But even beyond Santeria, the strong, conservative traditions of colonial Spanish Catholic culture have been re-formed in Puerto Rico's multicultural crucible.

IN THE SEMILITERATE CULTURE of the 16th-century Spanish colony, not unlike that of medieval Europe, representational religious art was vitally important. Humble communicants who could not read the gospel could still "read" the lessons in pictures and statues that evoked Bible stories and the lives of the saints. In the context of this religious devotion, energetically nourished by Spanish missionaries, a spirited crafts-based folk art developed.

Perhaps calling upon a cultural memory of the Taíno cemi, with perhaps just a

glance at Santeria imagery, artisans in the early colonial period fashioned small statues intended to be objects of veneration. And like the pre-Columbian cemi, these Christian figurines, called santos, are still given a place of honor in homes around the island. Fashioned of cedar wood, clay, stone, even gold, the first santos figurines took shape under the handmade tools of carvers who are known as santeros (not to be confused with the Santeria priests of the same name).

Not surprisingly, early carvers working in the long shadow of the Spanish baroque were influenced by that splendidly ornate style. Even today, it's not hard to imagine how dazzled those long-ago santeros must have been by lavish imported cargoes of richly ornamented sacred objects. But as time went on, the santeros came into their own. Later santos were simpler in design and more reflective of local culture and the natural materials at hand. The blue of the Holy Virgin's robes, for example, might have been achieved with carefully blended vegetable dyes, and her soft hair might be real.

While many art historians argue that santos carving peaked in the late 19th and early 20th centuries, the art form still flourishes. Indeed, experts make the case that these evocative santos continue to be the island's greatest contribution to sculpture.

Antique or contemporary, Puerto Rican santos are typically small in scale, averaging about eight inches in height. They are carved mostly by artisans with no formal training, although there might be a strong family or local carving tradition supporting their work. Certain villages and certain families are known for the artistry of their santos. San Germán, for example, in the southwestern part of the island, was a major center of colonial Spanish influence and has been associated with santo-making since the origins of the craft. Members of the extended Rivera family of central Puerto Rico have been carving for more than 150 years.

No matter where they were carved or by whom, many antique santos have been repainted, sometimes repeatedly over the years, by believers expressing their gratitude for a prayer answered or a favor granted. While these subsequent layers of paint might frustrate some collectors, they ultimately serve a protective purpose. With proper techniques, the original layer of col-ors can be revealed, unworn and unfaded, along with other hidden stylistic features.

Santeros have always endowed their figures with symbols, such as the Virgin's blue robes, and other characteristics that make them readily recognizable. The faithful can pick out St. Francis by the birds and animals with him, St. Barbara by her tower or the Holy Spirit by a hovering dove. San Juan, the patron saint of the island, is an ever-popular subject for the carvers, as is the panoply of the Nativity, which might be rendered as the Holy Family alone or with an entire supporting cast of herald angels, shepherds, sheep, and all sorts of other barnyard animals.

But the most requested carving has to be the Three Kings, Los Santos Reyes. Their feast day, January 6, is an important celebration in Puerto Rico, continuing for days on either side of the actual holiday, and it would be difficult to find a home that does not display some rendering of these Sacred Kings making their way to the Christ Child. While the three riders are often depicted carrying their traditional gifts of gold, frankincense, and myrrh, you'll often see a magi santo riding along strumming a *cuatro,* an island guitar.

Santos fashioned by contemporary carvers are still cherished as votive objects and prized by Puerto Ricans as examples of their cultural heritage. Modern collectors, too, appreciate the latest expressions of this traditional art form. But in Puerto Rico, even a craft with the history and cultural identity of saint-carving cannot be isolated from more far-flung cultural influences.

PUERTO RICO'S STRATEGIC LOCATION, which the magnificent Spanish forts guarding San Juan Harbor bear witness to, has meant that the three pillars of its modern culture—Spanish, African, and Indian—would be continually stirred by other influences. The island's political and geographic proximity to the United States, in particular, has made a huge impact, especially since 1898, as both islanders and mainlanders have traveled back and forth. Puerto Rican music, literature, and visual arts have all been enriched by influences introduced by a larger, increasingly more global culture. Two of the most prominent artists associated with Puerto Rico in the second half of the 20th century were, in fact, refugees from another hemisphere. Up-

rooted from the Old World, each found an artistic home in the welcoming diversity of Puerto Rico's arts scene.

The career of painter, sculptor, and printmaker Angel Botello, and the many strands in his work, mirror something of the essence of Puerto Rican culture. There is no one influence, there is no one style. Each piece of art he created may be strikingly different from the next in expression, scale, and medium, but each is no less a Botello.

Born in Spain in 1913, the artist studied in France, then in Madrid. When the Spanish Civil War ended, he left Spain for the Caribbean. By the time Botello had settled in Hispaniola he had already broken with his academic training and begun experimenting with different styles and movements. In sunlit Haiti, he married the daughter of the first Haitian governor and painted vibrant female figures in bright, tropical colors, earning his sobriquet, "the Caribbean Gauguin." In 1952 Botello moved to Puerto Rico, where he remained for the rest of his life.

In his adopted multifaceted culture, Botello was comfortable calling upon the various influences of a lifetime: a youth in Spain, an education in France, a mature career in the Caribbean. Other artists he admired, many of whom he knew personally, also influenced his work. Besides the studies of females so reminiscent of Gauguin, there are nudes that evoke Matisse and studies in cubism that recall Picasso. Botello was a friend of the masterful Mexican artist Diego Rivera, who tried to persuade Botello to leave Puerto Rico and join him farther west. But Botello remained in Old San Juan, restoring a colonial town house as his home and studio and continuing to paint prolifically, often working on several canvasses at once. From the late 1950s until his death in 1986, much of Botello's work focused on his three adopted children, and there are wonderful paintings and bronzes of round, winsome, childlike figures from this period.

Like many other artists of his era, Botello continued to experiment as he searched for a means of expression that would reflect the multifaceted world he knew. Innovative and energetic, Botello's art is right at home in his adopted culture: it is colorful and replete with many important influences that jostled and spun off each other to produce something that was always fresh.

Today, Botello's town-house studio at 208 Calle Cristo is a gallery that, appropriately, showcases many artistic movements and styles, from Rembrandt to Dr. Seuss—with a generous sprinkling of Botello's own work.

LIKE BOTELLO, CELLIST PABLO CASALS made his way to San Juan from a Spain in turmoil. Born in Catalonia in 1876, Casals was one of the most influential musicians of the 20th century. Also like Botello, Casals's studies took him beyond Spain to a multinational community of the arts, where he found himself at home in a world of many different influences and sensibilities.

Casals studied in Spain and Belgium, settled for a time in Paris, then returned to Barcelona. Tours in Europe, the United States, and South America brought him artistic and financial success and opportunities to collaborate with other prominent musicians. When the Spanish Civil War began, Casals was an internationally famous musician, teacher, and conductor, but he was also an outspoken supporter of a democratic Spain. Forced into exile by Franco's regime, Casals arrived in Puerto Rico, his mother's birthplace, in 1956. There, the 81-year-old maestro continued to work, teach, and lend his musical support to the cause of world peace. With his friend Albert Schweitzer, he appealed to the world powers to stop the arms race, and he made what many experts say is his greatest work, an oratorio titled "The Manger," his personal message of peace. Appropriately, Casals's name in Catalan is Pau, which means peace. Casals died in Puerto Rico in 1973.

Over the course of an exceptionally long career, Casals's controlled artistry made significant contributions to the world of music. For his favorite instrument, he changed the way the average person thinks of the cello. And for his adopted island, he established the Casals Festival of Classical Music, making it a home for sublime orchestral and chamber works. During two weeks each June, the Puerto Rico Symphony Orchestra is joined by musicians from all over the world, who add their input to an already diverse musical scene. It's not hard to imagine these classical virtuosos blending their melodic sounds with the bomba, merengue, salsa, and jazz that make Puerto Rico's highly textured music scene so interesting. Casals memorabilia, including his favorite instruments, recordings, and some of his many awards, are conserved in the Pablo Casals Museum in Old San Juan, at 101 Calle San Sebastian.

I N SAN JUAN, CASALS AND BOTELLO sought a place to live and work that was both congenial and inspirational. The multifaceted culture they found had an energy of its own that embraced fresh talent and innovation. Today, the arts in Puerto Rico are no less dynamic. But whether an artist is experimenting with the latest computer graphics or carving a figure from the Old Testament, he or she still draws upon a heritage that reaches back to the Spanish colonialists, uprooted Africans, and indigenous peoples. To paraphrase Casals's famous remark about children, since the beginning of the world there hasn't been, and until the end of the world there will not be, another culture quite like Puerto Rico's.

–Karen English

WHEN I WAS PUERTO RICAN

N HER BOOK When I Was Puerto Rican, *which is excerpted below, Esmeralda Santiago tells of her days growing up in the small town of Macún, west of San Juan. Her story reveals the rich, family-centered culture of Puerto Rico and the underlying tensions between the urban and the rural, the island and the mainland United States, that are intrinsic to Puerto Rican life.*

WALKED THE LAND from post to post, trying to place myself within its borders. Our house stood in the center, its shiny zinc roof splotched with rust at the corners. Next to the house was the kitchen shed, from which a thin curl of smoke wove into the air. Behind the house, under the breadfruit tree, there was a pigsty, now empty, the mud the pigs loved to bathe in dried into dusty ridges. The chicken coop squatted between the pigsty and the mango tree, a branch of which held one end of Mami's laundry line, the other end stretched to the trunk of an acerola bush. Away from the house, near Doña Ana's, the latrine with palm frond walls under a zinc roof was hidden from the road by hibiscus bushes and an avocado tree. The boundary between our land and Doña Ana's was bordered by eggplant bushes, and between us and Doña Lola by annatto, oregano, and yucca.

Behind our house was Lalao's *finca,* which stretched into the next town. Sometimes a herd of cows grazed on this land, or a man on horseback rode the borders, a *sombrero* shading his face, his shirt stained yellow with sweat. We were not allowed to go into Lalao's *finca,* which was surrounded by a well-maintained barbwire fence. Not three feet from our backyard, on the other side of this fence, was a fragrant grove of grapefruit trees. The grapefruits weighed on the branches, huge and

round, dark green speckled yellow. In the mornings, I heard them tumble from the trees, and it seemed a waste to let them rot under the branches when we could be enjoying them. But Mami and Papi made it clear that we were never to go into that grove, so I stood at the barbwire fence and stared at the fruits growing and ripening, then falling and rotting on the ground where they formed a pulpy wet mud, which I was sure was sour.

OOK, NEGI," MAMI SAID ONE DAY. "Take a look at what I found!"

She was gutting a chicken. It looked naked without its feathers, which she'd yanked off in between dips into boiling water. Inside the bloody entrails were globes that quivered as she lifted them out.

"What are they?"

"Eggs that haven't been laid yet. See? No shell."

They looked like soft marbles, pink shooters striated with red, inside of which an orange/yellow liquid gleamed and threatened to ooze out if the outer membrane broke.

"They're delicious in soup," Mami said, and I believed her, because Mami never lied about food.

That night she served *asopao* with a solid dark ball floating on top of each of our bowls. I bit into the firm center with my front teeth. It tasted like hard-boiled egg yolks mixed with liver. It coated the inside of my mouth with a dry, sticky paste, and the smell of feathers rose from the back of my throat into my nose. I had to scrape my teeth with my tongue several times before the flavor dissipated into the familiar bittersweet oregano and garlic. Mami watched me eat and smiled at me with her eyes. I smiled back. It was delicious, just like she said.

F YOU CLOSE YOUR EYES while they're crossed, they'll stay like that!"

Juanita Marín was distraught. She stared at me, her eyes wide. She had long

From *When I Was Puerto Rican* by Esmeralda Santiago, copyright © 1993 by Esmeralda Santiago. Reprinted by permission of Perseus Books Publishers, a member of Perseus Books, L.L.C.

lashes that curled up to her eyebrows, which now formed a single wiggly line from one temple to the other.

I shut my eyes, trying to keep them crossed. She held her breath. I rolled my eyes around my lids and pictured her staring at me in wonder. Then I opened my eyes, still crossed. Two Juanita Maríns gasped and brought up four hands to two mouths with gaps where teeth should have been. I uncrossed my eyes and burst out laughing. Her relief changed to anger, and she bopped me with her fist. That made me laugh harder, and she, in spite of herself, laughed with me.

Juanita was my best friend in Macún. She lived down the road from us, past Doña Lola's house, almost at the funnel end of the *barrio*. Every day we walked home from school together, chatting about what we were going to be when we grew up, and whose father could saw the most wood in the least amount of time. I had an advantage over Juanita. I had lived in Santurce, and I could tell her about things like electric light bulbs and shower nozzles. But Juanita, who had lived in Macún all her life, could tell me about the secret places in the *barrio* that even our mothers didn't know about. Places like the caves at the narrow end, and the breaks in Lalao's fence, and the shortcuts through the woods that led to the next *barrio* where all sorts of *pocavergüenzas* took place. A *pocavergüenza* was something you should be ashamed of but weren't.

It was in Jurutungo that all the women who seduced all the men in Macún lived. At least, that's the way it seemed to us, because every time we heard our mothers, or our mothers' friends complaining about their husbands' *pocavergüenzas*, they had happened in Jurutungo. It was there that their *sinvergüenza* husbands went when they'd just been paid and wanted to get drunk. It was there that their teenage sons disappeared when they reached a certain age and couldn't be controlled any longer. It was to Jurutungo that women who'd had a bad life retreated with bastard children. Juanita and I never wanted to go there. But we often staked out the secret path, hoping someday to catch someone in the act of sneaking into that ill-reputed *barrio*.

DON BERTO, JUANITA'S grandfather lived in a shed behind Juanita's house, and every time I saw him he was sitting on its front steps sharpening his machete. His skin was so black and wrinkled that it seemed to absorb light into its crevices, to be let out again in the most glorious smile I'd ever seen on anyone with no teeth. I was fascinated by his pink gums, the tongue spotted with white, the lips almost the same color as the rest of his skin. His gnarly hands stuck out of his shirt like gigantic hairless tarantulas, always moving, always searching for someplace to land. His palms, as pink as his gums, were calloused, and his fingertips were stained with age and soil.

We would sit at his feet listening to his *jíbaro* tales of phantasms, talking animals, and enchanted guava trees. While he spoke, he ran the tip of his machete back and forth, back and forth, over a stone, and we knew that if any of the creatures he talked about came to life, he would take care of it with one well-placed *machetazo*.

One morning, while I snapped on my uniform, Mami told me not to wait for Juanita because she wouldn't be coming to school.

"Why not?"

"Don Berto died last night, may he rest in peace."

"How do you know?" I was astonished at the way news travelled in the *barrio*. No neighbors ever appeared at the door to bring us up-to-date. It was as if whatever happened in the *barrio* was conveyed in the breeze to be picked up by whomever was alert enough.

"Never mind how I know! Hurry up and get ready or you'll be late for school."

I scrambled out, irritated, wondering why parents never answered questions but seemed to have all the answers. In school many of my classmates' seats were empty, and the teacher explained that Don Berto had died, and the children who were not there were his grandchildren and great-grandchildren, and that we must be extra nice to them when they returned because it was a very sad thing to lose a grandparent. She also said that she hoped we had all been nice to Don Berto when he was alive, because now we would never get another chance. I tried to remember if I'd ever been rude to him, or if I'd ever been in some small way disrespectful to Don Berto, but, to my relief, I couldn't come up with anything.

While I was in school, Mami was at the Marín house getting it ready for the *velorio*. Most of the *barrio's* women had put in some time dusting, washing the floors and walls, sprinkling *agua florida* all over, positioning wreaths, bathing Don Berto and laying him out in his box. By that night, when we came to the wake, the house looked festive, decorated with flowers and candles.

Don Berto was in the middle of the living room, dressed in a clean white shirt buttoned all the way up. His eyes were closed, and his hands, which I'd never seen without his machete, were clasped on his chest with a rosary wrapped around them so that the large cross covered his fingers. A mosquito net hung around the coffin, and every time a new person came to see him, someone would have to lift netting away. Chairs were set up along the walls of the house, and into the yard, and people from the neighborhood, and some I'd never seen before, sat quietly sipping coffee or talking in whispers. When Papi came in, people said hello to him and pulled their chairs closer to Don Berto. Juanita's mother brought a chair up for Papi, and he sat down, took a Bible that had been holding down the mosquito net, opened it, and pulled a rosary from his pocket, which he fingered in silence as the rest of the people bowed their heads and did the same thing.

"Let us pray," Papi said in a dramatic voice, and he began mumbling words that I couldn't understand, and the people repeated the same pattern of sounds, and each time they finished a prayer they'd say, "Amen" and click their rosary beads, but Papi would start over again, and they'd follow, mumbling and clicking their beads. This went on for a long time, so that even though I didn't want to, I fell asleep, and next thing, a rooster was crowing and I woke up next to Delsa.

"Don't put on your uniform because you're not going to school today," Mami said as I came out to the kitchen, rubbing my eyes and scratching myself.

"Why not?"

"You and Juanita are going to lead the procession to the cemetery."

"Why?"

Mami gave me an exasperated look. "Just do as I tell you and don't talk back."

Héctor toddled out, stepped out of his diaper, and aimed his pee in a wide arc toward the chickens pecking at worms near the acerola tree. He grinned toward us happily, and Mami and I had to giggle.

MAMI STARCHED AND IRONED my best dress, which was white with blue flowers on the collar. We walked to the Marín house right after breakfast. Juanita wore a white dress too, with pale pink flowers along the hem. The rest of her family was dressed in black or gray, their hair neatly combed, the boys' heads shimmering with brilliantine. Juanita and I were given a heavy wreath to carry. It was held together with wires, two of which had been twisted into handles at either side. Juanita's mother wrapped handkerchiefs around the sharp ends so that our hands wouldn't get scratched.

We walked in the hot dust from Juanita's place to the mouth of the *barrio*. Black-clad people came out of the houses along the way to join the procession in back of us, many of them carrying homemade wreaths tied with purple ribbons. At the highway, traffic was stopped so that the procession could move into the middle of the road. As we passed, men took off their hats and bowed their heads and women crossed themselves.

It was a long walk to the cemetery. Behind us, Don Berto's sons carried the coffin on their shoulders and didn't set it down all the way there. The world was still, except for the shuffling footsteps of mourners, the hum of prayers, the click-clack of rosaries. The wreath we carried weighed on us, pulled on our skinny arms, strained our shoulders. But it would have been disrespectful to complain, or to let the ribbon with Don Berto's name drag on the ground. Every so often Juanita looked at me with sad eyes. I'd never lost a loved one, so I took on her grief as if it were mine, tried it on to see if I could feel anything for the old man who had made me so happy with his tales and the hypnotizing movement of his machete across the stone. An echoing hollowness pressed against my ribs and threatened to escape like air from a balloon. I felt light-headed, empty, and I held on to the wreath so that it would anchor me to the ground, so that I could not fly up into the sky, above the trees, into the clouds where Don Berto's soul waited, machete in hand. He had become a ghost, a creature that could haunt my nights and see my every move, like the phantasms he told us about when we sat at his feet, listening to his stories.

At the cemetery, El Cura said a few words, and then the coffin was lowered, as Juanita's mother and aunts wailed about what a good man he was and how he didn't deserve to die. They shovelled dirt on top of the box, red moist earth not unlike the dirt I used for making mud people, and I wondered what would happen to him under there, with all that weight on him. I thought about this as we walked back to Macún behind Don Berto's daughters, who were overcome with an attack of *los nervios*, so that their sons ended up half carrying them, half dragging them home.

PAPI WAS TO LEAD the novenas for Don Berto. After dinner he washed and put on a clean white shirt, pulled a rosary and a Bible from his dresser, and started out the door.

"Do you want to come?" he asked me.

"¡Sí! I would! ¡Sí!"

"Only if you bring a long-sleeve shirt," Mami said. "I don't want you sick from the night air."

We walked on the pebbled road as the sun set behind the mountains. Toads hopped out of our way, their dark brown bodies bottom heavy. The air smelled green, the scents of peppermint, rosemary, and verbena wafting up from the ground like fog.

"Papi, what's a soul?"

"The soul is that part of us that never dies."

"What do you mean?"

"When people die, it's just the body that dies. The soul goes up to the sky."

"I know. Mami told me that already."

He laughed. "Okay, so what more do you want to know?"

"What does the soul do?"

"It goes to live with Papa Dios in Paradise."

"When people are alive . . . what does the soul do?"

He stopped and stared at the tip of his work shoes. "Let's see, what does it do?" He massaged his forehead as if that would make the answer come out quicker. "Well, it is the soul of a person that writes poetry."

"How?"

He pinched his lower lip with his thumb and index finger, and pulled it back and forth in small tugs. He dropped his hand and took mine in his then began walking again.

"The soul lives inside a person when he's alive. It's the part of a person that feels. A poet's soul feels more than regular people's souls. And that's what makes him write poetry."

Clouds had formed above the mountains in streaks, like clumps of dough that had been stretched too thin.

"What does the soul look like?"

He let out a breath. "Well, it looks like the person."

"So my soul looks like me and your soul looks like you?"

"Right!" He sounded relieved.

"And it lives inside our bodies?"

"Yes, that's right."

"Does it ever come out?"

"When we die . . ."

"But when we're alive . . . does it ever come out?"

"No, I don't think so." The doubt in his voice let me know that I knew something he didn't because my soul travelled all the time, and it appeared that his never did. Now I knew what happened to me when I walked beside myself. It was my soul wandering.

The sun dipped behind the mountains, leaving flecks of orange, pink, and turquoise. In the foreground, the landscape had become flat, without shadow, distanceless.

"Papi, what happens to the body when it's buried?"

"It decomposes," he said. "It becomes dust."

We were joined by a group of mourners on their way to the Marín house. They wished us all a good evening, and the rest of the way we walked in dreadful silence.

Papi settled into his place in front of the house, next to an altar with a picture of Don Berto holding his machete. I wondered if his soul had already gone to live with Papa Dios, or if he was floating around watching to see if his daughters and sons were paying him the proper respect now that his body was rotting under the ground. I tried to send my soul up, to meet him halfway between heaven and earth, but I couldn't get out, held by the fear that if he saw my soul he might try to take it with him.

S OMEONE IS COMING TO TAKE your lap, freckles," Doña Lola cuddled Alicia. We sat in her kitchen, sipping coffee from blue enamel tin cups. Mami had told me to take the baby when I brought a bag of pigeon peas to Doña Lola, who would give us coffee in return. She grew it in the crags that rose behind her kitchen, up the hill from the latrine. I had helped her pick the red, swollen fruit, and she had roasted them in a giant frying pan on her *fogón* then laid the blackened beans out to cool before storing them in an odd assortment of cans and jars.

"Papi said by the time the new baby is born we will have electricity."

"Ah, yes," Doña Lola sighed, "electricity. Pretty soon they'll bring water, too, and then they'll pave the road and bring cars, buses maybe. Ah, yes."

"Buses, Doña Lola?"

"Trucks and buses. And then the *Americanos* will come looking for *artesanías.*" She spit into the yard and chuckled as if remembering a private joke. "Those *Americanos* are really something. . . ."

"Do you know any?"

"Oh, I've known a few. Yes. A few. You know, it's an *Americano* that owns the *finca* back there."

"Lalao's *finca*?"

"Bah! *A otro perro con ese hueso.* That *finca* doesn't belong to Lalao. That man doesn't own the hole to lay his corpse in."

"But everyone says . . ."

"*Del dicho al hecho hay un gran trecho.*"

"What does that mean?"

"It means there's a long way between what people say and what is. That *finca* belongs to Rockefela."

"Who's he?"

"An *Americano* from the *Nueva Yores*. He's going to build a hotel back there." The *finca* stretched across the road to the horizon, the tall grass broken now and then by groves of lemon, orange, and grapefruit trees, herds of cattle, and, in the distance, a line of coconut palms.

"What will they do with all those cows?"

Doña Lola guffawed. "You're worried about the cows? What about us?"

"Well, we don't live on the *finca* . . ."

"Do you think they will let us stay here if they build a hotel?"

"Why not?"

"*Yo conozco al buey que faja y a la víbora que pica.*" She swallowed the last drop of coffee and got up from her stool brusquely, startling Alicia, who reached her arms out to me and clung to my neck the minute she was close enough.

I loved Doña Lola's *refranes,* the sayings she came up with in conversation that were sometimes as mysterious as the things Papi kept in his special dresser. "I know the bull that charges and the serpent that stings" could only mean that she distrusted Americans, and that this mistrust had come from experience.

But in the time I'd lived in Macún I'd never seen an American, nor had I ever heard mention of a Rockefela, nor plans for a hotel in what everyone called Lalao's *finca.*

When I came home, Alicia on my hip, a can of freshly roasted coffee in my hand, Mami was peeling *ñame* and *yautía* tubers for that night's supper.

"Mami, is it true that they're going to build a hotel on Lalao's *finca*?"

"That will be the day!"

"Doña Lola said they'll make us all move."

"They've been talking about bringing electricity here since before you were born. And the rumor about a hotel in Lalao's *finca* is older than the hopes of the poor. Your granddaughters will be *señorita* before anything like that happens around here."

I was relieved we wouldn't have to move and helped Mami peel the sweet potatoes.

"Where are *los Nueva Yores*?" I asked later as I tore the fish bones out of the soaking salted codfish.

"That's where Tata lives." Tata was my mother's mother, who had left Puerto Rico while I was still a toddler. Every so often Mami received a letter from her with a money order, or a package with the clothes my cousins in the United States had outgrown. "It's really called *Nueva Yor,* but it's so big and spread out people sometimes call it *los Nueva Yores.*"

"Have you ever been there?"

"No, I haven't. . . . Maybe someday . . . ," she mused as she set a pot of water to boil on the fire. "Maybe."

A Y! DIOS MÍO SANTO, AYÚDAME. ¡Ay!" Mami was having another baby. I was in charge of the younger kids, having been told to stay in the yard and out of the house until Doña Ana, our next-door neighbor, came to get us. Even from the far corner of the yard we heard Mami screaming, and Doña Lola and the midwife urging her. Every so often one of them came out and grabbed hot water from a big caldron in the *fogón* or poured a cup of coffee from the pot on the embers. They'd go back in and shut the door behind them, not allowing us even a peek into our mother's pain.

At dusk Doña Ana and her daughter Gloria came to get us, and we walked through the path that connected our yards, Héctor on my hip, Delsa carrying Alicia, Norma dragging a change of clothes for us bundled into a pillowcase, just in case we had to spend the night.

Mami's screams got louder and more shrill as we walked away from the house, as if she could feel us leaving. Norma whimpered; Héctor's eyes darted back and forth, and a solemn expression was on his usually smiling face. Alicia happily sucked her thumb and pointed at everything we passed, chirping, "What's that? What's that?" Delsa tried to comfort everyone, or perhaps just herself. "Don't worry," she

repeated over and over. "It's just Mami having a baby, that's all. It's just a baby. Mami will be all right." But none of us were comforted that easily, although by now we had learned not to make a fuss.

We ate Doña Ana's rice and beans with stringy fried chicken and waited in the yard, huddled together. I told stories learned from Don Berto or made up some of my own, none so scary as to chase away sleep. The next morning we were herded back to our own yard, into our house, where Mami was propped up on pillows nursing our new baby sister, and Papi, in the kitchen, installed a kerosene cookstove.

E VERYBODY, TAKE OFF YOUR clothes!" It was the middle of the afternoon, the first week in May. The air had cooled in a matter of seconds. A whisper of rain was beginning through a sunny sky, distant black clouds not close enough to throw the valley into darkness. Mami ran from the window, her face glowing, to the basket of house clothes and slipped out of her flowered dress into a faded shift.

"Quickly! Keep your panties on, girls, just take off your shirts. Hurry!" She helped us undress one by one while we laughed and asked her why. She didn't answer just giggled and took our clothes and stacked them on her rocking chair. She carried Edna, who was a few days old, to the threshold, and let a few sprinkles of rain dot her forehead, and rubbed them over the baby's face and shoulders before returning her to her cradle.

"Come. Follow me." She ran and stood in the middle of the yard smiling. The black clouds raced across the valley, but where she was standing, it was still bright. Light rain fell like dew on her, moistening her dress against her shoulders, her rounded belly, her hips. She raised her head to the sky and let the rain fall on her face, and she pushed the drops into her hair, down her neck, into the crevice between her breasts. We clustered on the threshold.

"What's she doing?" Delsa whispered.

"She's taking a bath," Norma answered, her yellow eyes enormous.

"What are you waiting for? Mami sang to us from the yard.

"But it's raining, Mami," Delsa said, sticking her hand out as if to prove her point.

"Yes," Mami said. "It's the first rain in May. It's good luck to get wet by the first May rain."

She took Delsa's hand, and Héctor's; he was holding on to the door frame as if glued there. She waltzed them to the yard then danced them around in circles. The rest of us stepped out gingerly, watching the black clouds crest the mountain and drop into the valley. Rain fell in thick drops now, exploding craters in the dry earth, banging against the zinc walls.

We held hands because it seemed the right thing to do, circled around as the ground became mud and the rain fell harder, cascading down our faces, into our mouths. We circled and sang a school yard rhyme:

> *¡Que llueva, que llueva!*
> *La Virgen en la cueva,*
> *los pajaritos cantan,*
> *la Virgen se levanta.*
> *¡Que llueva, que llueva!*

> Let it rain, let it rain!
> The Virgin in the cave.
> Birds sing,
> The Virgin rises.
> Let it rain, let it rain!

Mami let go our hands and ran under the roof overhang, where water fell in a thick stream. She gave us each a turn at being massaged by the torrent, which banged against our skinny bodies and bounced off in silver fans onto the ground. She rubbed the water into our scalps, behind our ears, under our arms, then sent us to chase one another in the slippery mud. We squished our toes and fingers into it, rubbed it on our arms, our bellies, behind our knees, then let the rain wash it off in long streams of red and orange that dribbled back into the soft earth. We squealed and laughed and sang silly rhymes, until the first bolt of lighting broke open the clouds, and thunder sent us all scampering inside, shivering, to be dried off by a laughing Mami, her eyes bright, her face flushed.

For the rest of the month, the rains came, heavy, angry downpours called *vaguadas* that soaked into the ground, turning our yard into a slippery, muddy swamp. Thunder and lightning seemed to strike just over our heads, the sound magnified by the metal roof and walls. The low-slung clouds threw the valley into twilight, and we had to keep the *quinqués* lit all day so we could find our way in the shuttered house.

Papi couldn't leave for work if the rains started early, and he passed the time reading magazines he retrieved from his special dresser. If the rains began after he'd left for work, however, we wouldn't see him for days. Mami didn't seem as bothered by his absence and fed us soups, or creamy rice with milk, or hot *sancochos* made up of whatever leftovers she could fit into the pot. When she wasn't feeding us, she sewed, if she had fabric, or polished the bedstead and Papi's dresser, or mended whatever was worn, ripped, or needed patching.

We slept long hours, the rain drumming against the walls, the angry rolls of thunder galloping over our zinc roof. We collected rain in barrels that filled up, topped off, overspilled, and still the *vaguadas* came like a once-welcome guest that couldn't stay away, eroding the ground into deep furrows that the summer sun burned into long, dry scars, deep wounds that never healed.

—Esmeralda Santiago

CITY OF LIGHT

THE LIGHT IS ALWAYS YELLOW in the morning streets. Even in the soft, drizzling rains of summer or the fierce, wind-driven storms of early fall, I feel bathed in that luminous yellow light. It seeps from the walls of the old houses—a light formed by the centuries, an antique light, a light that once held conquistadores and slaves, sugar kings and freebooters, the light of old gold and vanished supremacies—the light of San Juan.

When I say San Juan, I don't mean that great urban sprawl, with its population of more than a million, that makes up the modern capital of the island of Puerto Rico. That San Juan, with its office towers and traffic jams, raw concrete-block factories and heartless condominia, is just another city of the 20th century. When I think of San Juan, I mean the old town, called San Juan Antiguo by the formal, but more affectionately referred to as Viejo San Juan by those who know it and love it and have been warmed by its yellow light.

My San Juan, the old town I first saw in the late 1950s and have been visiting ever since, fills a mere seven square blocks on a promontory hooked around to face the great harbor that made the Spanish christen this island Rich Port. Across the centuries, it has been battered by unnamed tropical storms, and, in 1989, felt the power of Hurricane Hugo. But Viejo San Juan endures.

Whenever I visit Puerto Rico, arriving on a screaming jet at the airport in Isla Verde, I always go first to the old town. It centers me, in an island society that is too often culturally and politically schizophrenic. It grants me a sense of proportion. The modern city vanishes and much of the 20th century goes with it. Few places on this earth make me as happy.

The past is part of the reason. In many American cities now, we seem to be living in an eternal present tense, as insubstantial as the images on television screens. Too many events flash across our minds in unconnected fragments; today's crises are forgotten tomorrow; we hear too much and see too much and never listen for the whispering of ghosts. But there has been a San Juan since 1521, one hundred years before the first Dutchman mortared two bricks together to begin making New York. When the American Revolution began, San Juan had been there for 255 years.

SO IT IS NO ACCIDENT that when I walk from Plaza de Colón (with its statue of Columbus disguised as Dean Rusk) into Calle San Francisco, my sense of time shifts. The past asserts itself and I am reminded that for a long time before the rise of the United States this was a Spanish-speaking hemisphere. I hear the conversations of Puerto Ricans, delivered in the staccato-rhythms of port people, full of jokes and innuendo and untranslatable local words. The air is thick with vowels. From the old mortar of the walls, the past murmurs: Wait, slow down, listen, have a glass of rum, and remember old sins, the folly of man, the futility of despair.

Columbus discovered America in 1492, and on his second voyage the following year, the Admiral of the Ocean Sea landed at the site of the present town of Aguadilla on the northwest coast of the island. There were then about 30,000 Taíno Indians living on the island, which they called Borinquén. There was little gold to plunder, and those first Spaniards quickly moved on. Their first settlement was established at Caparra in 1509, but was soon abandoned to the mosquitoes. The Spaniards moved out of the marshes to the promontory beside the great bay and began to build a town they called San Juan Bautista, for St. John the Baptist, who remains the island's patron saint. They built from memory, combining the Islamic clarity and the proportions of Andalusia with houses glimpsed in the Canary Islands before the passage across the fierce Atlantic. They used brick and the ax-breaking hardwood called *ausubo* as well

"City of Light," by Pete Hamill, was originally published in Travel Holiday. *Copyright © 1990 by Pete Hamill. Reprinted by permission of the author.*

as iron forged in their own shops. They built the place to last.

The city they made evolved over centuries, of course, and even today the urban archaeologists of the Institute of Puerto Rican Culture are trying to chart its transformations. This is no simple task. Although minibuses now move through the old town, and taxis can take you to some key points (other streets are blocked to cars), the best way to see San Juan is on foot.

As you walk the streets, you tread upon blue-slag bricks called *adoquines*. Some guides insist they were originally ballast in the sailing ships of the 17th and 18th centuries, dumped here as the ships took on cargoes of sugar and tobacco for the markets of Europe; others tell you they arrived in San Juan from England as late as 1890. But they feel as if they had been here from the beginning, glistening with spring rain, perfect complements to the suffused yellow light.

Ni modo; it doesn't matter. They are part of San Juan forever. So is the feeling that here you might be safe. Three fortresses guard the city: La Fortaleza—the oldest executive mansion in the hemisphere, now occupied by the island's governor—overlooking the bay on the southwest of the promontory; San Cristóbal, to the right as you enter the old town from the hotels of the Condado; the magnificent El Morro on the tip, its cannon pointing northwest into the Atlantic. Walls surround the city, linking the three great fortresses, walls of stone.

THESE WALLS AND FORTS were not empty adornment; they were, like most things of beauty, a necessity. San Juan was established in an age of international gangsterism, and, since it was usually the last stop for Spanish galleons groaning with the loot of Mexico and Peru, hijackers saw it as an obvious target. Today, you can walk along the edge of El Morro, on walls that are 20 feet thick and rise 140 feet above the sea, and imagine what it was like when unfriendly sails on the horizon could mean death and destruction.

The fort was completed in 1589 by a team of military engineers headed by Juan Bautista Antonelli. The noted English gangster, Francis Drake, appeared in 1595 and was battered by the fort's six levels of cannons, along with fire from the smaller guns of La Fortaleza. Ten of Drake's ships were sunk, and more than 400 sailors were sent to the bottom of the harbor. But, three years later, another English hood, the Earl of Cumberland, arrived and came upon the city from the land side with a force of a thousand soldiers. He occupied San Juan, looted it, and then was forced to abandon it as more than 400 of his men perished from disease. El Morro never was captured again, although the Dutch tried in 1625, managing to burn a number of buildings in San Juan, including the finest private library then in existence in the New World. American naval gunners blasted away at the walls in 1898, during the war against Spain that made Puerto Rico an American colony. They never did take the fortress.

Today, you can visit El Morro on foot, with better luck than Cumberland's doomed soldiers. You go through the 27-acre park grounds, where soldiers once drilled and lovers now meet and fathers play ball with their sons. Hugo did its best against the park, damaging some 50 Australian pines that once lined its entrance. The National Park Service subsequently cut them down.

The hurricane also caused minor damage to the fort, but across the centuries it has survived well. Its walls are the color of lions, its arches painted white, and you cross a dry moat to enter the interior. From the ramparts, you can look down upon crashing surf, or you can visit the museum and souvenir shop, or examine the restored lighthouse, or photograph the domed sentry boxes called *garitas*. You can watch the pretty girls. Or you can simply surrender to the sense of time.

N THE AREA OF EL MORRO, I always save an hour to wander through the 19th-century cemetery below the fortress walls; here lie many of the most famous Puerto Rican political leaders, the martyred revolutionaries, some of the old Spanish *peninsulares* (who lived lives of leisure while slaves did the work), and ordinary folk, too; shopkeepers and blacksmiths, shoemakers and chefs, and the artisans and craftsmen who built the town and died at home. Or I visit a while in La Casa Blanca, the oldest house on the island, built for Ponce de León in 1521. Ponce was a mixture of romantic and conqueror. He dreamed, as they all did in that generation of Spanish adventurers, of gold. In Puerto Rico, he found little of it—certainly nothing on the scale of the great treasures of Mexico. He stayed on for a while as governor, watching the Taínos die of European diseases or flee to the jungled hills or depart down through the islands in great hand-hewn boats.

They were strange, those dark-skinned pagans; they simply would not agree to be slaves. So Ponce de León departed for Florida in search of the Fountain of Youth, almost certainly a fabrication invented by an Indian. Ponce was still searching in Florida when he was killed in a skirmish with Indians much fiercer than the pacific Taínos. His body was first taken to Cuba, then to San Juan, and his bones are now in the Metropolitan Cathedral. But the elegant Casa Blanca remained in the Ponce family until the late 18th century. The town rose around them. Streets were laid out, fountains constructed, churches built. The energy of the first generation of conquistadores waned throughout the vast Spanish empire; adventurers were replaced with clerks and grandees. The family grew rich, was battered by history, and departed after 250 years. A series of Spanish and then American military commanders lived here, strutting around the lovely courtyard and the splashing fountains. The house is now occupied by the Institute for Advanced Studies.

As an object made by men, a collective work of sculpture, El Castillo de San Cristóbal is, to me, preferable to El Morro. You can walk to it along the city walls, looking down at La Perla, the most picturesque slum under the American flag (it was described in detail in anthropologist Oscar Lewis's book *La Vida*). In ordinary times, the green-tar-paper roofs of La Perla, and the flags of the island's political parties, stand precariously between the city walls and the sea. But Hugo blew the flags into eternity, ripped the tar paper from many rooftops, and battered some of the frailer structures. This was nothing new. Houses have been washed away by storms in the past, but the people of La Perla always come back and build again. Now, children run in the streets and winos flake out against the sides of houses. Years ago, I used to visit friends down here, but they don't live in La Perla anymore. And in the age of crack

cocaine I no longer have the courage to wander its impoverished streets.

INSTEAD, **I GO TO** San Cristóbal, designed by two of those Irishmen known as the "wild geese"—the men and women who scattered around the world after the English conquest of their home island. Two who came to Puerto Rico were Alejandro O'Reilly and Thomas O'Daly, and, in the employ of the Spanish Army, they designed a fort laced with tunnels, secret traps, blind walls, gates, and pickets. The intention was to protect San Juan from land invasions similar to Cumberland's. There are forts within forts here, like watertight compartments in ships. An invader might take part of the fortress, but would pay a bloody and ferocious price to take it all.

I love the view from the ramparts of this fort, looking east toward the beaches and gigantic clouds that gather above the rain forest of the mountain called El Yunque. I like to think of O'Reilly and O'Daly, with their noses peeling, standing in the great blinding light of the summer sun, far from home, on a promontory cooled by the trade winds, speaking in Irish about one final go with the hated English.

Within the city's walls, there are streets that resemble those of New Orleans, with elaborately scrolled iron balconies attached to three-story houses that loom imperiously above their smaller neighbors. Most were built in the 17th and 18th centuries by the hidalgos who grew rich from tobacco, sugar, and horses. The ceiling beams and front doors are cut from the ausubo tree, so hard that is has been known to make restoration workers cry. The austere walls are humanized by the bright colors of the Caribbean: lime green, aqua, cerulean blue, rose, and, of course, those warm ochres and yellows. In other places, such colors might seem garish; here, they are as natural and permanent as the sky and the sea.

But some things do change. When I first came to San Juan, there was always music coming from those scrolled balconies, through the open doors of apartments: The Trio Los Panchos and Tito Rodriguez, Augustin Lara and Lucho Gatica, music romantic and bittersweet, occasionally punctuated by the tougher rhythms of mambo. There is less music in the streets now because prosperity has brought air conditioning to Viejo San Juan, and, as everywhere in the world, air conditioning closes windows and doors.

But if there is less to hear, there is still much to see. You gaze into patios that are like snatches of Seville: small fountains, bird cages, polished-iron implements, flowers. All manner of flowers grow in elaborate terra-cotta pots: philodendron, orchids, the yellowing vines called canarios, bougainvillea spilling from balconies, and hibiscus—mounds, garlands, bowers of hibiscus. There is an occasional flamboyant tree, with its scarlet flowers, imprisoned in its city garden; or a flowering oleander or frangipani preening for the hibiscus. You see palm trees, too, those immigrants from Africa, with terns rattling in the fronds.

Most windows are shuttered, the mute houses implying that in the great Spanish centuries, the densest human life was lived behind them. The town was too small then, too bourgeois, too formal for public melodramas.

Today, life is more public. San Juan is not a museum, and as you wander the streets you can see old men playing dominoes in small, shaded squares, middle-aged women shopping in the boutiques or stopping in La Bombonera on Calle San Francisco for splendid coffee and oversweet pastries, and young people everywhere. I'm not much of a shopper; I'd rather look and imagine than own. So I ignore the shops and follow no set route on my wanderings through Viejo San Juan. I want to be reassured and surprised.

ALWAYS GO TO the Cristo Chapel on the city walls overlooking the harbor. Almost always it is as I saw it last, closed off by an iron gate, four potted palms within its small interior, the masonry peeled off parts of the walls to reveal the thin brick of the past. The palms were demolished by Hugo; they will be replaced. One need not share the belief that inspired the chapel to be charmed by its proportions and modesty. As always, the little park beside it is filled with children and pigeons. A plaque tells me that the chapel was built between 1753 and 1780 and that "legend traces its origin to a miraculous happening at the site." It doesn't describe the miracle, but it is said that in 1753 a rider in a holy festival made a mistake, plunged over the wall into the sea, and lived. Not

exactly a major miracle, I suppose, but good enough to get the chapel built. The plaque bears the seal of Lions International.

As in most Latin countries, the sacred and the profane are at war here. All over Old San Juan, there are dozens of little bars. On the corner of San Sebastián and San Justo there is a bar called Aquí Se Puede, which means "here you can," and in its cool, dark interior the name seems more an act of reporting than of enticement.

A FEW BLOCKS AWAY is the Church of San José—spare, controlled, set facing a square out of de Chirico. It is the oldest church still in active use in the Americas, built by Dominican friars in the 1530s. But the mood within is of an austere European Catholicism exiled to the tropics. Plainsong comes from a hidden sound system. Natural light falls from openings in the cupolas of side chapels. The wooden pews are severe. The stations of the cross, with their ancient tale of sacrifice and pain, are bichromes of blue and white. Most afternoons, there is an eerie silence in the place, perhaps for good reason; archives suggest that as many as four thousand people—including most of the descendants of Ponce de León—might be buried beneath the tile floors.

On hot days, I used to stop for a while in the Plaza de Armas, to sit under the shade trees and talk to the taxi drivers and lounging cops and gold-toothed old men. They all told fabulous lies, and, across the street, vendors sold flowers under the arches of City Hall. There were department stores on the harbor side and pretty girls everywhere. The stores and pretty girls remain; all the rest is changed.

In 1988, a mayor named Balthasar Corrado del Río insisted on remodeling the plaza his way. Citizens protested, but he went ahead anyway—the shade trees were chain sawed at four in the morning. A cheap phone kiosk was erected. And now the Plaza de Armas is a bald, bright plain.

Now, if it's a hot day, I walk across the plaza to the corner of the New York Department Store, toward the harbor along Calle San José. I go into The Bookstore, which is air conditioned and has a fine selection of books in English, along with the latest volumes from Mexico, Buenos Aires, and Barcelona, and the works of such fine

Puerto Rican writers as Pedro Juan Soto, Luis Rafael Sanchez, and Rene Marquez. Here I can also pick up a copy of *The New York Times*. Then I go next door into the Café de Los Amigos for the best coffee in the old town. A sign sets out one of the rules: *No Discuta Politica Aquí.*

There are other plazas, churches, and museums, of course; your legs will carry you to all of them, or, in revolt, will persuade you to see them at some later date. But the people are as important as the buildings. On Saturday nights, the young people of the other San Juan show up to party in Viejo San Juan; handsome young men in the pretty-boy *guapo* style—hair slicked, wearing New York fashions, playing out roles that they haven't earned; the young women, voluptuous, made up to look like Madonna or one of the stars of Spanish television, their bodies bursting from tight skirts, T-shirts, and blouses.

There is something sad about them, as they preen for each other in the ancient rituals. They seem like so many tropical flowers blooming briefly before the swift move into adulthood. On these weekend evenings, they stand outside the Daiquiri Factory on Calle San Francisco, or Joseph's Café next door, some of them drinking and dancing inside while MTV plays on giant screens. They come to Viejo San Juan from the modern city of plastic and cement, as if subconsciously seeking to discover who they are by temporarily inhabiting the places from which their families came.

The perfumed rituals are enacted amidst the colliding symbols of the island's general cultural schizophrenia: Kentucky Fried Chicken, Burger King, and McDonald's, along with El Convento and the Plaza Salvador Brau, where there is a statue of a man named Patricio Rijos, who was known in life as "Toribio, King of the Guiro." The guiro is a grooved gourd played as a rhythm instrument with a wire fork. It is never seen on MTV.

And as the children of those San Juan nights careen away to various appointments, the music gradually stops, doors are shuttered, the traffic departs. At 104 Calle Fortaleza, on one such evening, I stopped to look at a marble plaque that identified the building as: THE HOUSE WHERE IN 1963 THE PIÑA COLADA WAS CREATED BY DON RAMON PORTA MINGOT. It was now a perfume shop called Barrachina. I smiled, thinking that in Viejo San Juan, all of the important things are remembered, when a small, wiry man came up to me.

"*Es una mentira,*" he said. "It's a lie. It was the bar of the Caribe Hilton, 1958."

Without another word, he walked off on unsteady legs, humming an old song. I went back to the hotel, to dream of yellow light.

—Pete Hamill

A GAMBLING PRIMER

ASINOS ARE NO LONGER AS LARGE A PART OF THE TOURISM
experience in Puerto Rico as they once were—but that's due
more to growth in other areas than to a decline in the casinos themselves. If gambling is your thing, or if you're feeling yourself
drawn to the "action" for the first time, Puerto Rico's resort-based casinos provide an attractive setting for trying your luck.

The most popular games have their rules, etiquette, odds, and strategies. If you're new to gambling, take a reconnaissance stroll through
the casino, read up on the games here, and choose the one that best
suits your style. If you take the time to learn the basics and fine points
thoroughly, you'll be adequately prepared to play with as much of an
edge as the game allows.

Baccarat

The most "glamorous" game in the casino, baccarat (pronounced *bah-kuh-rah*) is a version of *chemin de fer,* popular in European gambling
halls. The Italian word *baccara* means "zero"; this refers to the point
value of 10s and picture cards. The game is run by four pit personnel.
Two dealers sit side by side at the middle of the table; they handle the
winning and losing bets and keep track of each player's "commission"
(explained below). The "caller" stands at the middle of the other side
of the table and dictates the action. A pit boss supervises the game and
acts as final judge if any disputes arise.

How to Play

Baccarat is played with eight decks of cards dealt from a large "shoe"
(or card holder). Each player is offered a turn at handling the shoe and
dealing the cards. Two two-card hands are dealt: the "player" and the
"bank" hands. The player who deals the cards is called the banker,
though the house, of course, banks both hands. The players bet, before the deal, on which hand, player or banker, will come closer to adding
up to 9 (a "natural"). The cards are totaled as follows: Ace through 9
retain face value, while 10s and picture cards are worth zero. If a hand
adds up to more than 10, the number 10 is subtracted from the total.
For example, if one hand contains a 10 and a 4, the hand adds up to
4. If a hand holds an ace and 6, it adds up to 7. If a hand has a 7 and
9, it adds up to 6.

Depending on the two hands, the caller either declares a winner and
loser (if either hand actually adds up to 8 or 9), or calls for another card
for the player hand (if it totals 1, 2, 3, 4, 5, or 10). The bank hand then
either stands pat or draws a card, determined by a complex series of rules
depending on what the player's total is and dictated by the caller. When
one or the other hand is declared a winner, the dealers go into action to
pay off the winning wagers, collect the losing wagers, and add up the
commission (usually 5%) that the house collects on the bank hand. Both
bets have a house advantage of slightly more than 1%.

The player-dealer (or banker) continues to hold the shoe as long as the
bank hand wins. As soon as the player hand wins, the shoe moves counterclockwise around the table. Players are not required to deal; they
can refuse the shoe and pass it to the next player. Most players bet on
the bank hand when they deal, since they "represent" the bank, and
to do otherwise would seem as if they were betting "against" themselves. This isn't really the case.

Baccarat Strategy

Making a bet at baccarat is very simple. All you have to do is place your money in either the bank, player, or tie box on the layout, which appears directly in front of where you sit at the table. If you're betting that the bank hand will win, you put your chips in the bank box; bets for the player hand go in the player box. (Betting on a tie is a sucker bet.)

Because the caller dictates the action, the player responsibilities are minimal. It's not necessary to know any of the card-drawing rules, even if you're the banker. Playing baccarat is a simple matter of guessing whether the player or banker hand will come closer to 9, and deciding how much to bet on the outcome.

Blackjack

Blackjack is the most popular table game in the casino. It's easy to learn, it's fun to play, and it involves skill, and therefore rewards those who learn its nuances. Blackjack also has one of the lowest house advantages. Because blackjack is the only table game in the casino in which players can gain a long-term advantage over the house, it is the only table game in the casino (other than poker) that can be played professionally. And because blackjack can be played professionally, it is the most written-about and discussed casino game. Dozens of how-to books, trade journals, magazines, newsletters, computer programs, videos, theses, and novels are available on every aspect of blackjack, from how to add to 21 to how to play against a variety of shuffles, from when to stand or hit to the Level-Two Zen Count. Of course, training someone to play blackjack professionally is beyond the scope of this guide. Contact the Gambler's Book Club (☎ 800/552–1777) for a catalog of gambling books, software, and videotapes, including the largest selection on blackjack around.

The Rules

Basically, here's how it works: You play blackjack against a dealer, and whichever one of you comes closest to a card total of 21 without going over is the winner. Number cards are worth their face value, picture cards count as 10, and aces are worth either 1 or 11. (Hands with aces in them are known as "soft" hands. Always count the ace first as an 11; if you also have a 10, your total will be 21, not 11.) If the dealer has a 17 and you have a 16, you lose. If you have an 18 against a dealer's 17, you win (even money). If both you and the dealer have a 17, it's a tie (or "push") and no money changes hands. If you go over a total of 21 (or "bust"), you lose immediately, even if the dealer also busts later in the hand. If your first two cards add up to 21 (a "natural"), you're paid 3 to 2. However, if the dealer also has a natural, it's a push. A natural beats a total of 21 achieved with more than two cards.

You're dealt two cards, either face down or face up, depending on the custom of the particular casino. Two cards go to the dealer—one face down and one face up. Depending on your first two cards and the dealer's up card, you can:

stand, or refuse to take another card.

hit, or take as many cards as you need until you stand or bust.

double down, or double your bet and take one card.

split a like pair; if you're dealt two 8s, for example, you can double your bet and play the 8s as if they're two hands.

buy insurance if the dealer is showing an ace. Here you're wagering half your initial bet that the dealer does have a natural; if so, you lose your initial bet but are paid 2 to 1 on the insurance (which means the whole thing is a push).

surrender half your initial bet if you're holding a bad hand (known as a "stiff") such as a 15 or 16 against a high up-card like a 9 or 10.

Basic Blackjack Strategy

Playing blackjack is not only about knowing the rules—it's also about knowing *how* to play. Many people devote a great deal of time to learning strategies based on complicated statistical schemes. However, if you don't have the time, energy, or inclination to get that seriously involved, the following basic strategies, which cover more than half the situations you'll face, should allow you to play the game with a modicum of skill and a paucity of humiliation:

- When your hand is a stiff (a total of 12, 13, 14, 15, or 16) and the dealer shows 2, 3, 4, 5, or 6, always stand.

- When your hand is a stiff and the dealer shows a 7, 8, 9, 10, or ace, always hit.

- When you hold 17, 18, 19, or 20, always stand.

- When you hold a 10 or 11 and the dealer shows a 2, 3, 4, 5, 6, 7, 8, or 9, always double down.

- When you hold a pair of aces or a pair of 8s, always split.

- Never buy insurance.

Craps

Craps is a dice game played at a large rectangular table with rounded corners. Up to 12 players can crowd around the table, all standing. The layout is mounted at the bottom of a surrounding "rail," which prevents the dice from being thrown off the table and provides an opposite wall against which to bounce the dice. It's important, when you're the "shooter," to roll the dice hard enough so that they bounce off the end wall of the table; this ensures a random bounce and shows that you're not trying to control the dice with a "soft roll." The layout grid is duplicated on the right and left side of the table, so players on either end will see exactly the same design. The top of the railing is grooved to hold the bettors' chips; as always, keep a close eye on your stash to prevent victimization by rail thieves.

It can require up to four pit personnel to run an action-packed, fast-paced game of craps. Two dealers handle the bets made on either side of the layout. A "stickman" wields the long wooden stick, curved at one end, which is used to move the dice around the table; the stickman also calls the number that's rolled and books the proposition bets (☞ *below*) made in the middle of the layout. The "boxman" sits between the two dealers and oversees the game; he settles any disputes about rules, payoffs, mistakes, etc. A slow crap game is often handled by a single employee, who performs stick, box, and dealer functions. A portable end wall can be placed near the middle of the table so that only one side is functional.

How to Play

To play, just join in, standing at the table wherever you can find an open space. You can start betting casino chips immediately, but you have to wait your turn to be the shooter. The dice move around the table in a clockwise fashion: The person to your right shoots before you, the one to the left after. (The stickman will give you the dice at the appropriate time.) If you don't want to roll the bones, motion your refusal to the stickman and he'll skip you.

Playing craps is fairly straightforward; it's betting on it that's complicated. The basic concepts are as follows: If the first roll turns up a 7 or 11, that's called a "natural"—an automatic win. If a 2, 3, or 12 comes up on the first throw (called the "come-out roll"), that's termed "crapping out"—an automatic loss. Any other total on a first roll is known as a "point": The shooter keeps rolling the dice until the point comes up again. If a 7 turns up before the point does, the shooter loses. When either the point (the original number thrown) or a 7 is rolled, this is known as a "decision"; one is made on average every 3.3 rolls.

But "winning" and "losing" rolls of the dice are entirely relative in this game, depending on how you bet. There are two ways you can bet at craps: "for" the shooter or "against" the shooter. Betting for means that the shooter will "make his point" (win). Betting against means that the shooter will "seven out" (lose). (Either way, you're actually betting against the house, which books all wagers.) If you're betting "for" on the come-out, you place your chips on the layout's "pass line." If a 7 or 11 is rolled, you win even money. If a 2, 3, or 12 (craps) is rolled, you lose your bet. If you're betting "against" on the come-out, you place your chips in the "don't pass bar." A 7 or 11 loses; a 2 or 3 wins (a 12 is a push). A shooter can bet for or against himself or herself.

At the same time, you can make roughly two dozen wagers on any single roll of the dice. Besides the "for" and "against" (pass and don't pass) bets, you can also make the following wagers at craps:

Come/Don't Come: After a pass-line point is established, the come bet renders every subsequent roll of the dice a come-out roll. When you place your chips in the come box, it's the same as a pass line bet. If a 7 or 11 is rolled, you win even money. If a 2, 3, or 12 is rolled, you've crapped out. If a 4, 5, 6, 8, 9, or 10 is rolled, it becomes another point, and the dealer moves your chips into the corresponding box on the layout. Now if that number comes up before the 7, you win the come bet. The opposite (almost) is true for the don't come box: 7 and 11 lose, 2 and 3 win (12 is a push), and if 7 is rolled before the point, you win.

Odds: The house allows you to take odds on whether or not the shooter will make his or her point, once it's established. Since the house pays off these bets at "true odds," rather than withholding a unit or two to its advantage, these are the best bets in a crap game. Odds on the 6 and 8 pay off at 6 to 5, on the 5 and 9 at 3 to 2, and on the 4 and 10 at 2 to 1. "Back up" your pass line bets with single, double, triple, or up to 109 times odds (depending on the house rules) by placing your chips behind your line bet. For example, if the point is a 10 and your bet is $5, backing up your bet with single odds ($5) returns $25 ($5 + $5 on the line and $5 + $10 single odds); taking triple odds returns $55 ($5 + $5 on the line and $15 + $30). To take the odds on a come bet, toss your chips onto the layout and tell the dealer, "Odds on the come."

Place: Instead of waiting for a point to be rolled on the come, you can simply lay your bet on the point of your choice. Drop your chips on the layout in front of you and tell the dealer to "place" your number. The dealer puts your chips on the point; when it's rolled you win. The 6 and 8 pay 7 to 6, the 5 and 9 pay 7 to 5, and the 4 and 10 pay 9 to 5. In other words, if you place $6 on the 8 and it hits, you win $7. Place bets don't pay off at true odds, which is how the house maintains its edge (1.51% on the 6 and 8, 4% on the 5 and 9, and 6.66% on the 4 and 10). You can "call your place bet down" (take it back) at any time; otherwise the place bet will "stay up" until a 7 is rolled.

Buy: Buy bets are the same as place bets, except that the house pays off at true odds and takes a 5% commission if it wins. Since buy bets have an edge of 4.7%, you should only buy the 4 and 10 (rather than place them at a 6.6% disadvantage).

Big 6 and 8: Place your own chips in these boxes; you win if the 6 or 8 comes up, and lose on the 7. Since they pay off at even money, rather than true odds, the house edge is large—9.09%.

Field: This is a "one-roll" bet (a bet that's decided with each roll). Numbers 3, 4, 9, 10, and 11 pay even money, while 2 and 12 pay 2 to 1. The house edge on the field is 5.5%.

Proposition Bets: All proposition bets are booked in the grid in the middle of the layout by the stickman. "Hardways" means a matching pair of numbers on the dice (two 3s for a hardways 6, two 4s for a hardways 8, etc.). A hardways 4 or 10 pays 7 to 1 (11.1% edge), and 6 or 8 pays 9 to 1 (9.09%). If a 7 or a 4, 6, 8, or 10 is rolled the "easy way," hardways bets lose. "Any seven" is a one-roll wager on the 7, paying 4 to 1 with a whopping 16.6% edge. "Yo'leven" is also a one-roll wonder paying 14 to 1 with a 16.6% edge. "Any craps" is a one-roll bet on the 2, 3, or 12, paying 7 to 1 (11.1%). Other bad proposition bets include the "horn" (one-roll bet on 2, 3, 11, or 12 separately; 16.6%), and "c and e" (craps or 11; 11.1%).

Note: The players place their own pass line, field, Big 6 and 8, and come line bets. Players must drop their chips on the table in front of the dealers and instruct them to make their place and buy bets, and to take or lay the odds on their come bets. Chips are tossed to the stickman, who makes the hardways, any craps, any seven, and c and e bets in the middle of the layout.

Roulette

Roulette is a casino game that utilizes a perfectly balanced wheel with 38 numbers (0, 00, and 1 through 36), a small white ball, a large layout with 11 different betting options, and special "wheel chips." The layout organizes the 11 different bets into six "inside bets" (the single numbers, or those closest to the dealer) and five "outside bets" (the grouped bets, or those closest to the players).

The dealer stands between the layout and the roulette wheel, and chairs for five or six players are set around the roulette table. At crowded times, players also stand among and behind those seated, reaching over and around to place their bets. *Always* keep a close eye on your chips at these times to guard against "rack thieves," clever sleight-of-hand artists who can steal from your pile of chips right from under your nose.

To buy in, place your cash on the layout near the wheel. Inform the dealer of the denomination of the individual unit you intend to play (usually 25¢ or $1, but it can go up as high as $500). Know the table limits (displayed on a sign in the dealer area); don't ask for a 25¢ denomination if the minimum is $1. The dealer gives you a stack of wheel chips of a different color from those of all the other players and places a chip marker atop one of your wheel chips on the rim of the wheel to identify its denomination. Note that you must cash in your wheel chips at the roulette table before you leave the game. Only the dealer can verify how much they're worth.

The dealer spins the wheel clockwise and the ball counterclockwise. When the ball slows, the dealer announces, "No more bets." The ball drops from the "back track" to the "bottom track," caroming off built-in brass barriers and bouncing in and out of the different cups in the wheel before settling into the cup of the winning number. Then the dealer, who knows the winning bettors by the color of their wheel chips, places a marker on the number and scoops all the losing chips into his or her corner. Depending on how crowded the game is, the casino can count on roughly 50 spins of the wheel per hour.

How to Place Inside Bets

You can lay any number of chips (depending on the table limits) on a single number, 1 through 36 or 0 or 00. If the number hits, your pay-off is 35 to 1, for a return of $36 on a $1 bet. You could, conceivably, place a $1 chip on all 38 numbers, but the return of $36 would leave you $2 short, which divides out to 5.26%, the house advantage.

If you place a $1 chip on the line between two numbers and one of those numbers hits, you're paid 17 to 1 for a return of $18 (again, $2 short of the true odds).

Betting on three numbers returns 11 to 1, four numbers returns 8 to 1, five numbers pays 6 to 1 (this is the worst bet at roulette, with a 7.89% disadvantage), and six numbers pays 5 to 1.

How to Place Outside Bets

Lay a chip on one of three "columns" at the lower end of the layout next to numbers 34, 35, and 36; if the winning number falls in the column you've chosen, the payoff is 2 to 1. A bet placed in the first 12, second 12, or third 12 boxes also pays 2 to 1. A bet on red or black, odd or even, and 1 through 18 or 19 through 36 pays off at even money, 1 to 1. If you think you can bet on red *and* black, or odd *and* even, in order to play roulette and drink for free all night, think again: The green 0 or 00, which fall outside these two basic categories, will come up on average once every 19 spins of the wheel.

Slot Machines

At the beginning of the 20th century, Charlie Fey built the first mechanical slot in his San Francisco basement. Slot-machine technology has exploded in the past 20 years, and now there are hundreds of different models, which accept everything from pennies to specially minted $500 tokens. Electronically operated machines known as "multipliers" accept more than one coin (usually three to five, maximum) and have flashing lights, bells, and whistles, and spin, credit, and cash-out buttons. Multipliers frequently have a variety of pay lines: three horizontal for example, or five horizontal and diagonal.

The major advance in the game, however, is the progressive jackpot. Banks of slots within a particular casino are connected by computer, and the jackpot total is displayed on a digital meter above the machines. Generally, the total increases by 5% of the wager. If you're playing a dollar machine, each time you pull the handle (or press the spin button), a nickel is added to the jackpot.

How to Play

To play, insert your penny, nickel, quarter, silver dollar, or dollar token into the slot at the far right edge of the machine. Pull the handle or press the spin button; then wait for the reels to spin and stop one by one, and for the machine to determine whether you're a winner (occasionally) or a loser (the rest of the time). It's pretty simple—but because there are so many different types of machines nowadays, be sure you know exactly how the one you're playing operates.

The house advantage on slots varies widely from machine to machine, between 3% and 25%. Casinos that advertise a 97% payback are telling you that at least one of their slot machines has a house advantage of 3%. Which one? There's really no way of knowing. Generally, $1 machines pay back at a higher percentage than quarter or nickel machines. On the other hand, machines with smaller jackpots pay back more money more frequently, meaning that you'll be playing with more of your winnings.

One of the all-time great myths about slot machines is that they're "due" for a jackpot. Slots, like roulette, craps, keno, and the big six, are subject to the Law of Independent Trials, which means the odds are permanently and unalterably fixed. If the odds of lining up three sevens on a 25¢ slot machine have been set by the casino at 1 in 10,000, then those odds remain 1 in 10,000 whether the three 7s have been hit three times in a row or not hit for 90,000 plays. Don't waste a lot of time playing a machine that you suspect is "ready," and don't think that if someone hits a jackpot on a particular machine only minutes after you've finished playing on it that it was "yours."

Video Poker

Like blackjack, video poker is a game of strategy and skill, and at select times on select machines, the player actually holds the advantage, however slight, over the house. Unlike with slot machines, you can determine the exact edge of video poker machines (or in gambler's lingo, "handicap" the machine). Like slots, however, video poker machines are often tied into a progressive meter; when the jackpot total reaches high enough, you can beat the casino at its own game.

The variety of video poker machines is already large, and it's growing steadily larger. All of the different machines are played in a similar fashion, but the strategies are different. This section deals only with straight-draw video poker.

How to Play

The schedule for the payback on winning hands is posted on the machine, usually above the screen. It lists the returns for a high pair (generally jacks or better), two pair, three of a kind, a straight, flush, full house, straight flush, four of a kind, and royal flush, depending on the number of coins played—usually 1, 2, 3, 4, or 5. (The machine assumes you're familiar with poker and its terminology.) Look for machines that pay, with a single coin played, 1 coin for "jacks or better" (meaning a pair of jacks, queens, kings, or aces; any other pair is a stiff), 2 coins for two pairs, 3 for three of a kind, 4 for a straight, 6 for a flush, 9 for a full house, 25 for four of a kind, 50 for a straight flush, and 250 for a royal flush. This is known as a 9/6 machine: one that gives a nine-coin payback for the full house and a six-coin payback for the flush with one coin played. Other machines are known as 8/5 (8 for the full house, 5 for the flush), 7/5, and 6/5.

You want a 9/6 machine because it gives you the best odds: The return from a standard 9/6 straight-draw machine is 99.5%; you give up a half percent to the house. An 8/5 machine returns 97.3%. On 6/5 machines, the figure drops to 95.1%, slightly better than roulette. Machines with varying paybacks are scattered throughout the casinos. In some you'll see an 8/5 machine right next to a 9/6, and someone will be blithely playing the 8/5 machine!

As with slot machines, it's always optimal to play the maximum number of coins in order to qualify for the jackpot. You insert five coins into the slot and press the "deal" button. Five cards appear on the screen—say, 5, J, Q, 5, 9. To hold the pair of 5s, you press the "hold" buttons under the first and fourth cards. The word "hold" appears underneath the two 5s. You then press the "draw" button (often the same button as "deal") and three new cards appear on the screen—say, 10, J, 5. You have three 5s; with five coins bet, the machine will give you 15 credits. If you want to continue playing, press the "max bet" button: Five units will be removed from your number of credits, and five new cards will appear on the screen. You repeat the hold and draw process; if you hit a winning hand, the proper payback will be added to your credits. Those who want coins rather than credit can hit the "cash out" button at any time. Some older machines don't have credit counters and automatically dispense coins for a winning hand.

Video Poker Strategy

Like blackjack, video poker has a basic strategy that's been formulated by the computer simulation of hundreds of millions of hands. The most effective way to learn it is with a video poker computer program that deals the cards on your screen, then tutors you in how to play each hand properly. If you don't want to devote that much time to the study of video poker, memorizing these six rules will help you make the right decision for more than half the hands you'll be dealt:

- If you're dealt a completely "stiff" hand (no like cards and no picture cards), draw five new cards.

- If you're dealt a hand with no like cards but with one jack, queen, king, or ace, always hold on to the picture card; if you're dealt two different picture cards, hold both. But if you're dealt three different picture cards, only hold two (the two of the same suit, if that's an option).

- If you're dealt a pair, always hold it, no matter what the face value.

- Never hold a picture card ("kicker") with a pair of 2s through 10s.

- Never draw two cards to try for a straight or flush.

- Never draw one card to try for an inside straight.

SPANISH VOCABULARY

Words and Phrases

	English	Spanish	Pronunciation
Basics			
	Yes/no	Sí/no	see/no
	Please	Por favor	pore fah-**vore**
	May I?	¿Me permite?	may pair-**mee**-tay
	Thank you (very much)	(Muchas) gracias	(**moo**-chas) **grah**-see-as
	You're welcome	De nada	day **nah**-dah
	Excuse me	Con permiso	con pair-**mee**-so
	Pardon me	¿Perdón?	pair-**dohn**
	Could you tell me?	¿Podría decirme?	po-dree-ah deh-**seer**-meh
	I'm sorry	Lo siento	lo see-**en**-to
	Good morning!	¡Buenos días!	**bway**-nohs **dee**-ahs
	Good afternoon!	¡Buenas tardes!	**bway**-nahs **tar**-dess
	Good evening!	¡Buenas noches!	**bway**-nahs **no**-chess
	Goodbye!	¡Adiós!/¡Hasta luego!	ah-dee-**ohss**/**ah**-stah-**lwe**-go
	Mr./Mrs.	Señor/Señora	sen-**yor**/sen-**yohr**-ah
	Miss	Señorita	sen-yo-**ree**-tah
	Pleased to meet you	Mucho gusto	**moo**-cho **goose**-to
	How are you?	¿Cómo está usted?	**ko**-mo es-**tah** oo-**sted**
	Very well, thank you.	Muy bien, gracias.	**moo**-ee bee-**en**, **grah**-see-as
	And you?	¿Y usted?	ee oos-**ted**
	Hello (on the telephone)	Diga	**dee**-gah
Numbers			
	1	un, uno	oon, **oo**-no
	2	dos	dos
	3	tres	tress
	4	cuatro	**kwah**-tro
	5	cinco	**sink**-oh
	6	seis	saice
	7	siete	see-**et**-eh
	8	ocho	**o**-cho
	9	nueve	new-**eh**-vey
	10	diez	dee-**es**
	11	once	**ohn**-seh
	12	doce	**doh**-seh
	13	trece	**treh**-seh
	14	catorce	ka-**tohr**-seh

15	quince	**keen**-seh
16	dieciséis	dee-**es**-ee-**saice**
17	diecisiete	dee-**es**-ee-see-**et**-eh
18	dieciocho	dee-**es**-ee-**o**-cho
19	diecinueve	**dee-es**-ee-new-**ev**-ah
20	veinte	**vain**-teh
21	veinte y uno/veintiuno	**vain**-te-**oo**-noh
30	treinta	**train**-tah
32	treinta y dos	train-tay-**dohs**
40	cuarenta	kwah-**ren**-tah
43	cuarenta y tres	kwah-**ren**-tay-**tress**
50	cincuenta	seen-**kwen**-tah
54	cincuenta y cuatro	seen-**kwen**-tay **kwah**-tro
60	sesenta	sess-**en**-tah
65	sesenta y cinco	sess-**en**-tay **seen**-ko
70	setenta	set-**en**-tah
76	setenta y seis	set-**en**-tay **saice**
80	ochenta	oh-**chen**-tah
87	ochenta y siete	oh-**chen**-tay see-**yet**-eh
90	noventa	no-**ven**-tah
98	noventa y ocho	no-**ven**-tah-**o**-choh
100	cien	see-**en**
101	ciento uno	see-**en**-toh **oo**-noh
200	doscientos	doh-see-**en**-tohss
500	quinientos	keen-**yen**-tohss
700	setecientos	set-eh-see-**en**-tohss
900	novecientos	no-veh-see-**en**-tohss
1,000	mil	meel
2,000	dos mil	dohs meel
1,000,000	un millón	oon meel-**yohn**

Colors

black	negro	**neh**-groh
blue	azul	ah-**sool**
brown	café	kah-**feh**
green	verde	**ver**-deh
pink	rosa	**ro**-sah
purple	morado	mo-**rah**-doh
orange	naranja	na-**rahn**-hah
red	rojo	**roh**-hoh
white	blanco	**blahn**-koh
yellow	amarillo	ah-mah-**ree**-yoh

Days of the Week

Sunday	domingo	doe-**meen**-goh
Monday	lunes	**loo**-ness
Tuesday	martes	**mahr**-tess
Wednesday	miércoles	me-**air**-koh-less
Thursday	jueves	hoo-**ev**-ess

Friday	viernes	vee-**air**-ness
Saturday	sábado	**sah**-bah-doh

Months

January	enero	eh-**neh**-roh
February	febrero	feh-**breh**-roh
March	marzo	**mahr**-soh
April	abril	ah-**breel**
May	mayo	**my**-oh
June	junio	**hoo**-nee-oh
July	julio	**hoo**-lee-yoh
August	agosto	ah-**ghost**-toh
September	septiembre	sep-tee-**em**-breh
October	octubre	oak-**too**-breh
November	noviembre	no-vee-**em**-breh
December	diciembre	dee-see-**em**-breh

Useful Phrases

Do you speak English?	¿Habla usted inglés?	**ah**-blah oos-**ted** in-**glehs**
I don't speak Spanish	No hablo español	no **ah**-bloh es-pahn-**yol**
I don't understand (you)	No entiendo	no en-tee-**en**-doh
I understand (you)	Entiendo	en-tee-**en**-doh
I don't know	No sé	no seh
I am American/ British	Soy americano (americana)/ inglés(a)	soy ah-meh-ree-**kah**-no (ah-meh-ree-**kah**-nah)/ in-**glehs** **(ah)**
What's your name?	¿Cómo se llama usted?	koh-mo seh **yah**-mah oos-**ted**
My name is . . .	Me llamo . . .	may **yah**-moh
What time is it?	¿Qué hora es?	keh **o**-rah es
It is one, two, three . . . o'clock.	Es la una. . . . Son las dos, tres	es la **oo**-nah/sohn lahs dohs, tress
Yes, please/No, thank you	Sí, por favor/No, gracias	**see** pohr fah-**vor**/no **grah**-see-us
How?	¿Cómo?	**koh**-mo
When?	¿Cuándo?	**kwahn**-doh
This/Next week	Esta semana/ la semana que entra	**es**-teh seh-**mah**-nah/lah seh-**mah**-nah keh **en**-trah
This/Next month	Este mes/el próximo mes	**es**-teh mehs/el **proke**-see-mo mehs
This/Next year	Este año/el año que viene	**es**-teh **ahn**-yo/el **ahn**-yo keh vee-**yen**-ay
Yesterday/today/ tomorrow	Ayer/hoy/mañana	ah-**yehr**/oy/mahn-**yah**-nah
This morning/ afternoon	Esta mañana/ tarde	**es**-tah mahn-**yah**-nah/**tar**-deh

Tonight	Esta noche	**es**-tah **no**-cheh
What?	¿Qué?	keh
What is it?	¿Qué es esto?	keh es **es**-toh
Why?	¿Por qué?	pore **keh**
Who?	¿Quién?	kee-**yen**
Where is . . . ?	¿Dónde está . . . ?	**dohn**-deh es-**tah**
the train station?	la estación del tren?	la es-tah-see-**on** del **train**
the subway station?	la estación del Tren subterráneo?	la es-ta-see-**on** del trehn soob-tair-**ron**-a-o
the bus stop?	la parada del autobus?	la pah-**rah**-dah del oh-toh-**boos**
the post office?	la oficina de correos?	la oh-fee-**see**-nah deh koh-**reh**-os
the bank?	el banco?	el **bahn**-koh
the hotel?	el hotel?	el oh-**tel**
the store?	la tienda?	la tee-**en**-dah
the cashier?	la caja?	la **kah**-hah
the museum?	el museo?	el moo-**seh**-oh
the hospital?	el hospital?	el ohss-pee-**tal**
the elevator?	el ascensor?	el ah-**sen**-sohr
the bathroom?	el baño?	el **bahn**-yoh
Here/there	Aquí/allá	ah-**key**/ah-**yah**
Open/closed	Abierto/cerrado	ah-bee-**er**-toh/ ser-**ah**-doh
Left/right	Izquierda/derecha	iss-key-**er**-dah/ dare-**eh**-chah
Straight ahead	Derecho	dare-**eh**-choh
Is it near/far?	¿Está cerca/lejos?	es-**tah sehr**-kah/ **leh**-hoss
I'd like . . . a room	Quisiera . . . un cuarto/una habitación	kee-see-ehr-ah oon **kwahr**-toh/ **oo**-nah ah-bee-tah-see-**on**
the key	la llave	lah **yah**-veh
a newspaper	un periódico	oon pehr-ee-**oh**-dee-koh
a stamp	un sello de correo	oon **seh**-yo deh koh-**reh**-oh
I'd like to buy . . .	Quisiera comprar . . .	kee-see-**ehr**-ah kohm-**prahr**
cigarettes	cigarrillos	ce-ga-**ree**-yohs
matches	cerillos	ser-**ee**-ohs
a dictionary	un diccionario	oon deek-see-oh-**nah**-ree-oh
soap	jabón	hah-**bohn**
sunglasses	gafas de sol	**ga**-fahs deh sohl
suntan lotion	loción bronceadora	loh-see-**ohn** brohn-seh-ah-**do**-rah
a map	un mapa	oon **mah**-pah
a magazine	una revista	**oon**-ah reh-**veess**-tah

paper	papel	pah-**pel**
envelopes	sobres	**so**-brehs
a postcard	una tarjeta postal	**oon**-ah tar-**het**-ah post-**ahl**
How much is it?	¿Cuánto cuesta?	**kwahn**-toh **kwes**-tah
It's expensive/cheap	Está caro/barato	es-**tah kah**-roh/bah-**rah**-toh
A little/a lot	Un poquito/mucho	oon poh-**kee**-toh/**moo**-choh
More/less	Más/menos	mahss/**men**-ohss
Enough/too much/too little	Suficiente/demasiado/muy poco	soo-fee-see-**en**-teh/deh-mah-see-**ah**-doh/**moo**-ee poh-koh
Telephone	Teléfono	tel-**ef**-oh-no
Telegram	Telegrama	teh-leh-**grah**-mah
I am ill	Estoy enfermo(a)	es-**toy** en-**fehr**-moh(mah)
Please call a doctor	Por favor llame a un medico	pohr fah-**vor ya**-meh ah oon **med**-ee-koh
Help!	¡Auxilio!/¡Ayuda!/¡Socorro!	owk-**see**-lee-oh/ah-**yoo**-dah/soh-**kohr**-roh
Fire!	¡Incendio!	en-**sen**-dee-oo
Caution!/Look out!	¡Cuidado!	kwee-**dah**-doh

On the Road

Avenue	Avenida	ah-ven-**ee**-dah
Broad, tree-lined boulevard	Bulevar	boo-leh-**var**
Fertile plain	Vega	**veh**-gah
Highway	Carretera	car-reh-**ter**-ah
Mountain pass, Street	Puerto Calle	poo-**ehr**-toh **cah**-yeh
Waterfront promenade	Rambla	**rahm**-blah
Wharf	Embarcadero	em-bar-cah-**deh**-ro

In Town

Cathedral	Catedral	cah-teh-**dral**
Church	Templo/Iglesia	**tem**-plo/ee-**glehs**-see-ah
City hall	Casa de gobierno	kah-sah deh go-bee-**ehr**-no
Door, gate	Puerta portón	poo-**ehr**-tah por-**ton**
Entrance/exit	Entrada/salida	en-**trah**-dah/sah-**lee**-dah
Inn, rustic bar, or restaurant	Taverna	tah-**vehr**-nah
Main square	Plaza principal	plah-thah prin-see-**pahl**

Market	Mercado	mer-**kah**-doh
Neighborhood	Barrio	**bahr**-ree-o
Traffic circle	Glorieta	glor-ee-**eh**-tah
Wine cellar, wine bar, or wine shop	Bodega	boh-**deh**-gah

Dining Out

A bottle of . . .	Una botella de . . .	**oo**-nah bo-**teh**-yah deh
A cup of . . .	Una taza de . . .	**oo**-nah **tah**-thah deh
A glass of . . .	Un vaso de . . .	oon **vah**-so deh
Ashtray	Un cenicero	oon sen-ee-**seh**-roh
Bill/check	La cuenta	lah **kwen**-tah
Bread	El pan	el pahn
Breakfast	El desayuno	el deh-sah-**yoon**-oh
Butter	La mantequilla	lah man-teh-**key**-yah
Cheers!	¡Salud!	sah-**lood**
Cocktail	Un aperitivo	oon ah-pehr-ee-**tee**-voh
Dinner	La cena	lah **seh**-nah
Dish	Un plato	oon **plah**-toh
Menu of the day	Menú del día	meh-**noo** del **dee**-ah
Enjoy!	¡Buen provecho!	bwehn pro-**veh**-cho
Fixed-price menu	Menú fijo o turistico	meh-**noo fee**-hoh oh too-**ree**-stee-coh
Fork	El tenedor	el ten-eh-**dor**
Is the tip included?	¿Está incluida la propina?	es-**tah** in-cloo-**ee**-dah lah pro-**pee**-nah
Knife	El cuchillo	el koo-**chee**-yo
Large portion of savory snacks	Raciónes	rah-see-**oh**-nehs
Lunch	La comida	lah koh-**mee**-dah
Menu	La carta, el menú	lah **cart**-ah, el meh-**noo**
Napkin	La servilleta	lah sehr-vee-**yet**-ah
Pepper	La pimienta	lah pee-me-**en**-tah
Please give me	Por favor déme	pore fah-**vor deh**-meh
Salt	La sal	lah sahl
Savory snacks	Tapas	**tah**-pahs
Spoon	Una cuchara	**oo**-nah koo-**chah**-rah
Sugar	El azúcar	el ah-**thu**-kar
Waiter!/Waitress!	¡Por favor Señor/Señorita!	pohr fah-**vor** sen-**yor**/sen-yor-**ee**-tah

INDEX

NOTES

NOTES

NOTES

NOTES